IS IT WRONG TO TRY TO PICK UP GIRLS IN A DUNGEON? ⑩

Fujino Omori
Kunieda
Suzuhito Yasuda

Translation: Andrew Gaippe • Lettering: Rochelle Gancio

DUNGEON NI DEAI WO MOTOMERU NO WA MACHIGATTEIRUDAROUKA vol. 10
© Fujino Omori / SB Creative Corp. Character Design: Yasuda Suzuhito
© 2018 Kunieda / SQUARE ENIX CO., LTD.
First published in Japan in 2018 by SQUARE ENIX CO., LTD.
English translation rights arranged with SQUARE ENIX CO., LTD. and Yen Press, LLC through Tuttle Mori Agency, Inc.

English translation © 2019 by SQUARE ENIX CO., LTD.

Yen Press
1290 Avenue of the Americas
New York, NY 10104

Visit us at yenpress.com
facebook.com/yenpress
twitter.com/yenpress
yenpress.tumblr.com
instagram.com/yenpress

First Yen Press Edition: January 2019

Yen Press is an imprint of Yen Press, LLC.
The Yen Press name and logo are trademarks of Yen Press, LLC.

The publisher is not responsible for websites (or their content) that are not owned by the publisher.

Library of Congress Control Number: 2015288171

ISBNs: 978-1-9753-8358-9 (paperback)
       978-1-9753-8359-6 (ebook)

10 9 8 7 6 5 4 3 2 1

WOR

Printed in the United States of America

HE DOES NOT LET ANYONE ROLL THE DICE.

A young Priestess joins her first adventuring party, but blind to the dangers, they almost immediately find themselves in trouble. It's Goblin Slayer who comes to their rescue—a man who has dedicated his life to the extermination of all goblins by any means necessary. A dangerous, dirty, and thankless job, but he does it better than anyone. And when rumors of his feats begin to circulate, there's no telling who might come calling next...

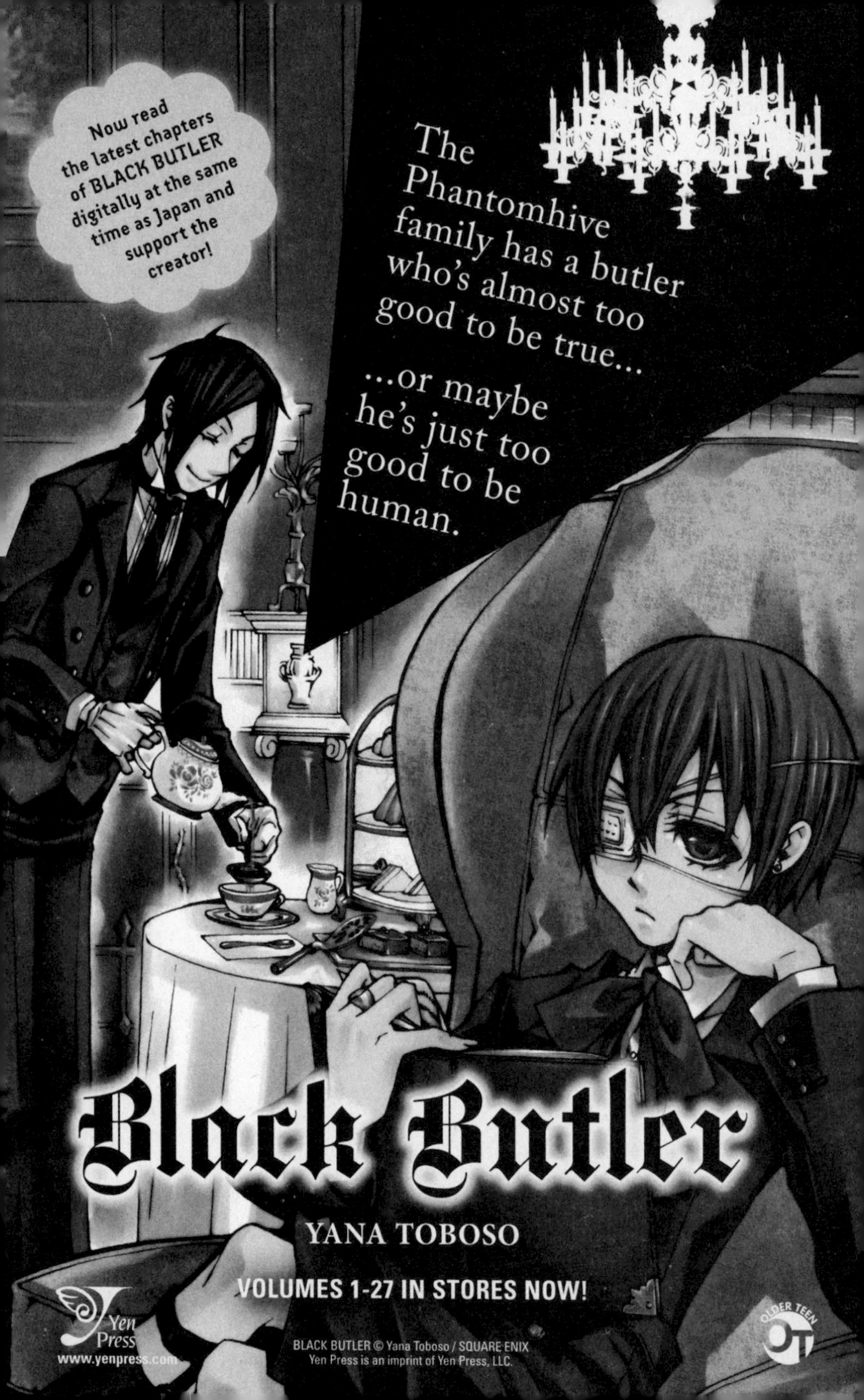
Now read the latest chapters of BLACK BUTLER digitally at the same time as Japan and support the creator!
The Phantomhive family has a butler who's almost too good to be true...
...or maybe he's just too good to be human.
Black Butler
YANA TOBOSO
VOLUMES 1-27 IN STORES NOW!
Yen Press
www.yenpress.com
BLACK BUTLER © Yana Toboso / SQUARE ENIX
Yen Press is an imprint of Yen Press, LLC.
OLDER TEEN
OT

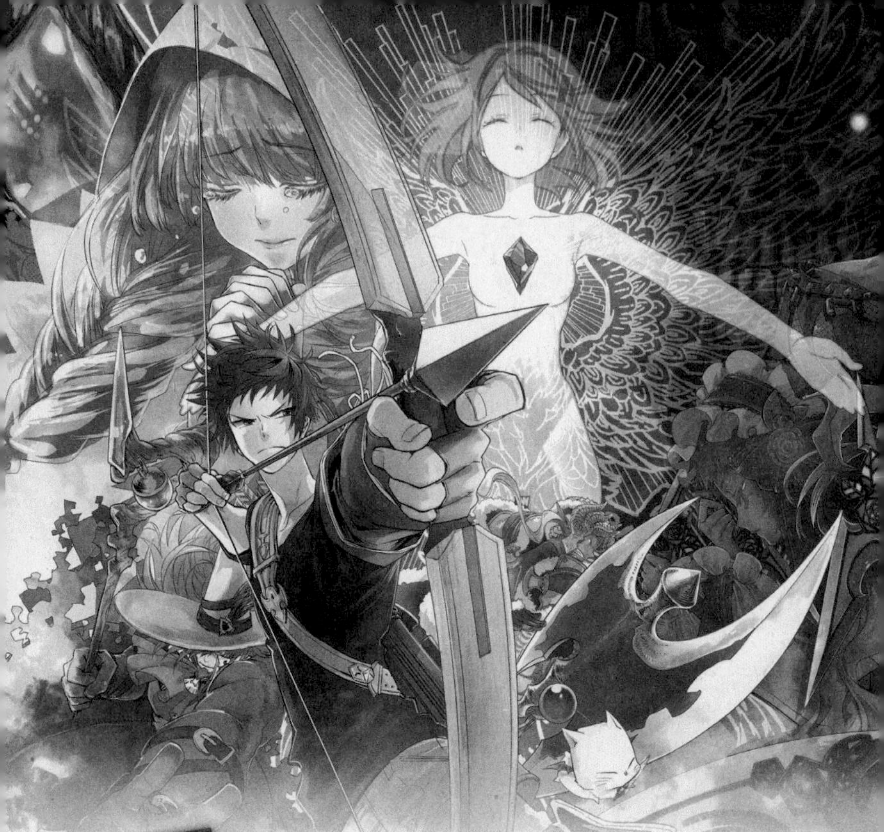

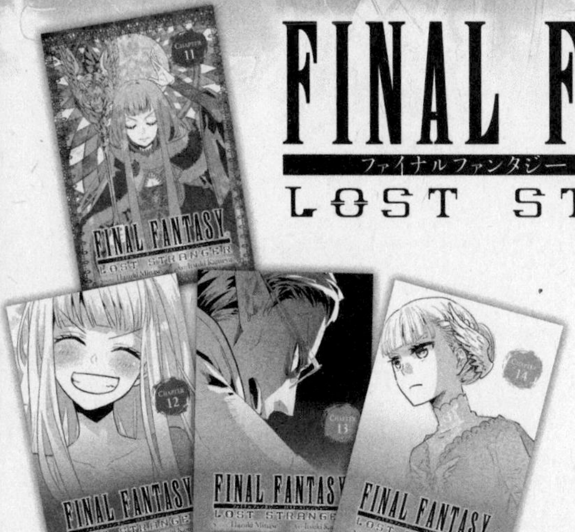
FINAL FANTASY
LOST STRANGER
FINAL FANTASY
LOST STRANGER
FINAL FANTASY
LOST STRANGER
FINAL FANTASY
LOST STRANGER

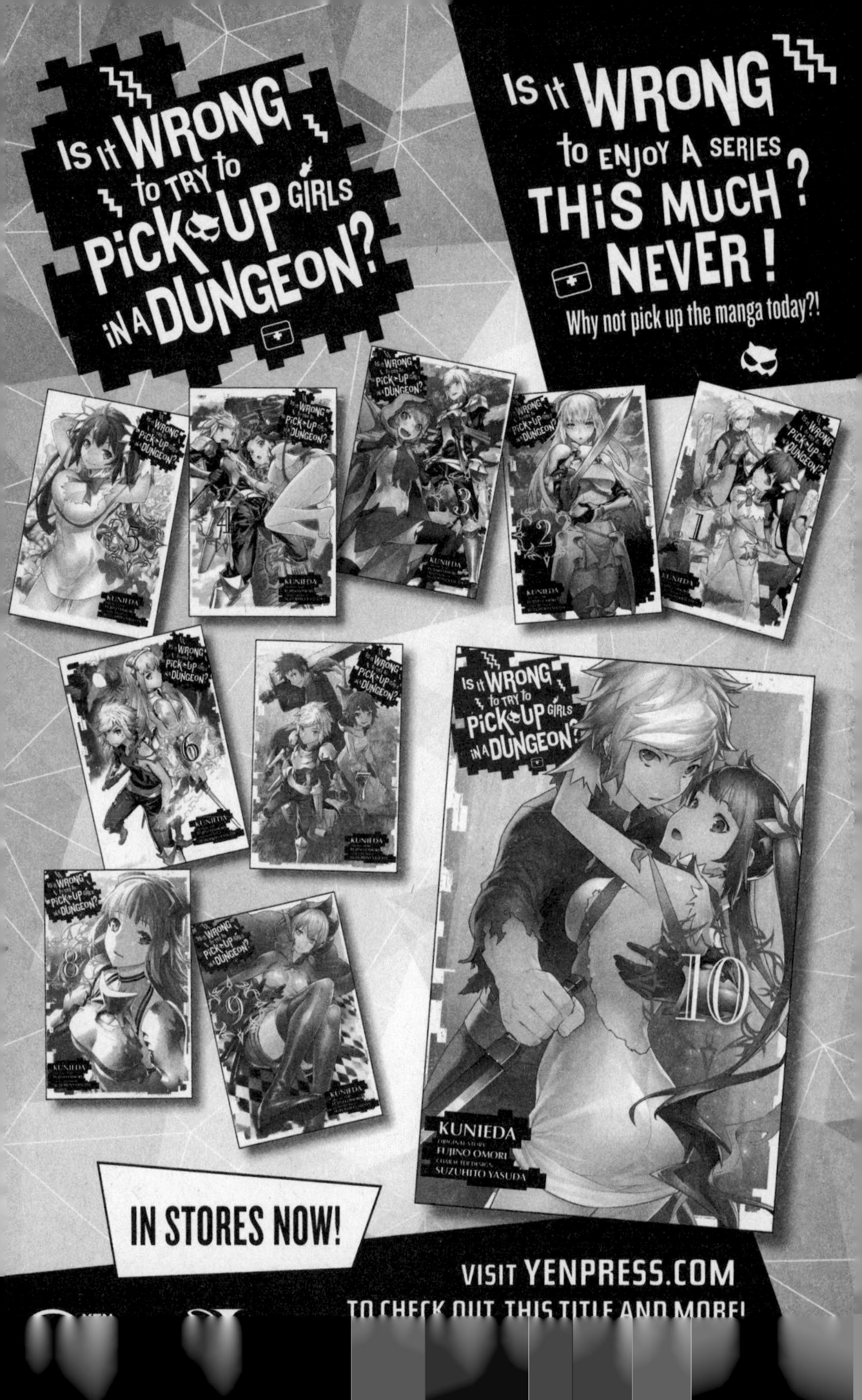

Is it WRONG to try to PICK UP GIRLS IN A DUNGEON?
Is it WRONG to ENJOY A SERIES THIS MUCH? NEVER!
Why not pick up the manga today?!
10
KUNIEDA
ORIGINAL STORY FUJINO OMORI
CHARACTER DESIGN SUZUHITO YASUDA
IN STORES NOW!
VISIT YENPRESS.COM TO CHECK OUT THIS TITLE AND MORE!

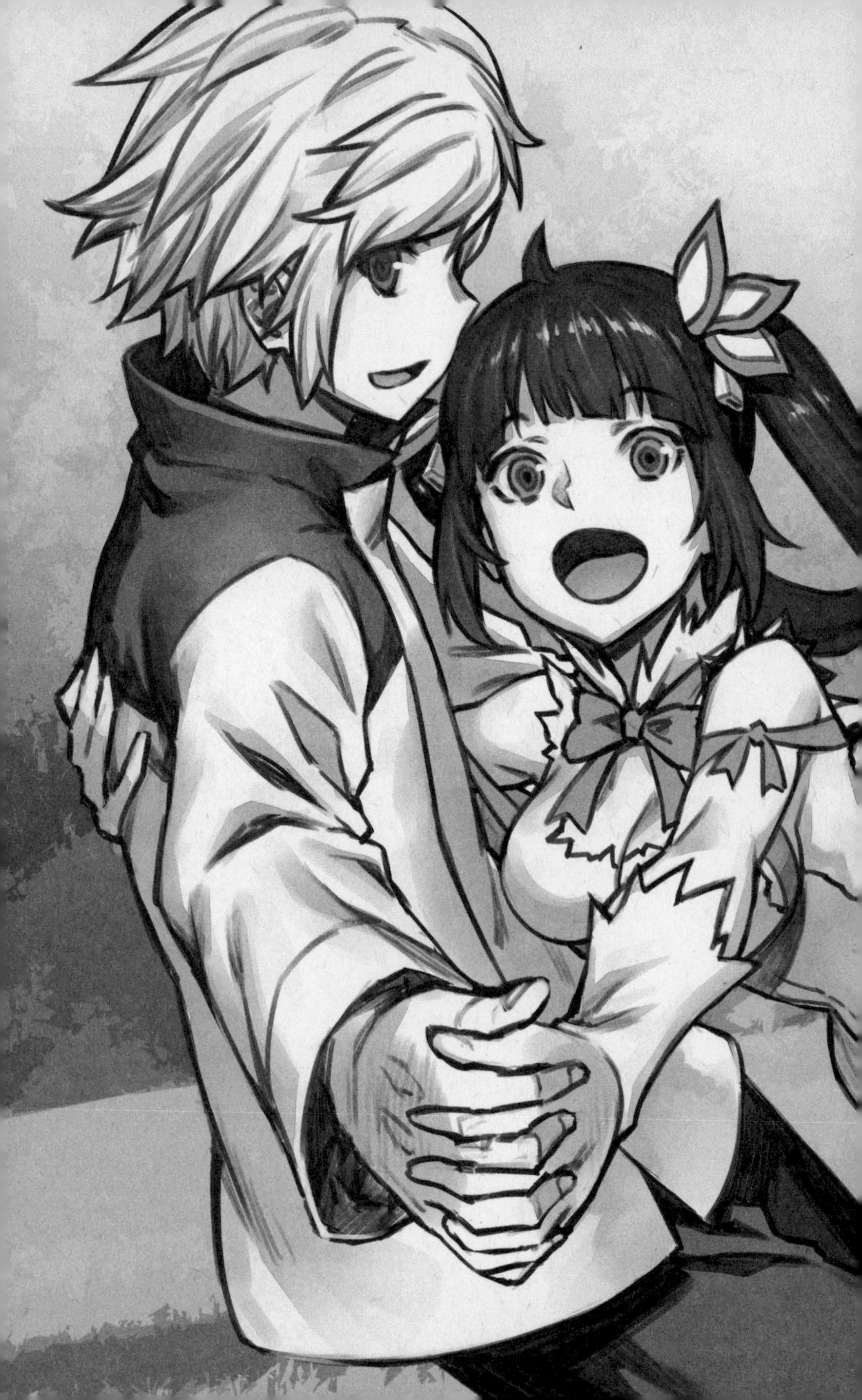

THANKS FOR PICKING UP VOLUME 10 OF THE MANGA!

THE BOSS FIGHT HAS ENDED, AND A NEW STORY ARC IS JUST BEGINNING.
BELL'S GETTING STRONGER BY THE DAY, BUT HIS ENEMIES KEEP GETTING MORE FORMIDABLE... THERE'S JUST NO END TO IT! WHAT A SCARY WORLD.

THE SCENE NOW SHIFTS FROM THE DUNGEON UP TO THE CITY ORARIO. THIS PART OF THE NOVEL SERIES WAS SO INTENSE, I WAS YELLING AT MY BOOK THE FIRST TIME I READ IT!

I'D LIKE TO MAINTAIN THAT SAME LEVEL OF INTENSITY IN MY WORK!

九二枝
KUNIEDA

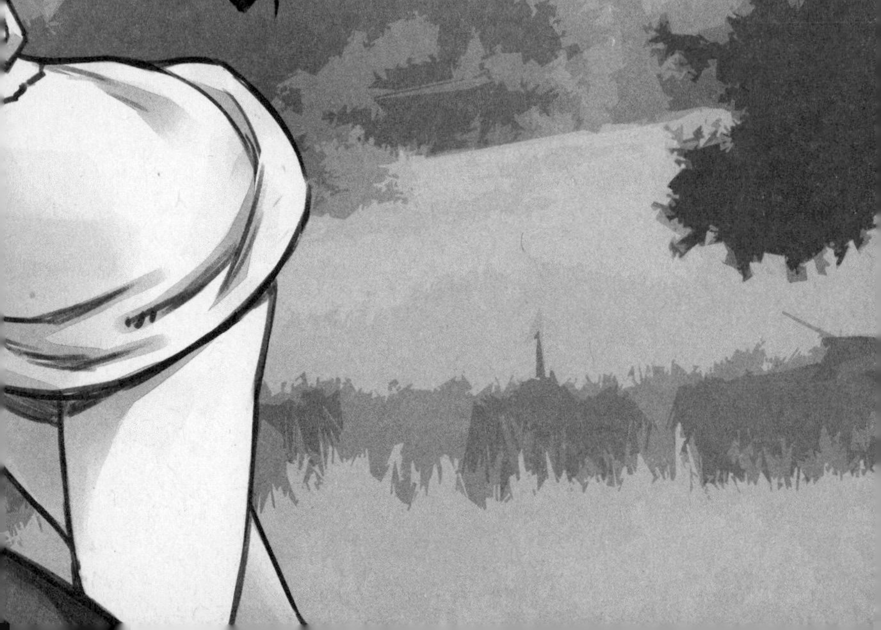

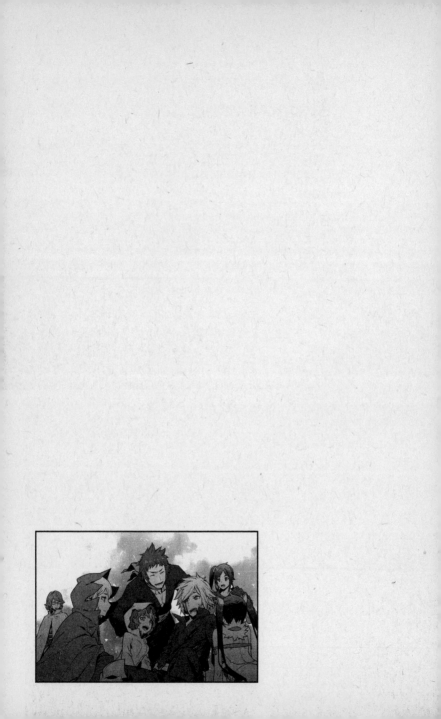

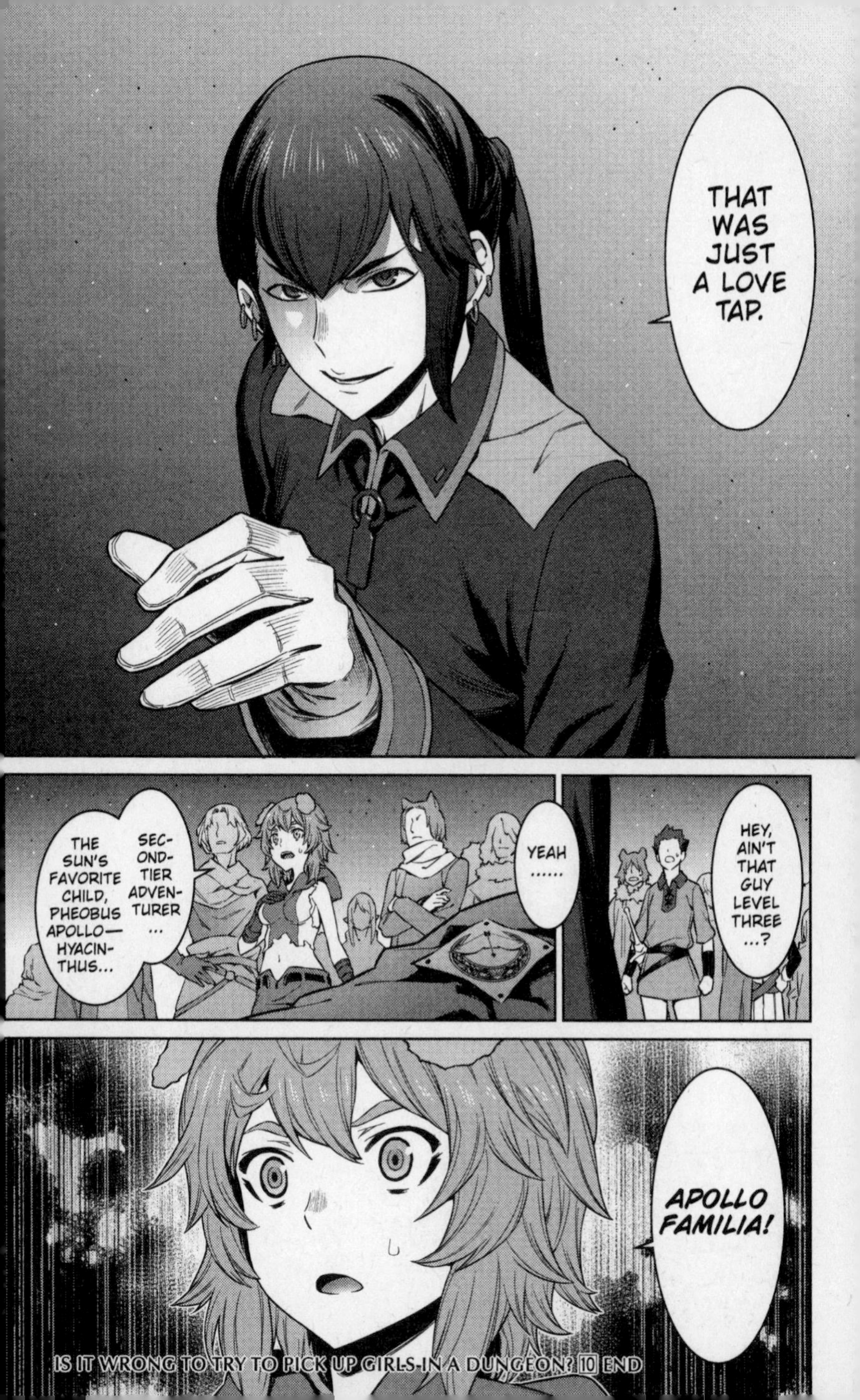
THAT WAS JUST A LOVE TAP.
HEY, AIN'T THAT GUY LEVEL THREE ...?
YEAH ......
SEC-OND-TIER ADVEN-TURER ...
THE SUN'S FAVORITE CHILD, PHEOBUS APOLLO—HYACIN-THUS...
APOLLO FAMILIA!
IS IT WRONG TO TRY TO PICK UP GIRLS IN A DUNGEON? 10 END

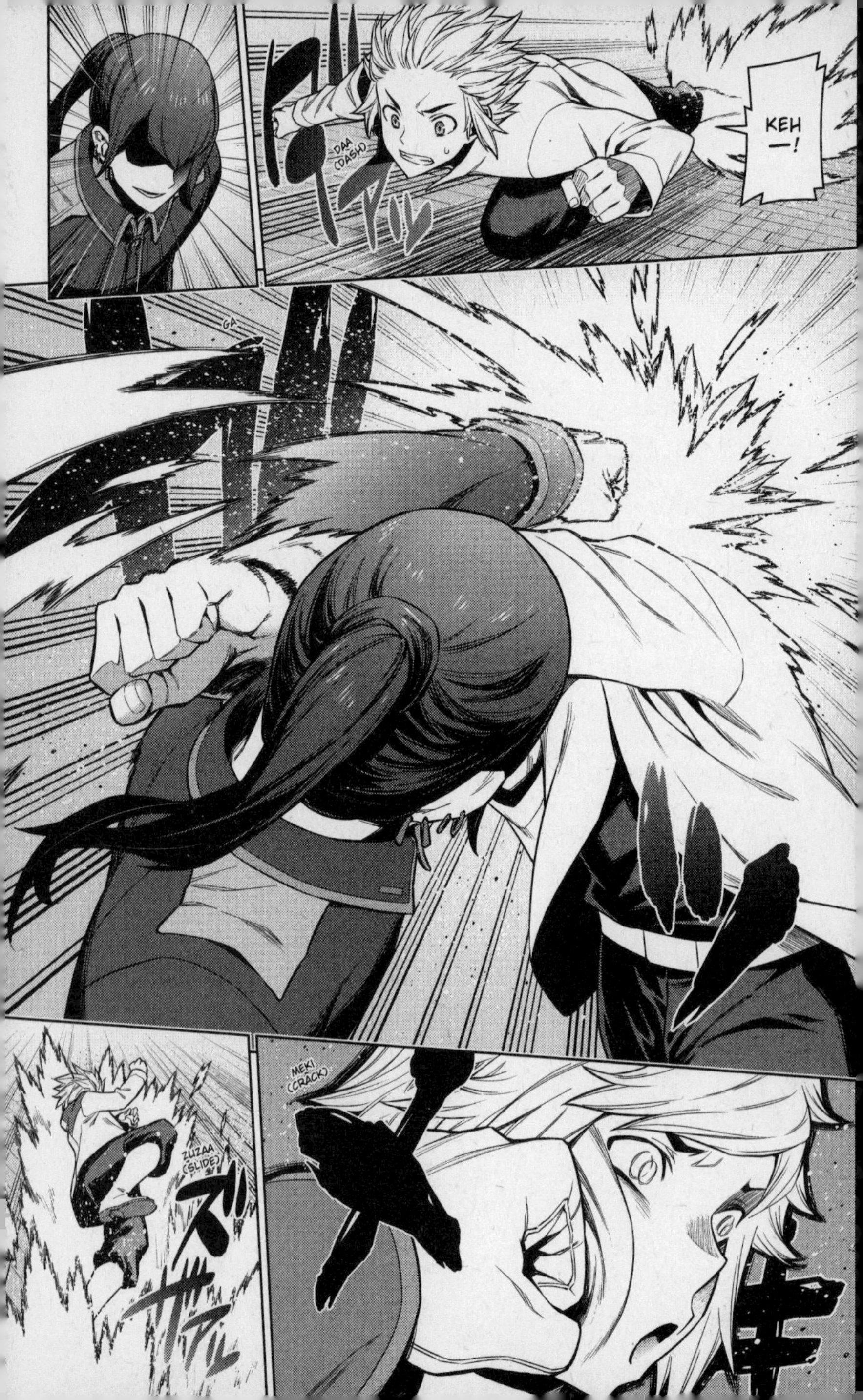
KEH—!
DAA (DASH)
GA
MEKI (CRACK)
ZUZAA (SLIDE)

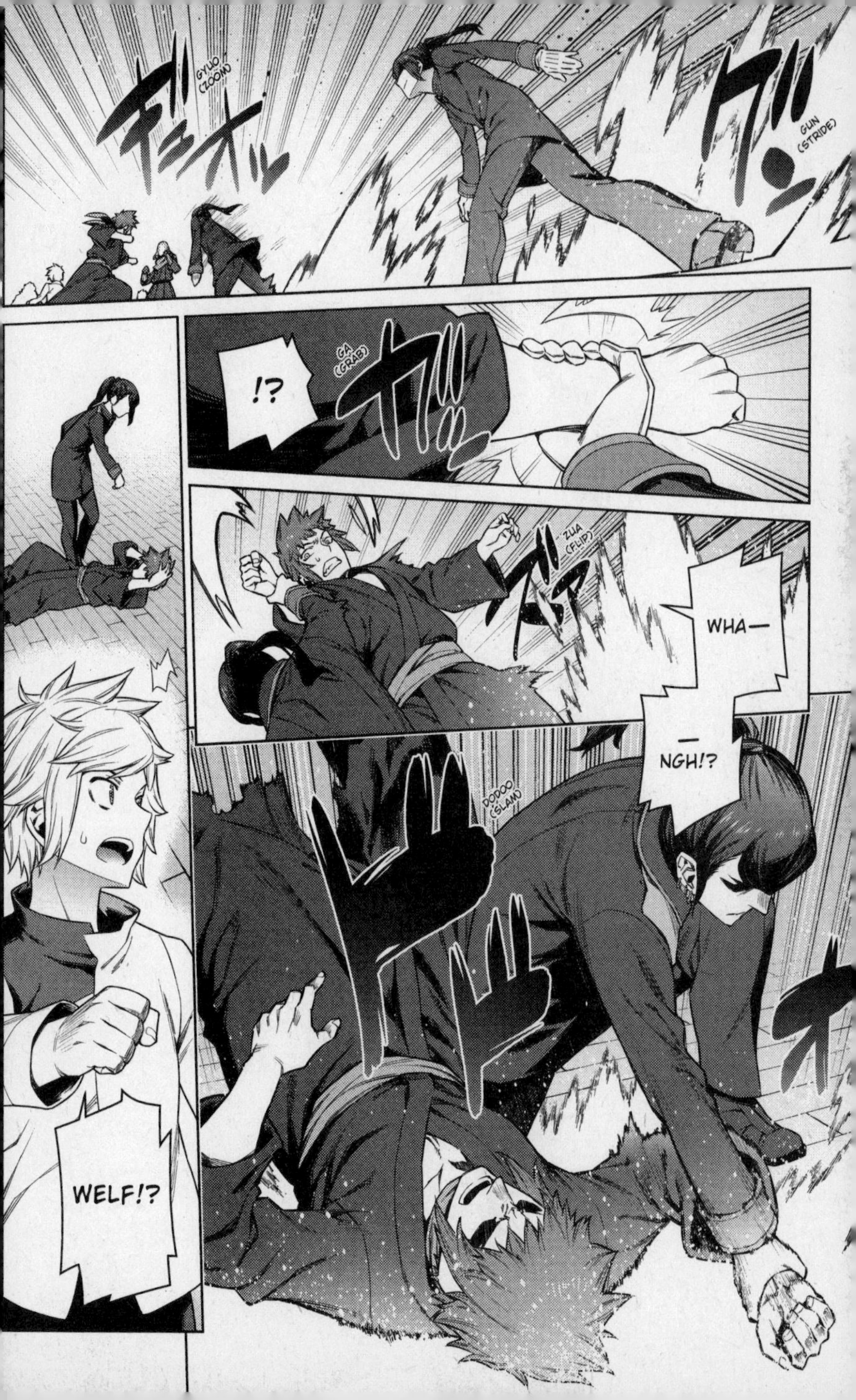
GUN
(STRIDE)
GYUO
(ZOOM)
!?
GA
(GRAB)
WHA—
ZUA
(FLIP)
—NGH!?
DODOO
(SLAM)
WELF!?

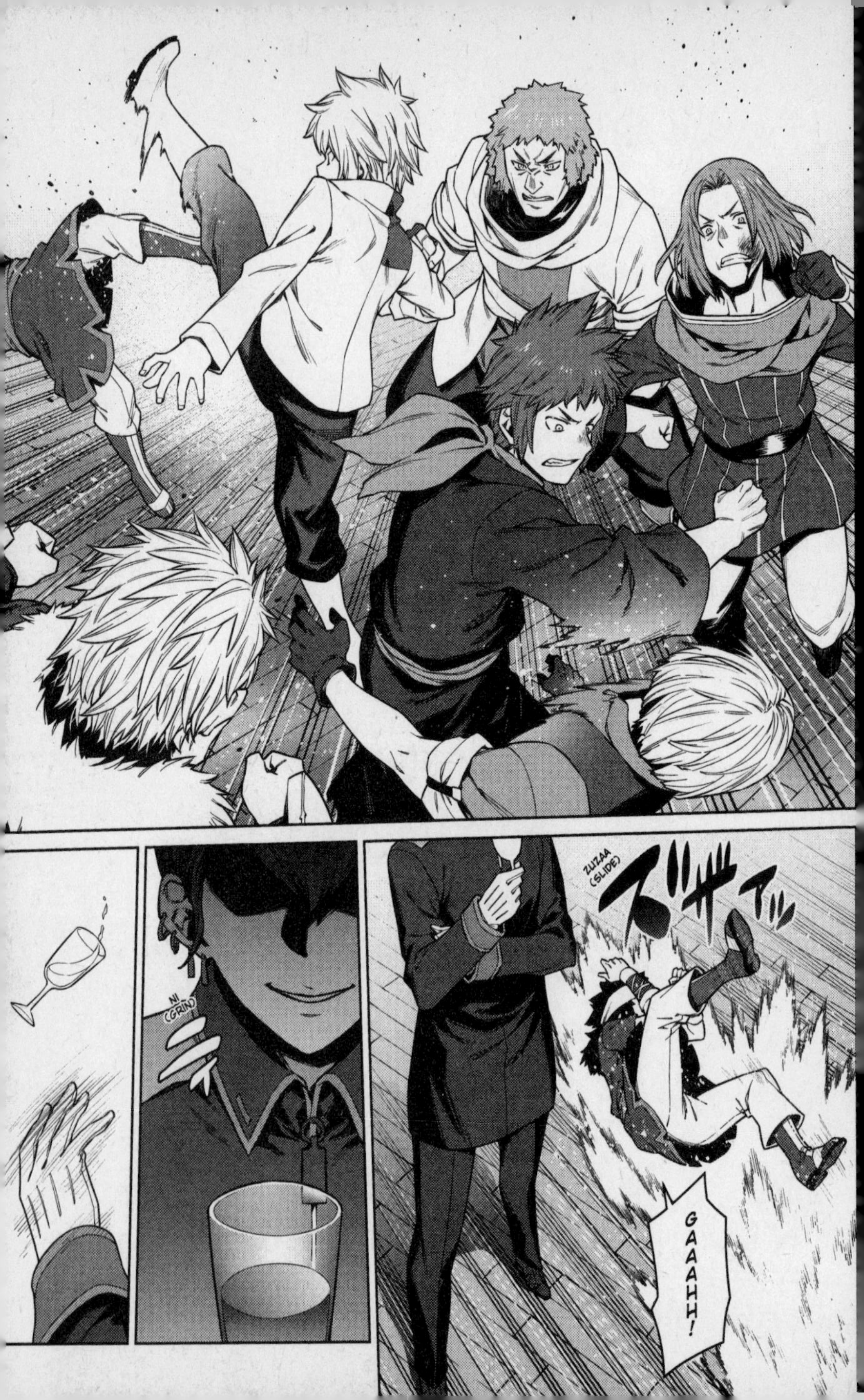
ZUZAA (SLIDE)
GAAAHH!
NI (GRIN)

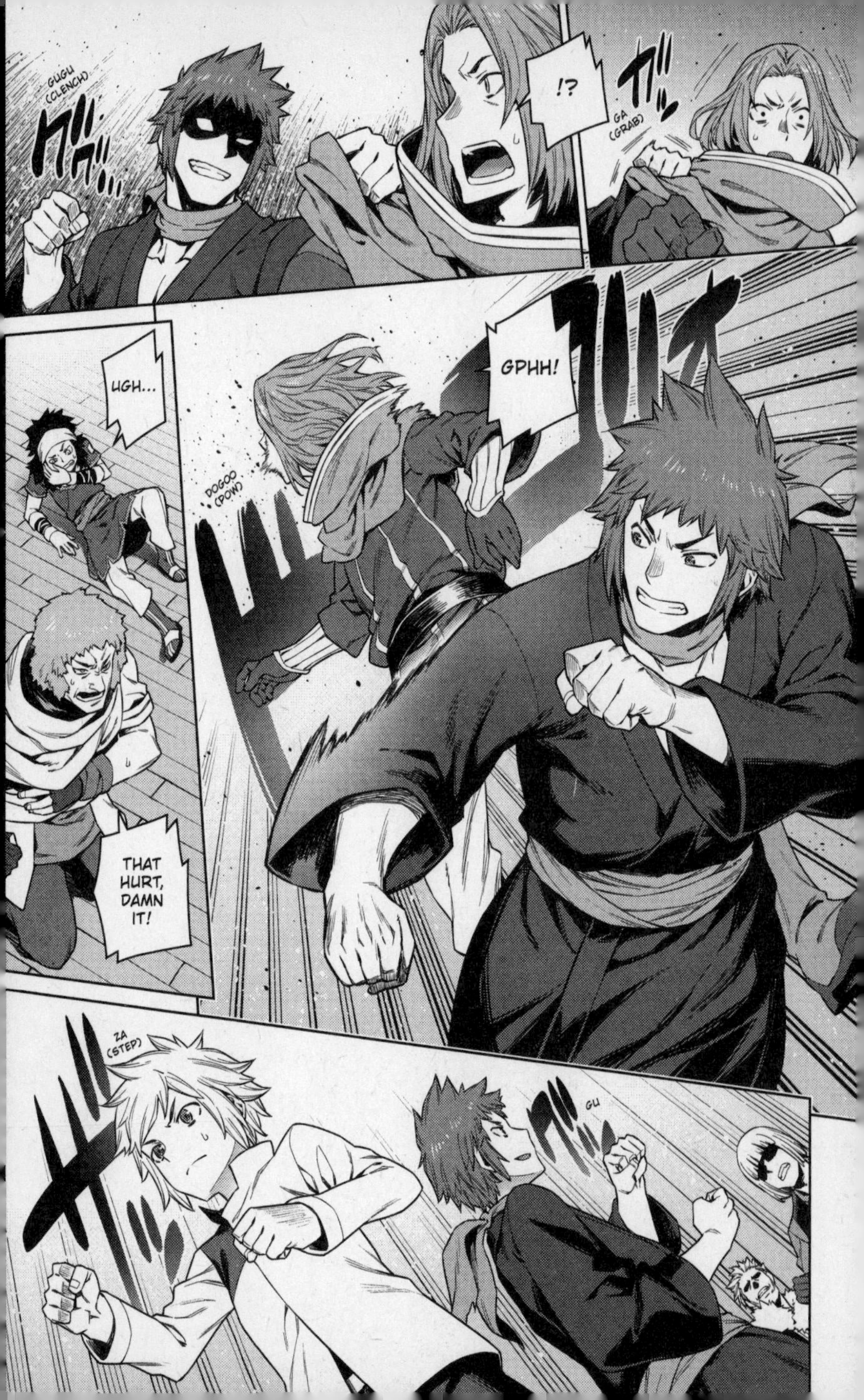
GA (GRAB)
!?
GUGU (CLENCH)
GPHH!
DOGOO (POW)
UGH...
THAT HURT, DAMN IT!
GU
ZA (STEP)

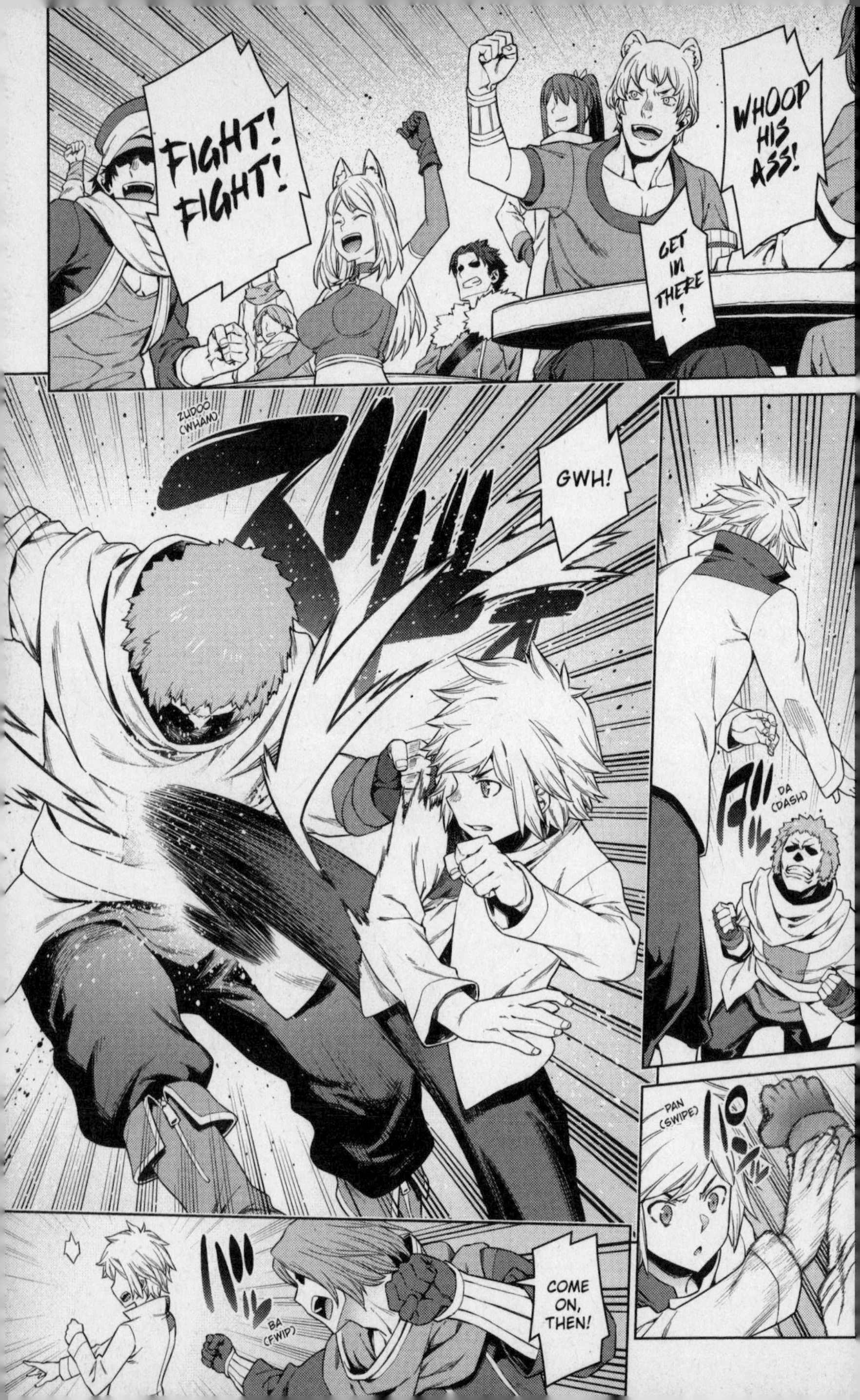
WHOOP HIS ASS!
GET IN THERE!
FIGHT! FIGHT!
DA (DASH)
PAN (SWIPE)
ZUDOO (WHAM)
GWH!
COME ON, THEN!
BA (FWIP)

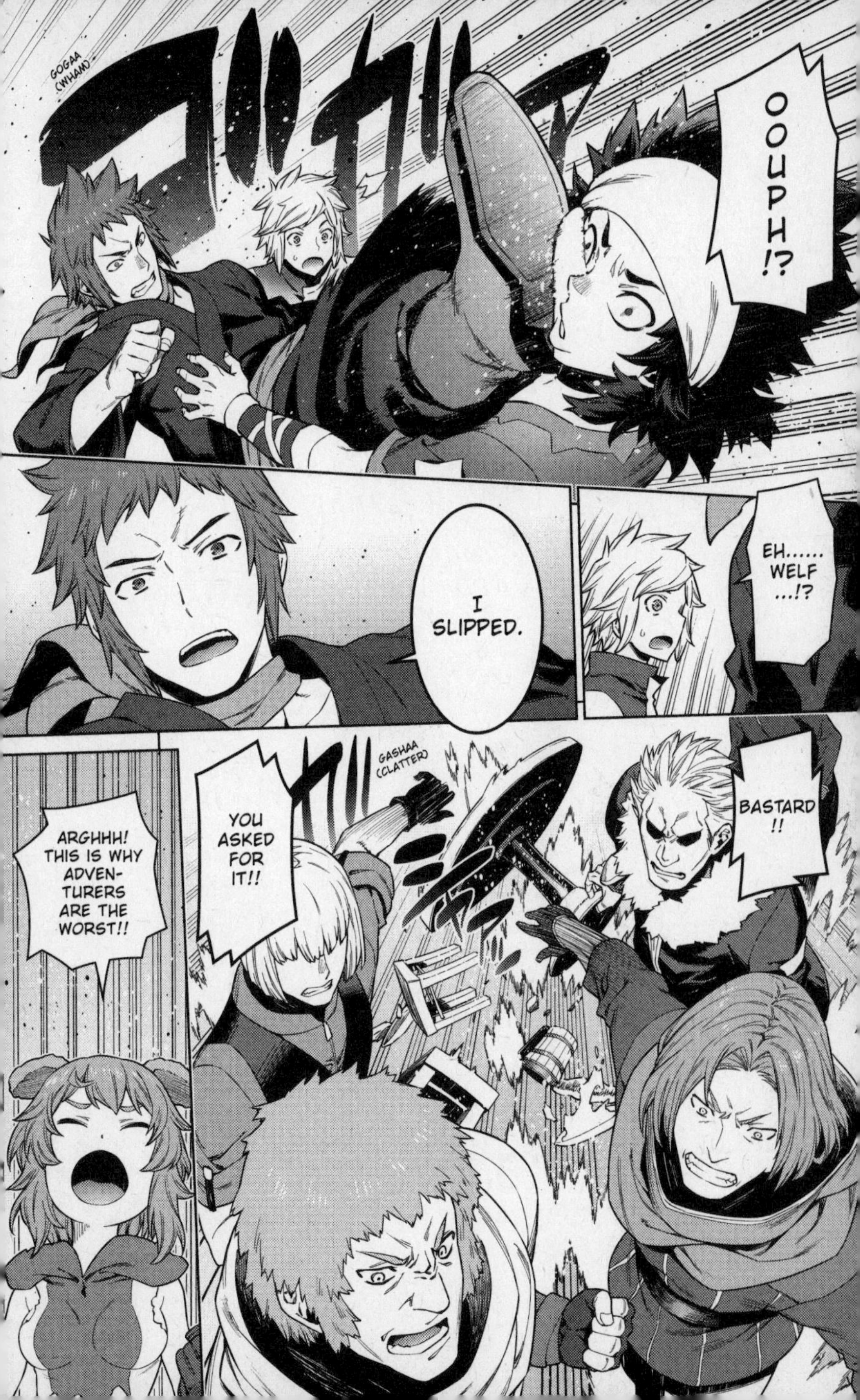
OOUPH!?
GOGAA (WHAM)
EH...... WELF ...!?
I SLIPPED.
BASTARD!!
GASHAA (CLATTER)
YOU ASKED FOR IT!!
ARGHHH! THIS IS WHY ADVEN-TURERS ARE THE WORST!!

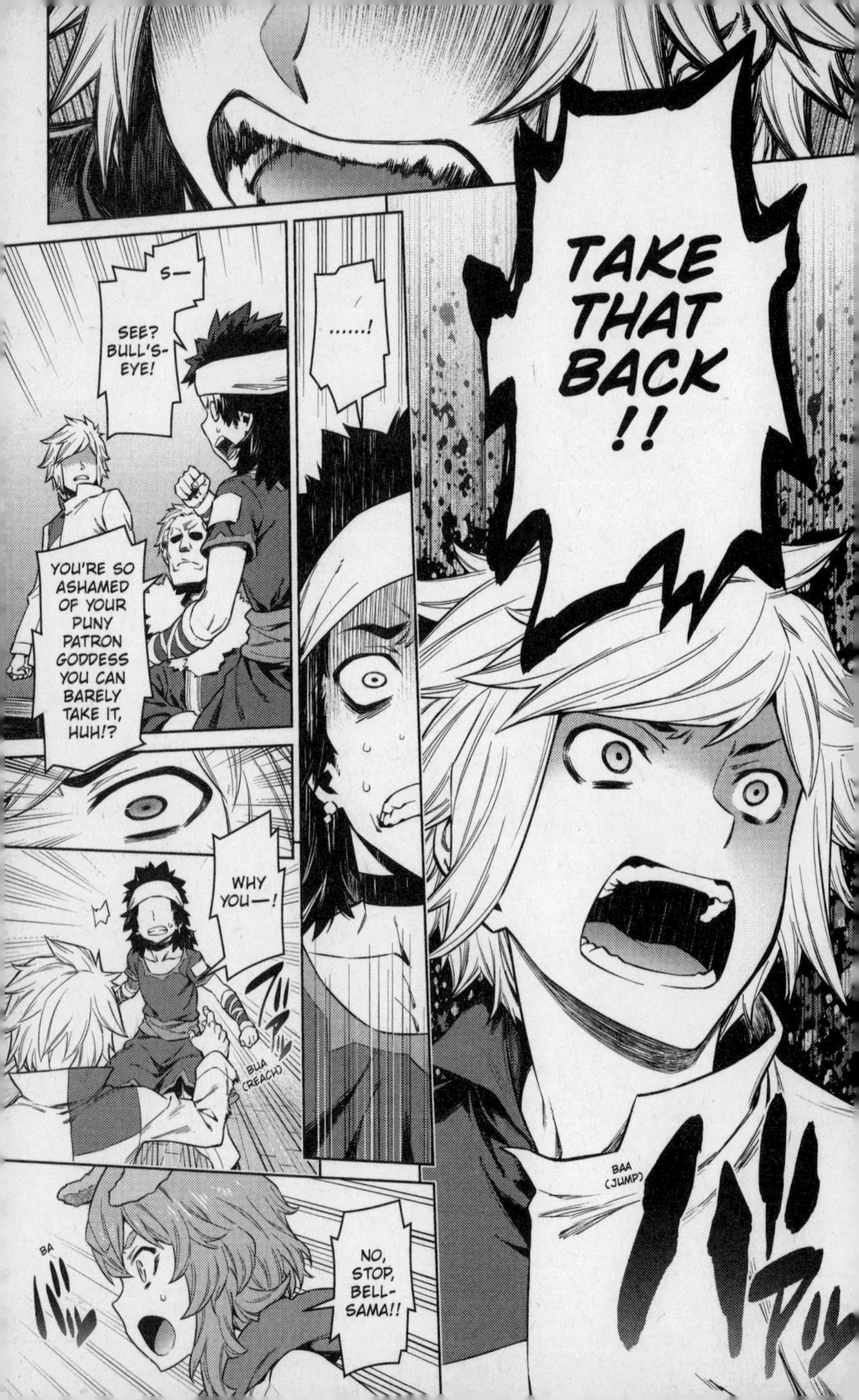
S—
SEE? BULL'S-EYE!
YOU'RE SO ASHAMED OF YOUR PUNY PATRON GODDESS YOU CAN BARELY TAKE IT, HUH!?
......!
TAKE THAT BACK!!
WHY YOU—!
BUA (REACH)
BAA (JUMP)
NO, STOP, BELL-SAMA!!
BA

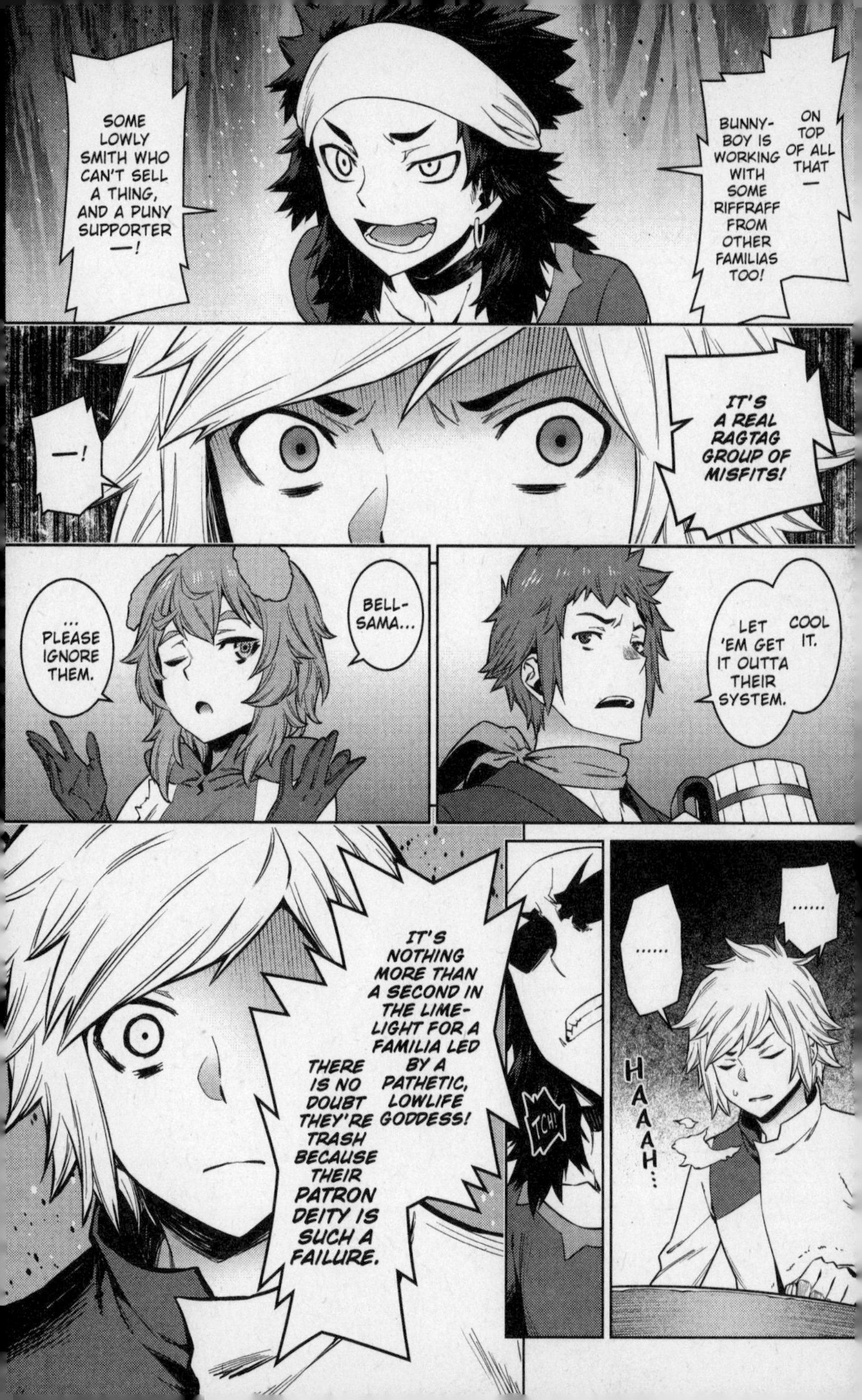
ON TOP OF ALL THAT—
BUNNY-BOY IS WORKING WITH SOME RIFFRAFF FROM OTHER FAMILIAS TOO!
SOME LOWLY SMITH WHO CAN'T SELL A THING, AND A PUNY SUPPORTER—!
IT'S A REAL RAGTAG GROUP OF MISFITS!
—!
COOL IT.
LET 'EM GET IT OUTTA THEIR SYSTEM.
BELL-SAMA...
...PLEASE IGNORE THEM.
......
......
HAAAH...
TCH!
IT'S NOTHING MORE THAN A SECOND IN THE LIME-LIGHT FOR A FAMILIA LED BY A PATHETIC, LOWLIFE GODDESS!
THERE IS NO DOUBT THEY'RE TRASH BECAUSE THEIR PATRON DEITY IS SUCH A FAILURE.

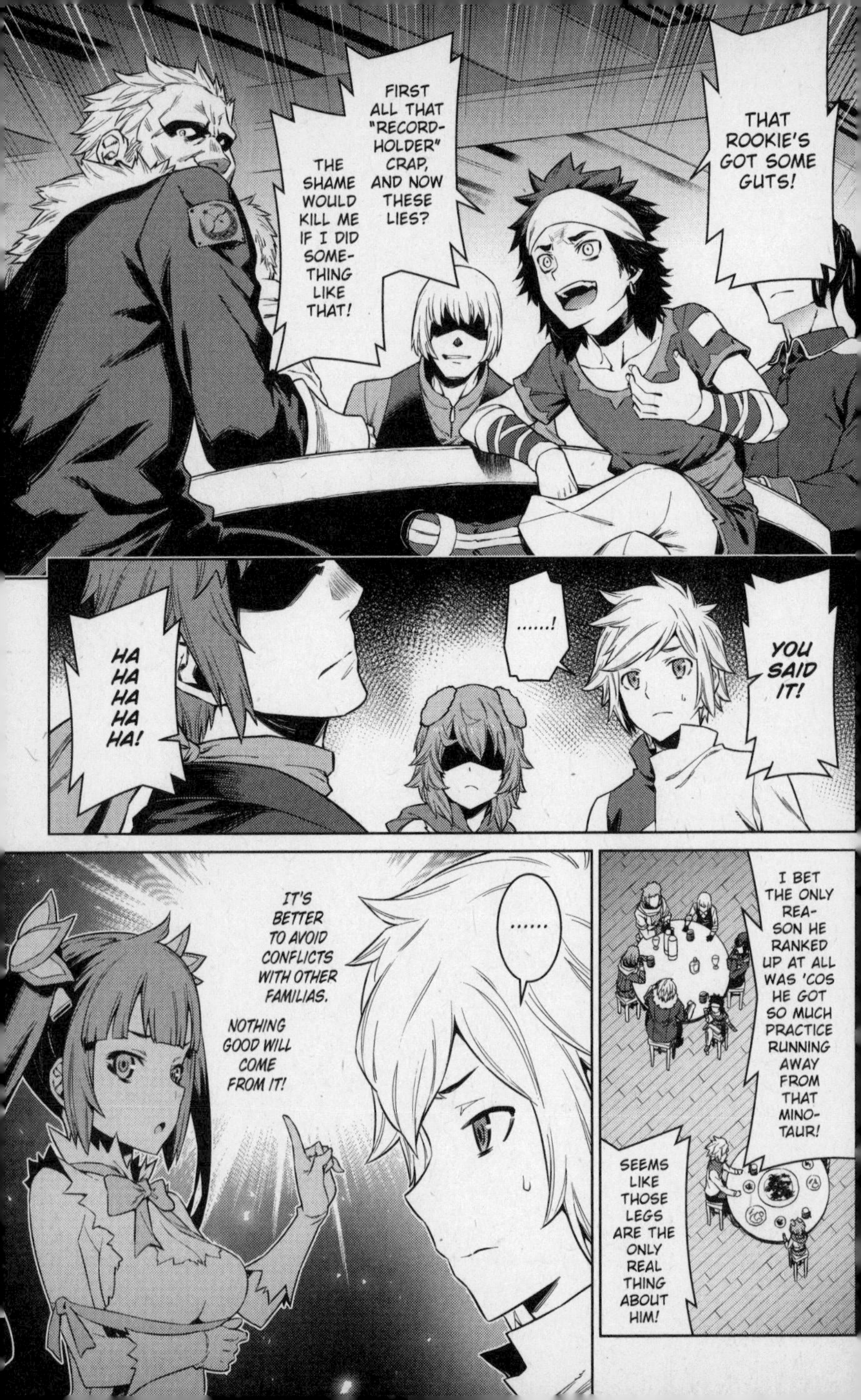

THAT ROOKIE'S GOT SOME GUTS!
FIRST ALL THAT "RECORD-HOLDER" CRAP, AND NOW THESE LIES?
THE SHAME WOULD KILL ME IF I DID SOMETHING LIKE THAT!
YOU SAID IT!
......!
HA HA HA HA HA!
I BET THE ONLY REASON HE RANKED UP AT ALL WAS 'COS HE GOT SO MUCH PRACTICE RUNNING AWAY FROM THAT MINOTAUR!
SEEMS LIKE THOSE LEGS ARE THE ONLY REAL THING ABOUT HIM!
......
IT'S BETTER TO AVOID CONFLICTS WITH OTHER FAMILIAS.
NOTHING GOOD WILL COME FROM IT!

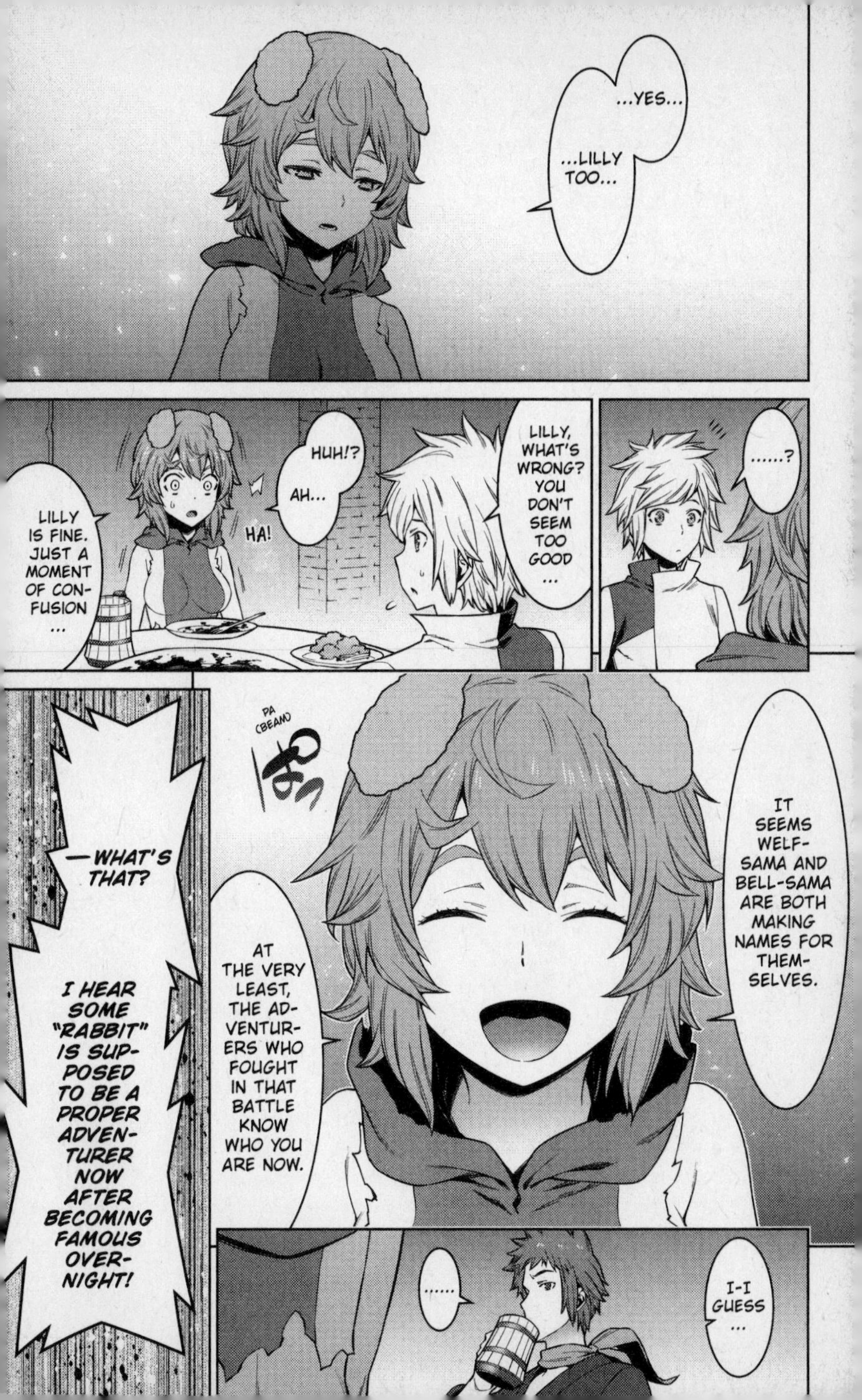

...YES...
...LILLY TOO...
......?
LILLY, WHAT'S WRONG? YOU DON'T SEEM TOO GOOD ...
HUH!?
AH...
HA!
LILLY IS FINE. JUST A MOMENT OF CONFUSION ...
PA (BEAM)
IT SEEMS WELF-SAMA AND BELL-SAMA ARE BOTH MAKING NAMES FOR THEMSELVES.
AT THE VERY LEAST, THE ADVENTURERS WHO FOUGHT IN THAT BATTLE KNOW WHO YOU ARE NOW.
I-I GUESS ...
......
—WHAT'S THAT?
I HEAR SOME "RABBIT" IS SUPPOSED TO BE A PROPER ADVENTURER NOW AFTER BECOMING FAMOUS OVERNIGHT!

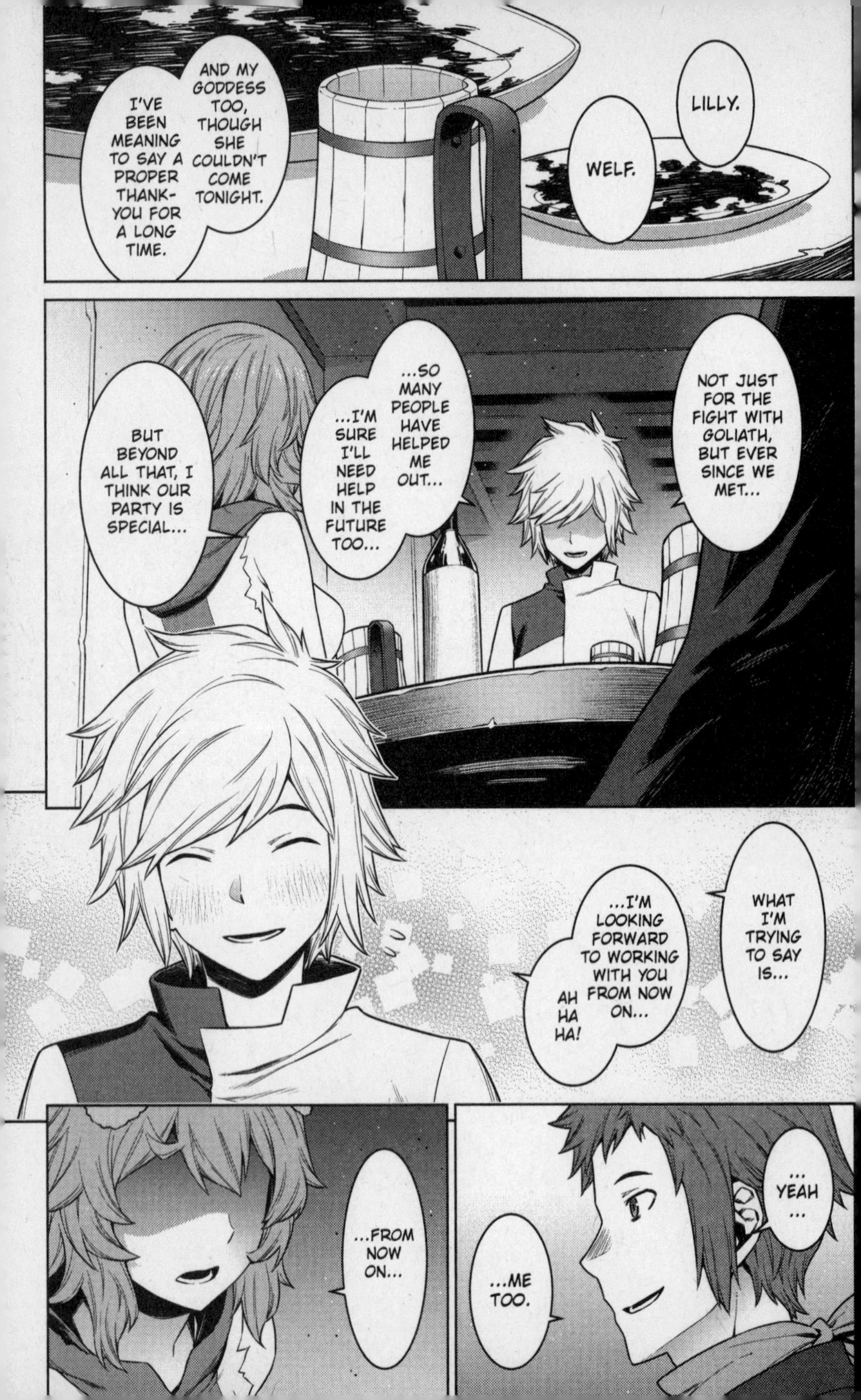
LILLY.
WELF.
AND MY GODDESS TOO, THOUGH SHE COULDN'T COME TONIGHT.
I'VE BEEN MEANING TO SAY A PROPER THANK-YOU FOR A LONG TIME.
NOT JUST FOR THE FIGHT WITH GOLIATH, BUT EVER SINCE WE MET...
...SO MANY PEOPLE HAVE HELPED ME OUT...
...I'M SURE I'LL NEED HELP IN THE FUTURE TOO...
BUT BEYOND ALL THAT, I THINK OUR PARTY IS SPECIAL...
WHAT I'M TRYING TO SAY IS...
...I'M LOOKING FORWARD TO WORKING WITH YOU FROM NOW ON...
AH HA HA!
...YEAH...
...ME TOO.
...FROM NOW ON...

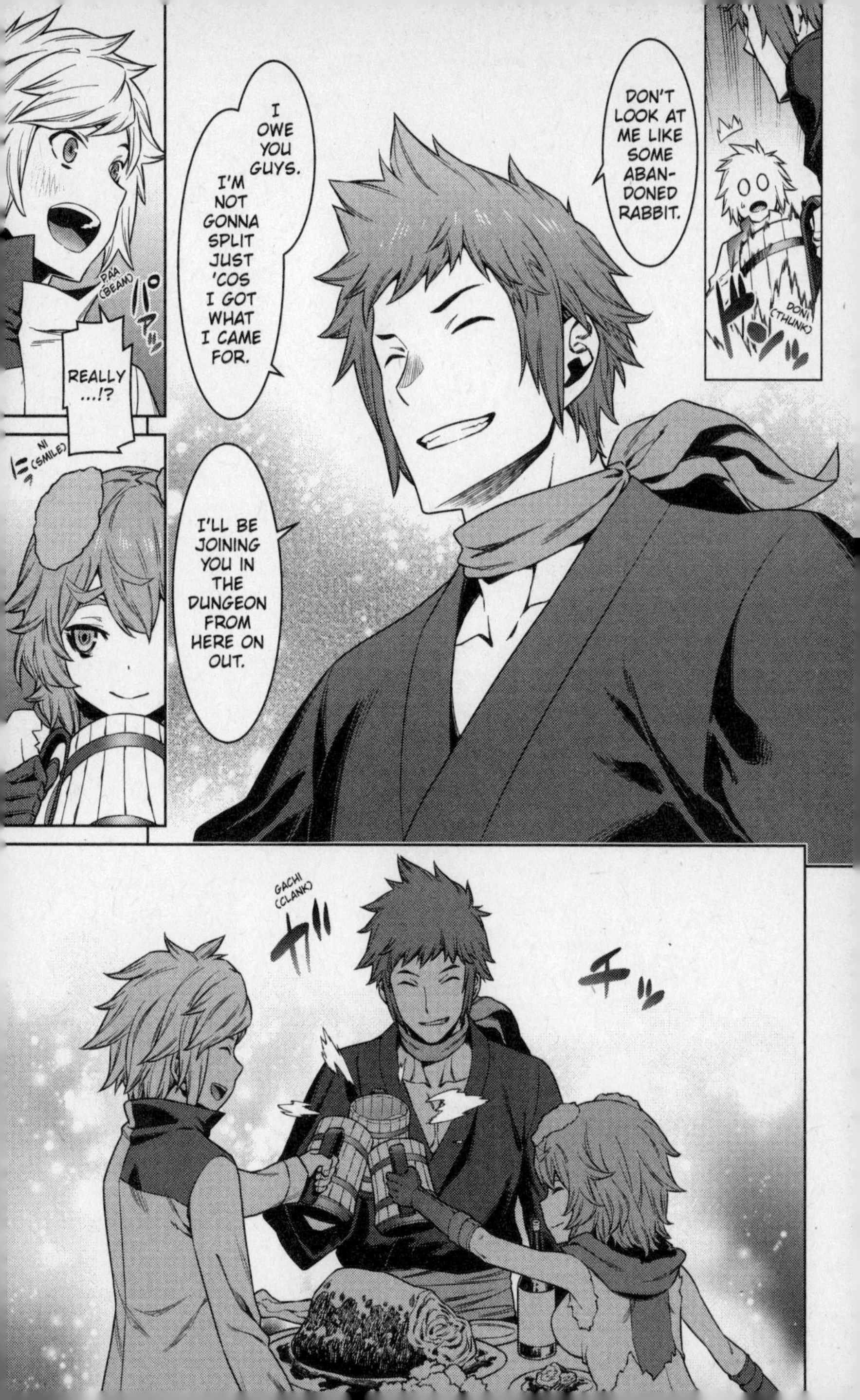
DONI (THUNK)
DON'T LOOK AT ME LIKE SOME ABAN-DONED RABBIT.
I OWE YOU GUYS.
I'M NOT GONNA SPLIT JUST 'COS I GOT WHAT I CAME FOR.
PAA (BEAM)
REALLY ...!?
I'LL BE JOINING YOU IN THE DUNGEON FROM HERE ON OUT.
NI (SMILE)
GACHI (CLANK)

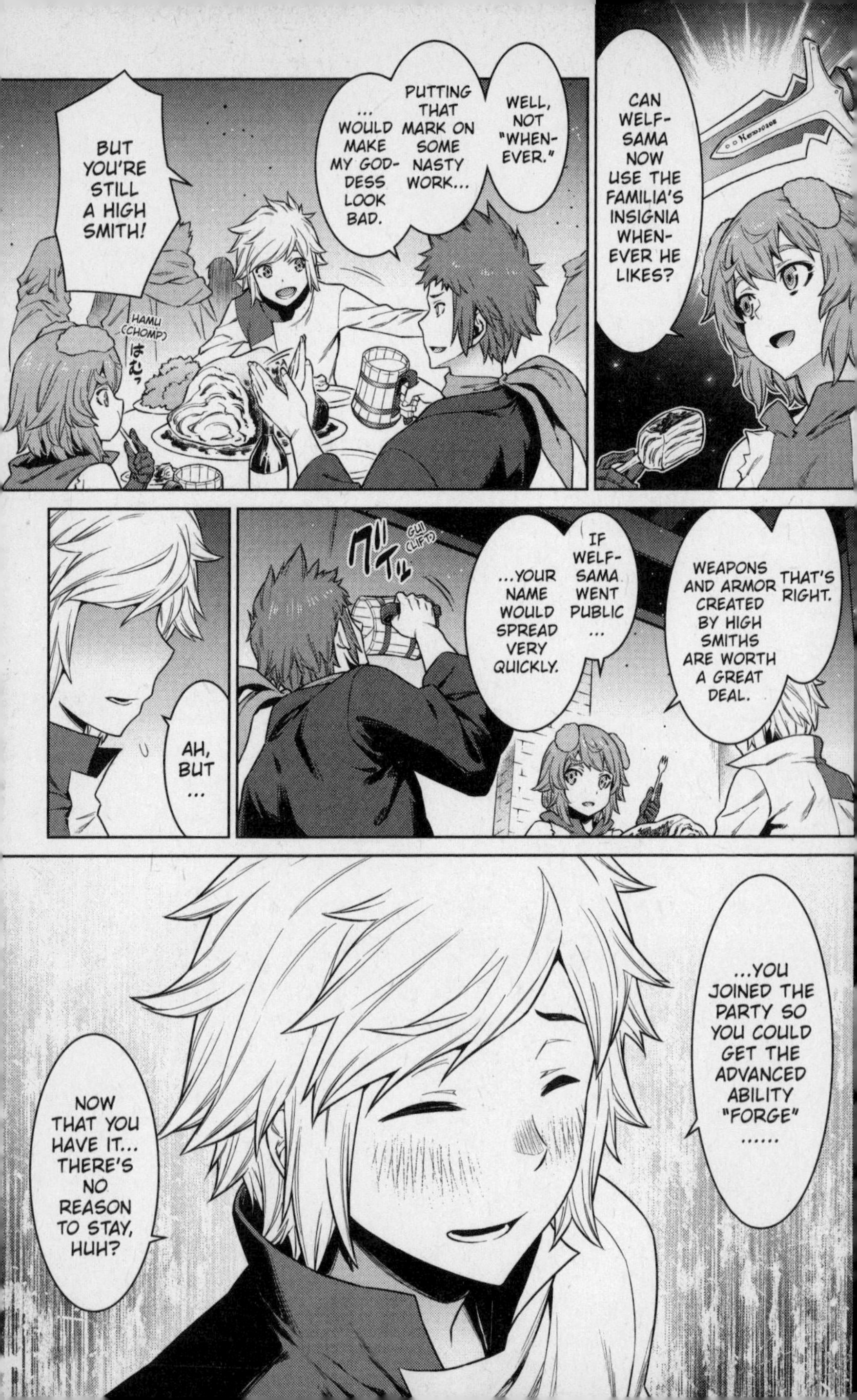
CAN WELF-SAMA NOW USE THE FAMILIA'S INSIGNIA WHENEVER HE LIKES?
WELL, NOT "WHENEVER."
PUTTING THAT MARK ON SOME NASTY WORK...
...WOULD MAKE MY GODDESS LOOK BAD.
BUT YOU'RE STILL A HIGH SMITH!
HAMU (CHOMP)
はむっ
THAT'S RIGHT.
WEAPONS AND ARMOR CREATED BY HIGH SMITHS ARE WORTH A GREAT DEAL.
IF WELF-SAMA WENT PUBLIC...
...YOUR NAME WOULD SPREAD VERY QUICKLY.
グイッ
GUI (LIFT)
AH, BUT...
...YOU JOINED THE PARTY SO YOU COULD GET THE ADVANCED ABILITY "FORGE"......
NOW THAT YOU HAVE IT... THERE'S NO REASON TO STAY, HUH?

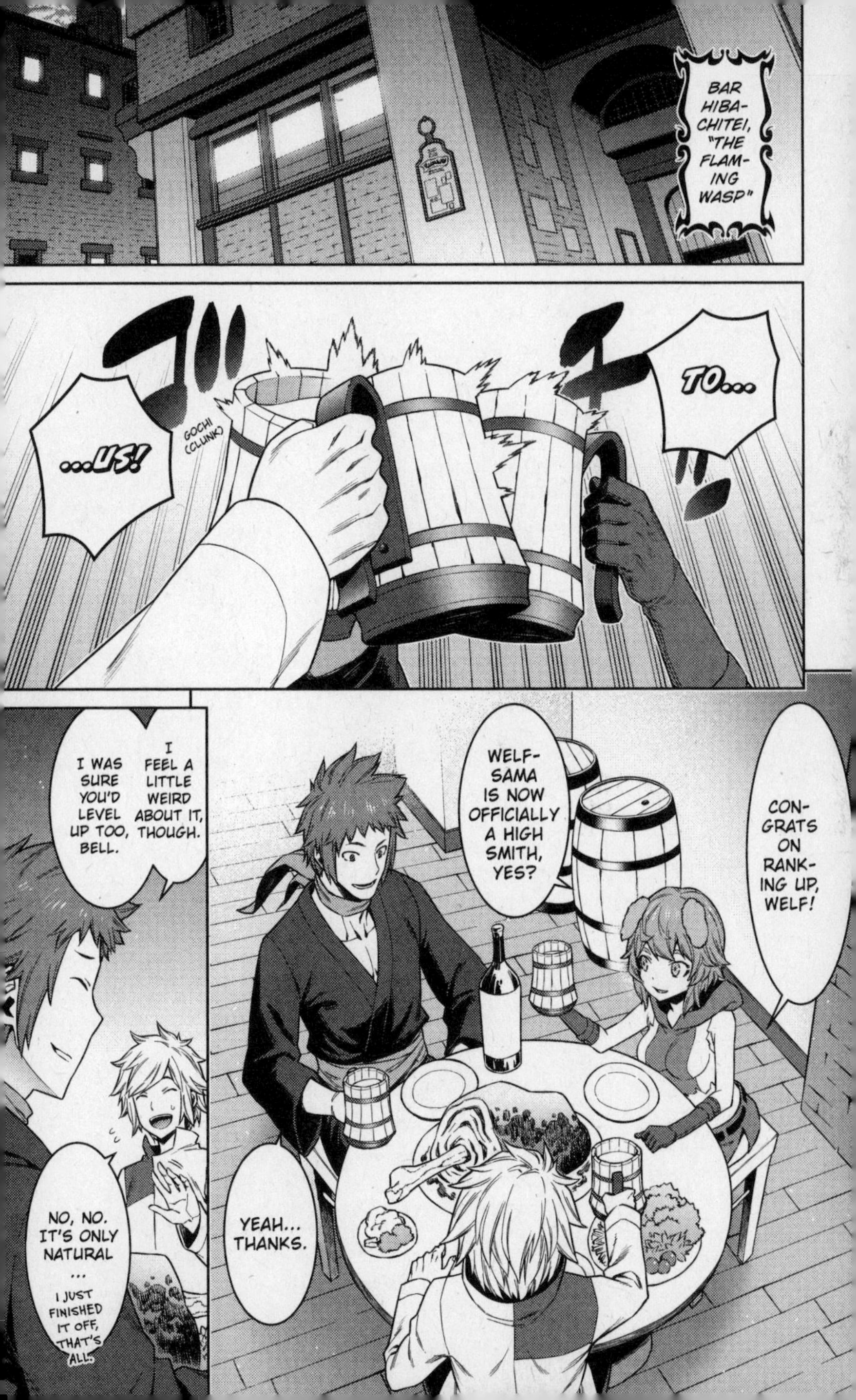
BAR HIBA-CHITEI, "THE FLAM-ING WASP"
TO...
GOCHI (CLUNK)
...US!
CON-GRATS ON RANK-ING UP, WELF!
WELF-SAMA IS NOW OFFICIALLY A HIGH SMITH, YES?
YEAH... THANKS.
I FEEL A LITTLE WEIRD ABOUT IT, THOUGH.
I WAS SURE YOU'D LEVEL UP TOO, BELL.
NO, NO. IT'S ONLY NATURAL ...
I JUST FINISHED IT OFF, THAT'S ALL.

STEP 86 ▶▶ COMPLICATIONS

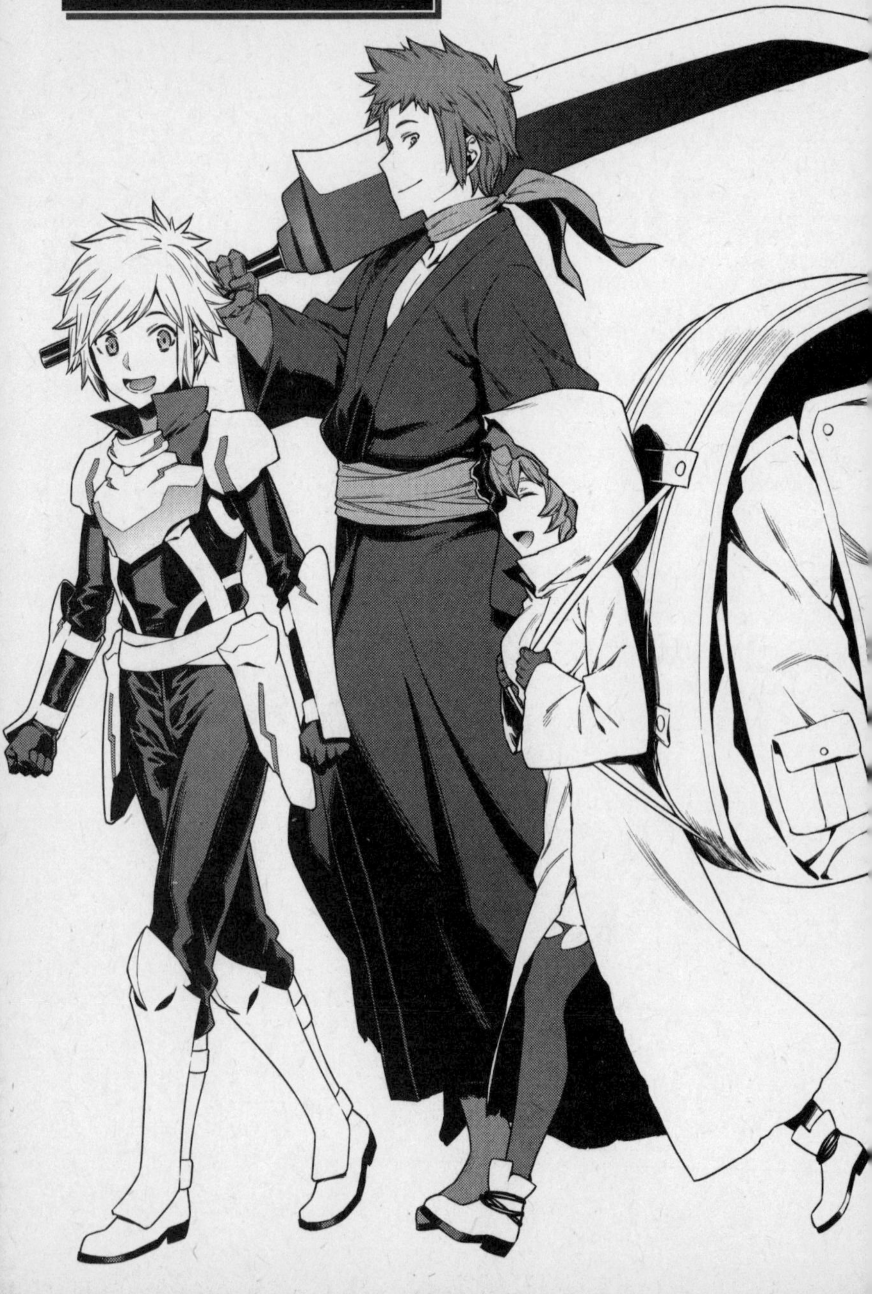

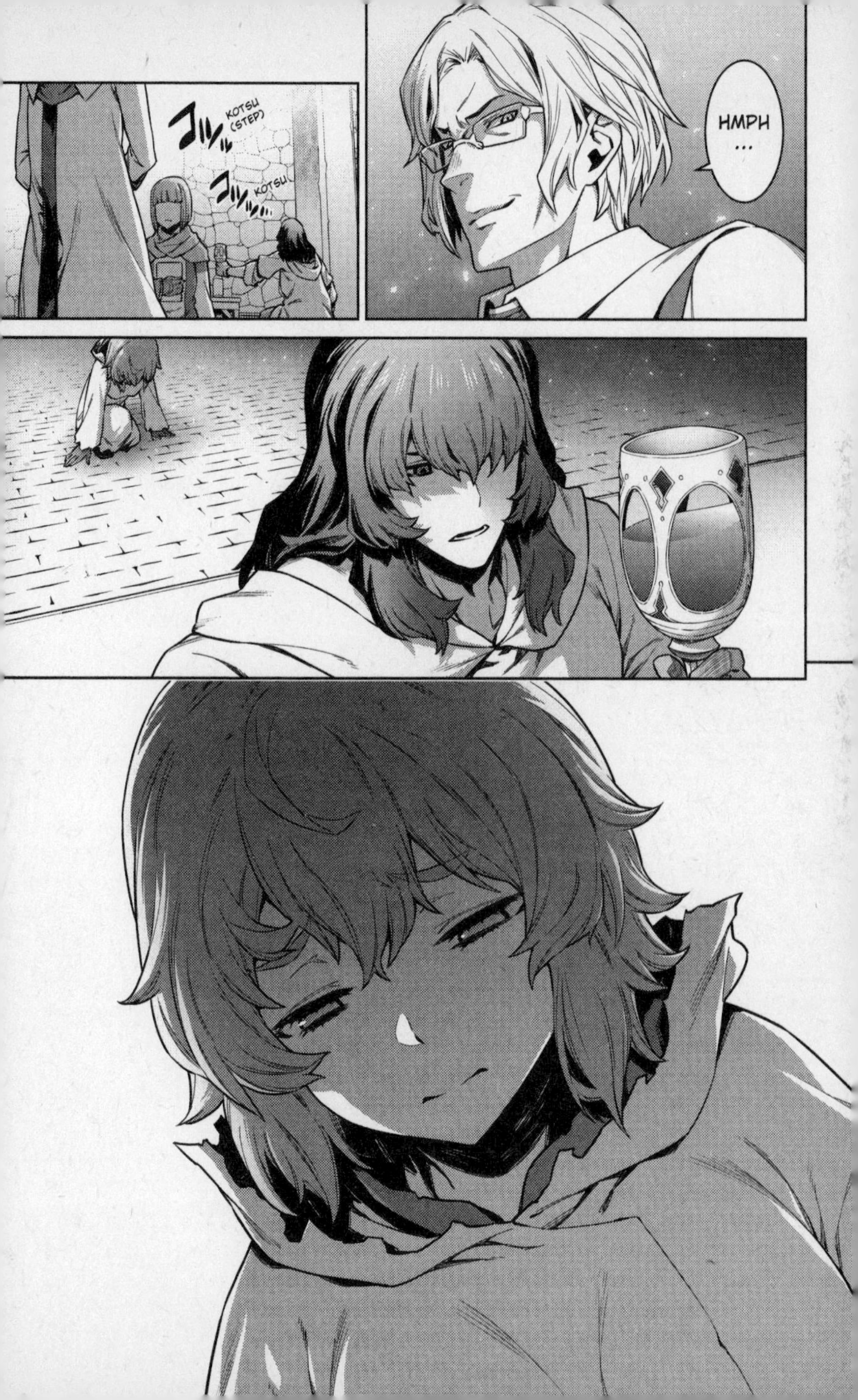
HMPH ...
KOTSU (STEP)
KOTSU

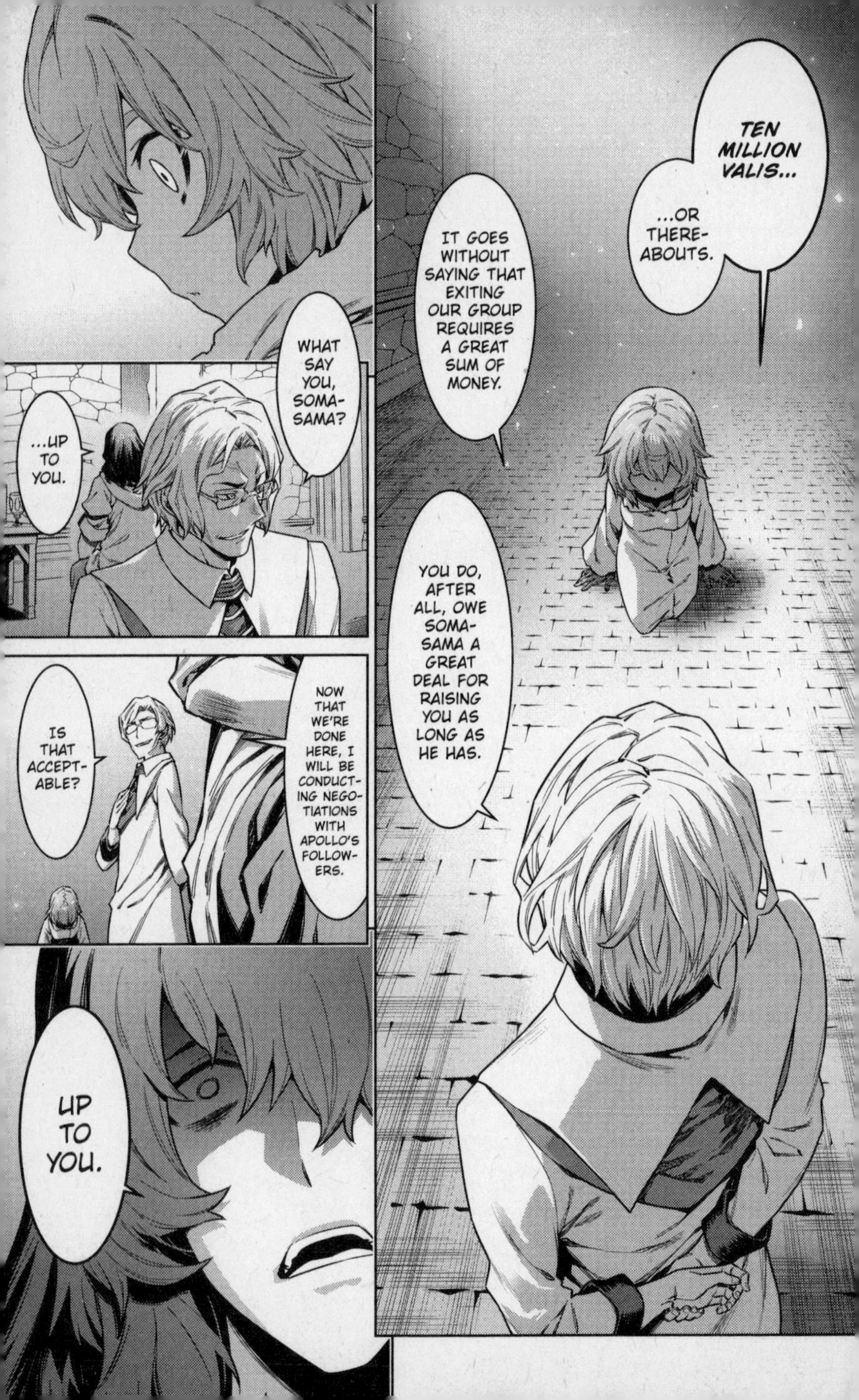
TEN MILLION VALIS...
...OR THERE-ABOUTS.
IT GOES WITHOUT SAYING THAT EXITING OUR GROUP REQUIRES A GREAT SUM OF MONEY.
YOU DO, AFTER ALL, OWE SOMA-SAMA A GREAT DEAL FOR RAISING YOU AS LONG AS HE HAS.
WHAT SAY YOU, SOMA-SAMA?
...UP TO YOU.
NOW THAT WE'RE DONE HERE, I WILL BE CONDUCTING NEGOTIATIONS WITH APOLLO'S FOLLOWERS.
IS THAT ACCEPTABLE?
UP TO YOU.

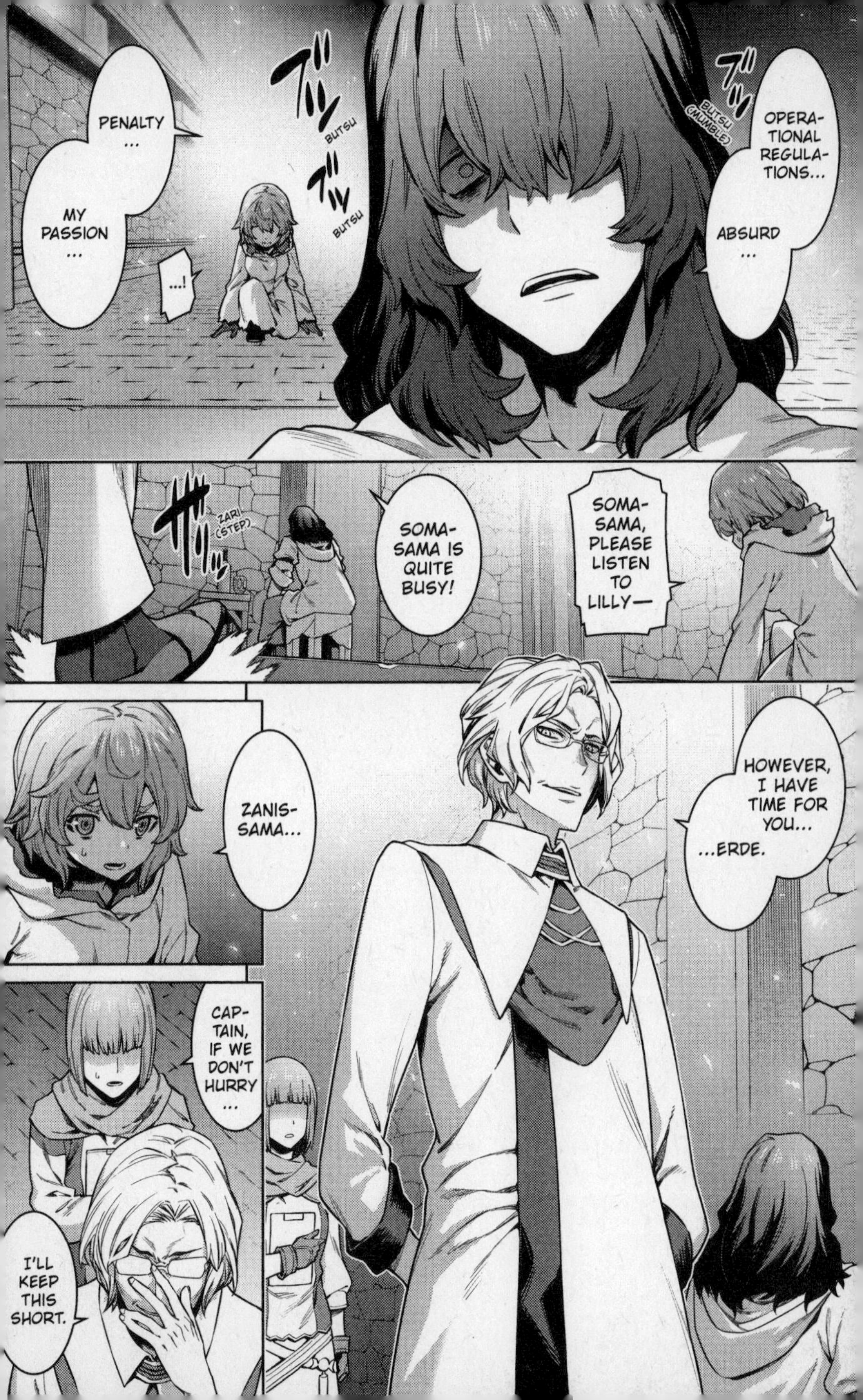
BUTSU (MUMBLE)
OPERATIONAL REGULATIONS...
ABSURD...
BUTSU
BUTSU
PENALTY...
MY PASSION...
...!
SOMA-SAMA, PLEASE LISTEN TO LILLY—
SOMA-SAMA IS QUITE BUSY!
ZARI (STEP)
HOWEVER, I HAVE TIME FOR YOU... ...ERDE.
ZANIS-SAMA...
CAPTAIN, IF WE DON'T HURRY...
I'LL KEEP THIS SHORT.

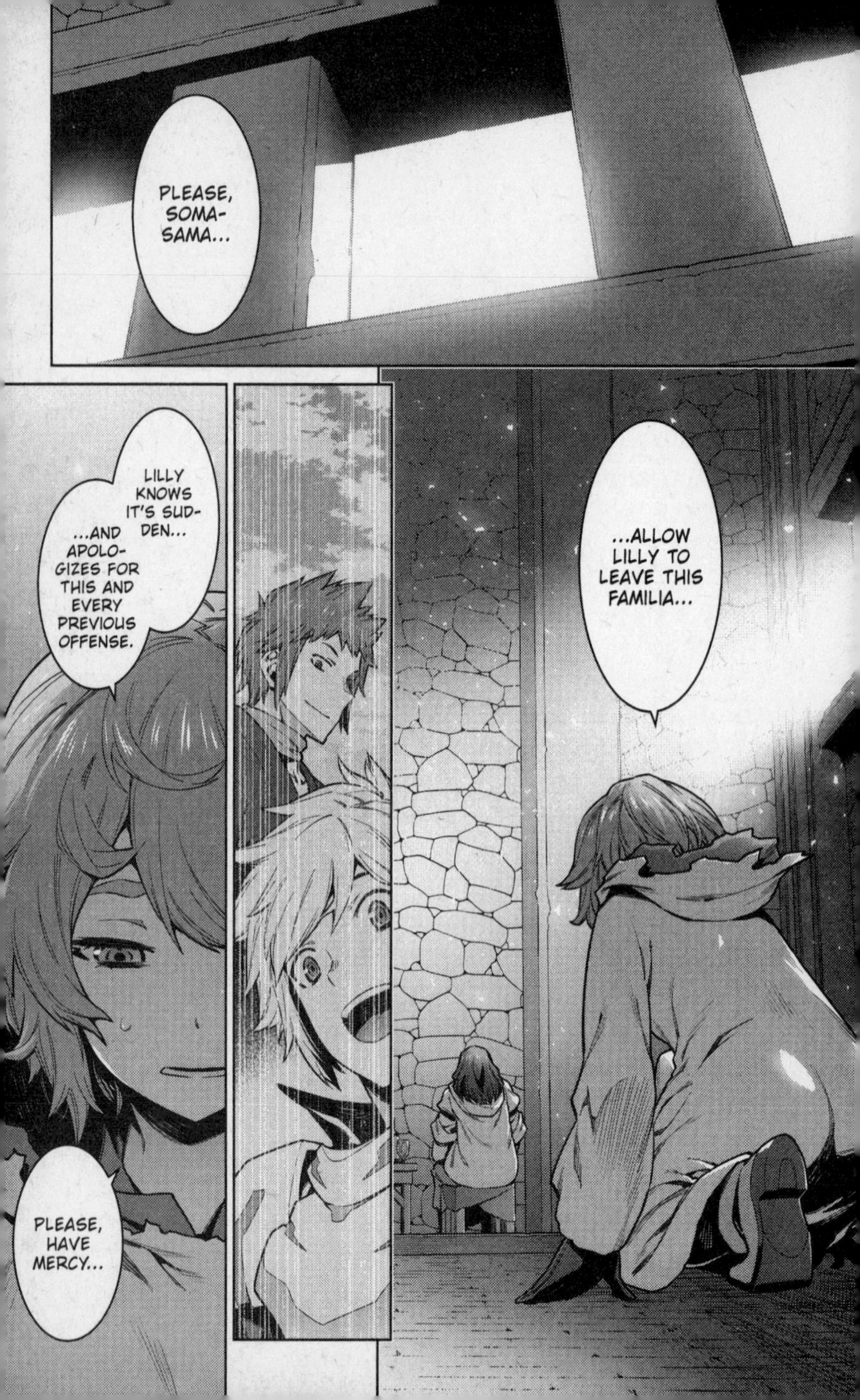
PLEASE, SOMA-SAMA...
...ALLOW LILLY TO LEAVE THIS FAMILIA...
LILLY KNOWS IT'S SUDDEN...
...AND APOLOGIZES FOR THIS AND EVERY PREVIOUS OFFENSE.
PLEASE, HAVE MERCY...

Is it WRONG to TRY to PiCK UP GiRLS iN A DUNGEON?

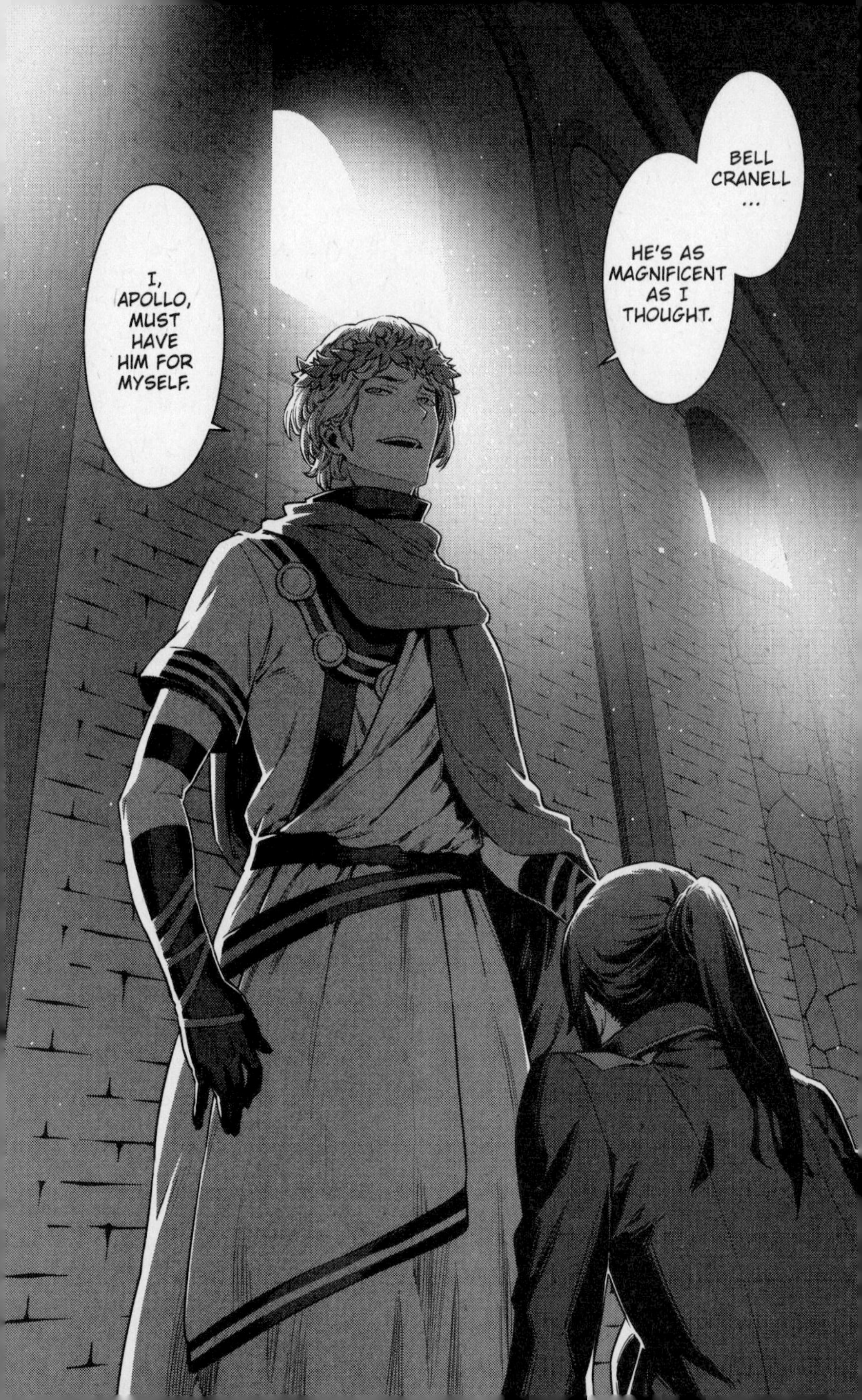
BELL CRANELL ...
HE'S AS MAGNIFICENT AS I THOUGHT.
I, APOLLO, MUST HAVE HIM FOR MYSELF.

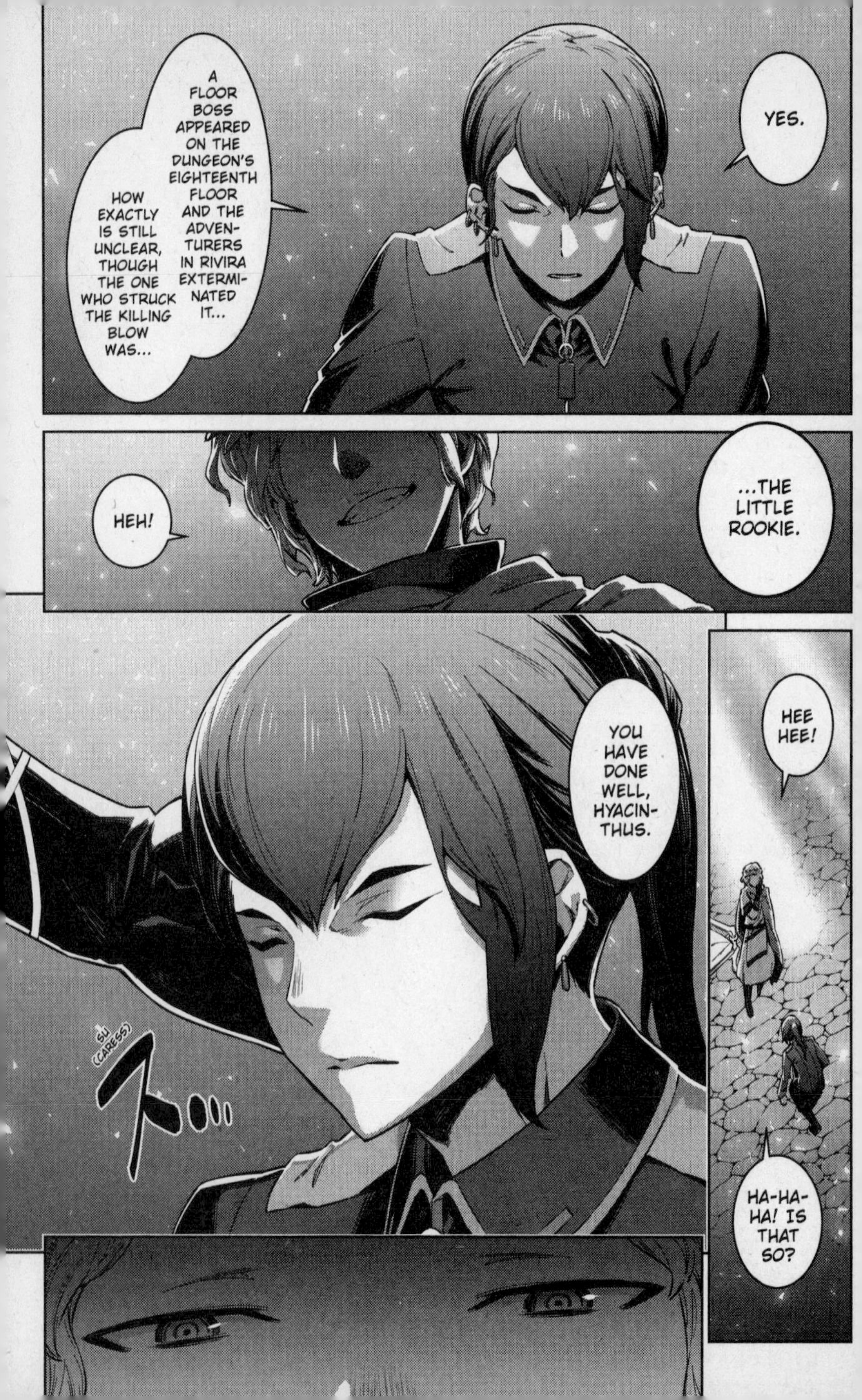
YES.
A FLOOR BOSS APPEARED ON THE DUNGEON'S EIGHTEENTH FLOOR AND THE ADVENTURERS IN RIVIRA EXTERMINATED IT... HOW EXACTLY IS STILL UNCLEAR, THOUGH THE ONE WHO STRUCK THE KILLING BLOW WAS...
...THE LITTLE ROOKIE.
HEH!
HEE HEE!
HA-HA-HA! IS THAT SO?
YOU HAVE DONE WELL, HYACINTHUS.
SU (CARESS)

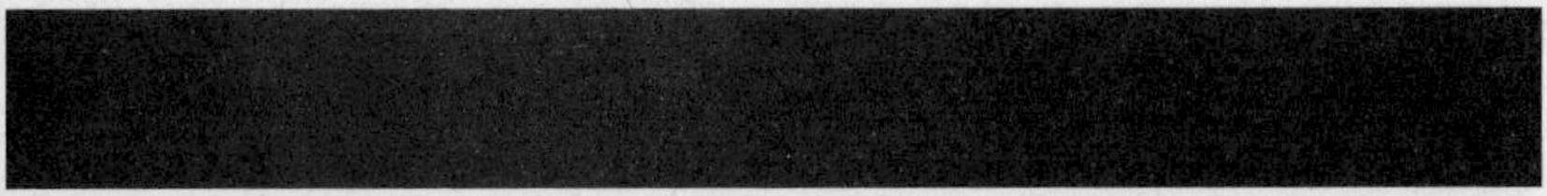
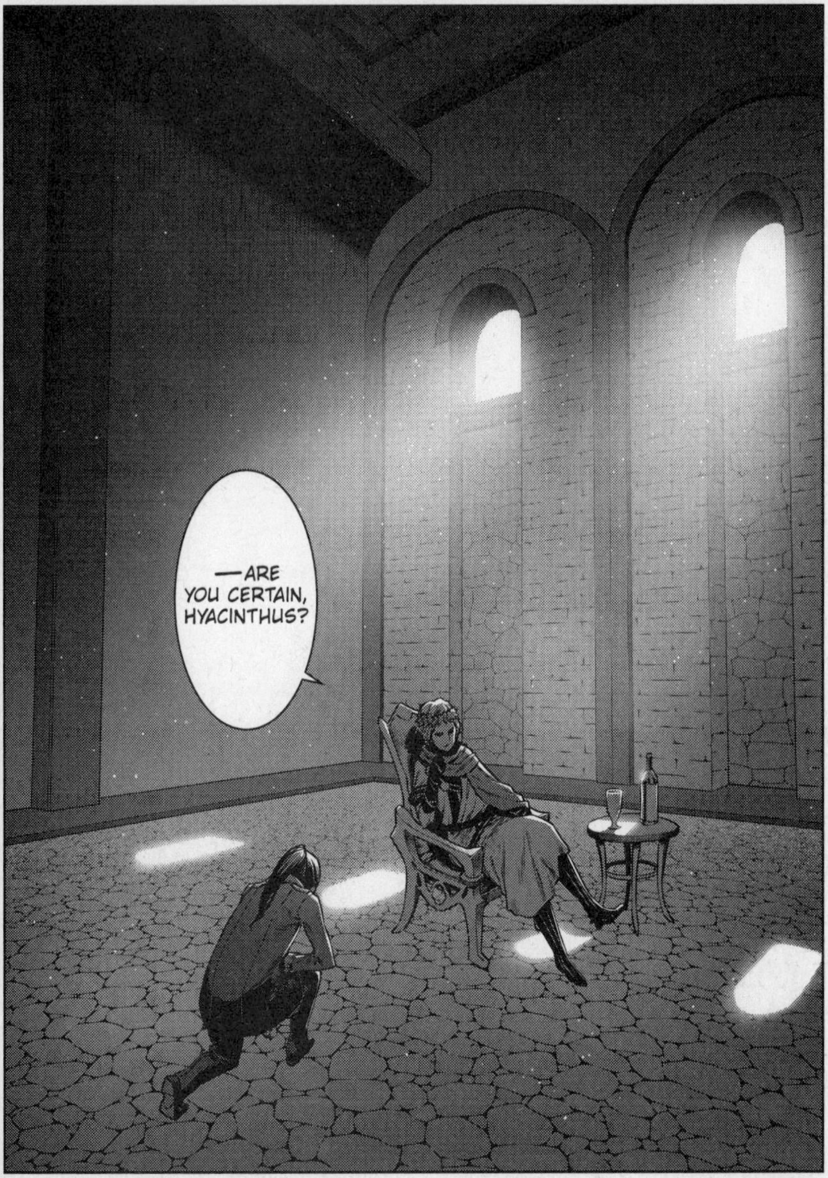
—ARE YOU CERTAIN, HYACINTHUS?

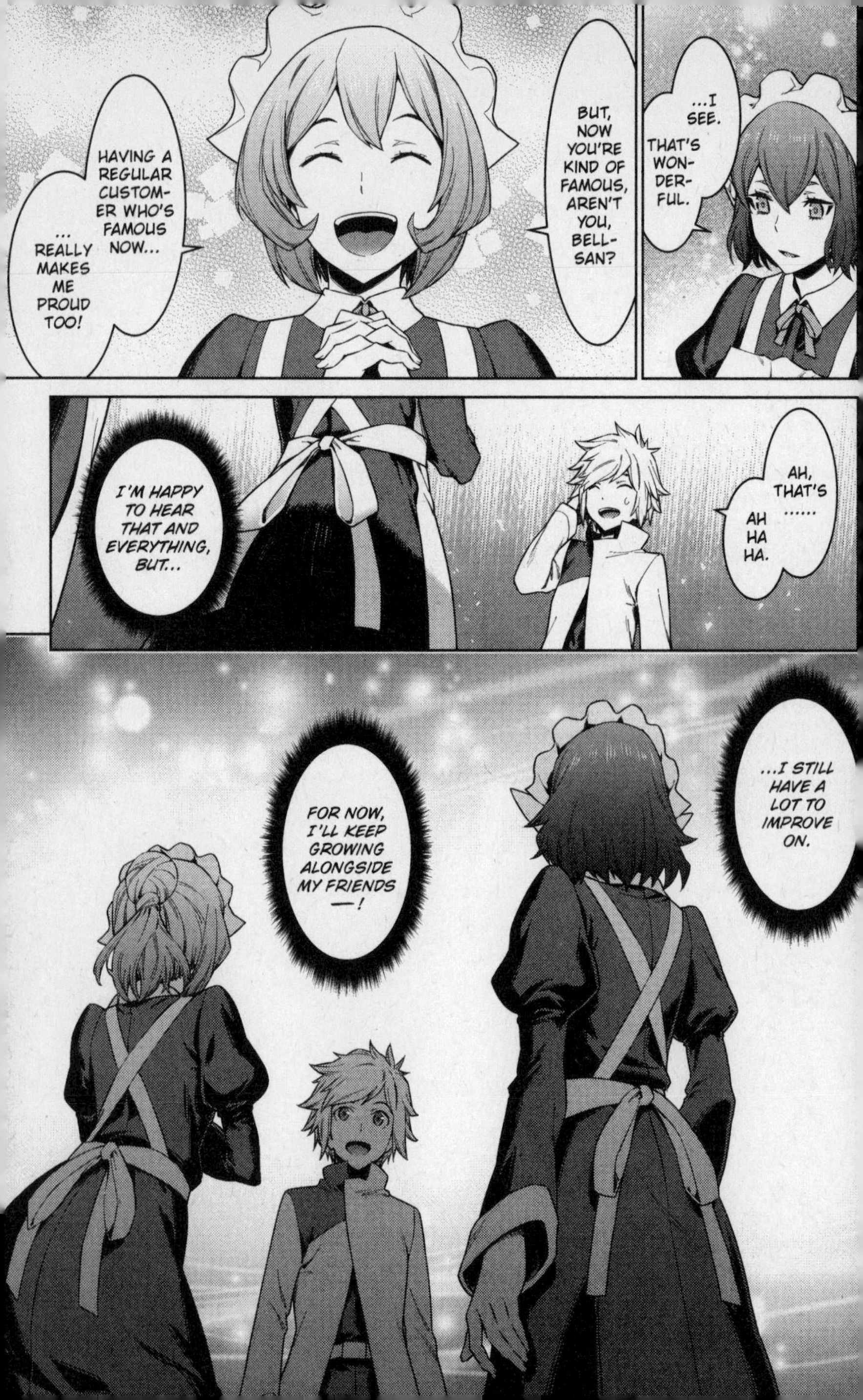
...I SEE. THAT'S WONDERFUL.
BUT, NOW YOU'RE KIND OF FAMOUS, AREN'T YOU, BELL-SAN?
HAVING A REGULAR CUSTOMER WHO'S FAMOUS NOW... ...REALLY MAKES ME PROUD TOO!
AH, THAT'S...... AH HA HA.
I'M HAPPY TO HEAR THAT AND EVERYTHING, BUT...
...I STILL HAVE A LOT TO IMPROVE ON.
FOR NOW, I'LL KEEP GROWING ALONGSIDE MY FRIENDS—!

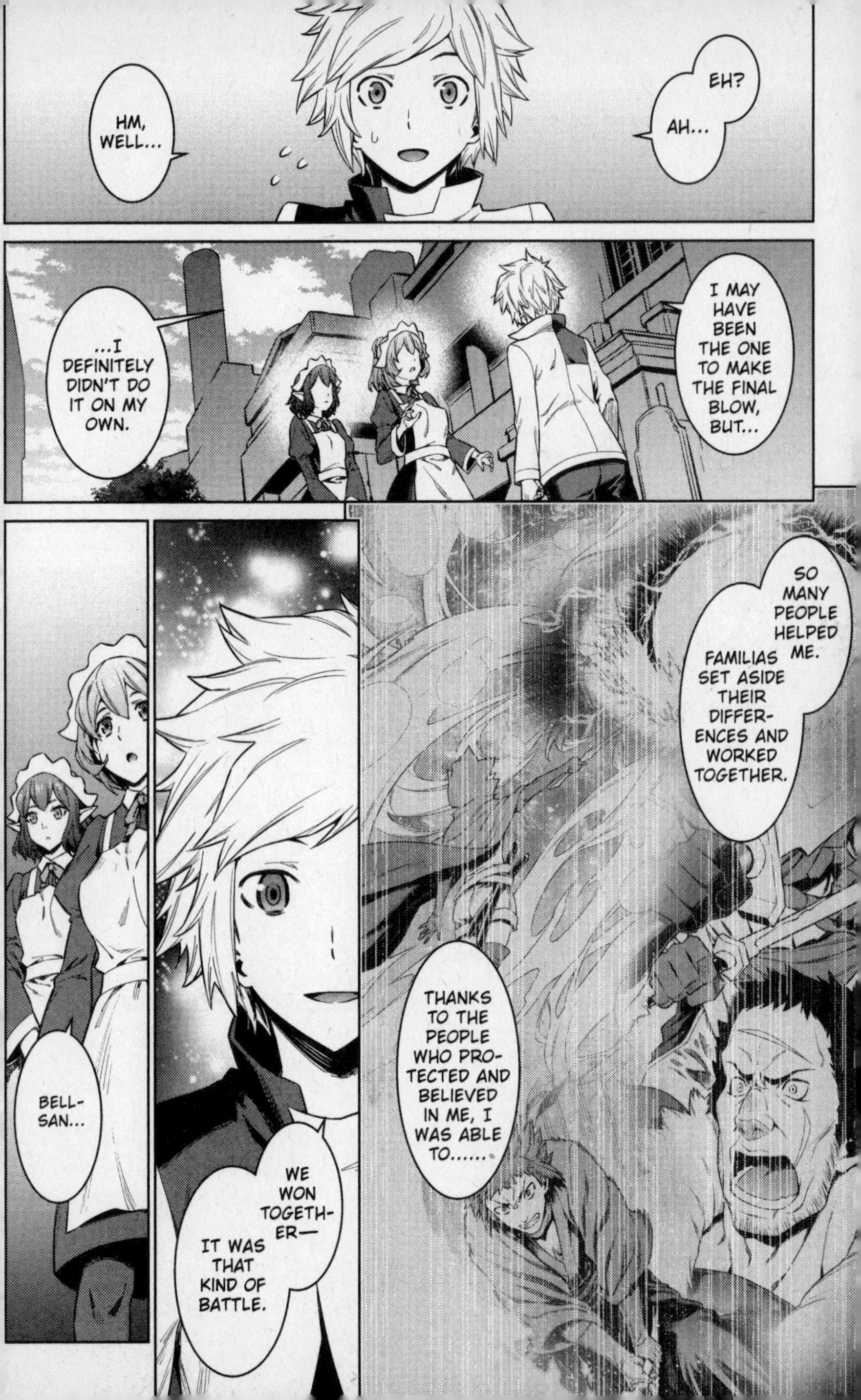
EH?
AH...
HM, WELL...
I MAY HAVE BEEN THE ONE TO MAKE THE FINAL BLOW, BUT...
...I DEFINITELY DIDN'T DO IT ON MY OWN.
SO MANY PEOPLE HELPED ME.
FAMILIAS SET ASIDE THEIR DIFFER-ENCES AND WORKED TOGETHER.
THANKS TO THE PEOPLE WHO PRO-TECTED AND BELIEVED IN ME, I WAS ABLE TO......
WE WON TOGETH-ER—
IT WAS THAT KIND OF BATTLE.
BELL-SAN...

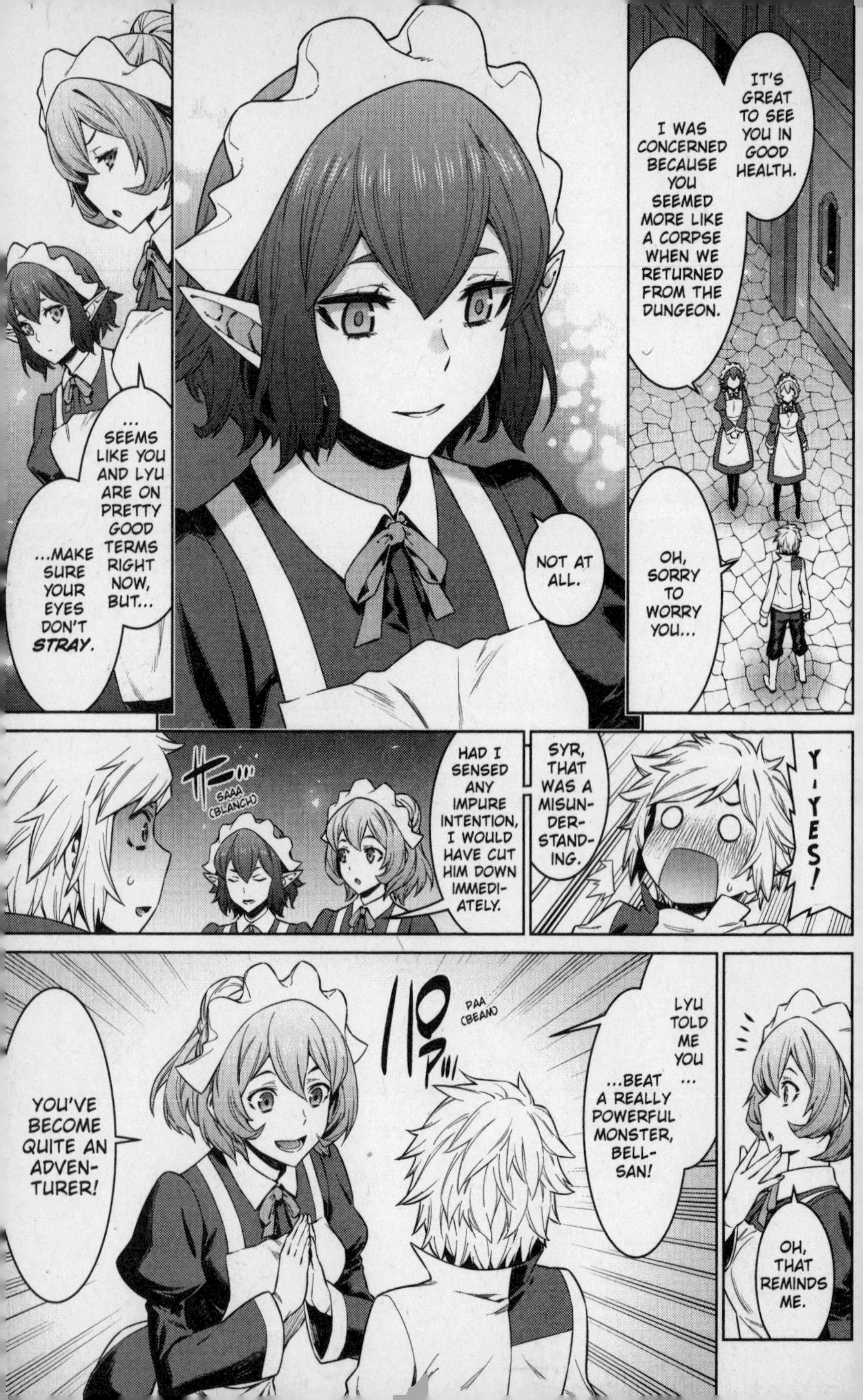
IT'S GREAT TO SEE YOU IN GOOD HEALTH.
I WAS CONCERNED BECAUSE YOU SEEMED MORE LIKE A CORPSE WHEN WE RETURNED FROM THE DUNGEON.
OH, SORRY TO WORRY YOU...
NOT AT ALL.
...SEEMS LIKE YOU AND LYU ARE ON PRETTY GOOD TERMS RIGHT NOW, BUT...
...MAKE SURE YOUR EYES DON'T STRAY.
Y-YES!
SYR, THAT WAS A MISUN-DER-STAND-ING.
HAD I SENSED ANY IMPURE INTENTION, I WOULD HAVE CUT HIM DOWN IMMEDI-ATELY.
SAAA (BLANCH)
OH, THAT REMINDS ME.
LYU TOLD ME YOU ... ...BEAT A REALLY POWERFUL MONSTER, BELL-SAN!
PAA (BEAM)
YOU'VE BECOME QUITE AN ADVEN-TURER!

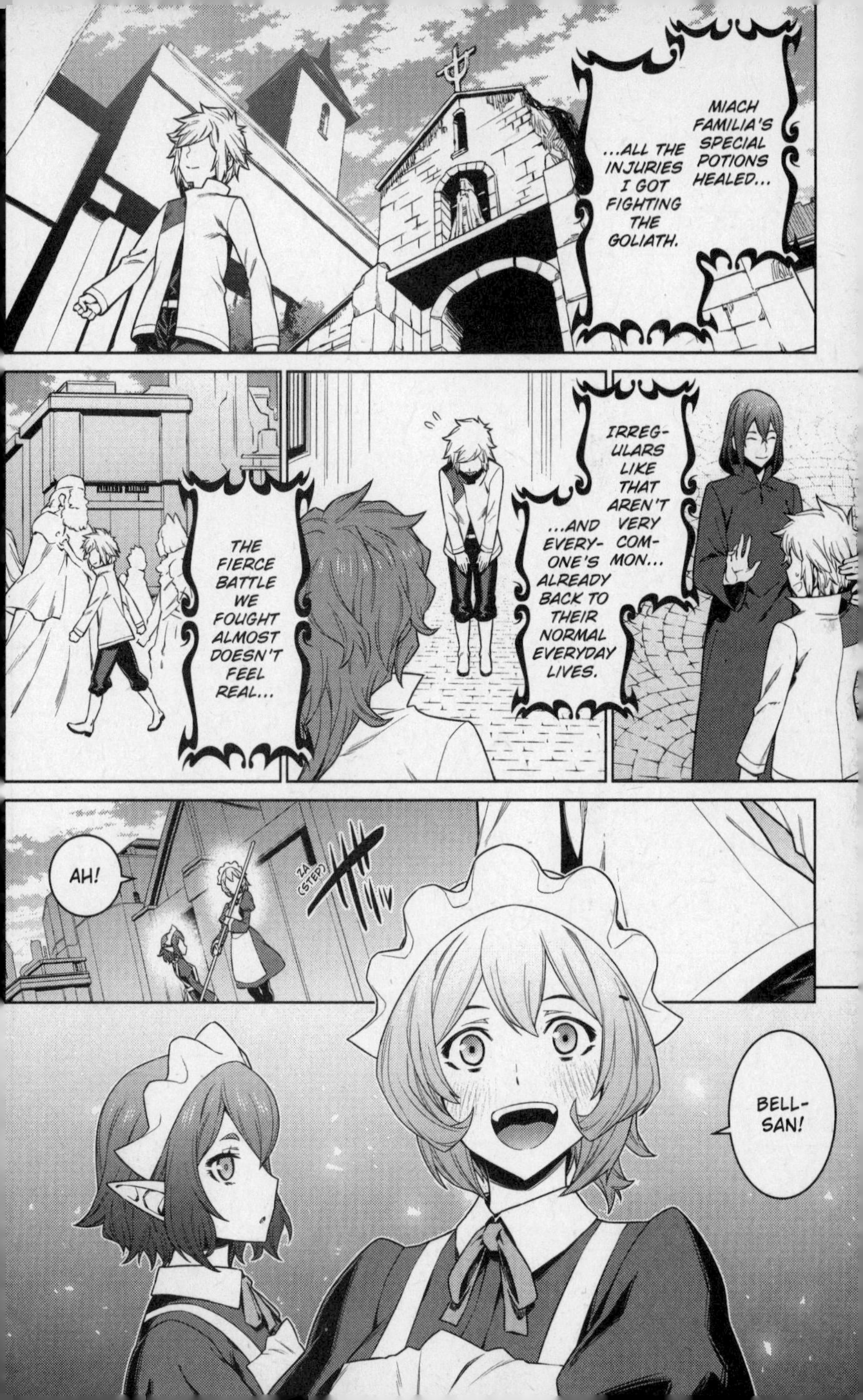
MIACH FAMILIA'S SPECIAL POTIONS HEALED...
...ALL THE INJURIES I GOT FIGHTING THE GOLIATH.
IRREGULARS LIKE THAT AREN'T VERY COMMON...
...AND EVERYONE'S ALREADY BACK TO THEIR NORMAL EVERYDAY LIVES.
THE FIERCE BATTLE WE FOUGHT ALMOST DOESN'T FEEL REAL...
ZA (STEP)
AH!
BELL-SAN!

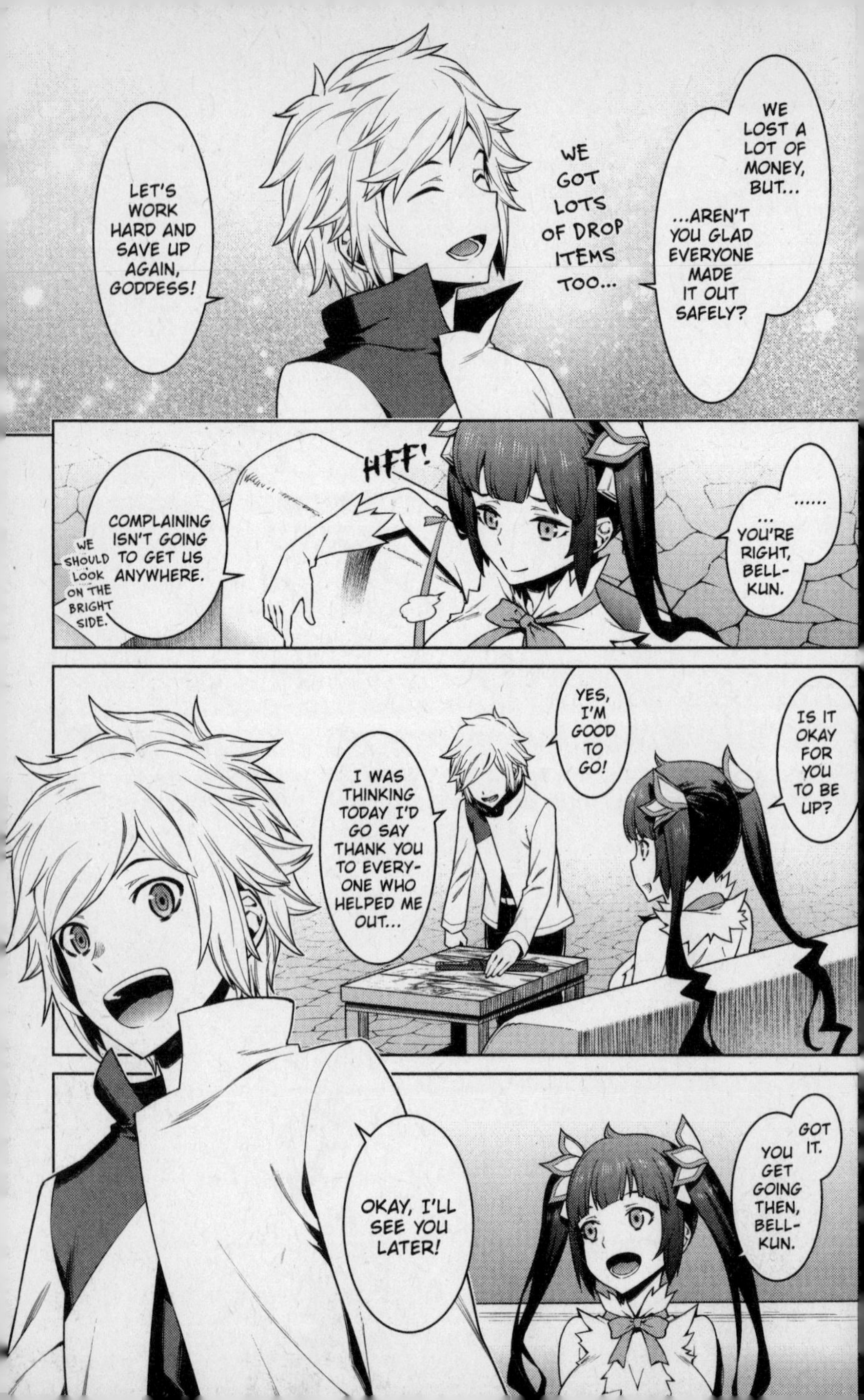
WE LOST A LOT OF MONEY, BUT... ...AREN'T YOU GLAD EVERYONE MADE IT OUT SAFELY?
WE GOT LOTS OF DROP ITEMS TOO...
LET'S WORK HARD AND SAVE UP AGAIN, GODDESS!
.... YOU'RE RIGHT, BELL-KUN.
HFF!
COMPLAINING ISN'T GOING TO GET US ANYWHERE.
WE SHOULD LOOK ON THE BRIGHT SIDE.
IS IT OKAY FOR YOU TO BE UP?
YES, I'M GOOD TO GO!
I WAS THINKING TODAY I'D GO SAY THANK YOU TO EVERY-ONE WHO HELPED ME OUT...
GOT IT. YOU GET GOING THEN, BELL-KUN.
OKAY, I'LL SEE YOU LATER!

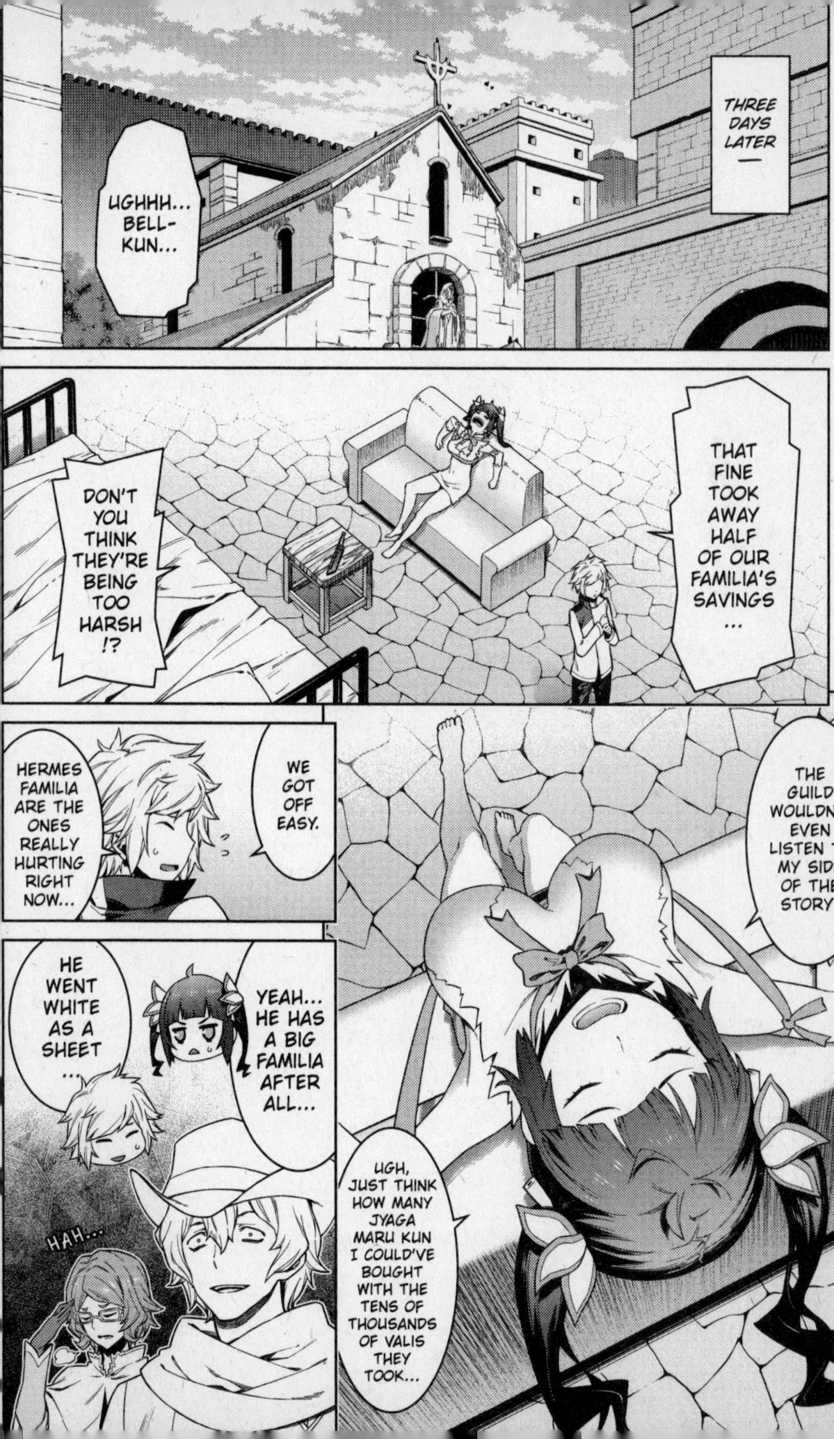
THREE DAYS LATER —
UGHHH... BELL-KUN...
THAT FINE TOOK AWAY HALF OF OUR FAMILIA'S SAVINGS...
DON'T YOU THINK THEY'RE BEING TOO HARSH!?
THE GUILD WOULDN'T EVEN LISTEN TO MY SIDE OF THE STORY!
UGH, JUST THINK HOW MANY JYAGA MARU KUN I COULD'VE BOUGHT WITH THE TENS OF THOUSANDS OF VALIS THEY TOOK...
WE GOT OFF EASY.
HERMES FAMILIA ARE THE ONES REALLY HURTING RIGHT NOW...
YEAH... HE HAS A BIG FAMILIA AFTER ALL...
HE WENT WHITE AS A SHEET...
HAH...

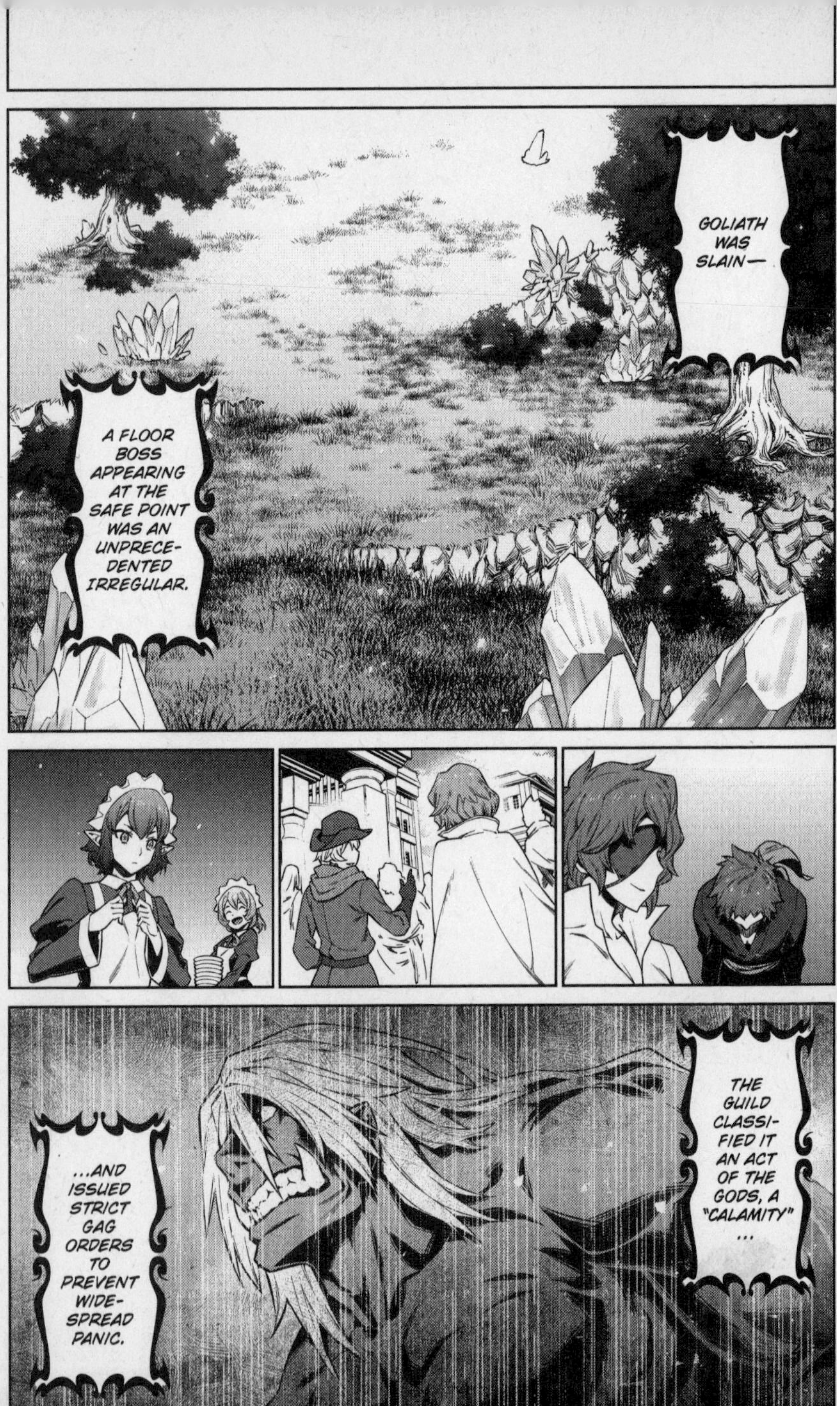
GOLIATH WAS SLAIN—
A FLOOR BOSS APPEARING AT THE SAFE POINT WAS AN UNPRECE-DENTED IRREGULAR.
THE GUILD CLASSI-FIED IT AN ACT OF THE GODS, A "CALAMITY"...
...AND ISSUED STRICT GAG ORDERS TO PREVENT WIDE-SPREAD PANIC.

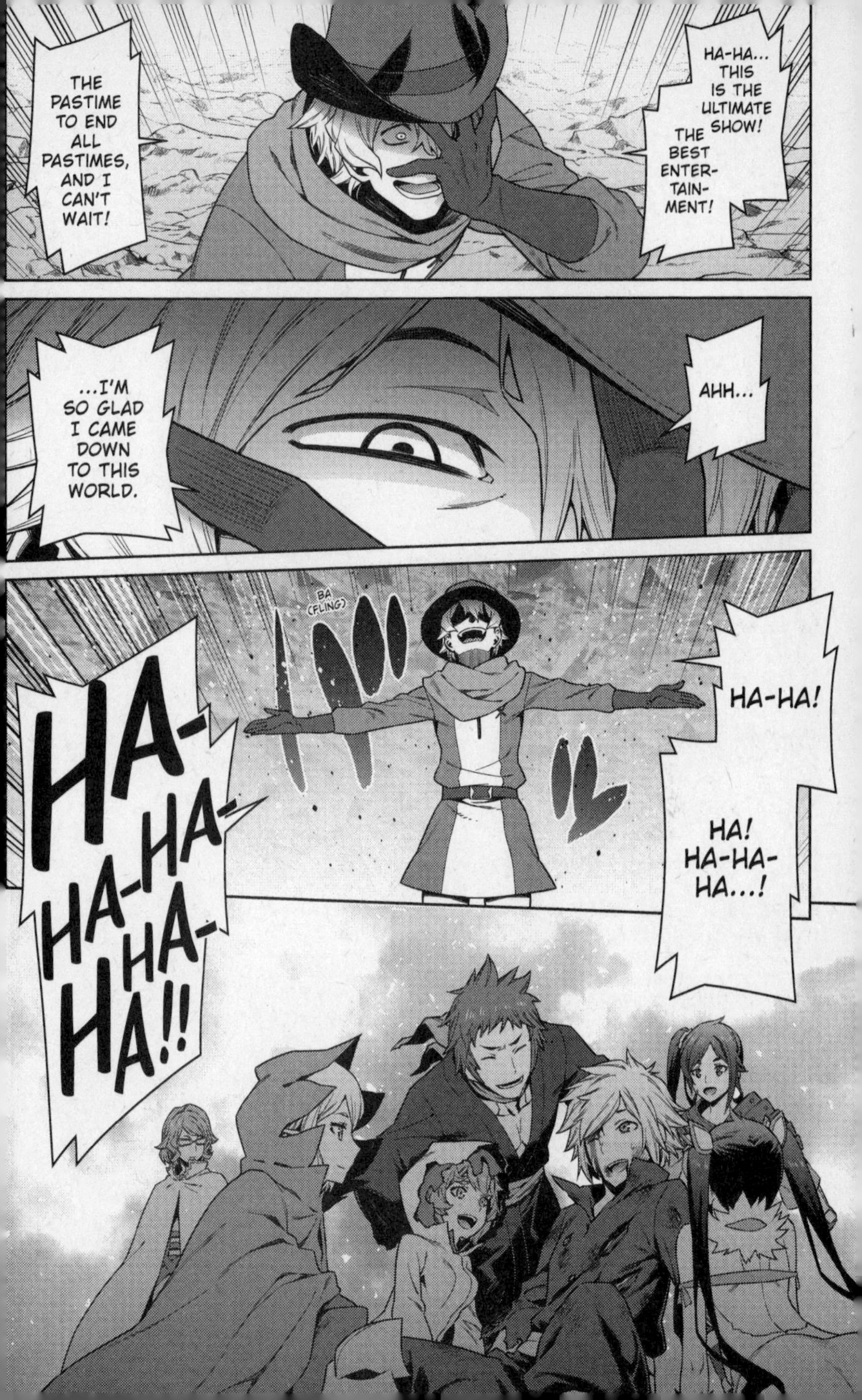
HA-HA... THIS IS THE ULTIMATE SHOW! THE BEST ENTERTAINMENT!
THE PASTIME TO END ALL PASTIMES, AND I CAN'T WAIT!
AHH...
...I'M SO GLAD I CAME DOWN TO THIS WORLD.
BA (FLING)
HA-HA!
HA! HA-HA-HA...!
HA-HA-HA-HA-HA-HA!!

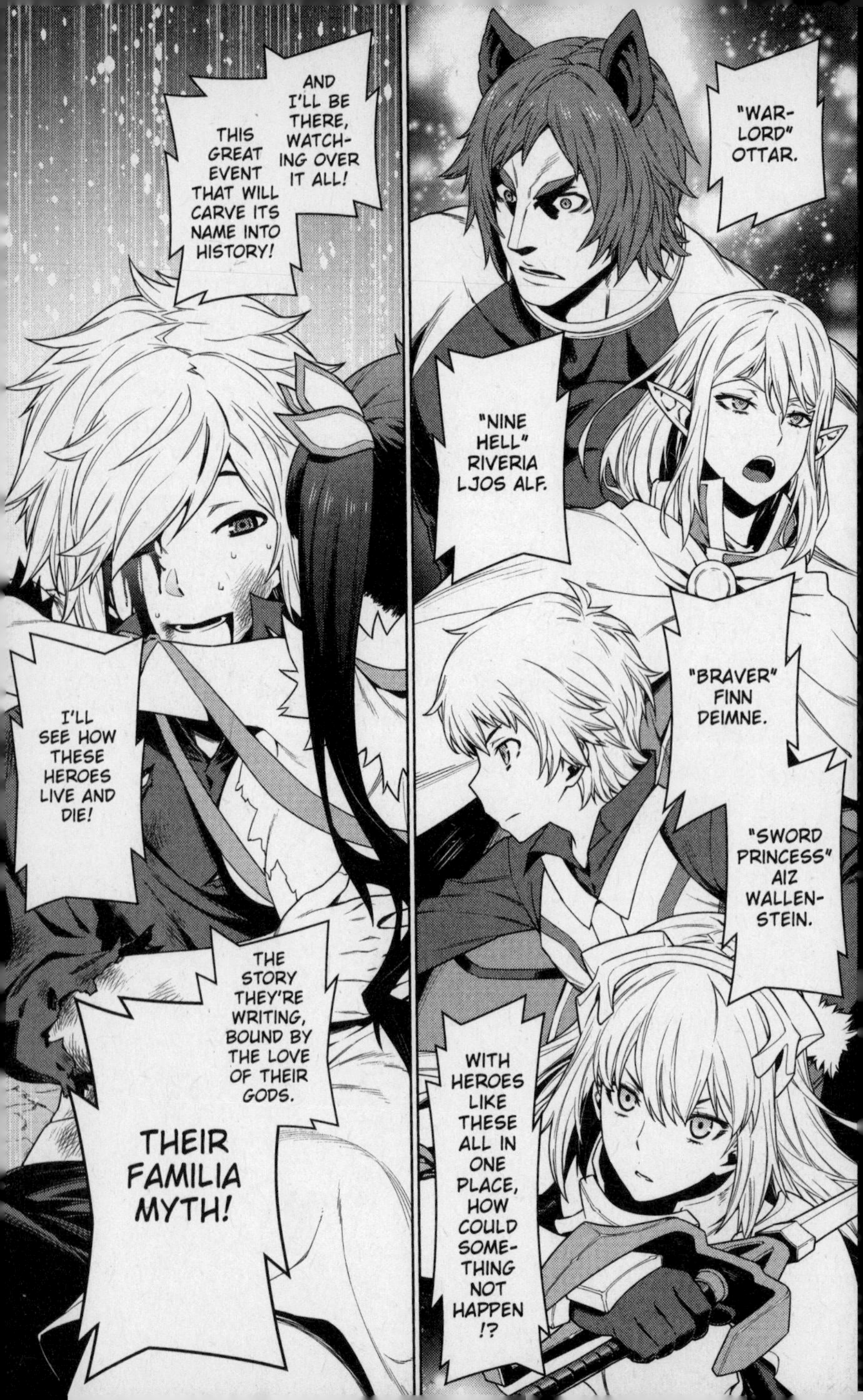
"WAR-LORD" OTTAR.
"NINE HELL" RIVERIA LJOS ALF.
"BRAVER" FINN DEIMNE.
"SWORD PRINCESS" AIZ WALLEN-STEIN.
WITH HEROES LIKE THESE ALL IN ONE PLACE, HOW COULD SOME-THING NOT HAPPEN !?
THIS GREAT EVENT THAT WILL CARVE ITS NAME INTO HISTORY!
AND I'LL BE THERE, WATCH-ING OVER IT ALL!
I'LL SEE HOW THESE HEROES LIVE AND DIE!
THE STORY THEY'RE WRITING, BOUND BY THE LOVE OF THEIR GODS.
THEIR FAMILIA MYTH!

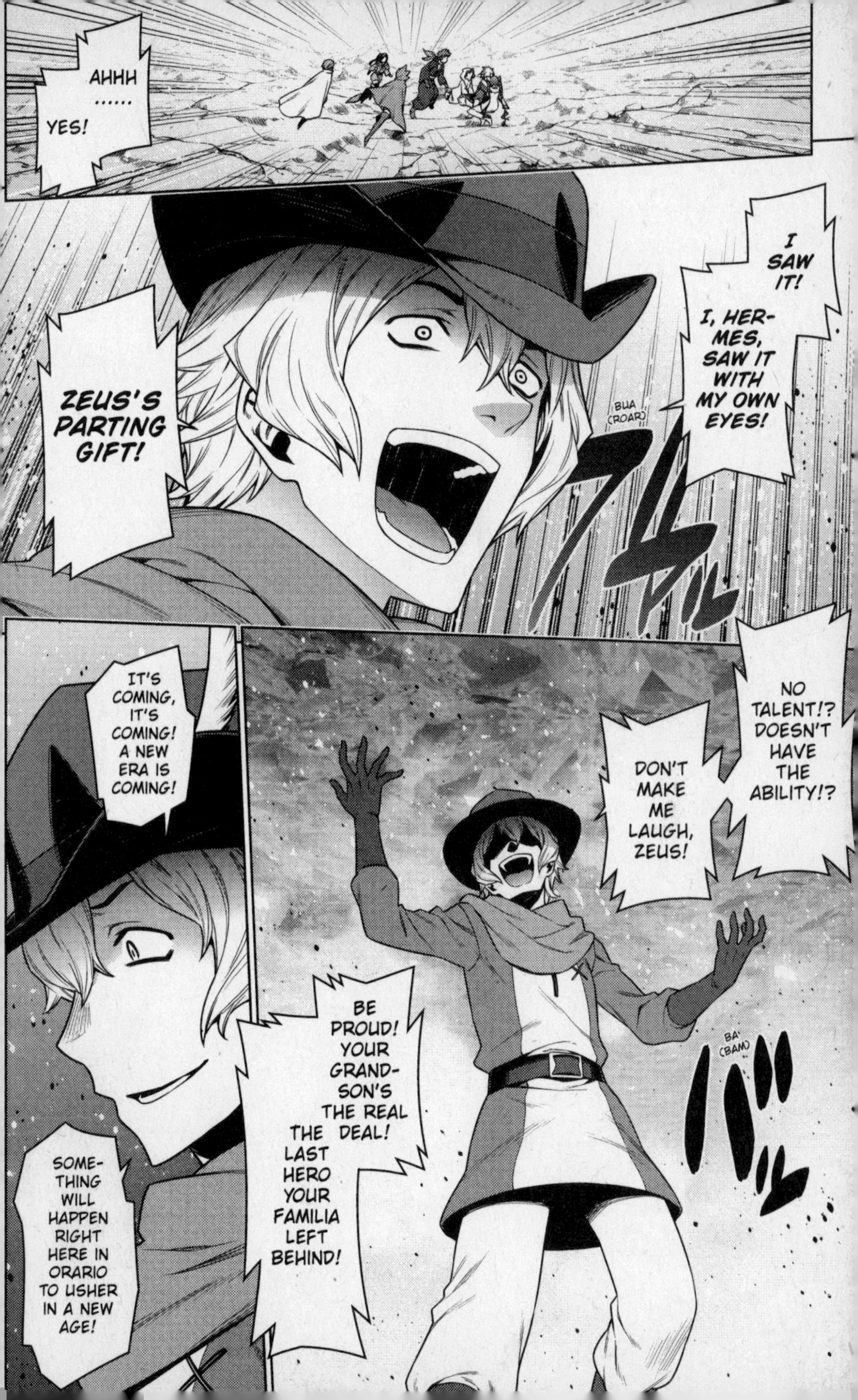
AHHH ...... YES!
I SAW IT! I, HERMES, SAW IT WITH MY OWN EYES!
BUA (ROAR)
ZEUS'S PARTING GIFT!
NO TALENT!? DOESN'T HAVE THE ABILITY!?
DON'T MAKE ME LAUGH, ZEUS!
BA (BAM)
BE PROUD! YOUR GRANDSON'S THE REAL DEAL!
THE LAST HERO YOUR FAMILIA LEFT BEHIND!
IT'S COMING, IT'S COMING! A NEW ERA IS COMING!
SOMETHING WILL HAPPEN RIGHT HERE IN ORARIO TO USHER IN A NEW AGE!

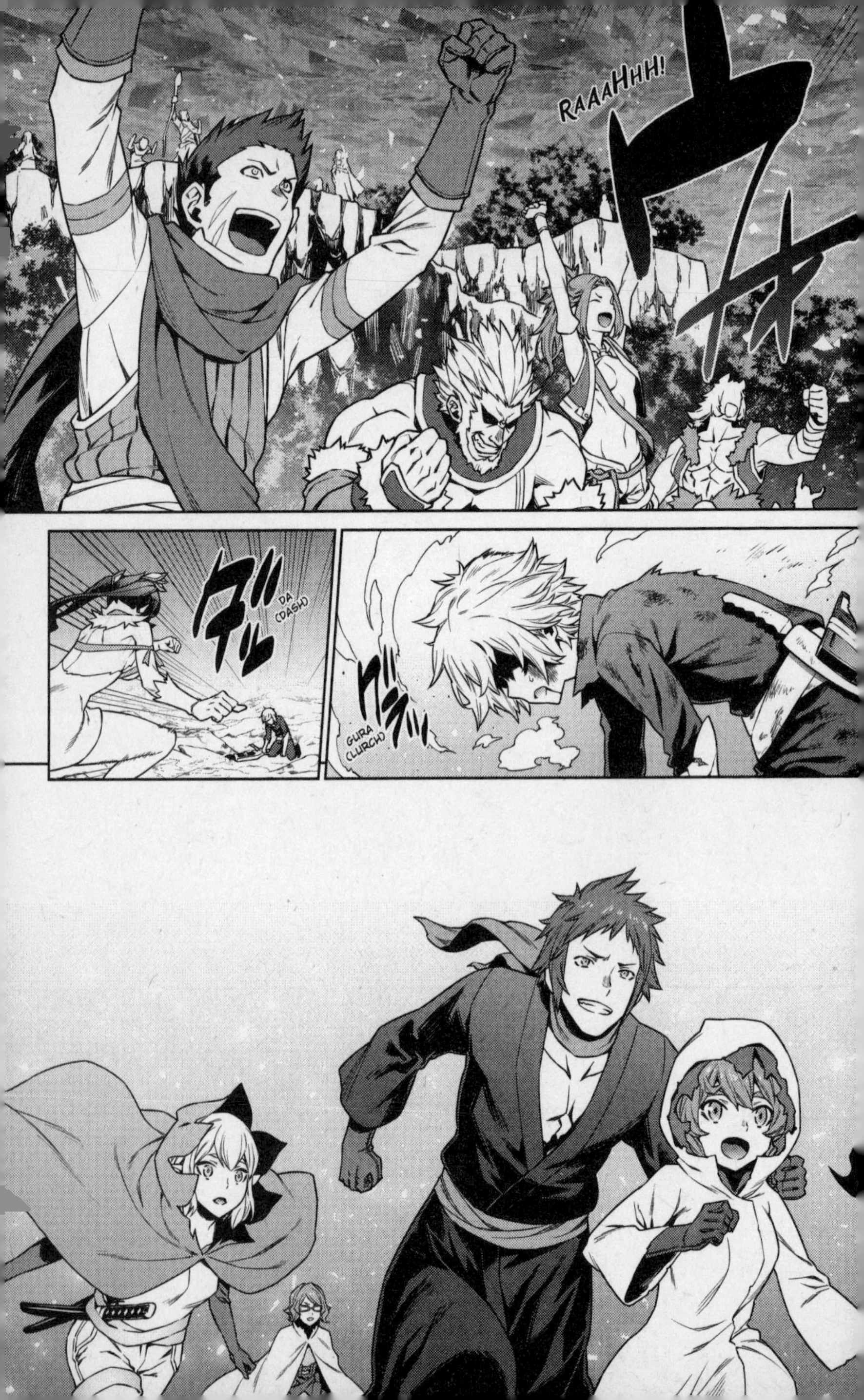
RAAAHHH!
GURA (LURCH)
DA (DASH)

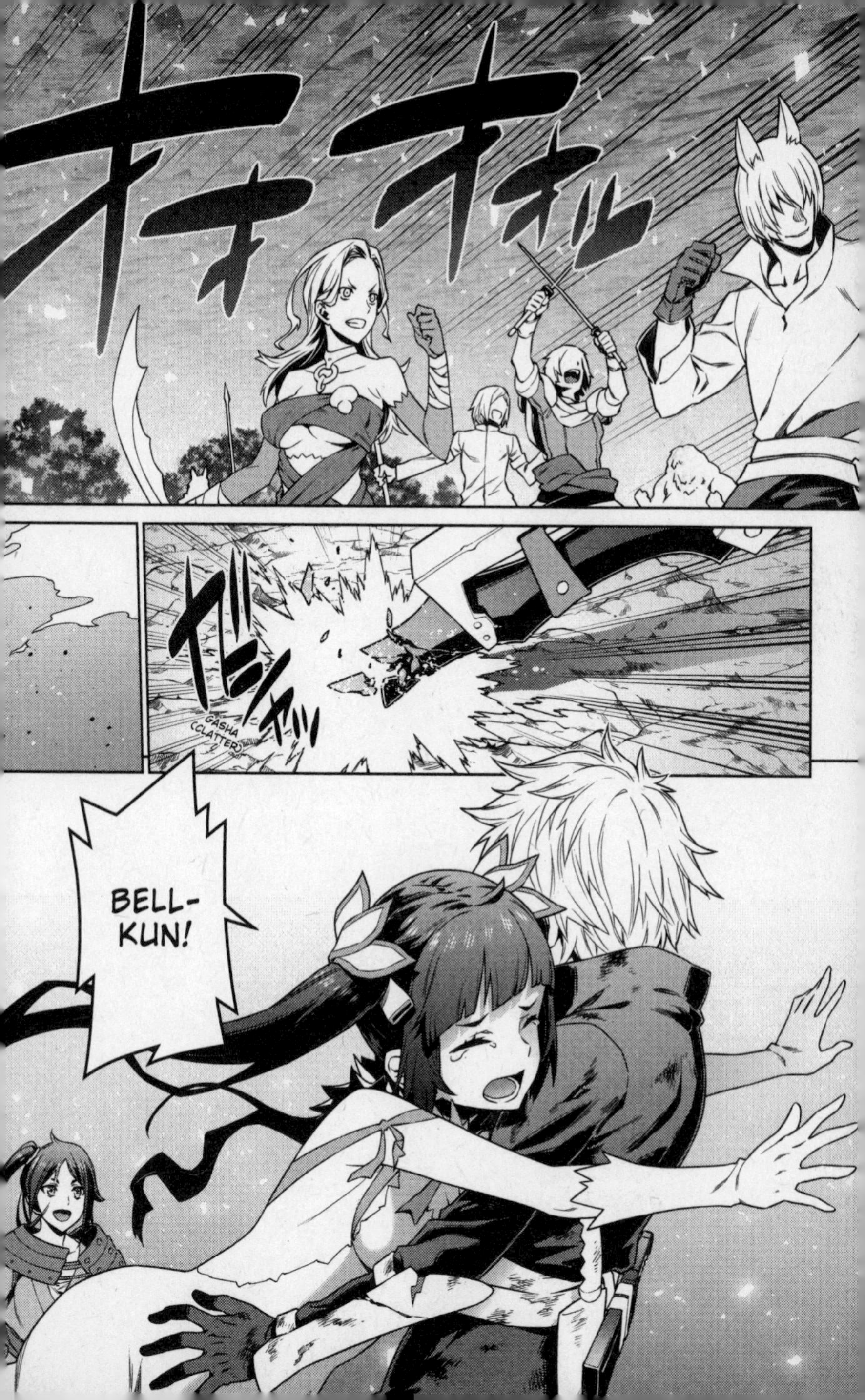
GASHA (CLATTER)
BELL-KUN!

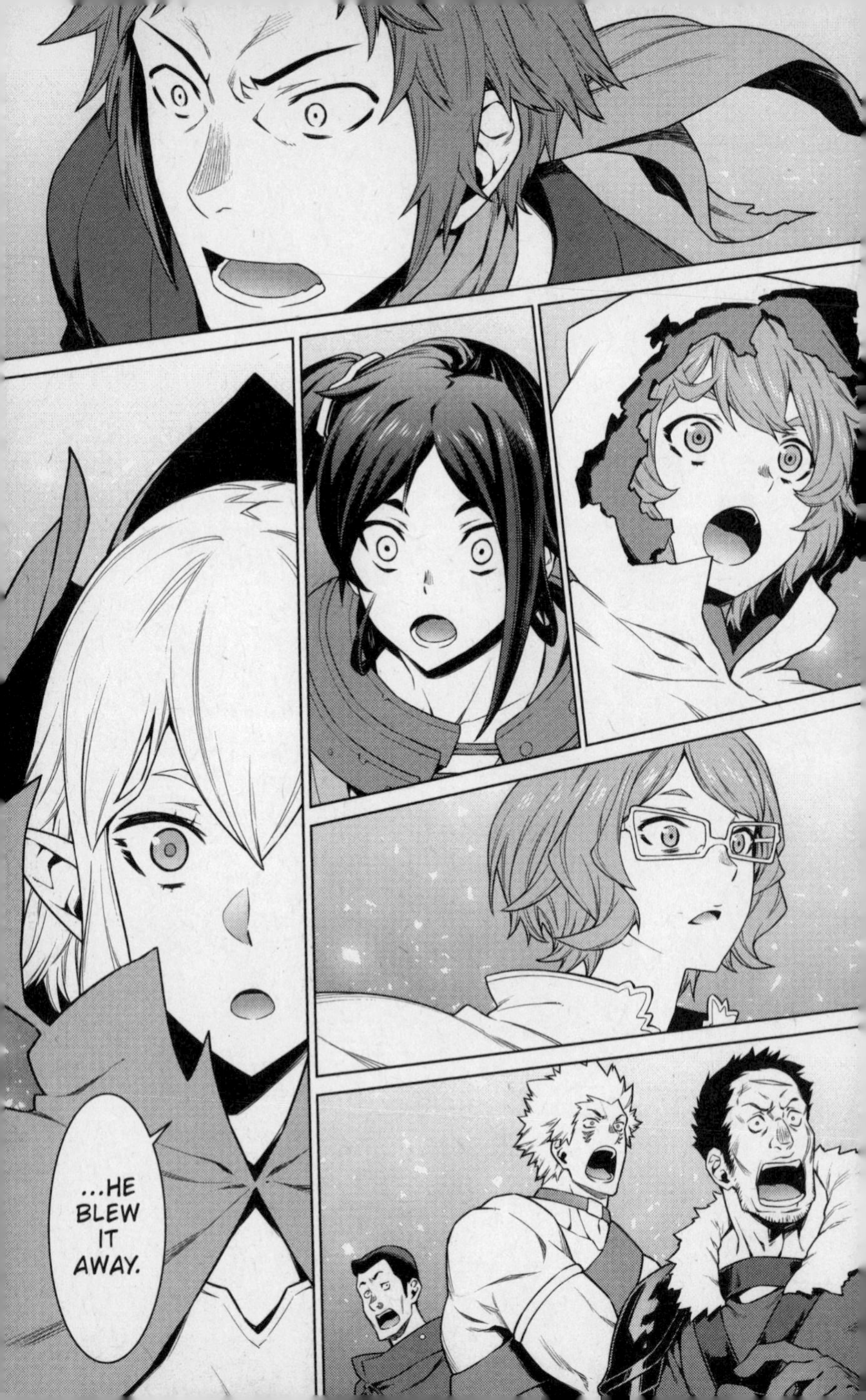
...HE BLEW IT AWAY.

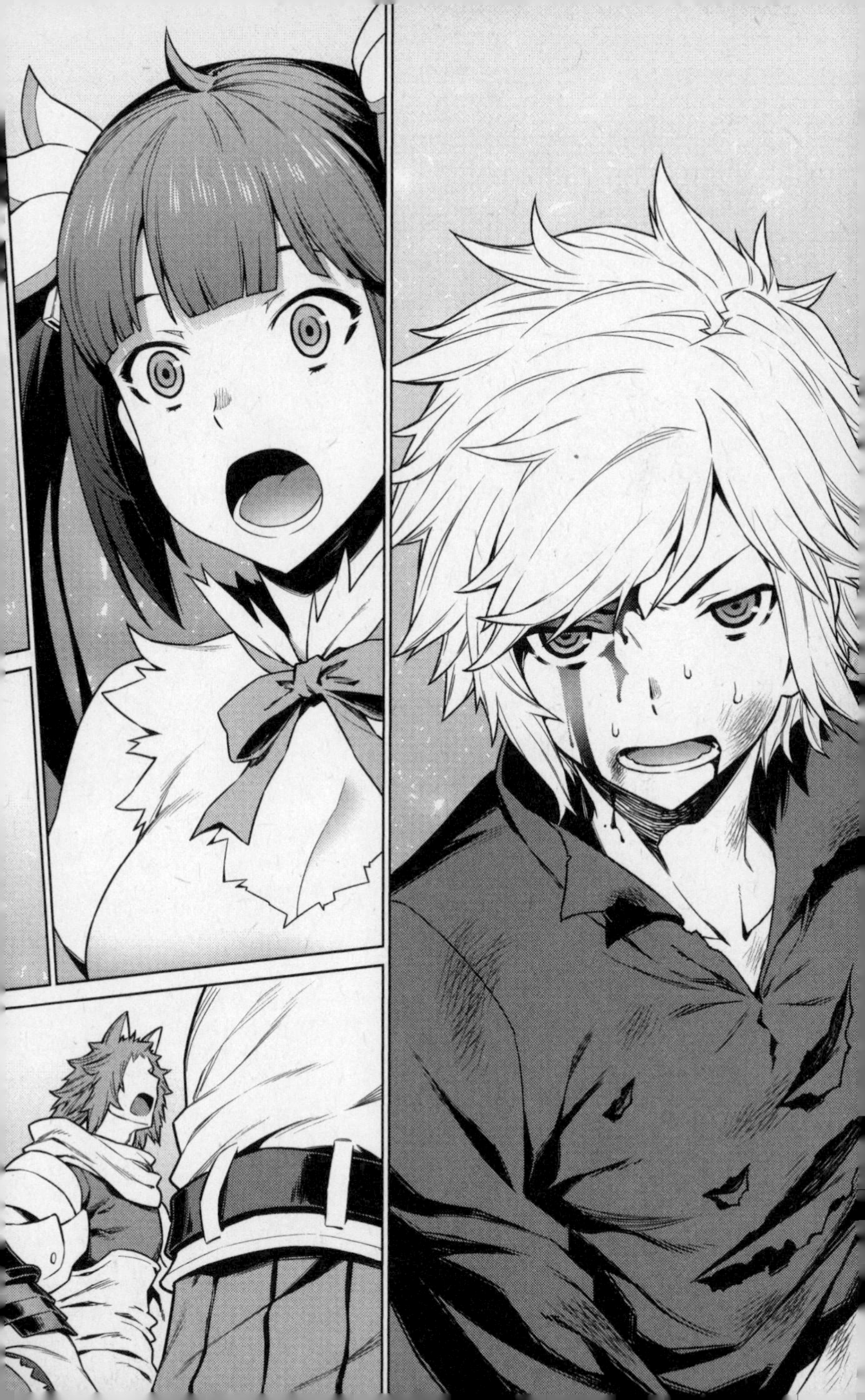

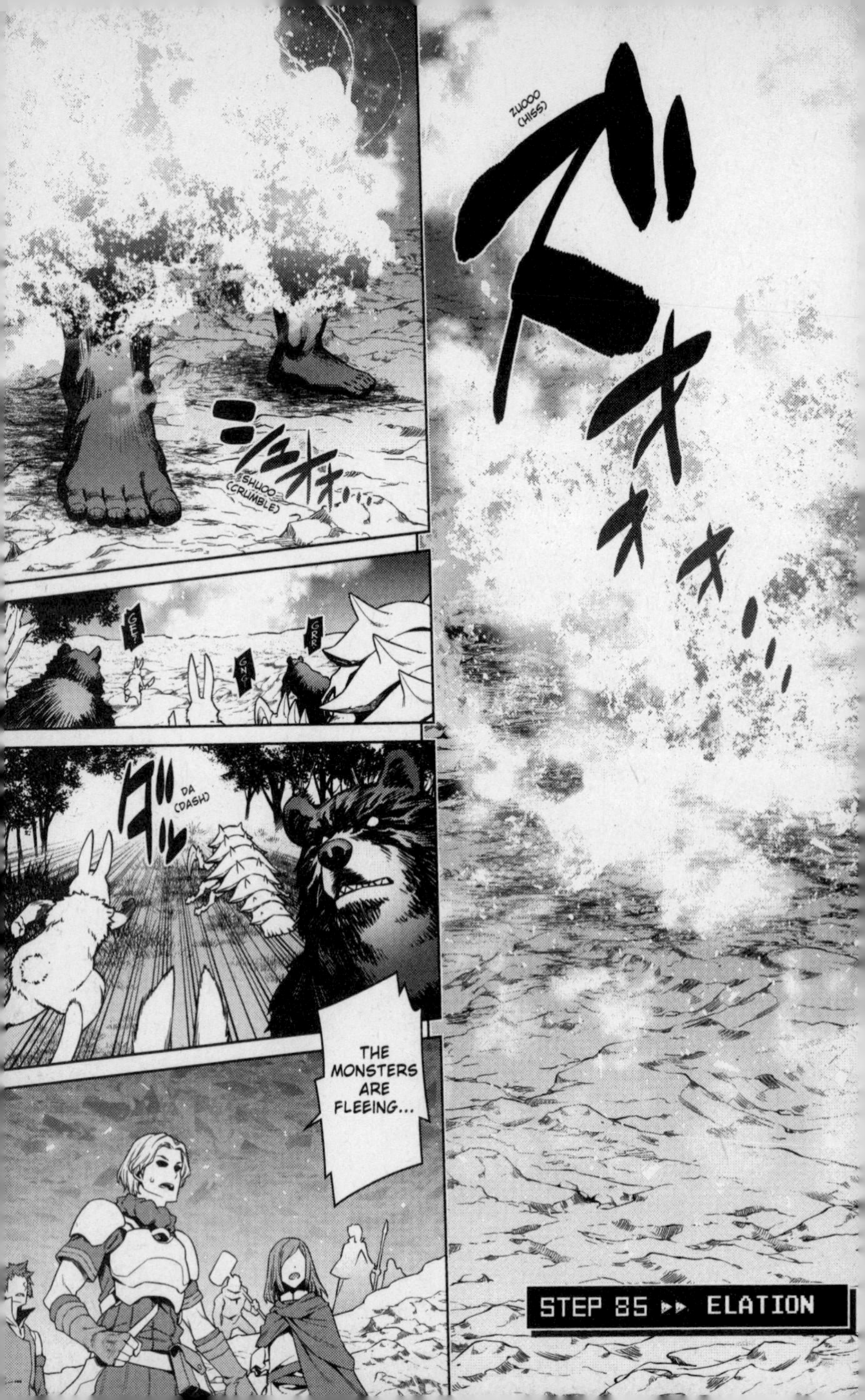
ZUOOO (HISS)
STEP 85 ▸▸ ELATION
SHUOO (CRUMBLE)
GRR
GN
GET
DA (DASH)
THE MONSTERS ARE FLEEING...

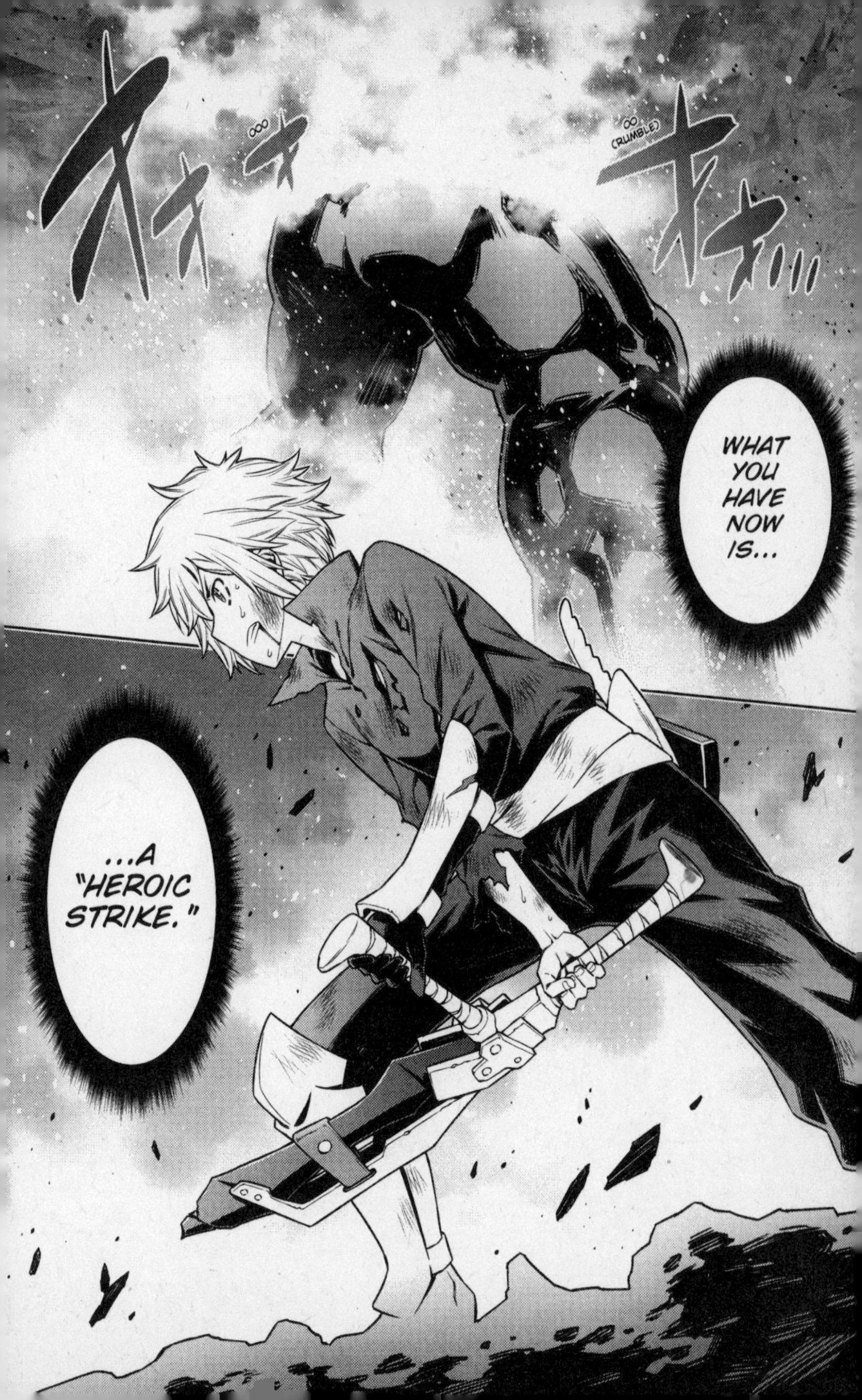
(RUMBLE)
WHAT YOU HAVE NOW IS...
...A "HEROIC STRIKE."

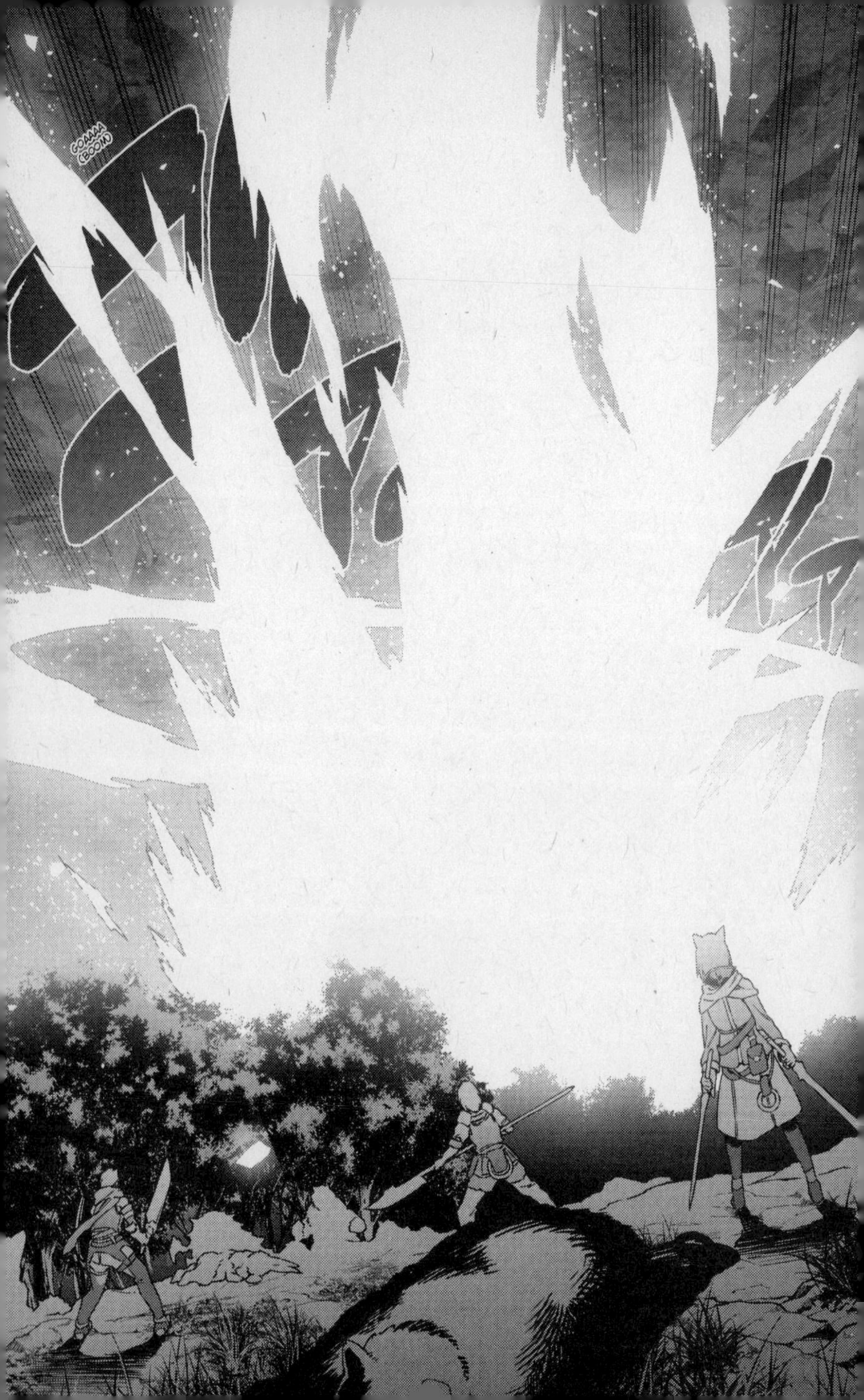
GOAAAA
(BOOM)

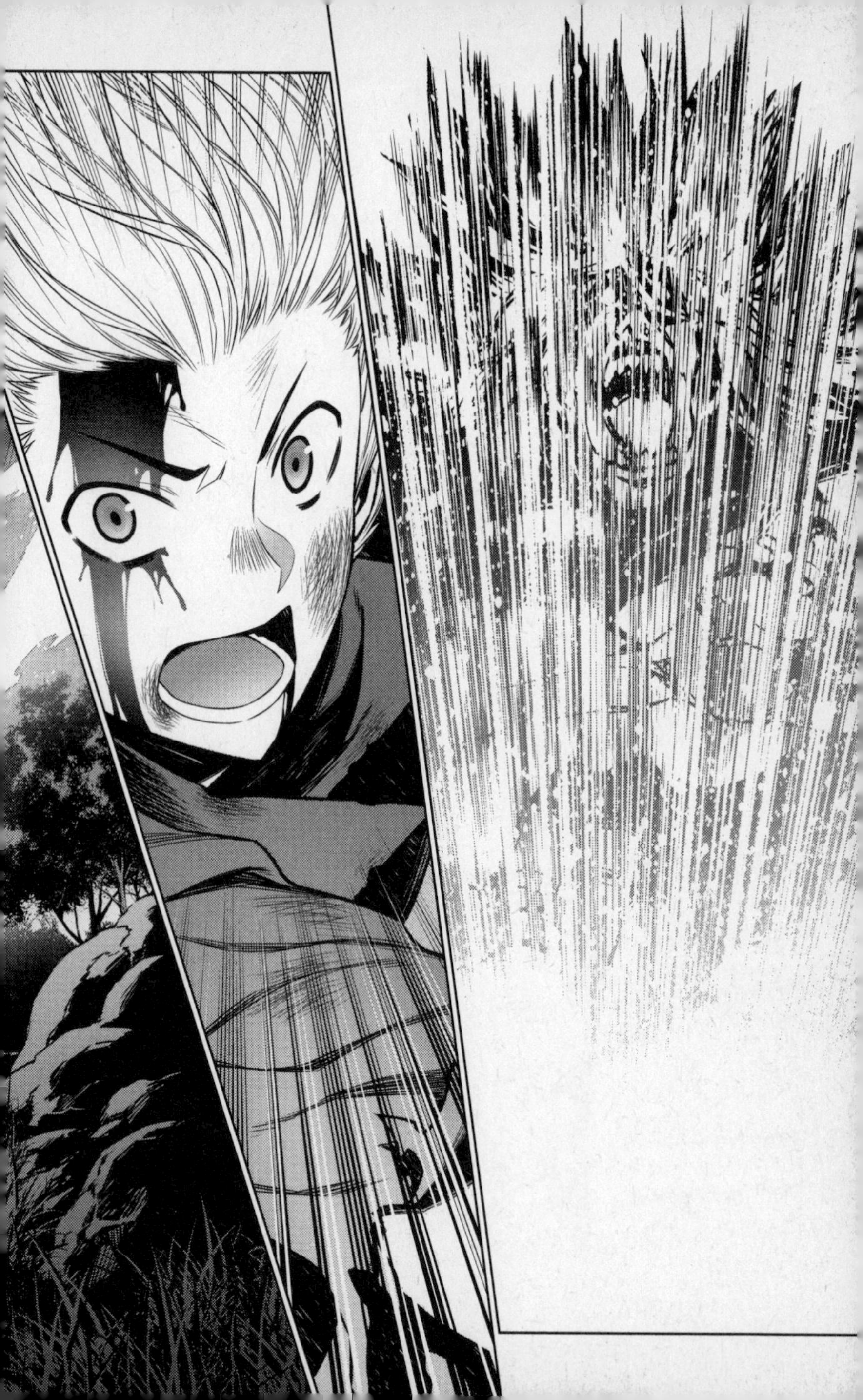

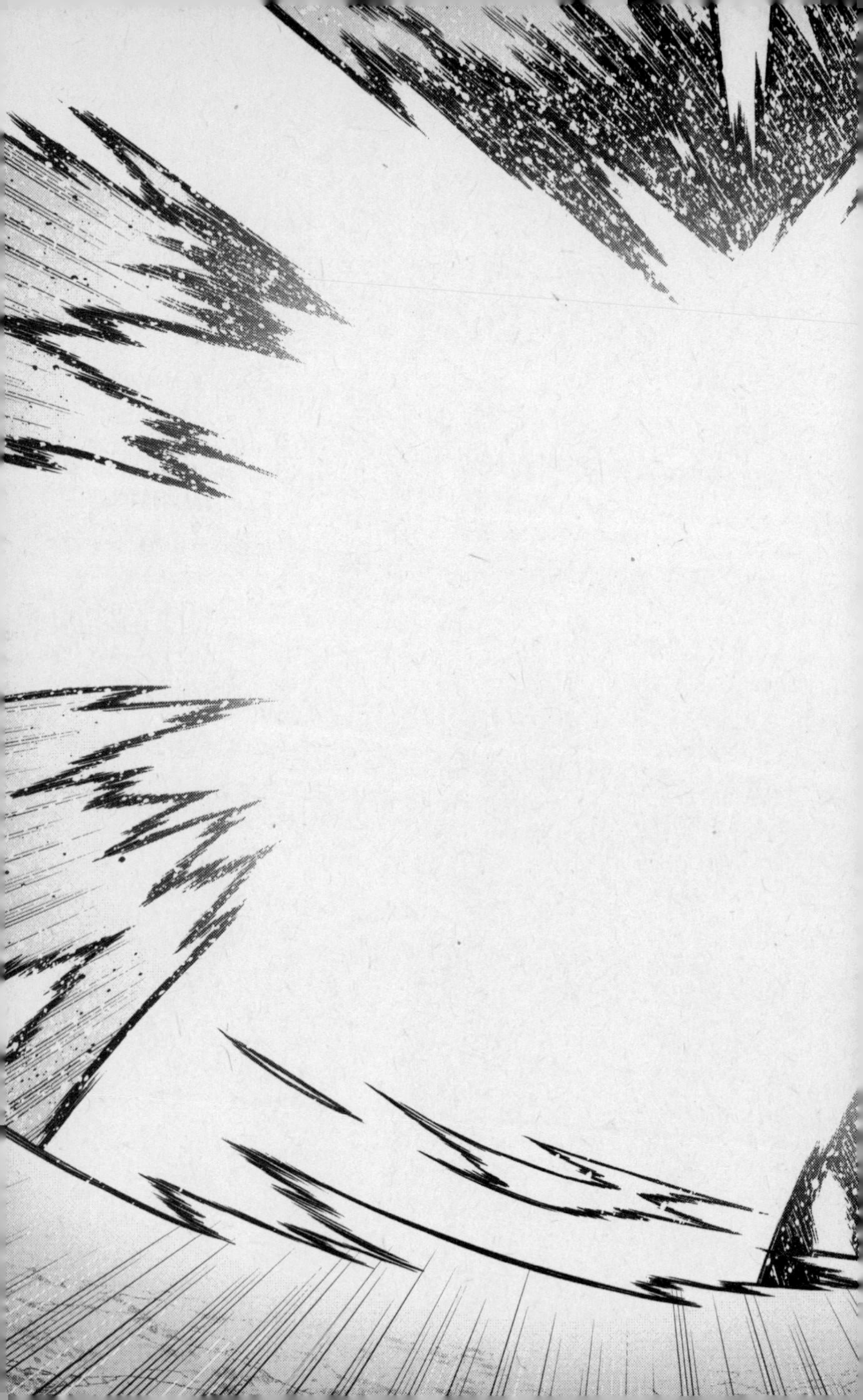

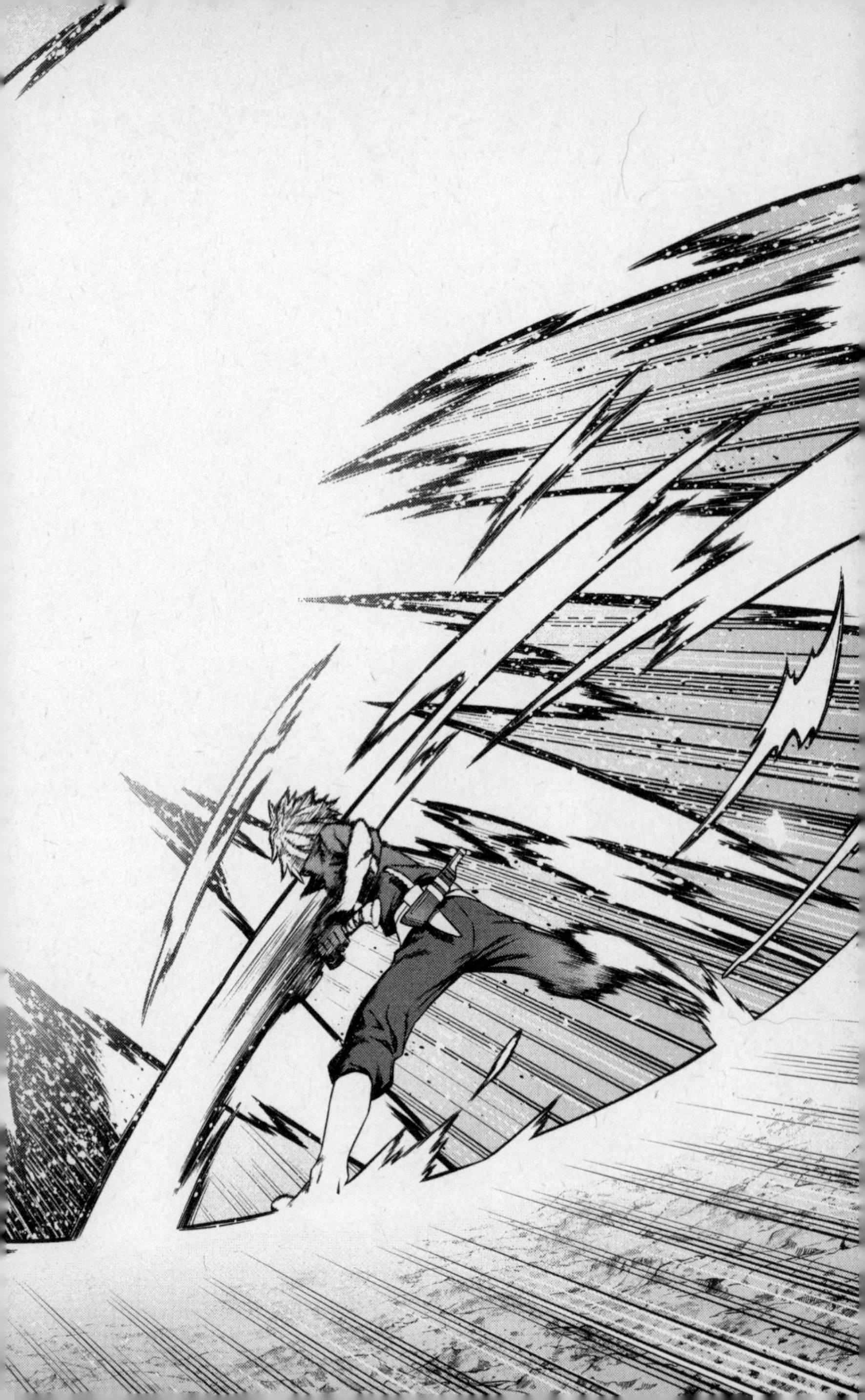

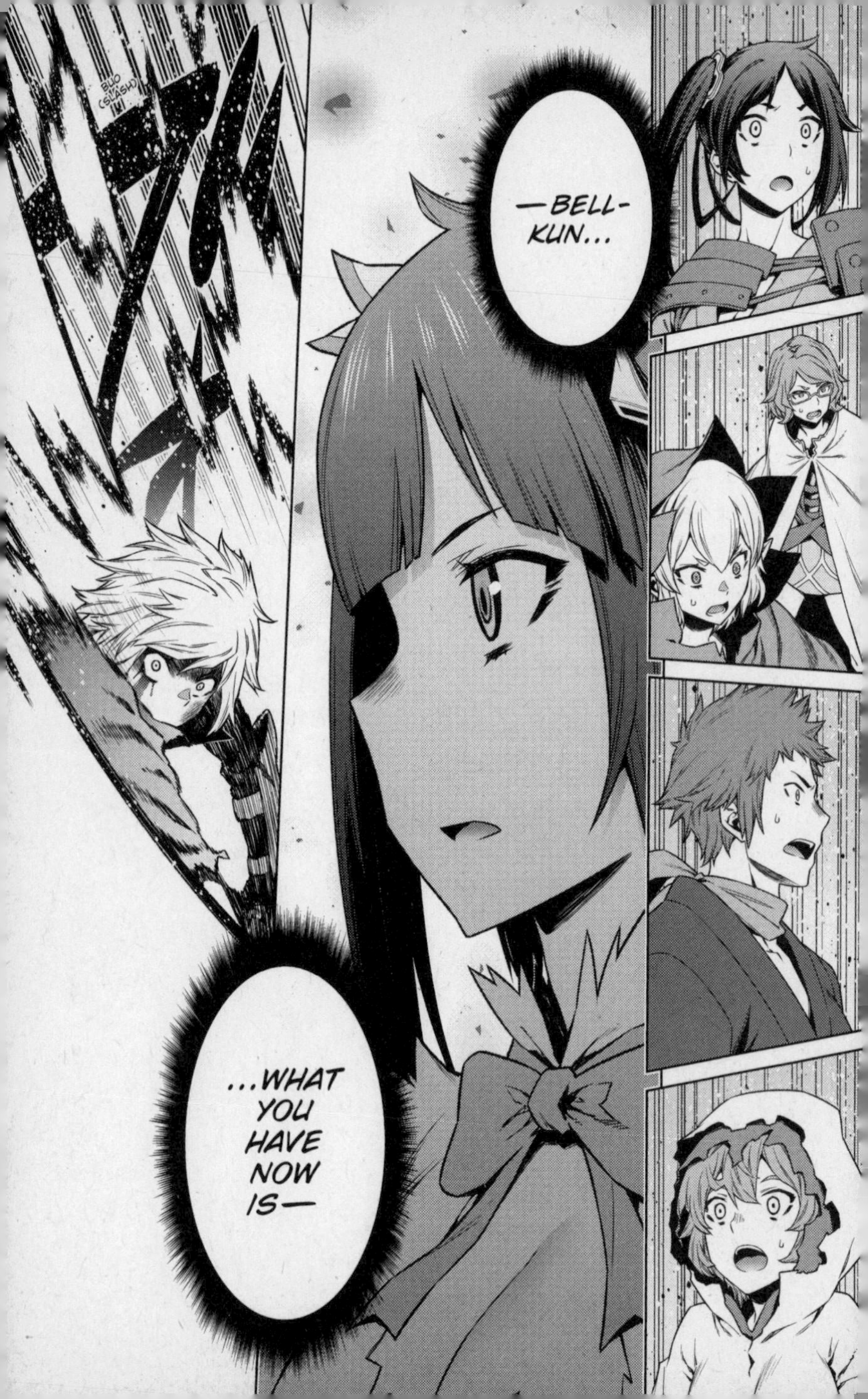
—BELL-KUN...
...WHAT YOU HAVE NOW IS—
BUO (SLASH)

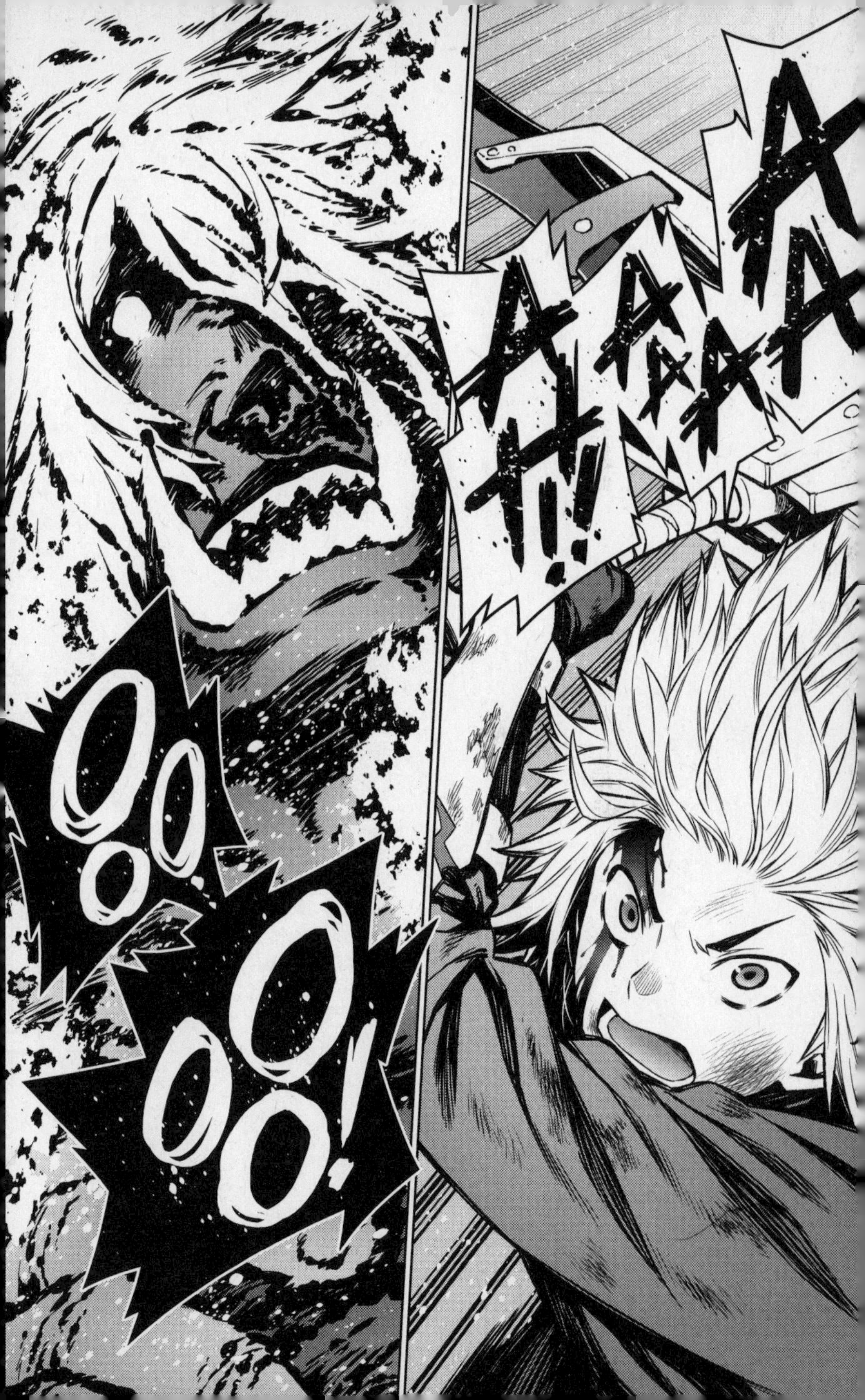
AAAAAAAH!!
OOOOOOOO!

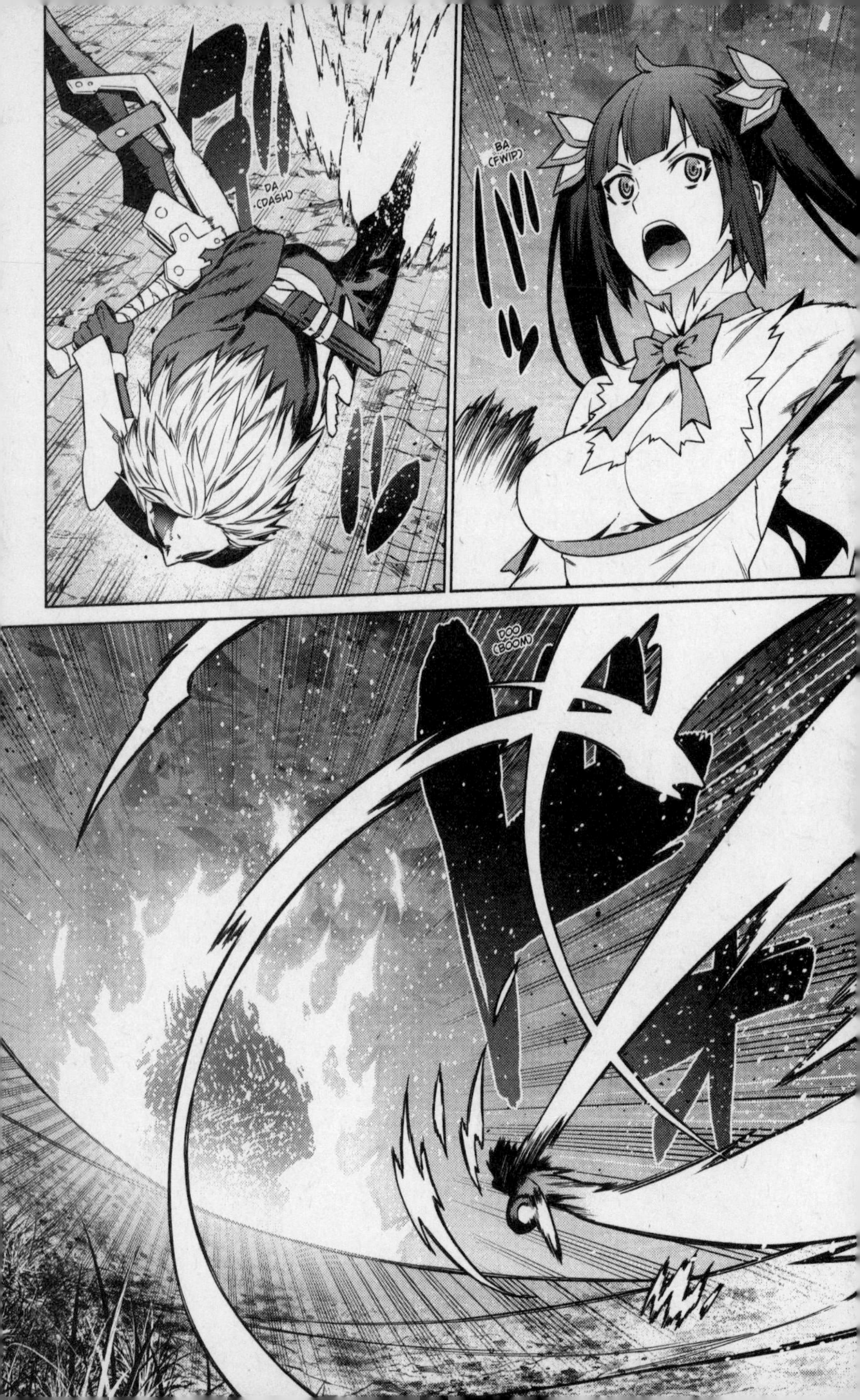
BA
(FWIP)
DA
(DASH)
DOO
(BOOM)

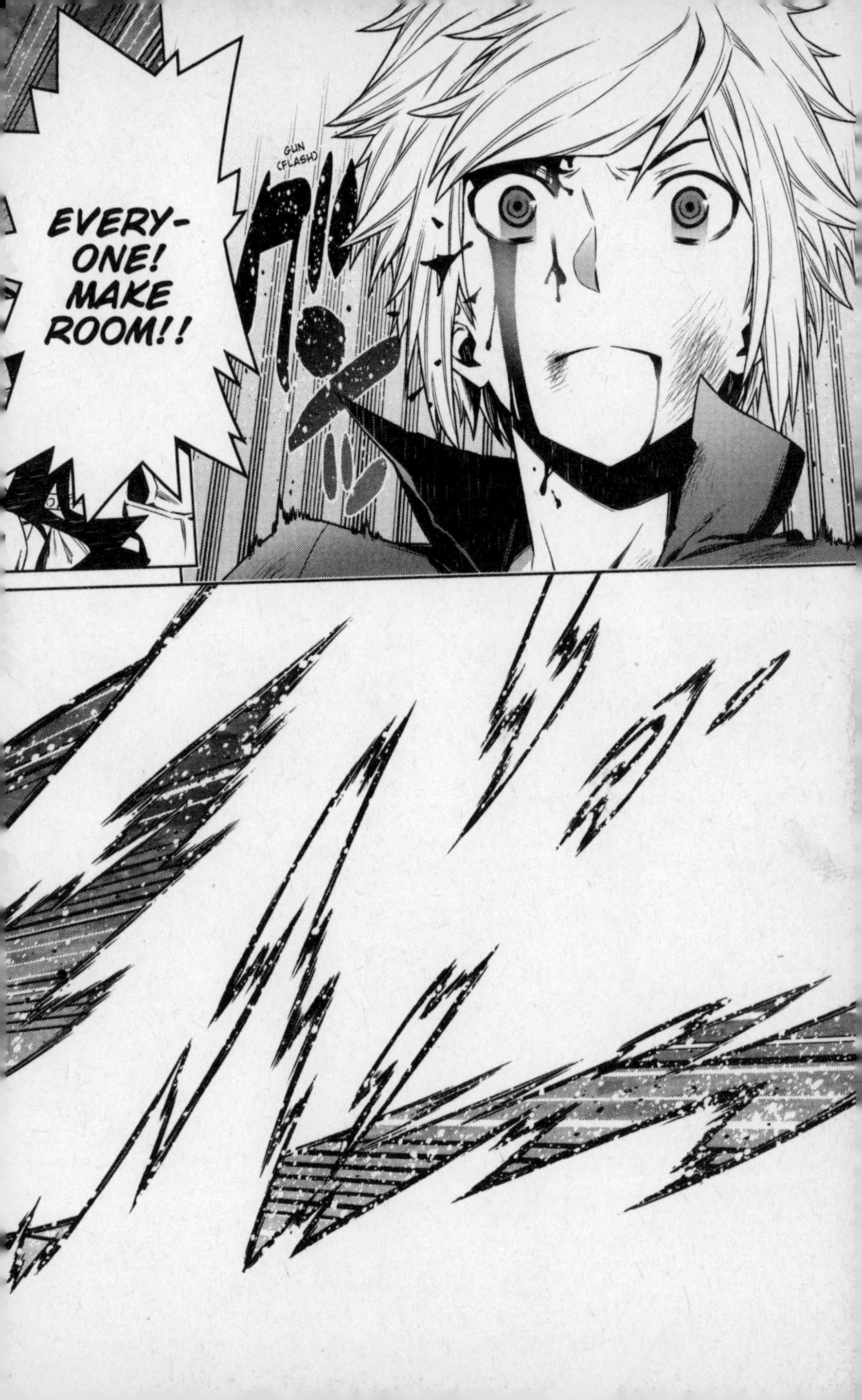
GUN
(FLASH)
EVERY-ONE! MAKE ROOM!!

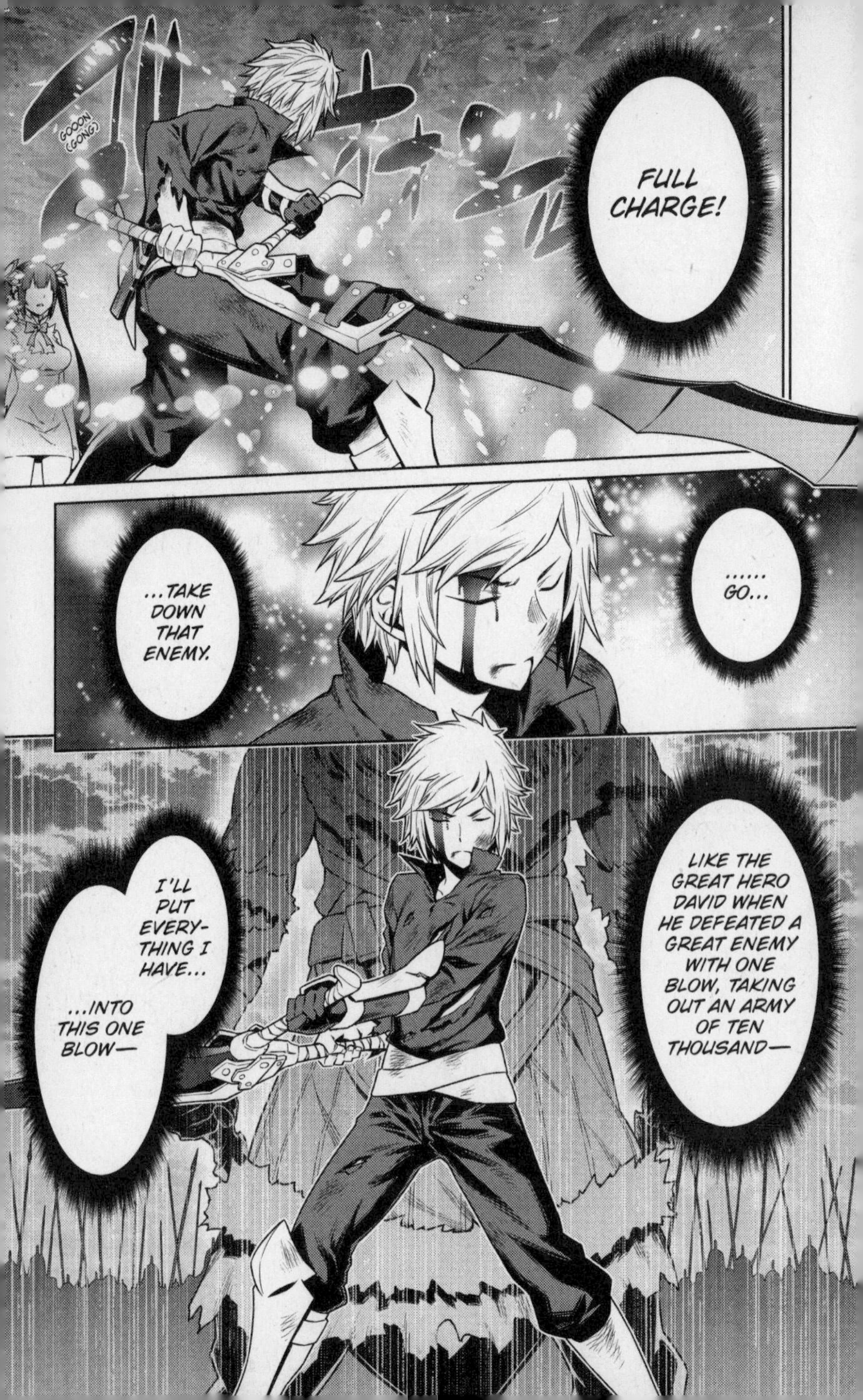
FULL CHARGE!
GOOOON (GONG)
......GO...
...TAKE DOWN THAT ENEMY.
LIKE THE GREAT HERO DAVID WHEN HE DEFEATED A GREAT ENEMY WITH ONE BLOW, TAKING OUT AN ARMY OF TEN THOUSAND—
I'LL PUT EVERYTHING I HAVE...
...INTO THIS ONE BLOW—

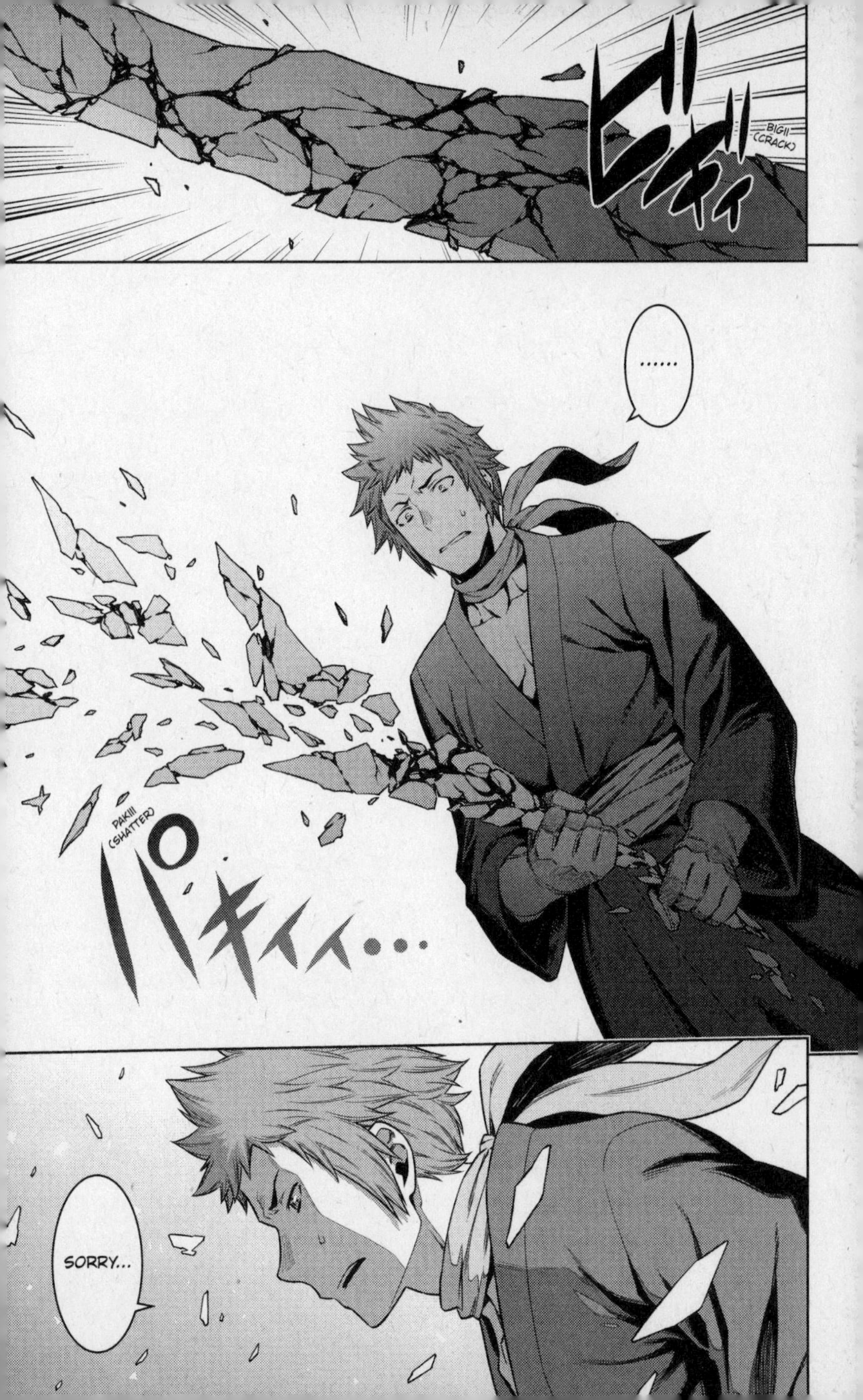

BIGII (CRACK)
......
PAKIII (SHATTER)
SORRY...

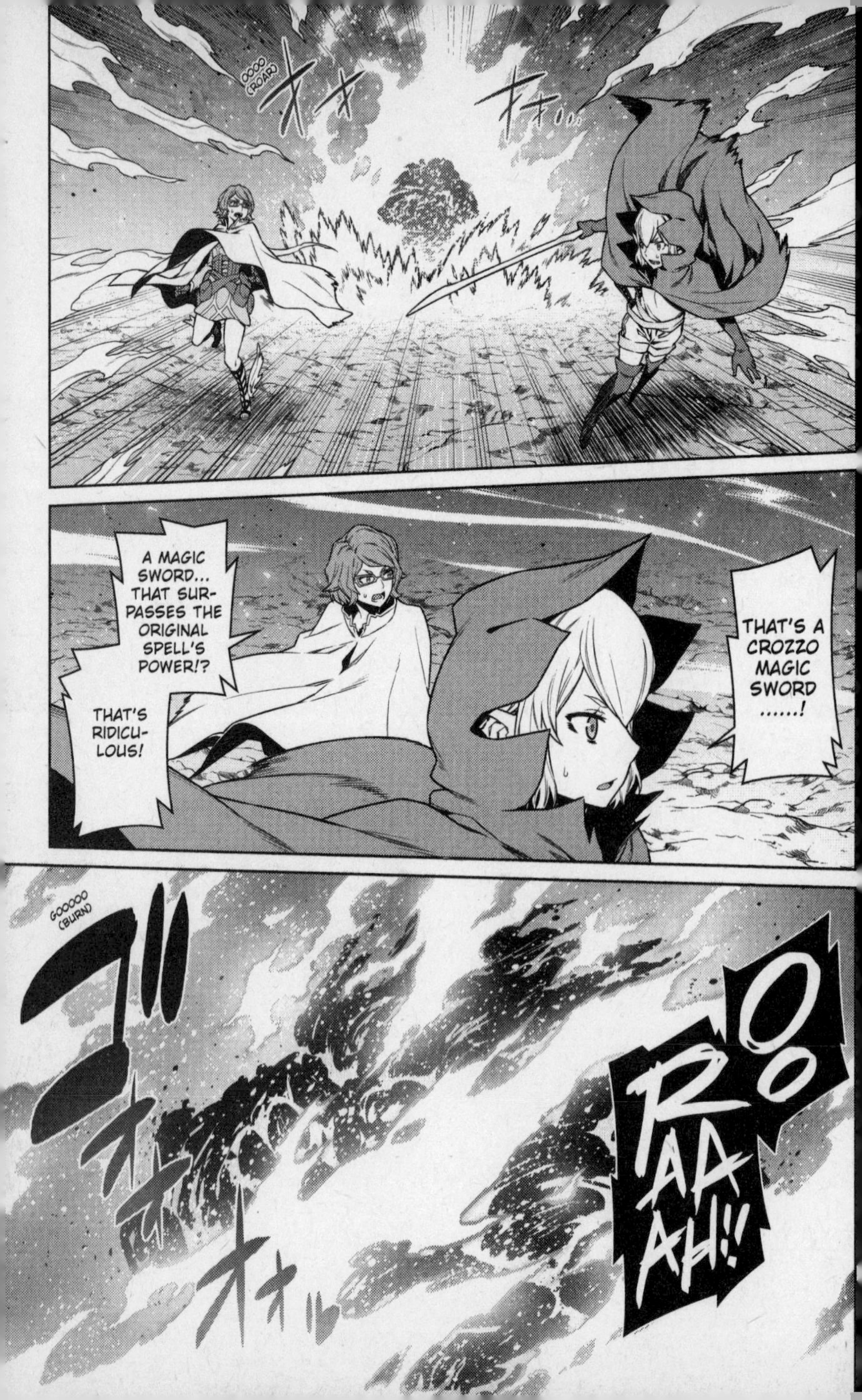
OOOO (ROAR)
THAT'S A CROZZO MAGIC SWORD ......!
A MAGIC SWORD... THAT SURPASSES THE ORIGINAL SPELL'S POWER!?
THAT'S RIDICULOUS!
GOOOOO (BURN)
ROOAAAH!!

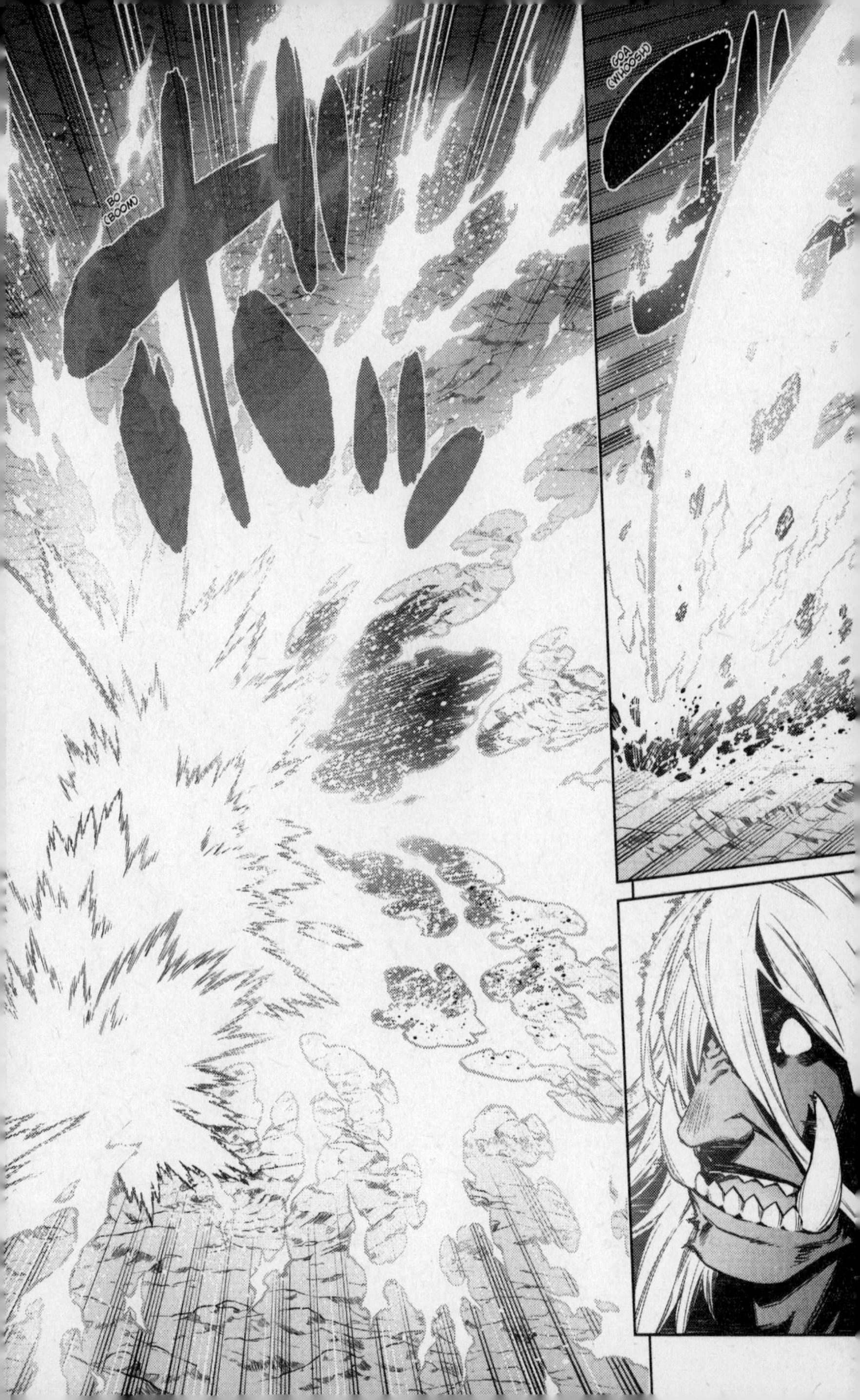
GOA (WHOOSH)
BO (BOOM)

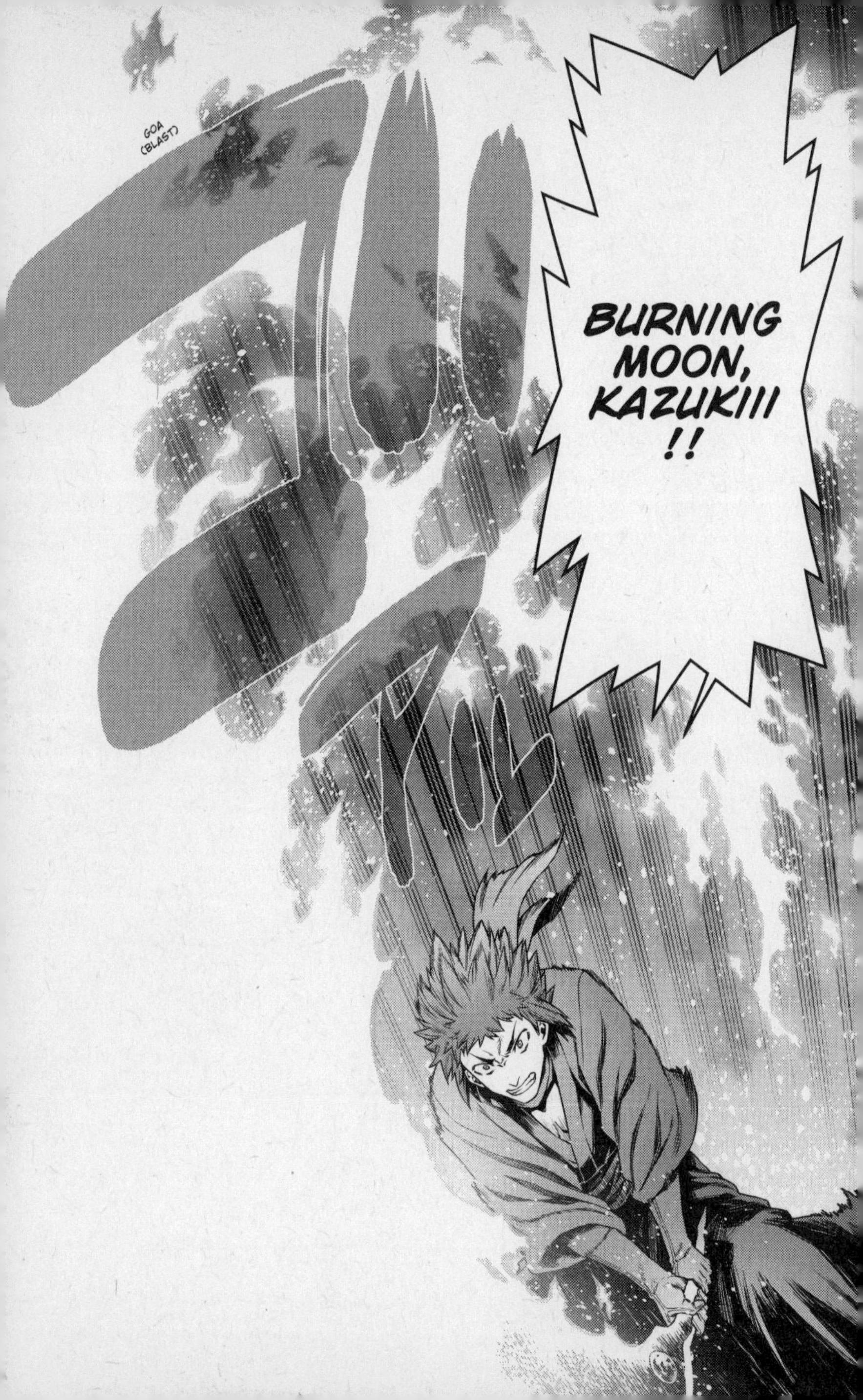
GOA (BLAST)
BURNING MOON, KAZUKIII !!

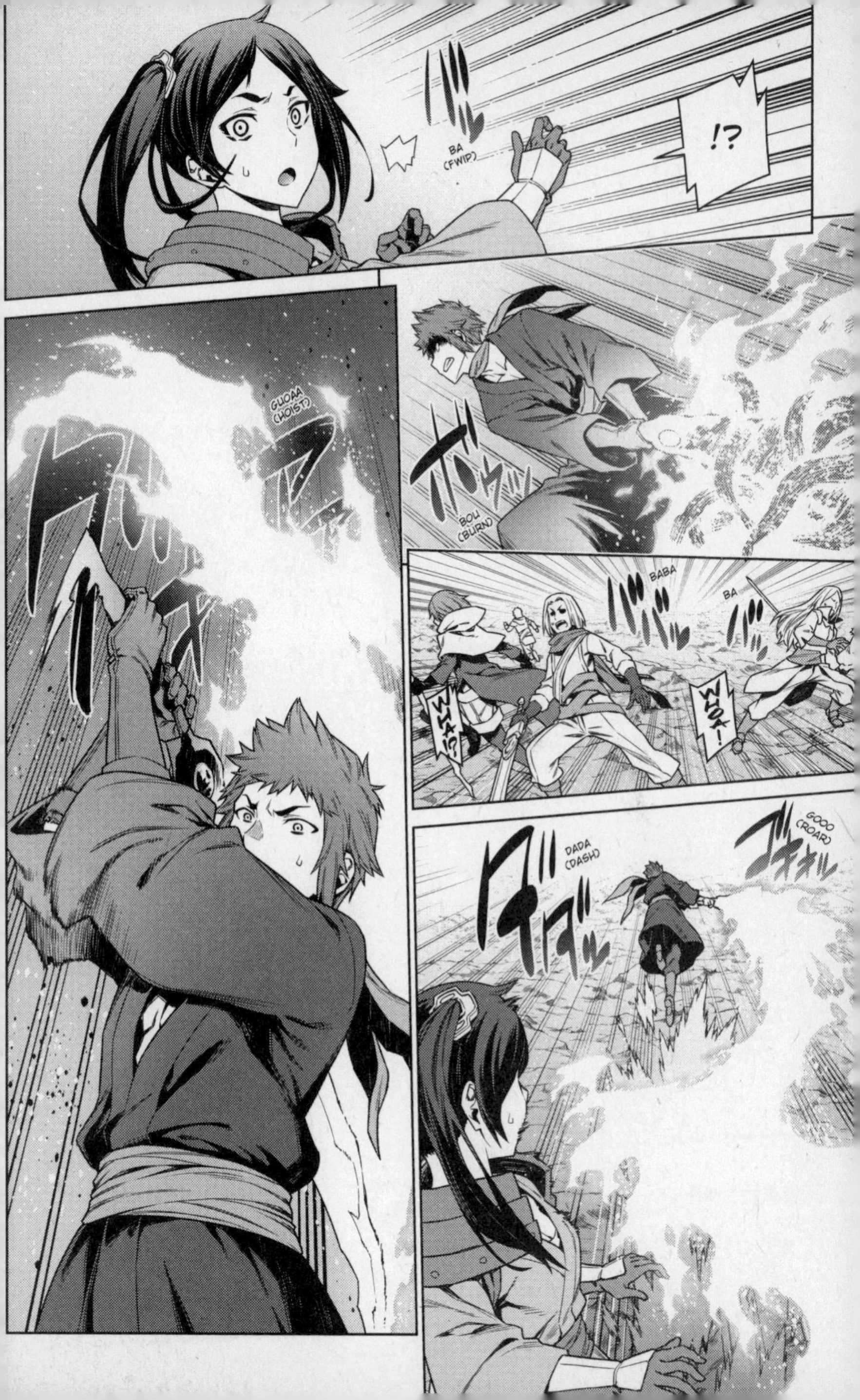
!?
BA
(FWIP)
BOU
(BURN)
BA
BABA
WHOA!
WHA!?
GOOO
(ROAR)
DADA
(DASH)
GUOAA
(HOIST)

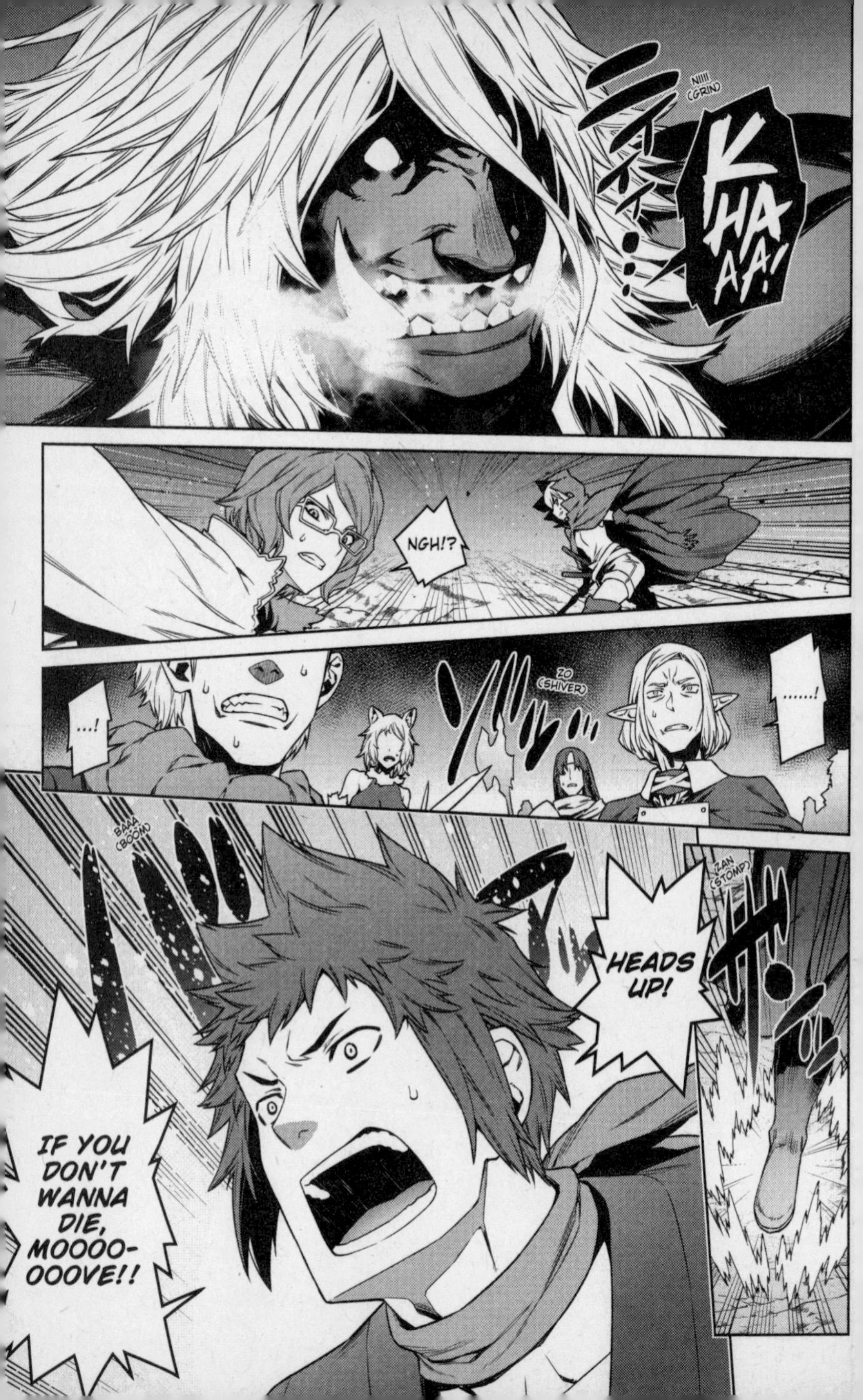
KHAAA!
NIIII (GRIN)
NGH!?
......!
ZO (SHIVER)
...!
ZAN (STOMP)
HEADS UP!
BAAA (BOOM)
IF YOU DON'T WANNA DIE, MOOOO-OOOVE!!

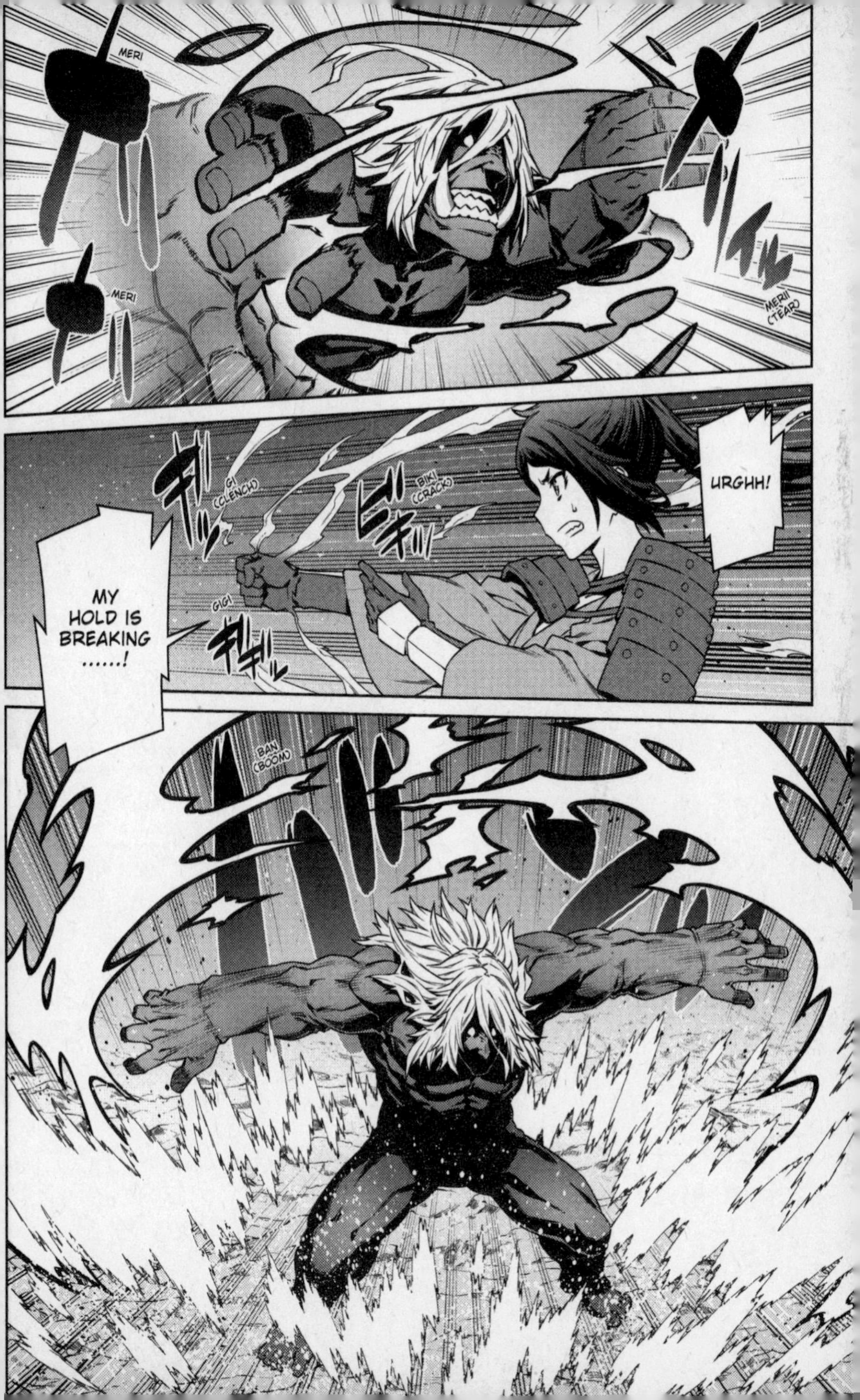
MERI! (TEAR)
MERI
MERI
URGHH!
BIKI (CRACK)
GI (CLENCH)
GIGI
MY HOLD IS BREAKING ......!
BAN (BOOM)

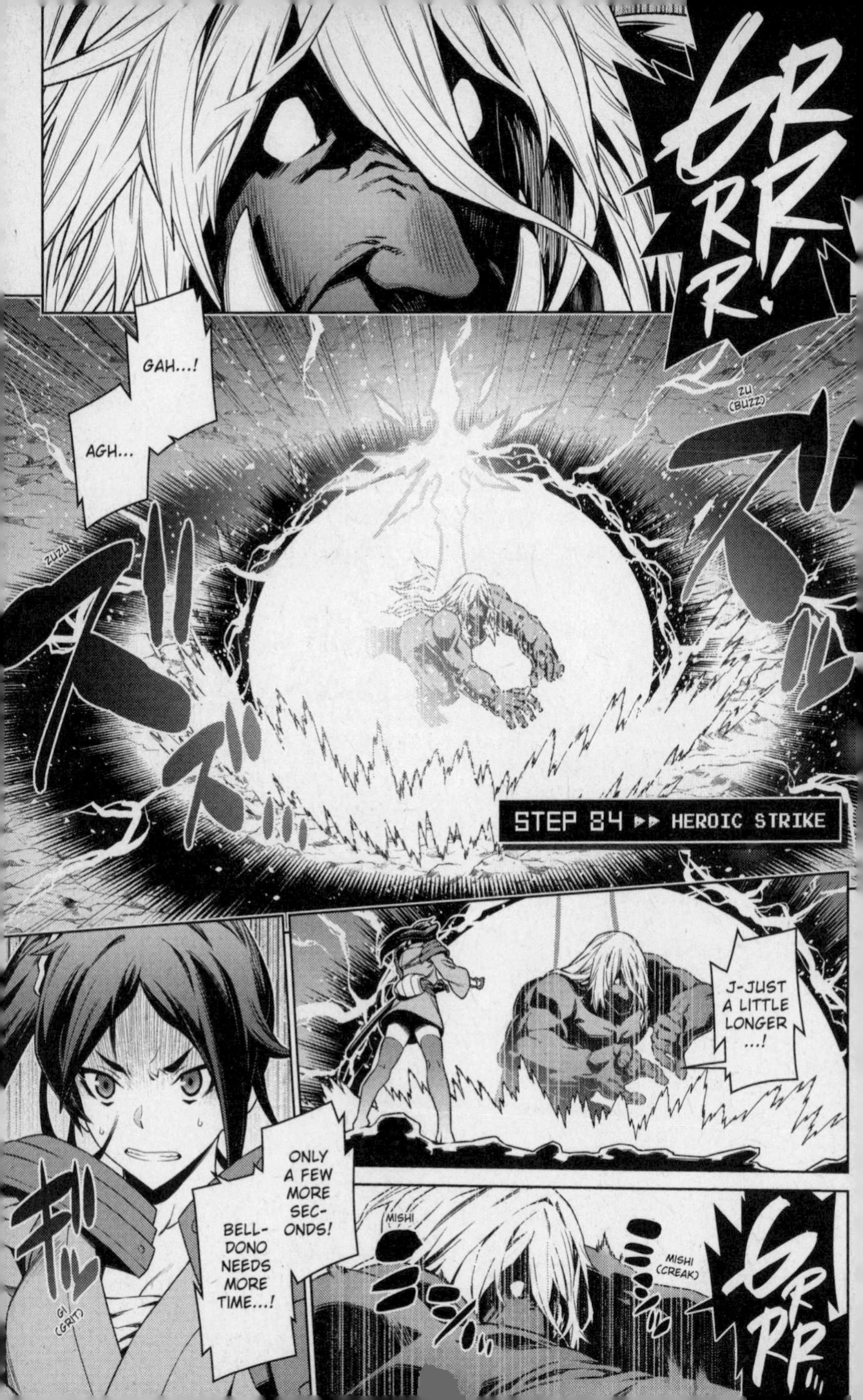
GRRRR!
ZU (BUZZ)
GAH...!
AGH...
ZUZU
STEP 84 ▸▸ HEROIC STRIKE
J-JUST A LITTLE LONGER...!
ONLY A FEW MORE SECONDS!
BELL-DONO NEEDS MORE TIME...!
GI (GRIT)
MISHI
MISHI (CREAK)
GRRR...

Is it WRONG to TRY to PICK UP GIRLS IN A DUNGEON?

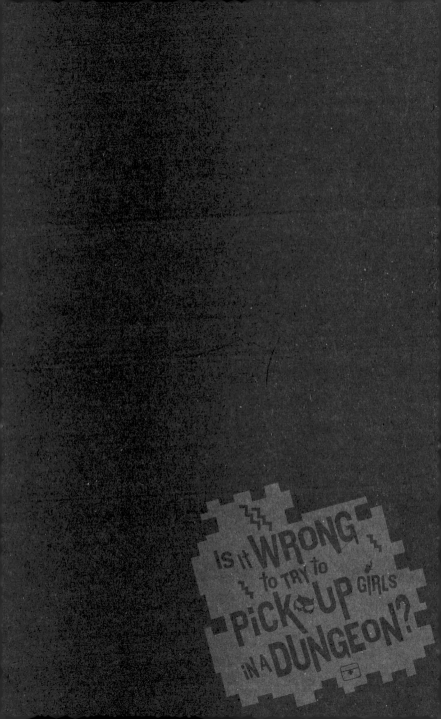

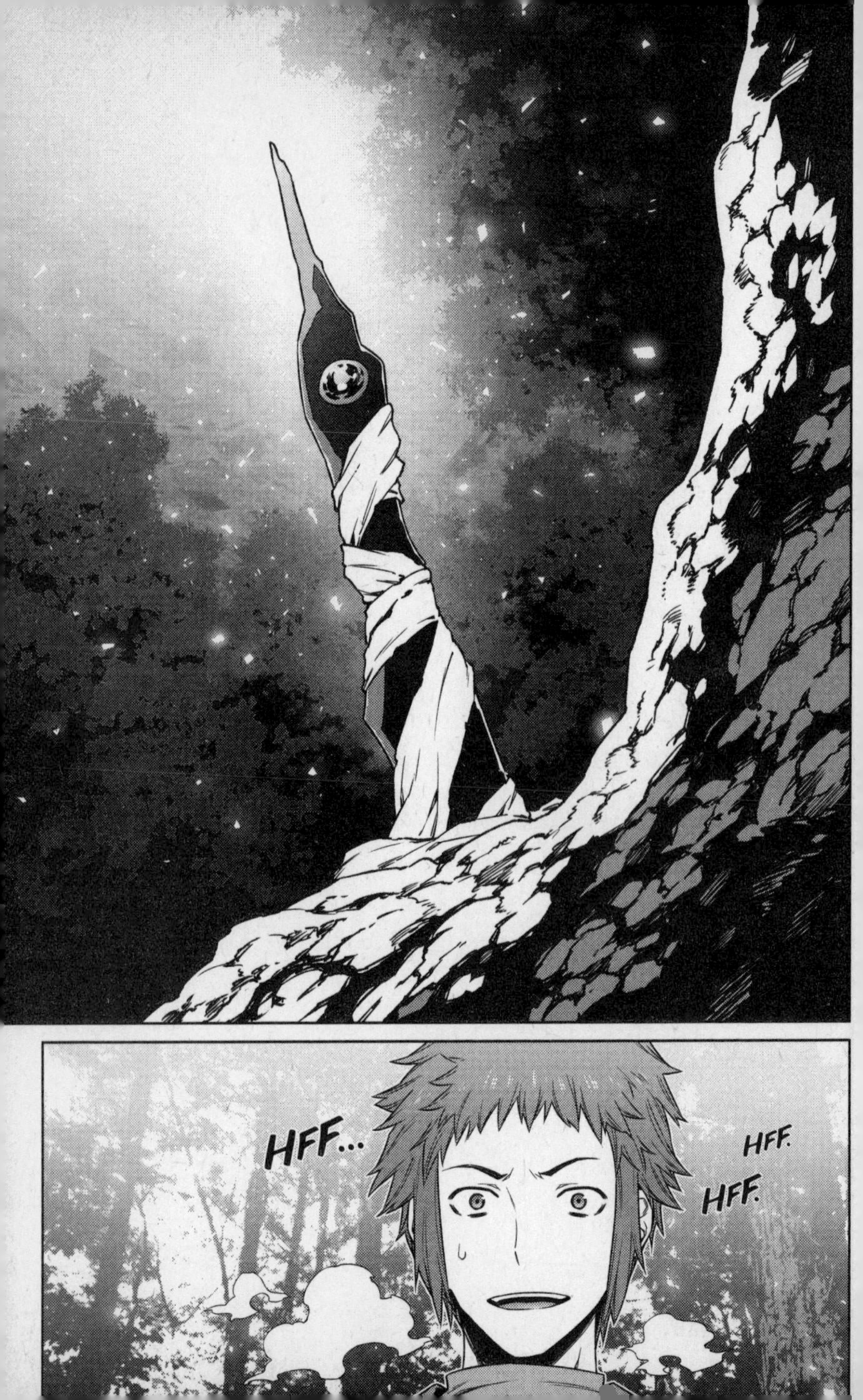
HFF.
HFF.
HFF...

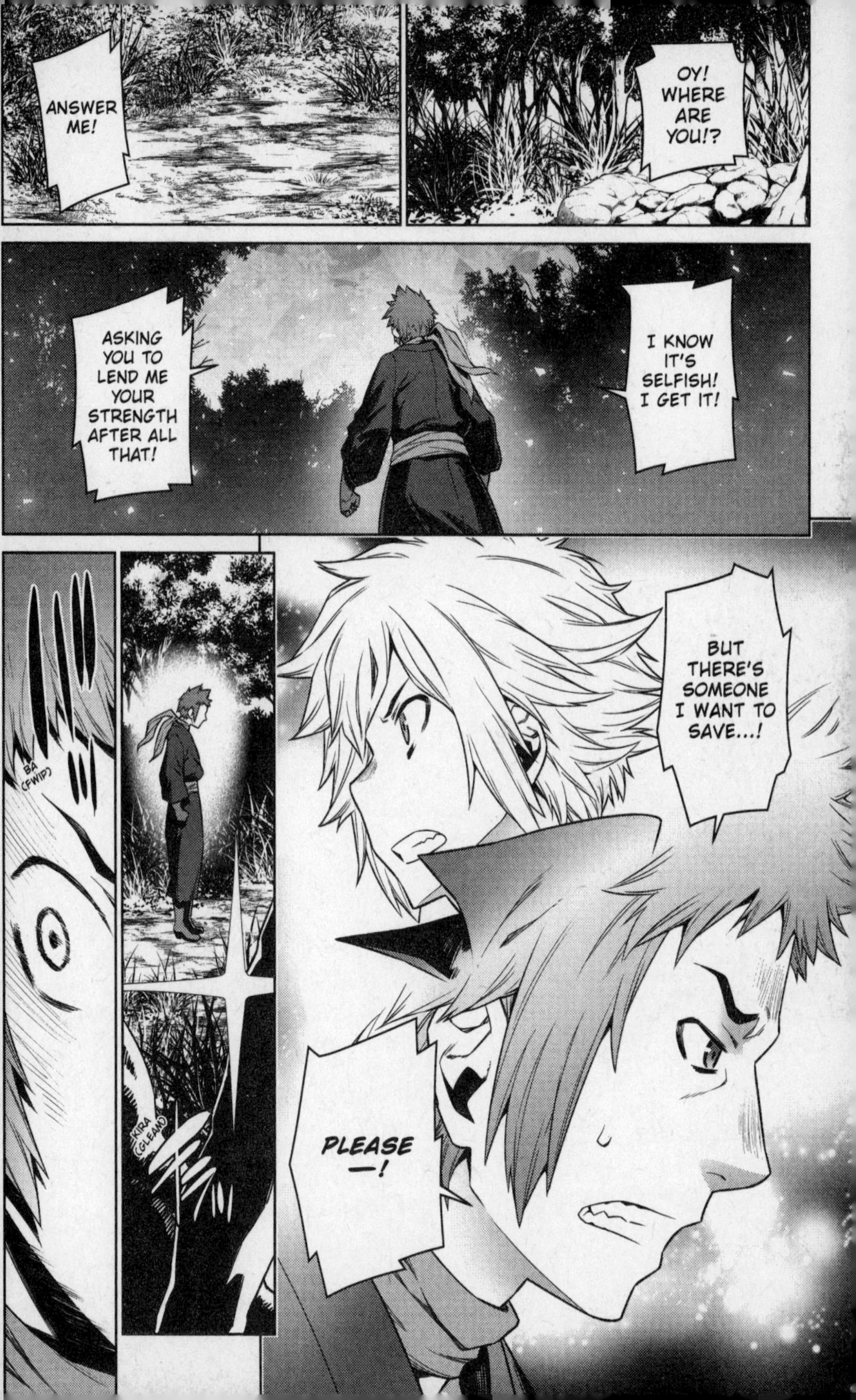
OY! WHERE ARE YOU!?
ANSWER ME!
I KNOW IT'S SELFISH! I GET IT!
ASKING YOU TO LEND ME YOUR STRENGTH AFTER ALL THAT!
BUT THERE'S SOMEONE I WANT TO SAVE...!
PLEASE—!
KIRA (GLEAM)
BA (FWIP)

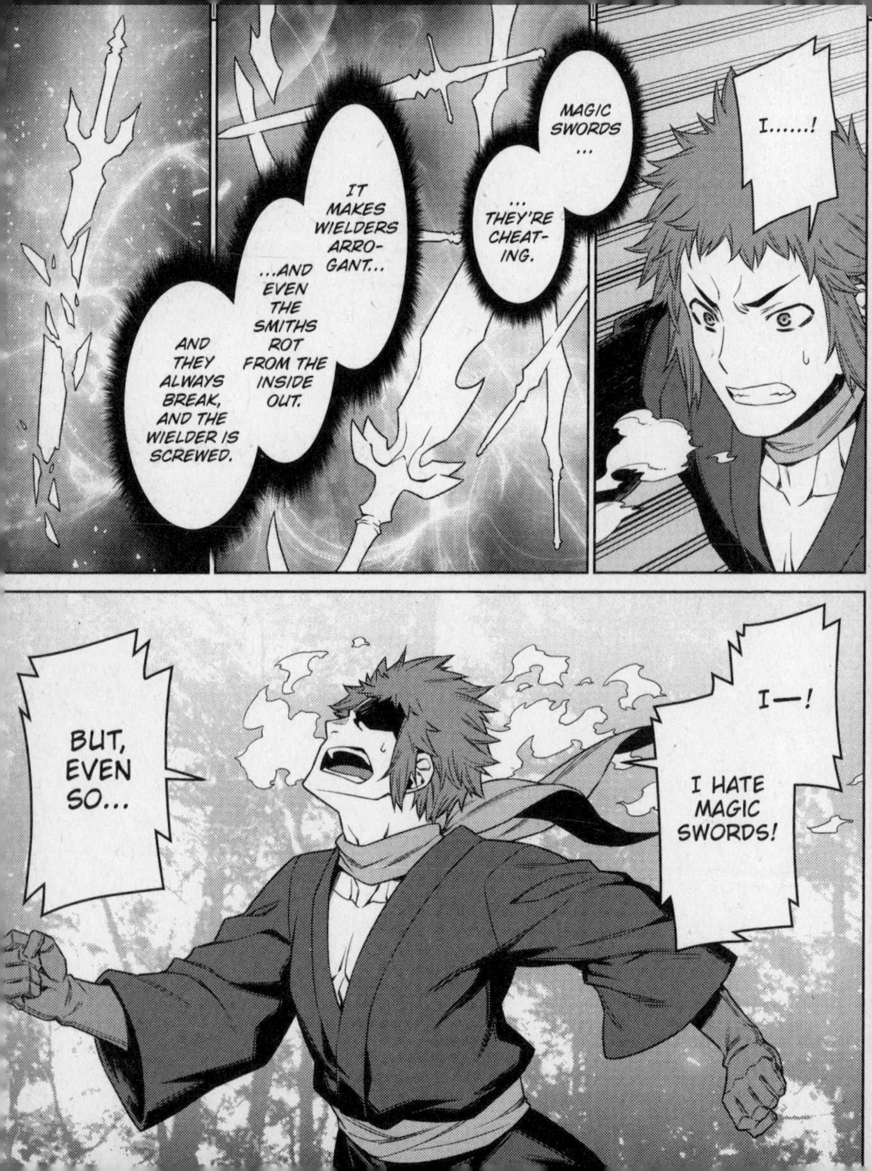
I......!
MAGIC SWORDS ...
... THEY'RE CHEAT-ING.
IT MAKES WIELDERS ARRO-GANT...
...AND EVEN THE SMITHS ROT FROM THE INSIDE OUT.
AND THEY ALWAYS BREAK, AND THE WIELDER IS SCREWED.
I—!
I HATE MAGIC SWORDS!
BUT, EVEN SO...

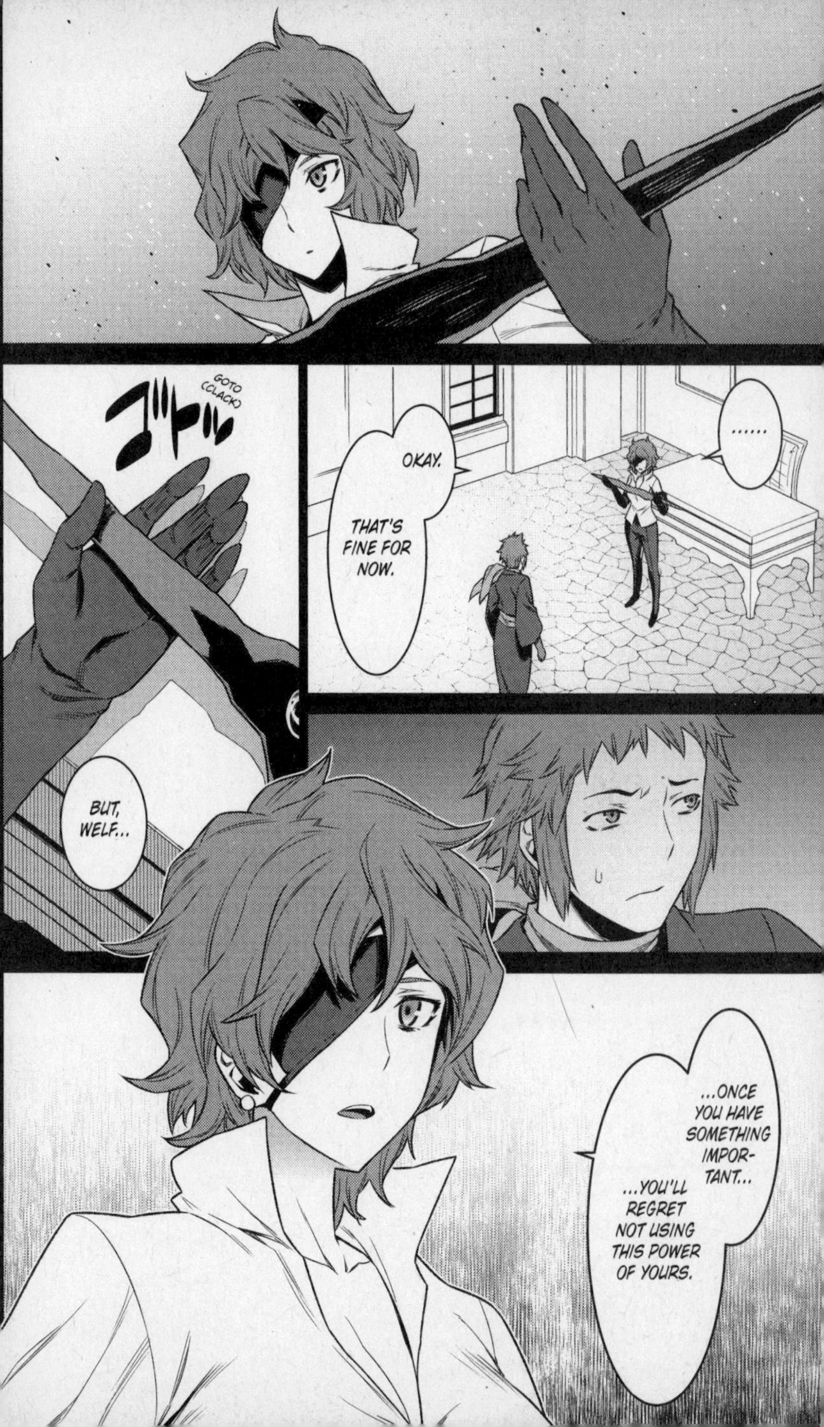
......
OKAY.
THAT'S FINE FOR NOW.
ゴトッ GOTO (CLACK)
BUT, WELF...
...ONCE YOU HAVE SOMETHING IMPOR-TANT...
...YOU'LL REGRET NOT USING THIS POWER OF YOURS.

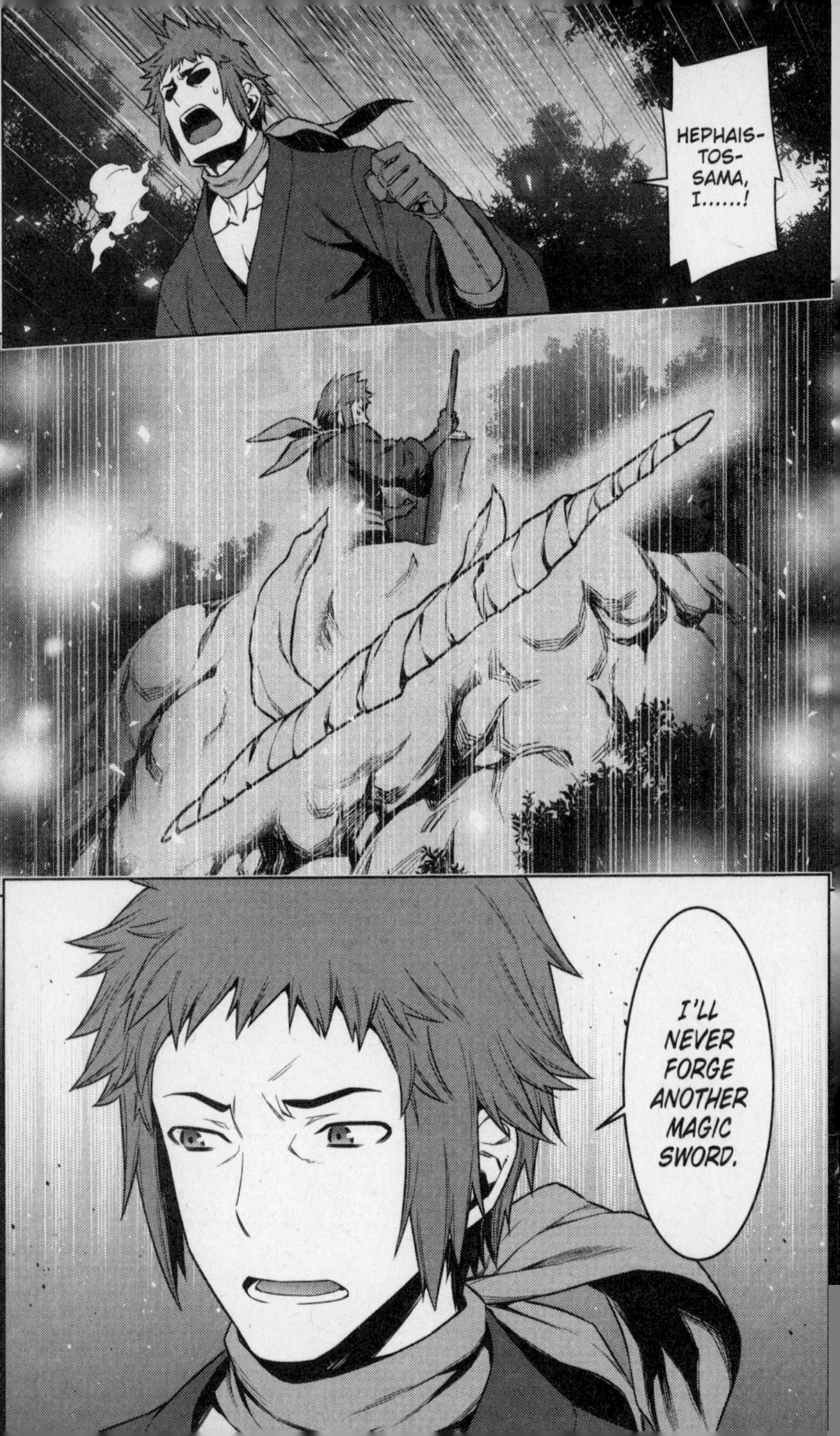
HEPHAIS-
TOS-
SAMA,
I......!
I'LL NEVER FORGE ANOTHER MAGIC SWORD.

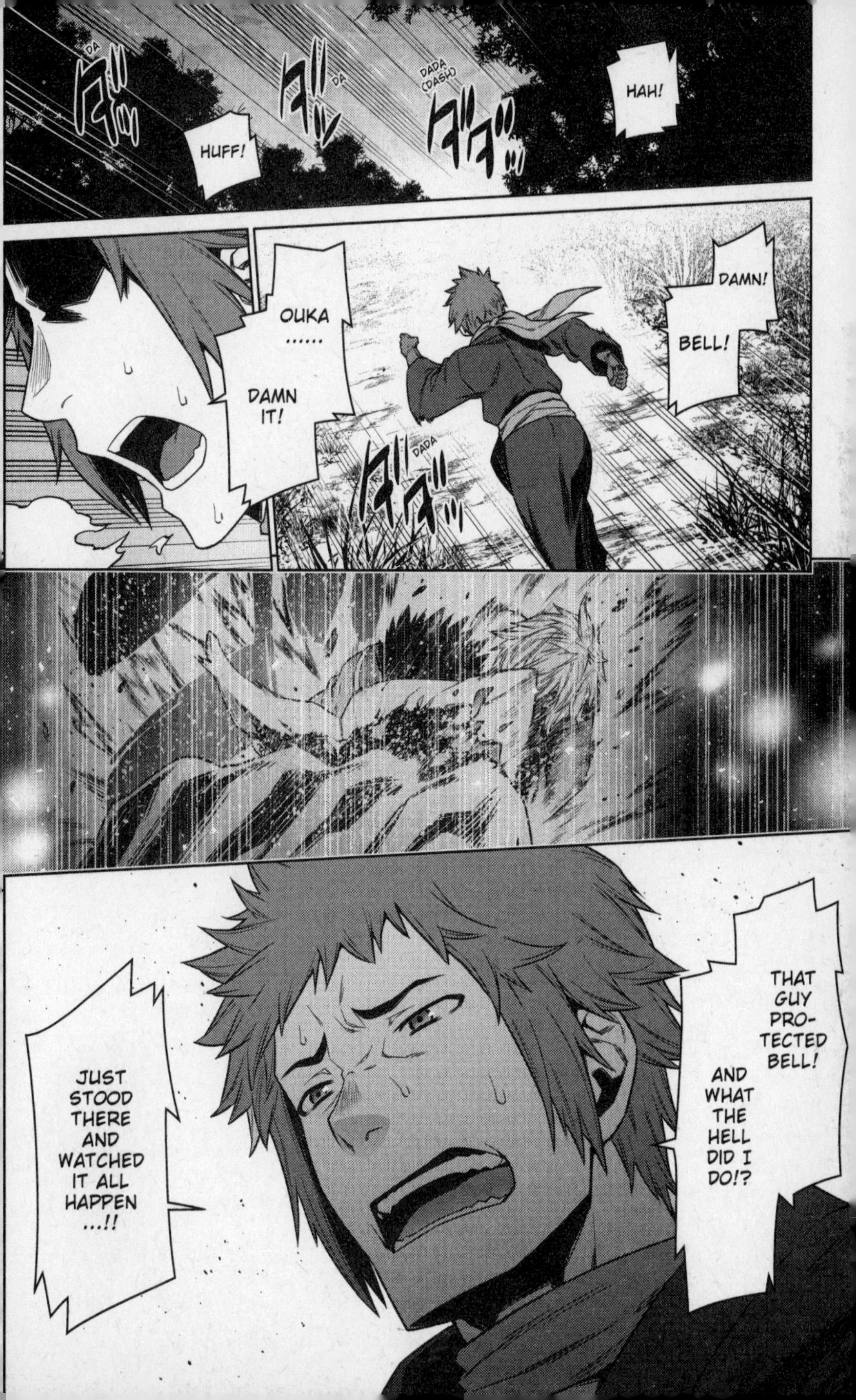
HAH!
DADA (DASH)
DA
HUFF!
DA
DAMN!
BELL!
DADA
OUKA ......
DAMN IT!
THAT GUY PROTECTED BELL!
AND WHAT THE HELL DID I DO!?
JUST STOOD THERE AND WATCHED IT ALL HAPPEN ...!!

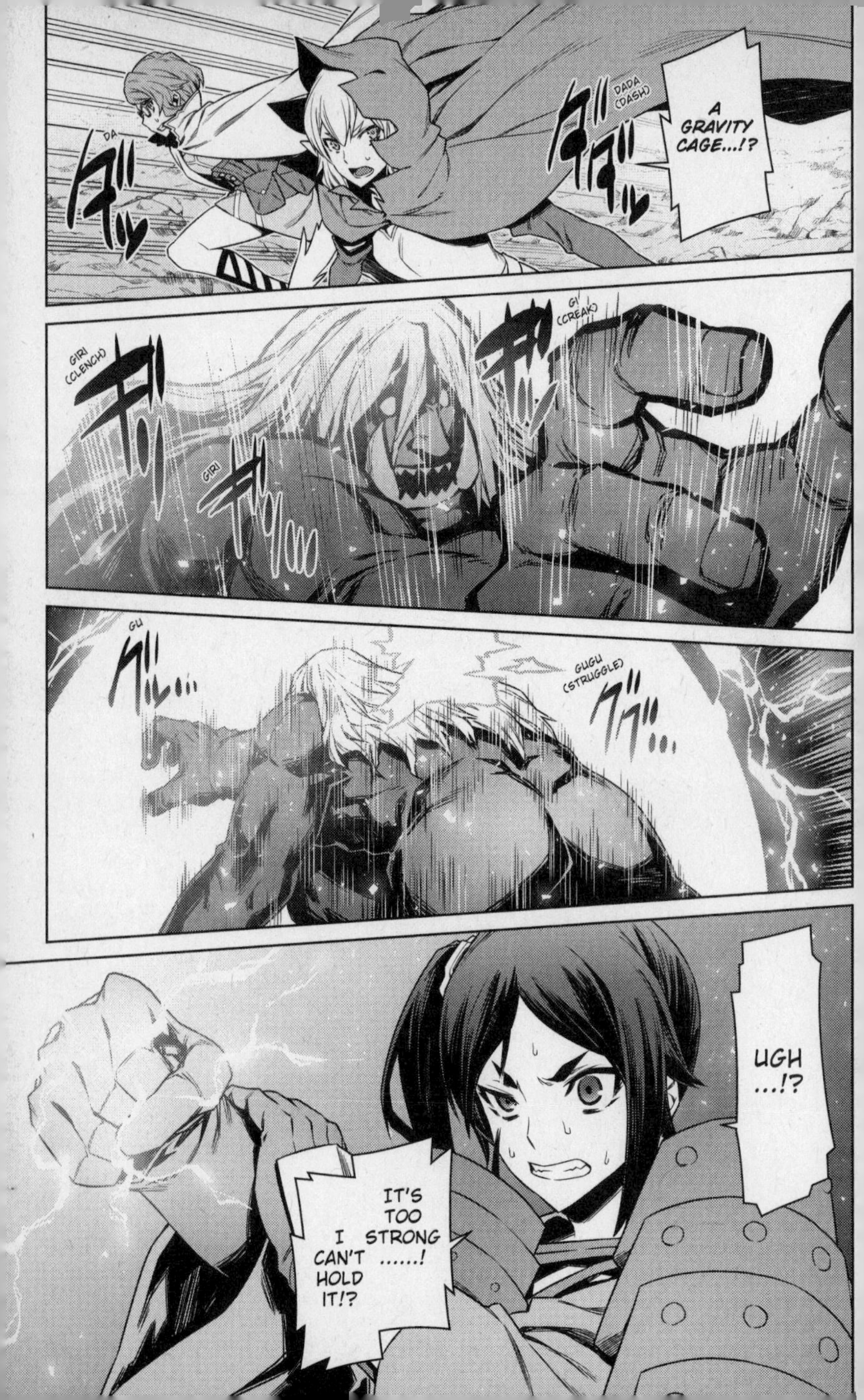
A GRAVITY CAGE...!?
DADA (DASH)
DA
GI' (CREAK)
GIRI (CLENCH)
GIRI
GUGU (STRUGGLE)
GU
UGH ...!?
IT'S TOO STRONG ......!
I CAN'T HOLD IT!?

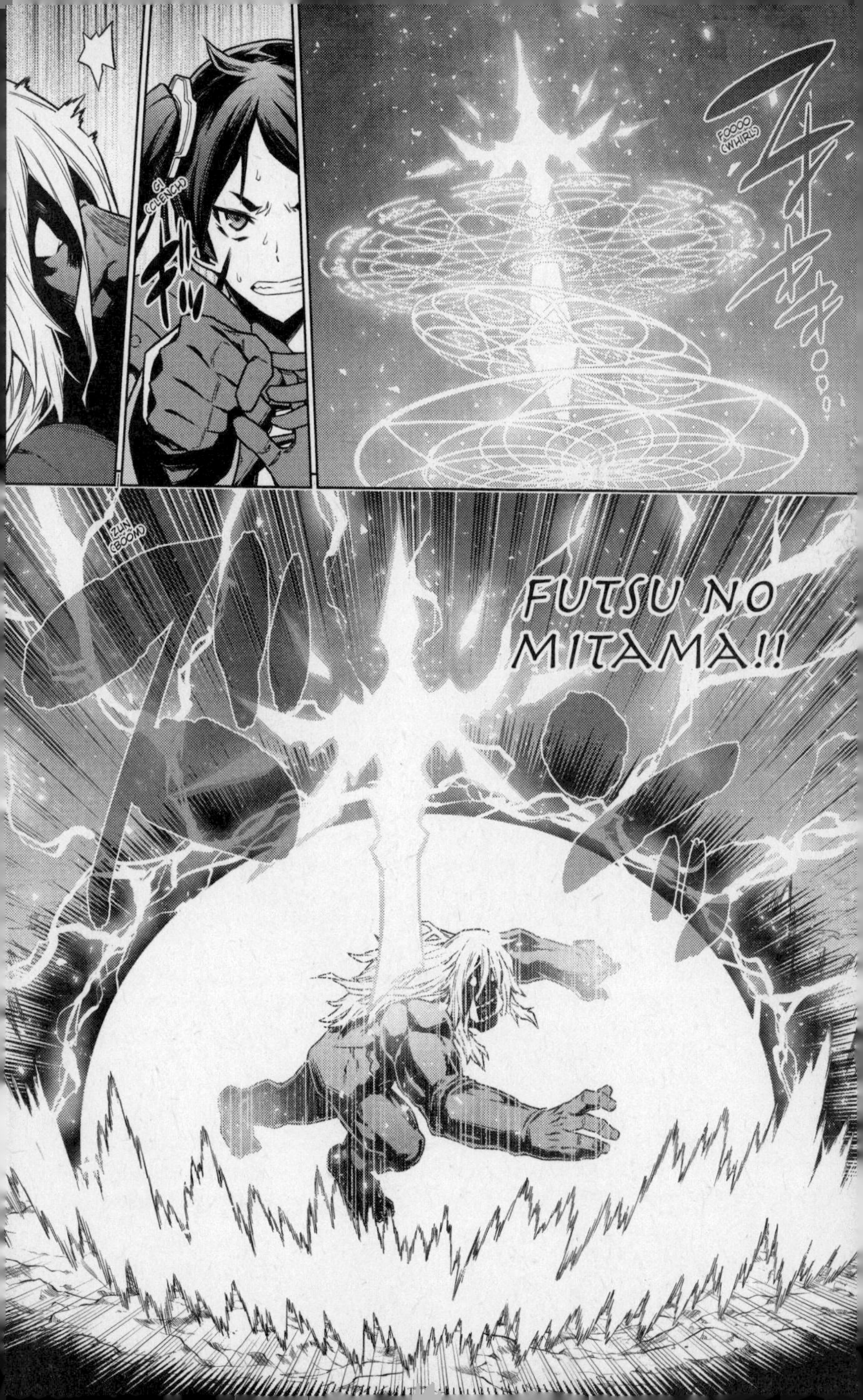
FOOOO (WHIRL)
GI (CLENCH)
ZUN (BOOM)
FUTSU NO MITAMA!!

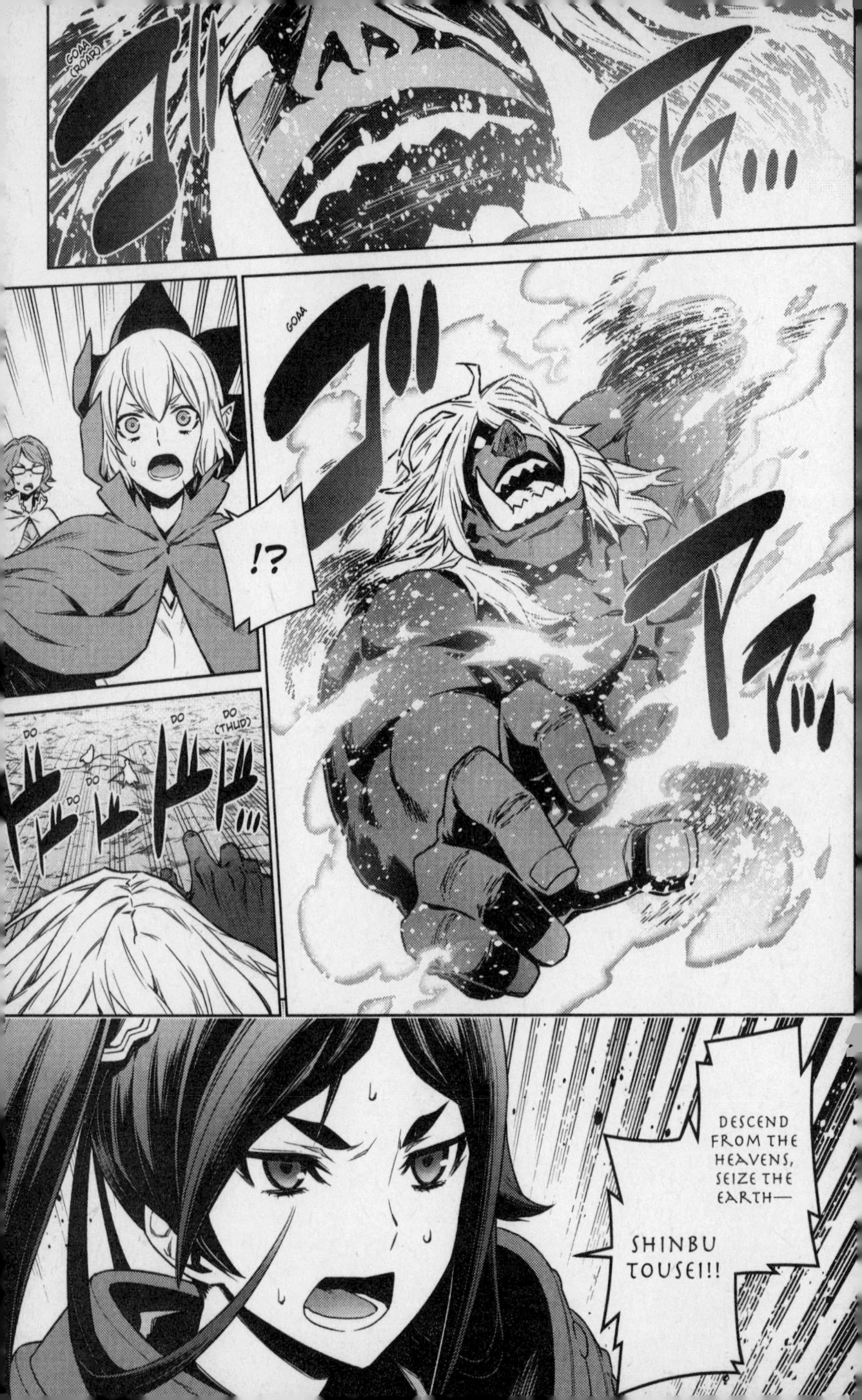
GOAA (ROAR)
GOAA
!?
DO DO DO DO DO (THUD)
DESCEND FROM THE HEAVENS, SEIZE THE EARTH—
SHINBU TOUSEI!!

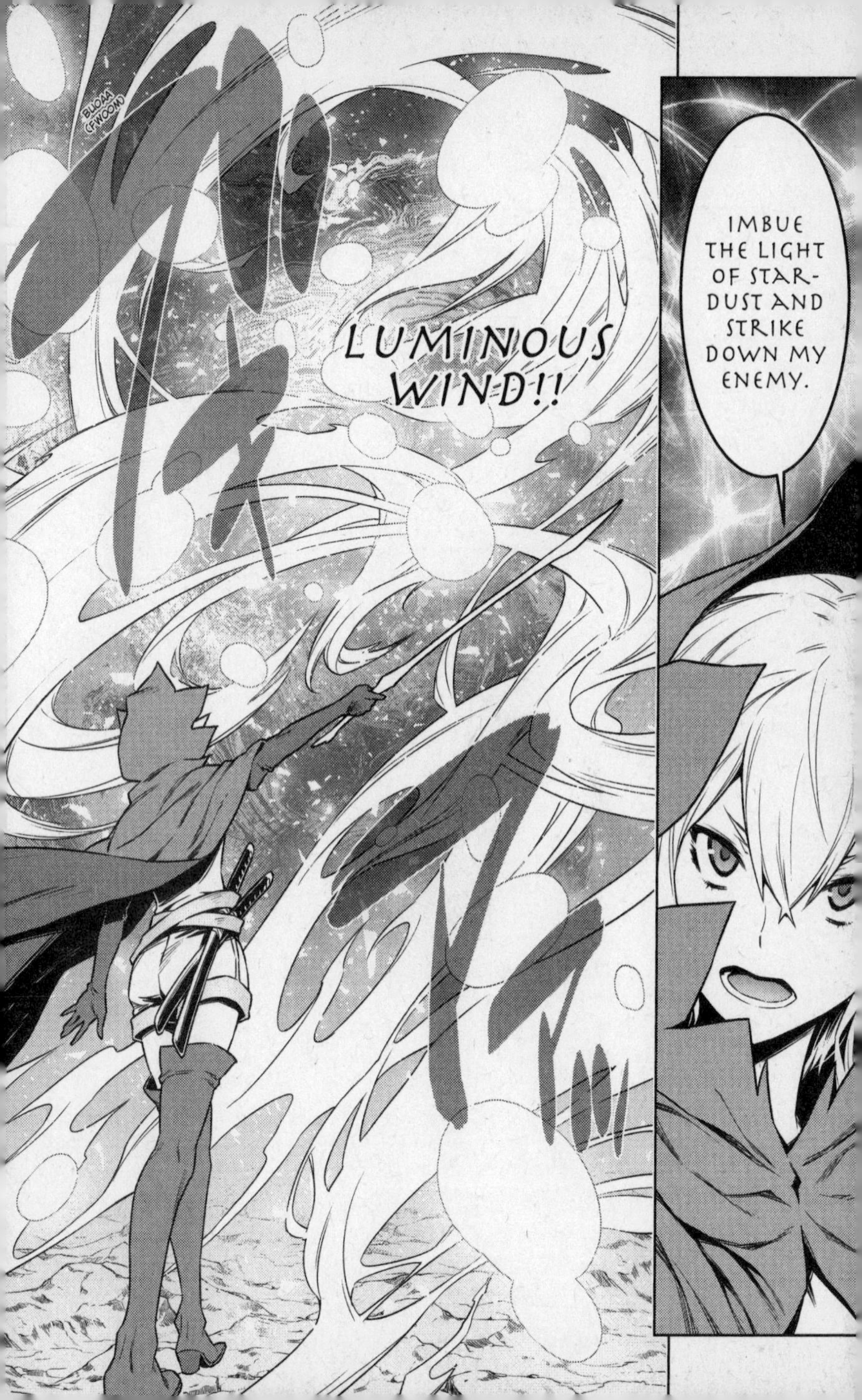
IMBUE THE LIGHT OF STAR-DUST AND STRIKE DOWN MY ENEMY.
BUOAA (FWOOM)
LUMINOUS WIND!!

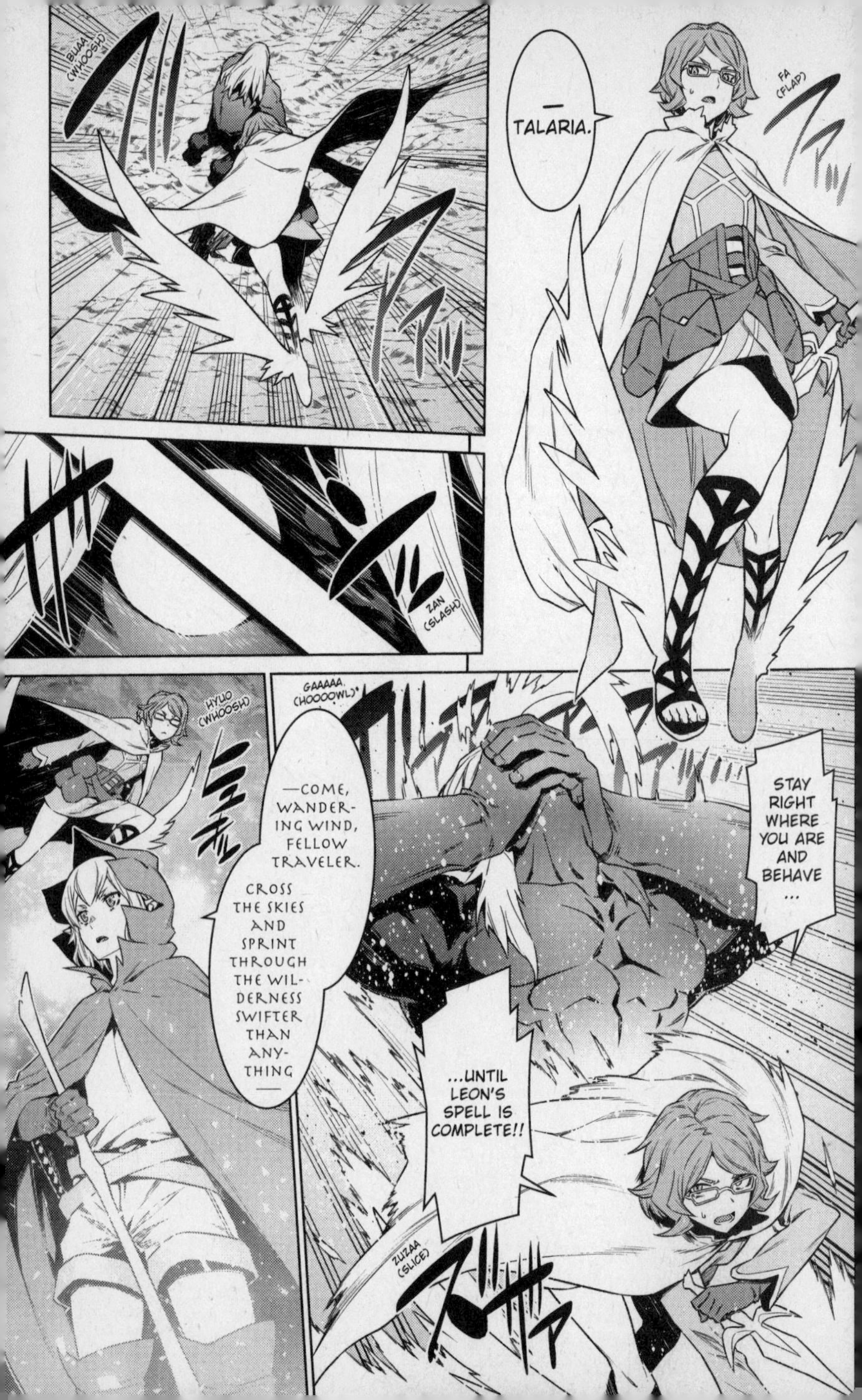
FA (FLAP)
—TALARIA.
BUAA (WHOOSH)
ZAN (SLASH)
STAY RIGHT WHERE YOU ARE AND BEHAVE...
GAAAAA (HOOOOWL)
—COME, WANDERING WIND, FELLOW TRAVELER.
CROSS THE SKIES AND SPRINT THROUGH THE WILDERNESS SWIFTER THAN ANYTHING—
...UNTIL LEON'S SPELL IS COMPLETE!!
ZUZAA (SLICE)
HYUO (WHOOSH)

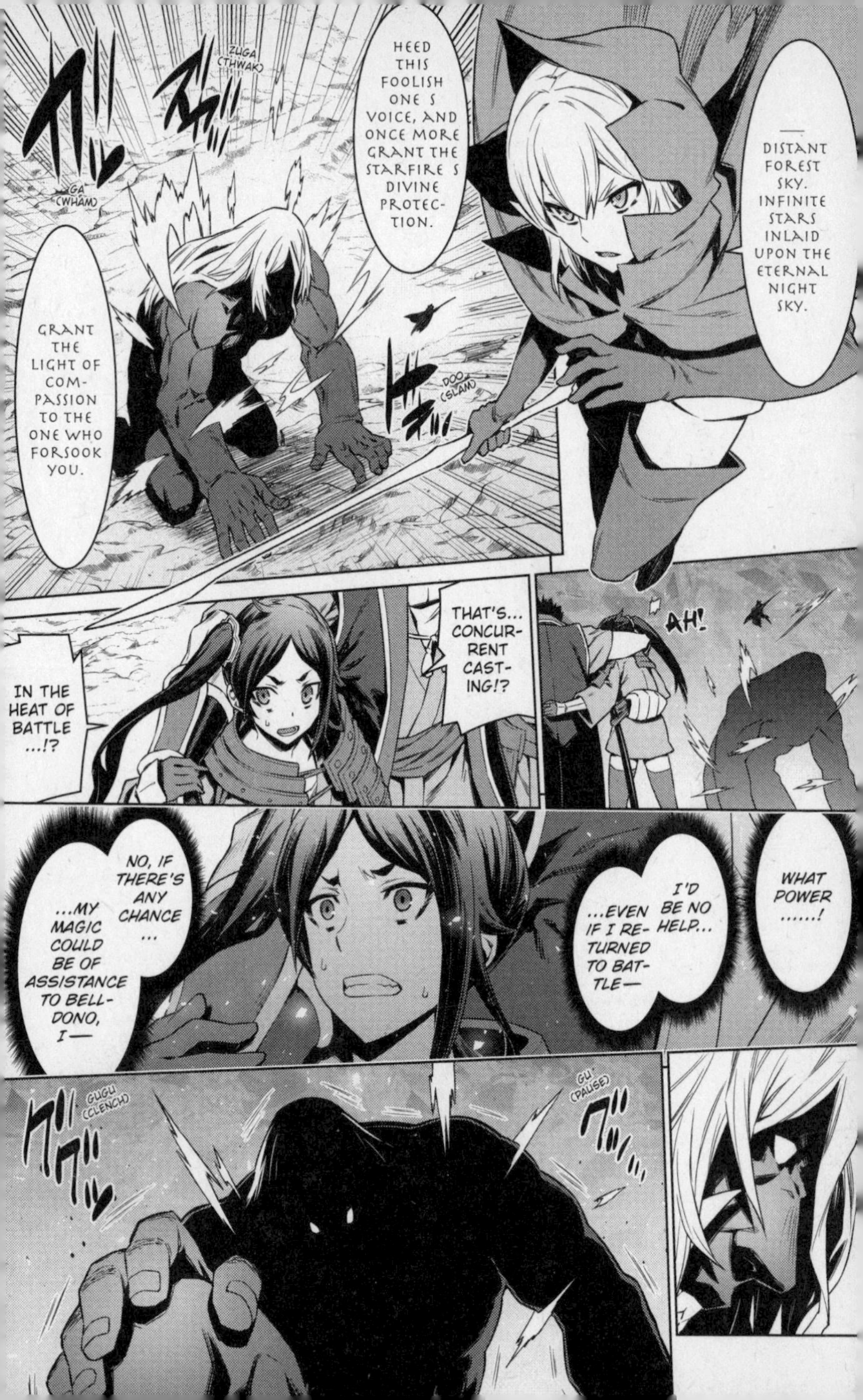

—DISTANT FOREST SKY. INFINITE STARS INLAID UPON THE ETERNAL NIGHT SKY.
HEED THIS FOOLISH ONE'S VOICE, AND ONCE MORE GRANT THE STARFIRE'S DIVINE PROTECTION.
ZUGA (THWAK)
GA (WHAM)
DOO (SLAM)
GRANT THE LIGHT OF COMPASSION TO THE ONE WHO FORSOOK YOU.
AH!
THAT'S... CONCURRENT CASTING!?
IN THE HEAT OF BATTLE ...!?
WHAT POWER ......!
I'D BE NO HELP...
...EVEN IF I RETURNED TO BATTLE—
NO, IF THERE'S ANY CHANCE ...
...MY MAGIC COULD BE OF ASSISTANCE TO BELL-DONO, I—
GU (PAUSE)
GUGU (CLENCH)

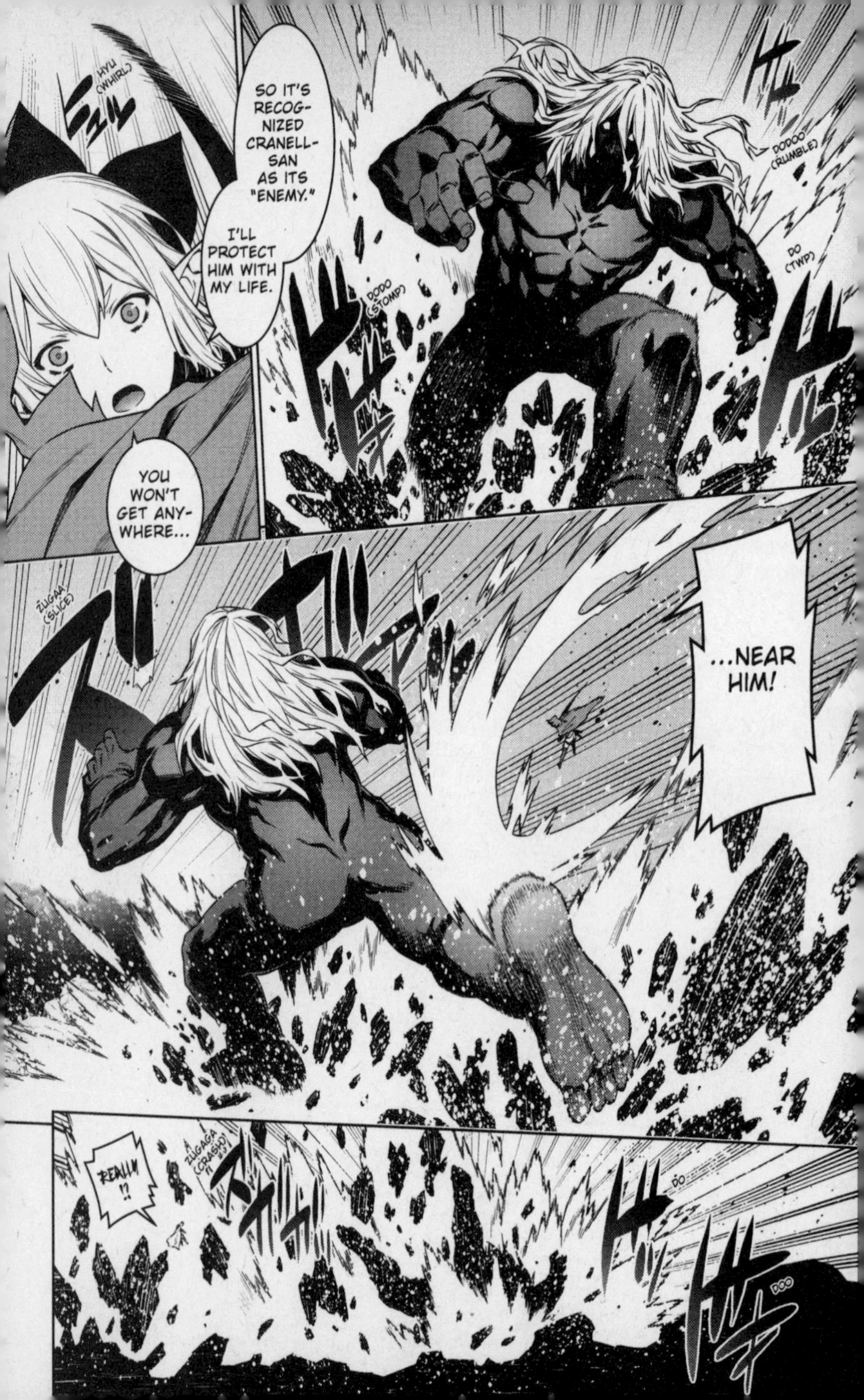
DODOO (RUMBLE)
DO (TWP)
DODO (STOMP)
HYU (WHIRL)
SO IT'S RECOGNIZED CRANELL-SAN AS ITS "ENEMY."
I'LL PROTECT HIM WITH MY LIFE.
YOU WON'T GET ANYWHERE...
...NEAR HIM!
ZUGAA (SLICE)
DO
DOO
ZUGAGA (CRASH)
REALLY!?

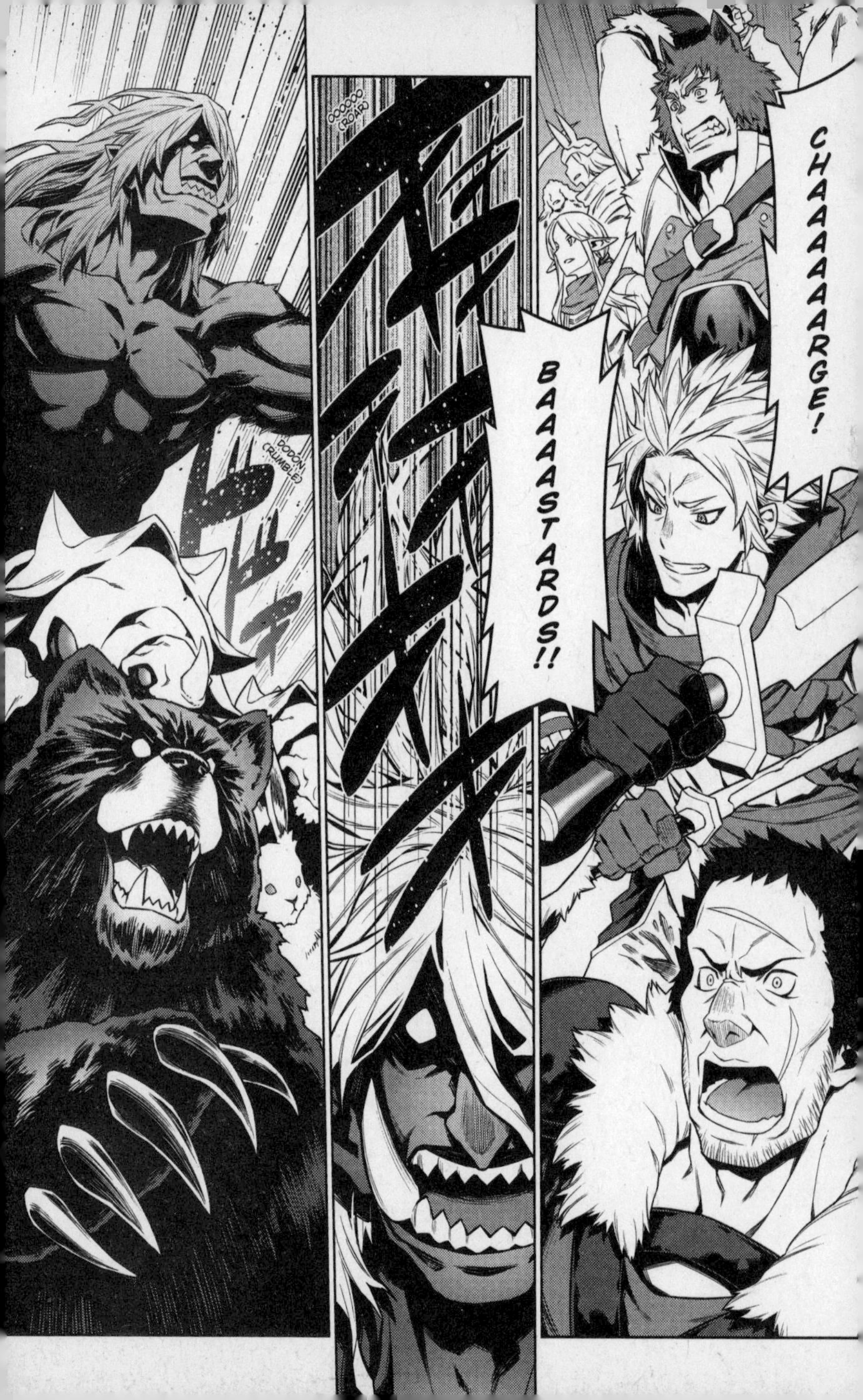
CHAAAAAAARGE!
BAAAASTARDS!!
OOOOOO (ROAR)
DODON (RUMBLE)

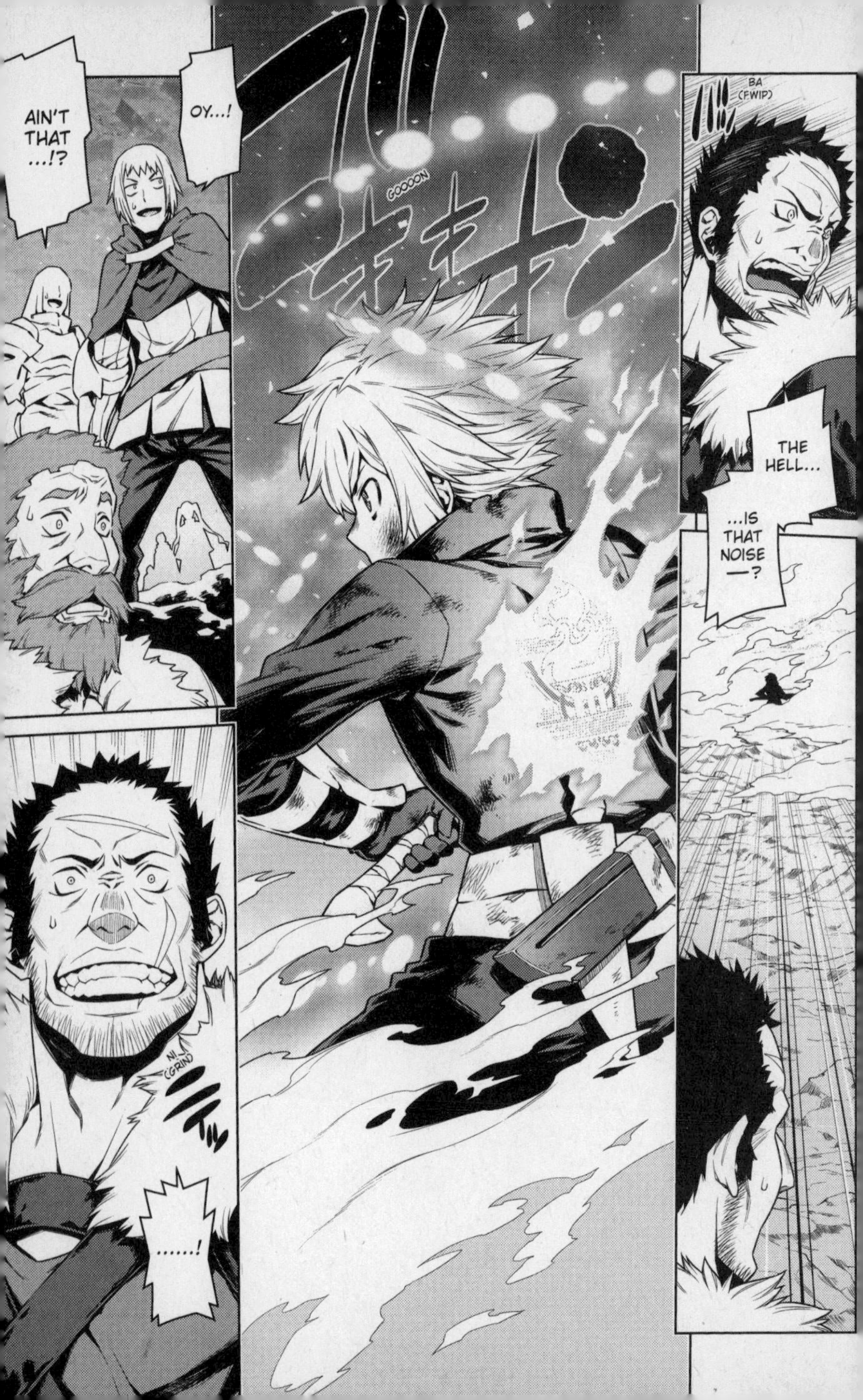
BA
(FWIP)
THE HELL...
...IS THAT NOISE—?
GOOOON
OY...!
AIN'T THAT ...!?
NI
(GRIN)
......!

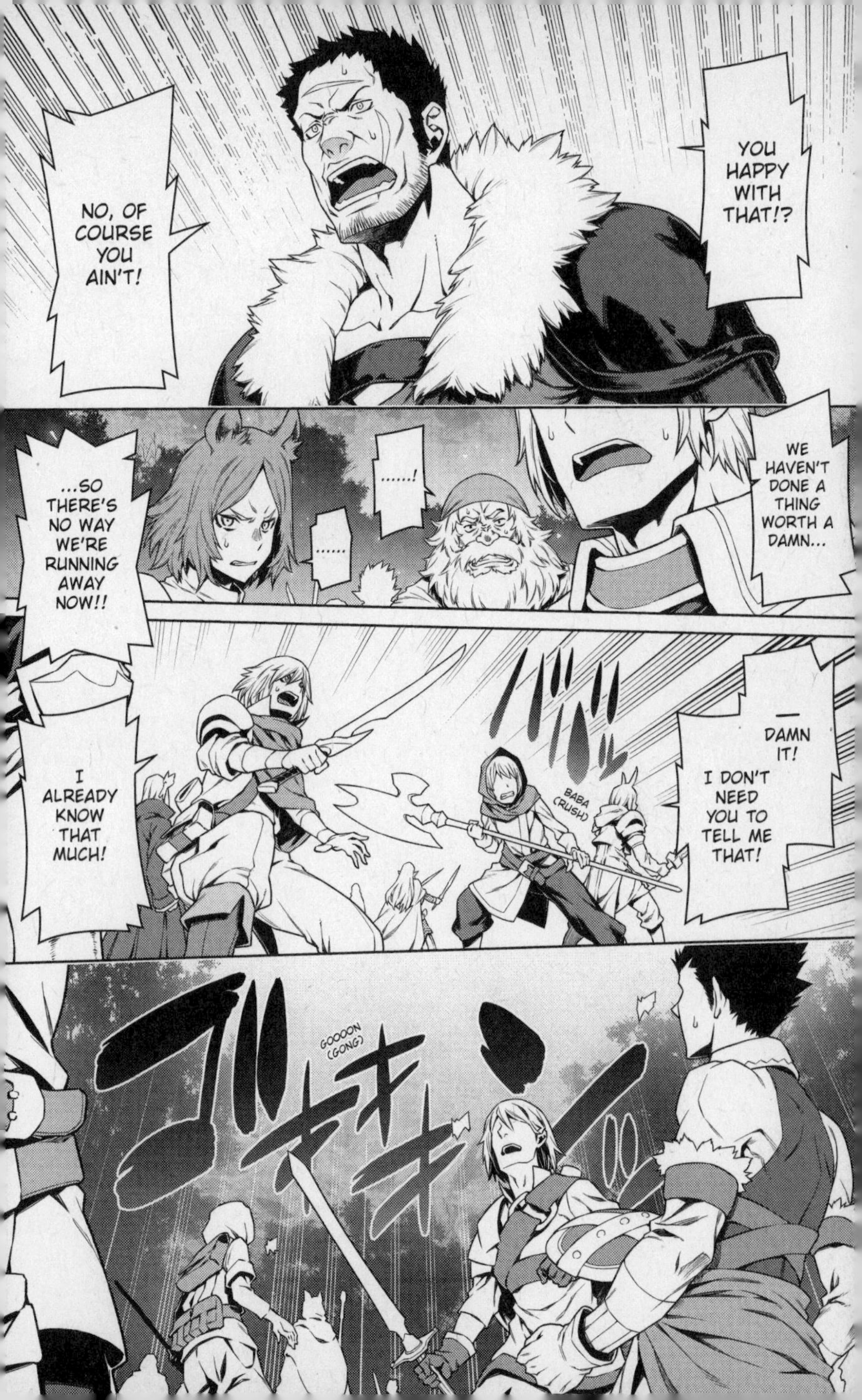
YOU HAPPY WITH THAT!?
NO, OF COURSE YOU AIN'T!
WE HAVEN'T DONE A THING WORTH A DAMN...
......!
......
...SO THERE'S NO WAY WE'RE RUNNING AWAY NOW!!
—DAMN IT!
I DON'T NEED YOU TO TELL ME THAT!
BABA (RUSH)
I ALREADY KNOW THAT MUCH!
GOOOON (GONG)

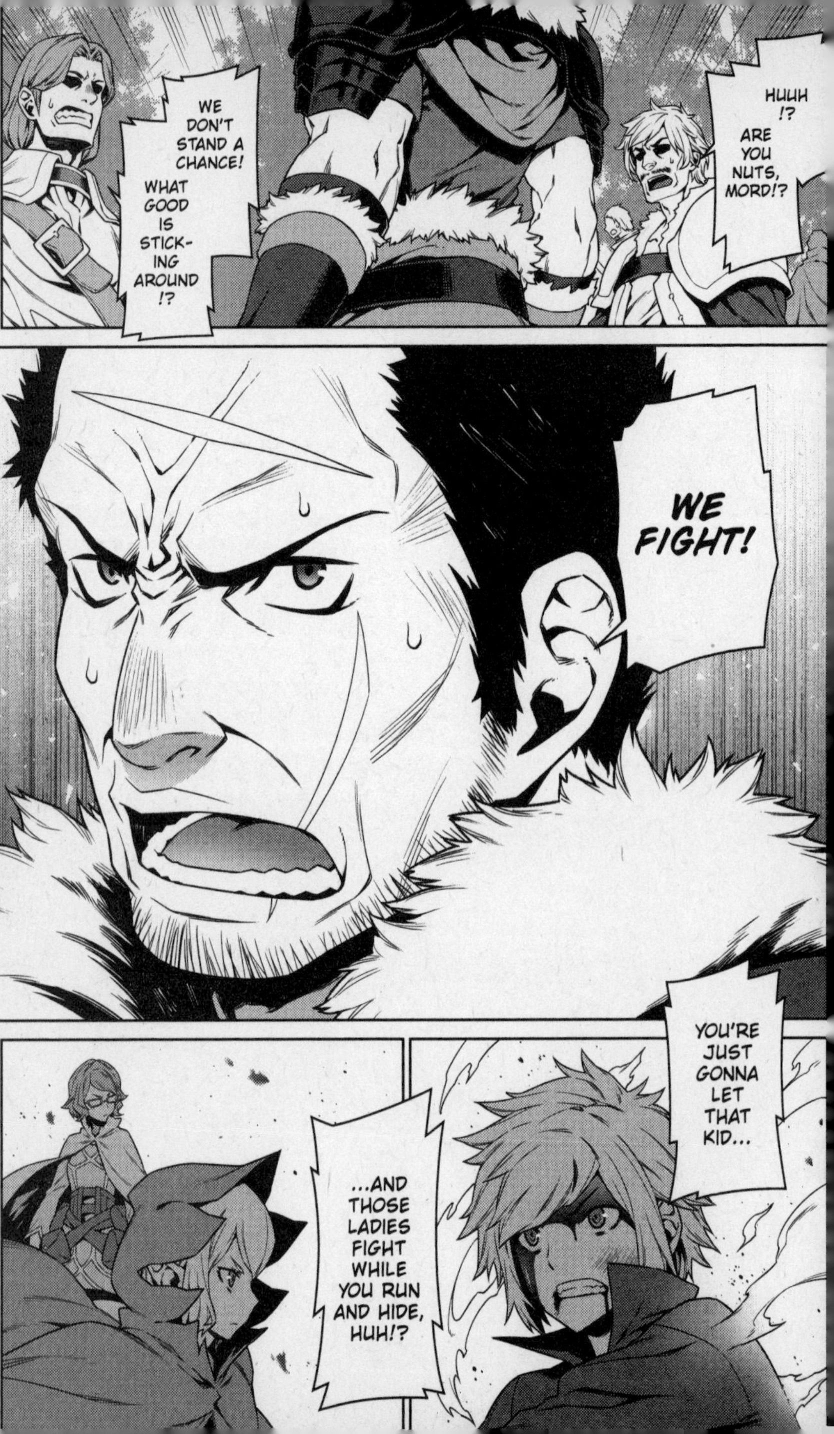
HUUH!? ARE YOU NUTS, MORD!?
WE DON'T STAND A CHANCE! WHAT GOOD IS STICK-ING AROUND!?
WE FIGHT!
YOU'RE JUST GONNA LET THAT KID...
...AND THOSE LADIES FIGHT WHILE YOU RUN AND HIDE, HUH!?

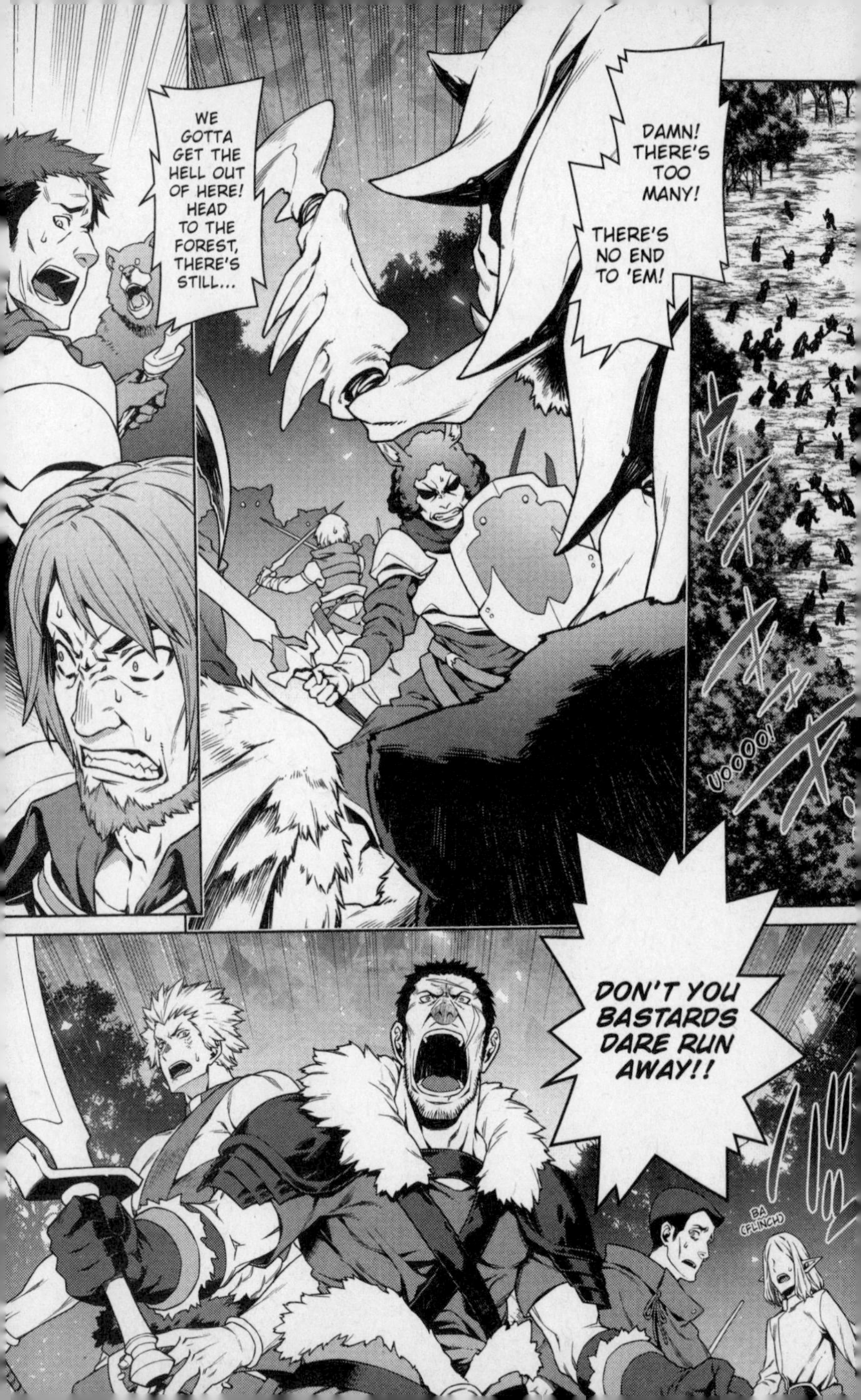
UOOOO!
DAMN! THERE'S TOO MANY!
THERE'S NO END TO 'EM!
WE GOTTA GET THE HELL OUT OF HERE! HEAD TO THE FOREST, THERE'S STILL...
DON'T YOU BASTARDS DARE RUN AWAY!!
BA (FLINCH)

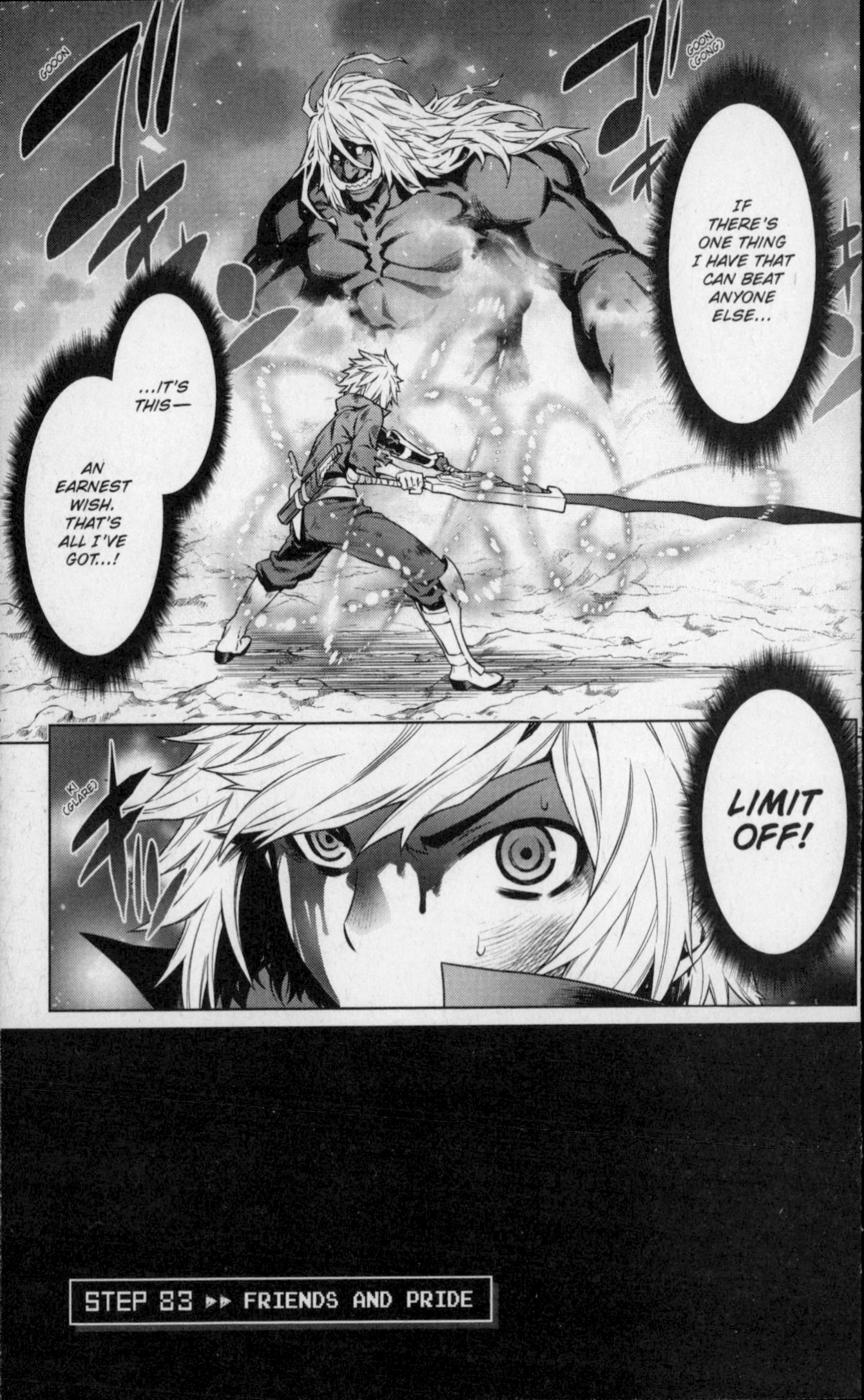
GOON (GONG)
IF THERE'S ONE THING I HAVE THAT CAN BEAT ANYONE ELSE...
GOOON
...IT'S THIS—
AN EARNEST WISH. THAT'S ALL I'VE GOT...!
LIMIT OFF!
KI (GLARE)

STEP 83 ▸▸ FRIENDS AND PRIDE

Is it WRONG to TRY to PiCK UP GIRLS iN A DUNGEON?

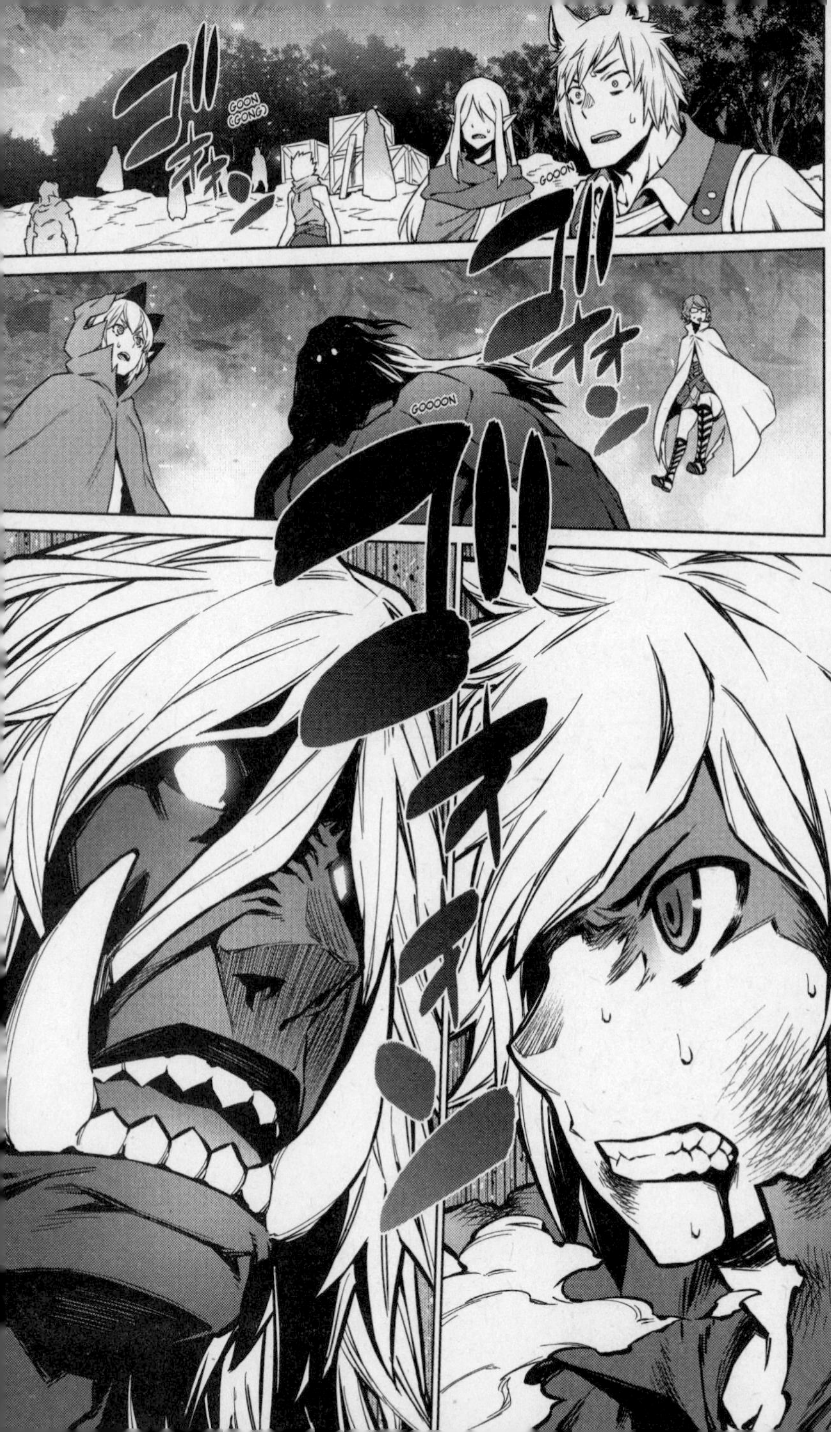
GOOON
GOON (GONG)
GOOOON

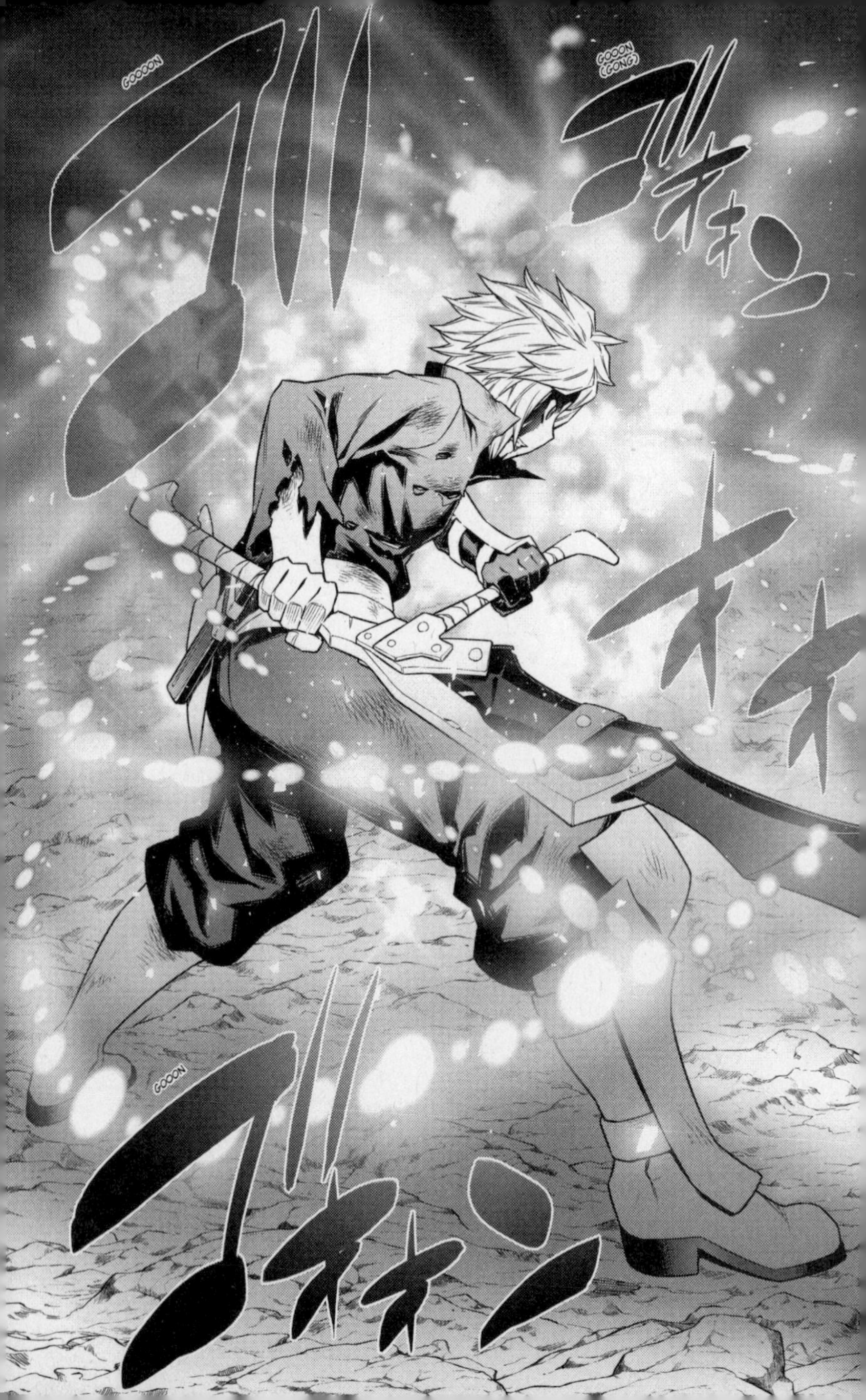
GOOON (GONG)
GOOOON
GOOON

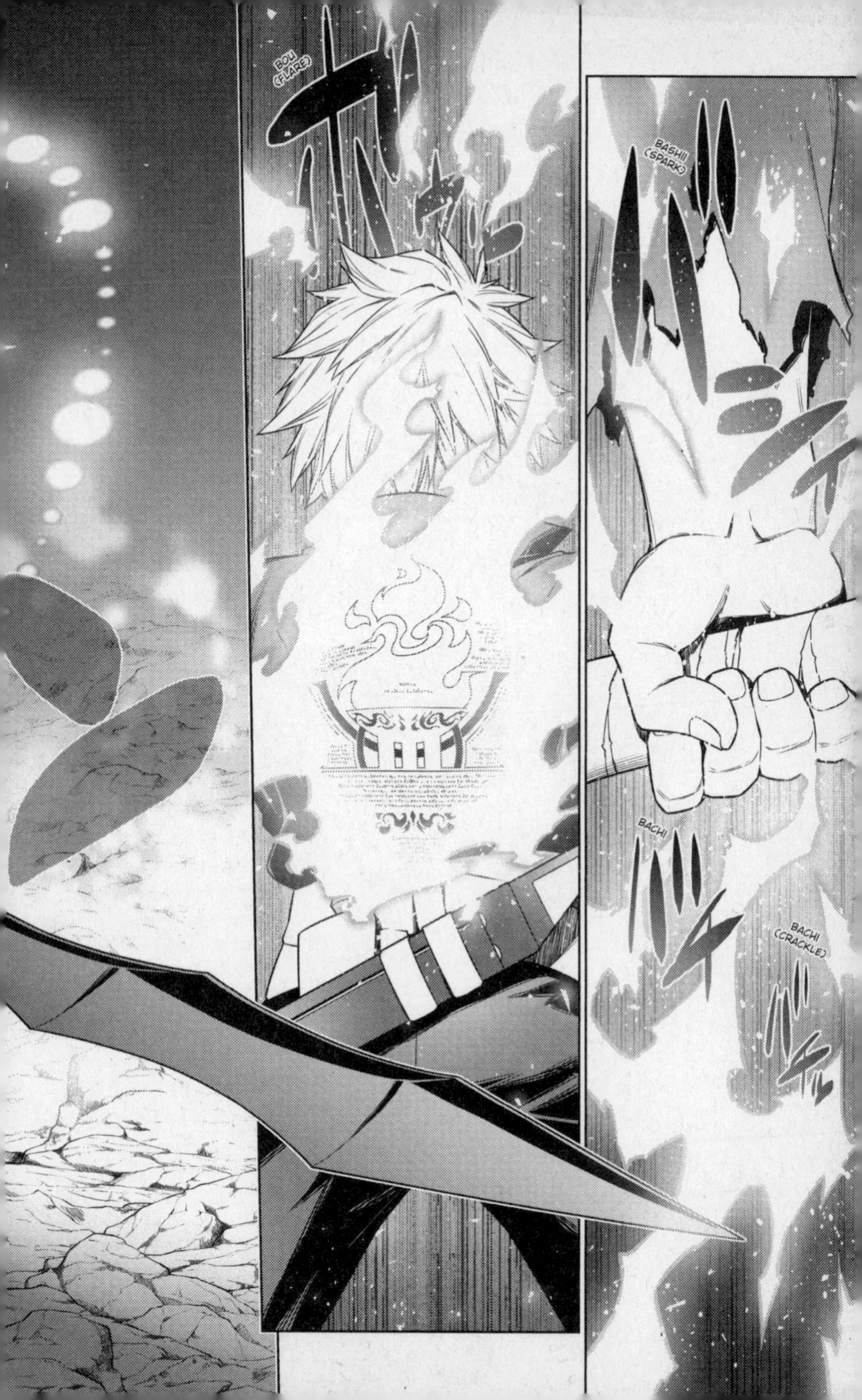
BASHII (SPARK)
BACHI
BACHI (CRACKLE)
BOU (FLARE)

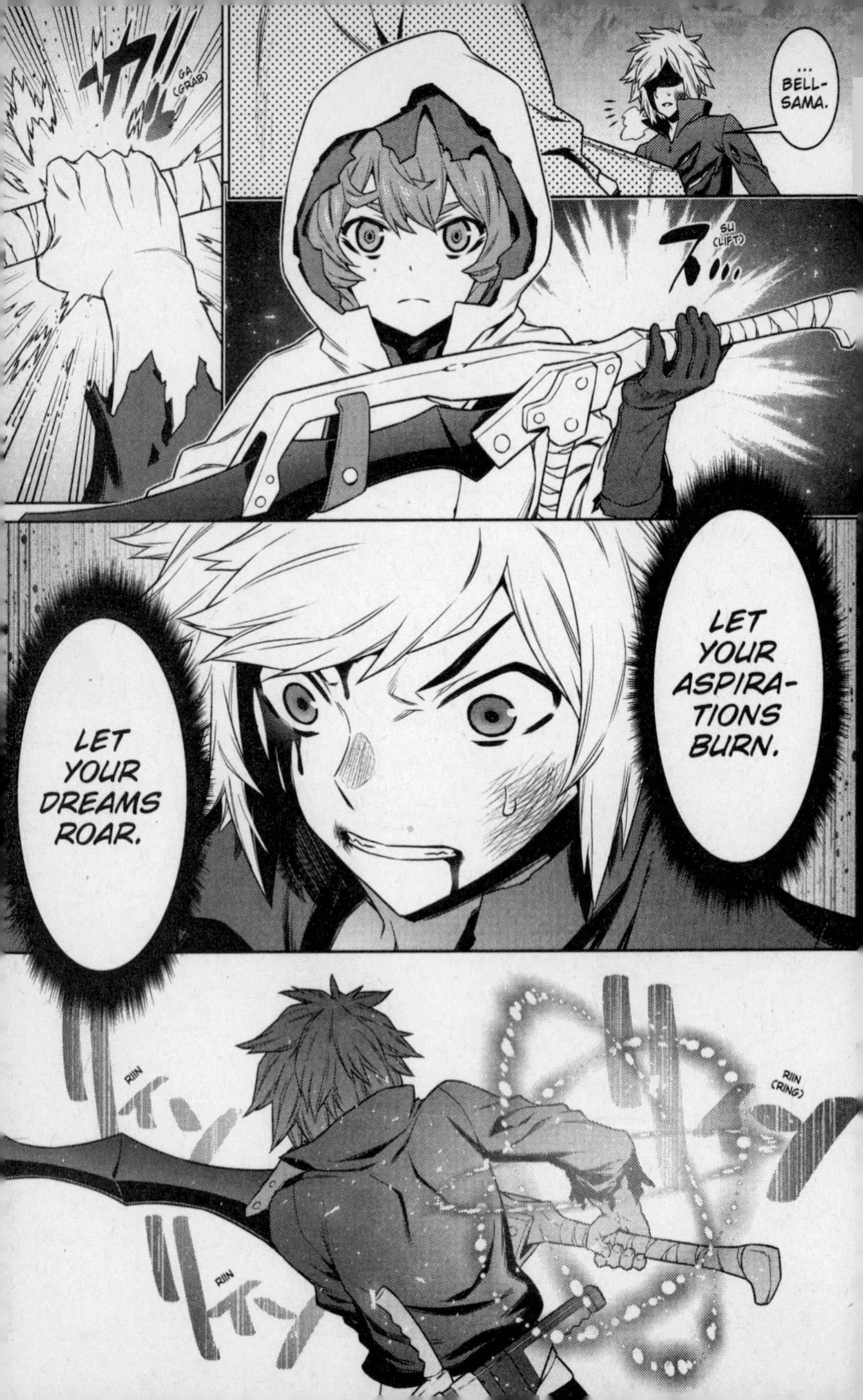

... BELL-SAMA.
SU (LIFT)
GA (GRAB)
LET YOUR ASPIRATIONS BURN.
LET YOUR DREAMS ROAR.
RIIN (RING)
RIIN
RIIN

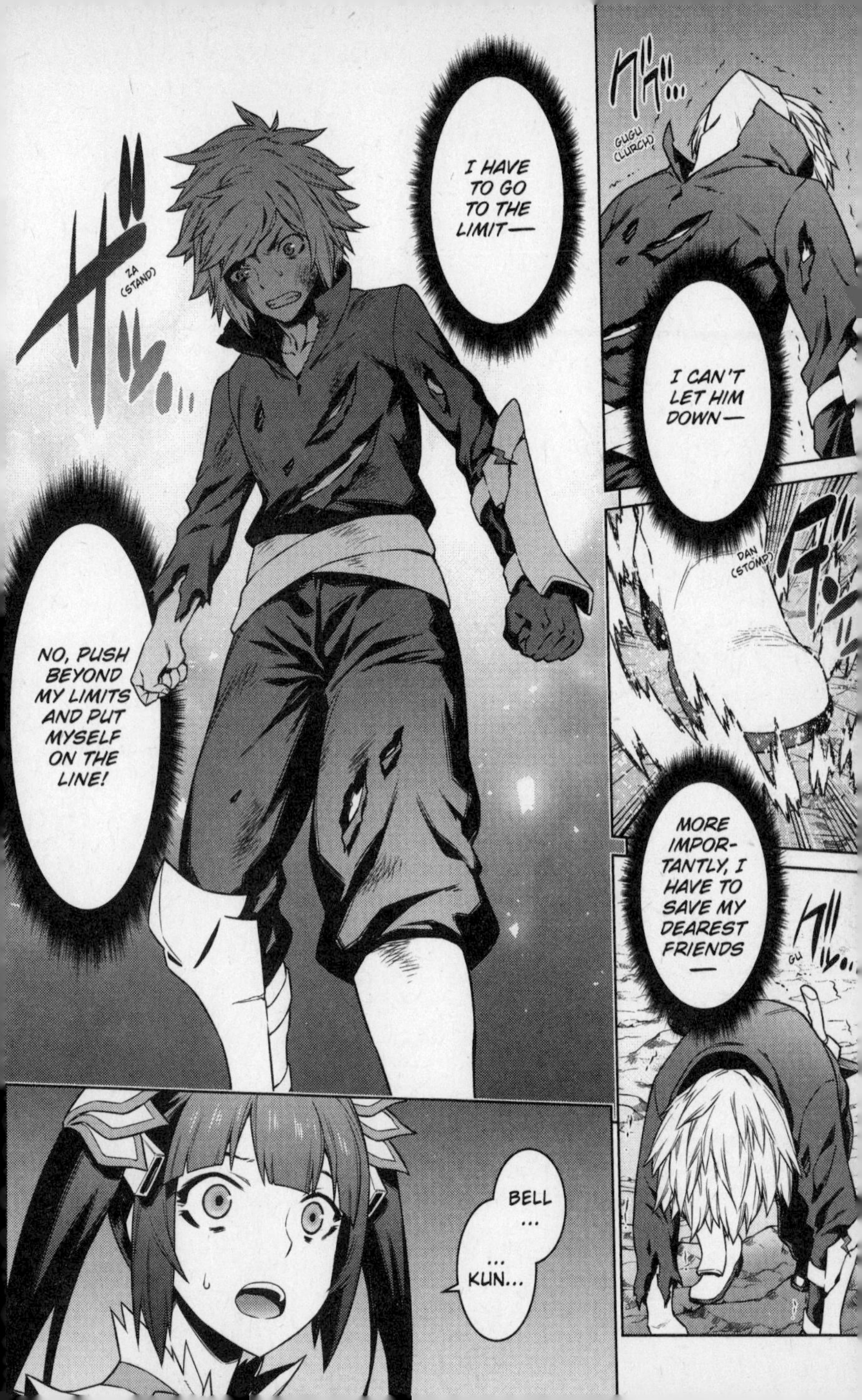
GUGU (LURCH)
I CAN'T LET HIM DOWN—
DAN (STOMP)
MORE IMPORTANTLY, I HAVE TO SAVE MY DEAREST FRIENDS—
GU
I HAVE TO GO TO THE LIMIT—
ZA (STAND)
NO, PUSH BEYOND MY LIMITS AND PUT MYSELF ON THE LINE!
BELL...
...KUN...

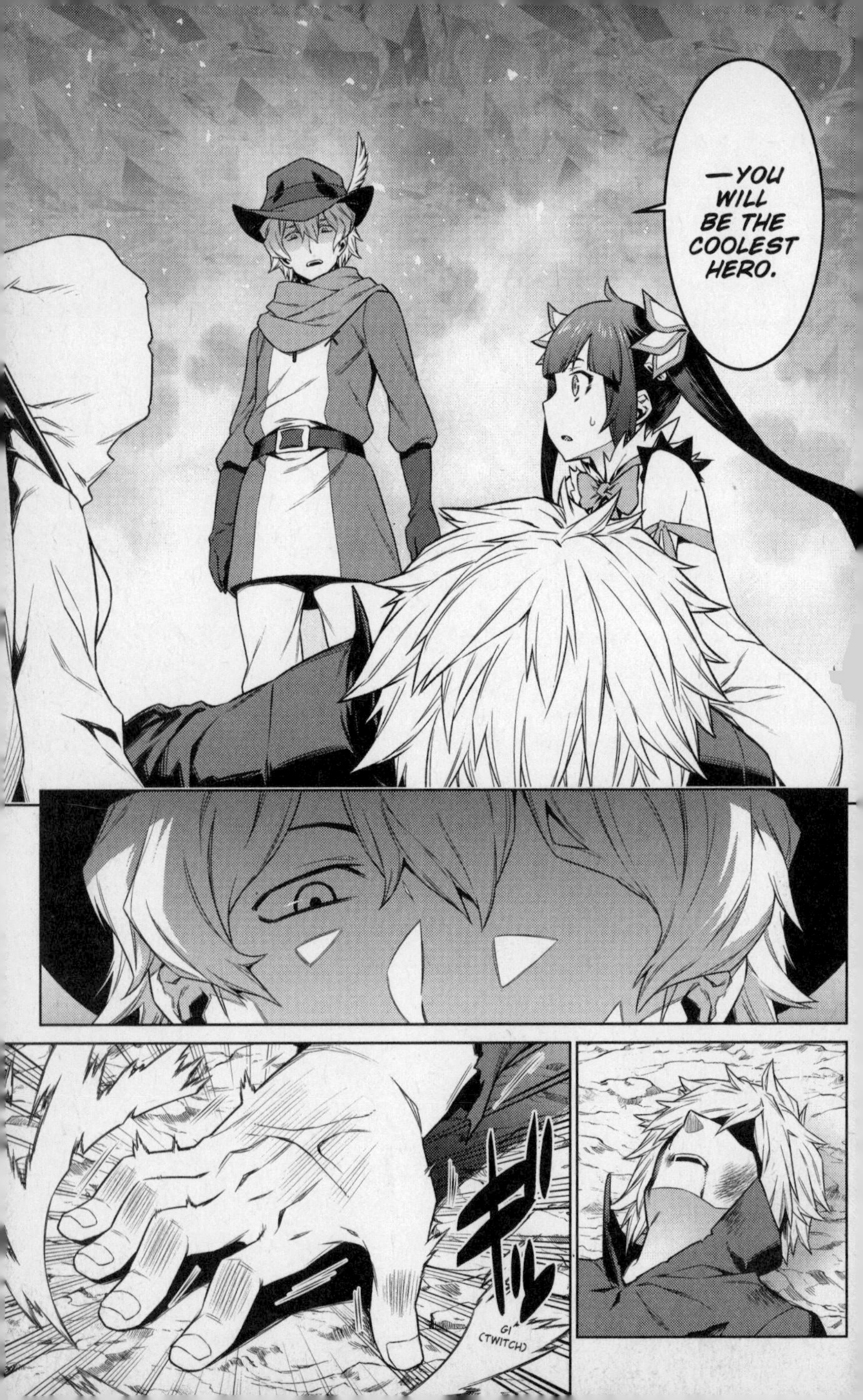
—YOU WILL BE THE COOLEST HERO.
GI (TWITCH)

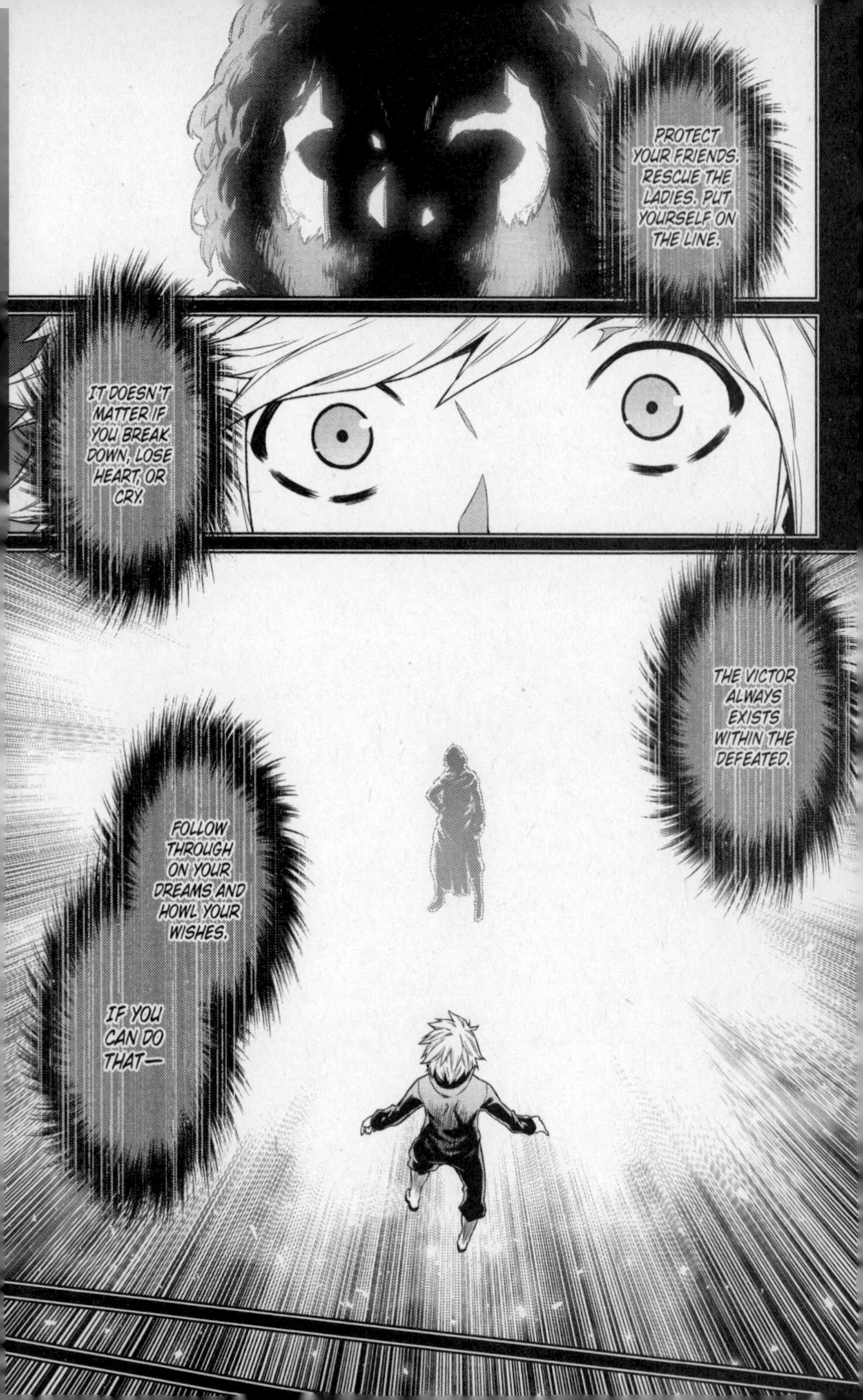
PROTECT YOUR FRIENDS. RESCUE THE LADIES. PUT YOURSELF ON THE LINE.
IT DOESN'T MATTER IF YOU BREAK DOWN, LOSE HEART, OR CRY.
THE VICTOR ALWAYS EXISTS WITHIN THE DEFEATED.
FOLLOW THROUGH ON YOUR DREAMS AND HOWL YOUR WISHES.
IF YOU CAN DO THAT—

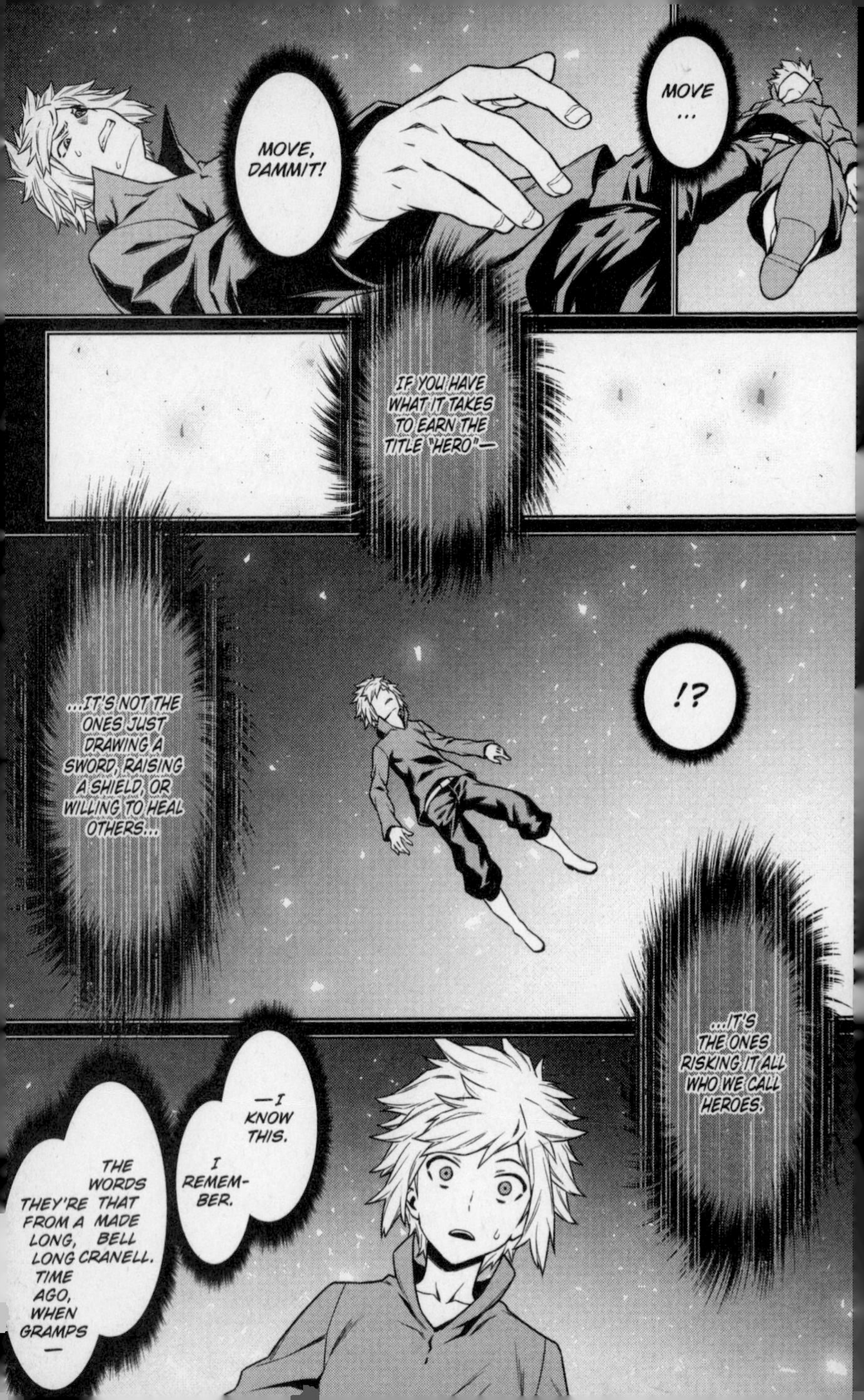
MOVE ...
MOVE, DAMMIT!
IF YOU HAVE WHAT IT TAKES TO EARN THE TITLE "HERO"—
!?
...IT'S NOT THE ONES JUST DRAWING A SWORD, RAISING A SHIELD, OR WILLING TO HEAL OTHERS...
...IT'S THE ONES RISKING IT ALL WHO WE CALL HEROES.
—I KNOW THIS.
I REMEMBER.
THE WORDS THAT MADE BELL CRANELL.
THEY'RE FROM A LONG, LONG TIME AGO, WHEN GRAMPS —

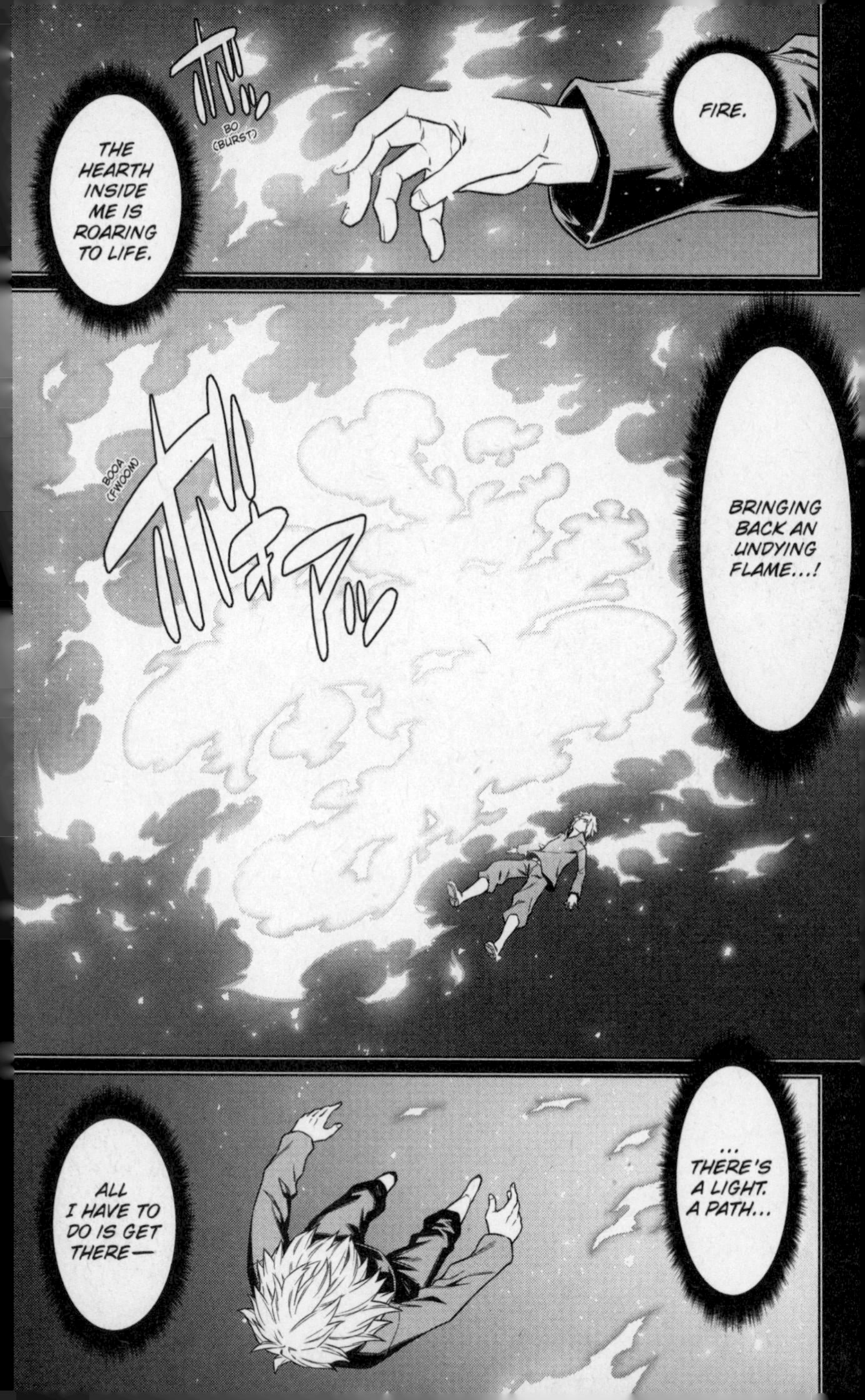
FIRE.
BO (BURST)
THE HEARTH INSIDE ME IS ROARING TO LIFE.
BRINGING BACK AN UNDYING FLAME...!
BOOA (FWOOM)
... THERE'S A LIGHT. A PATH...
ALL I HAVE TO DO IS GET THERE—

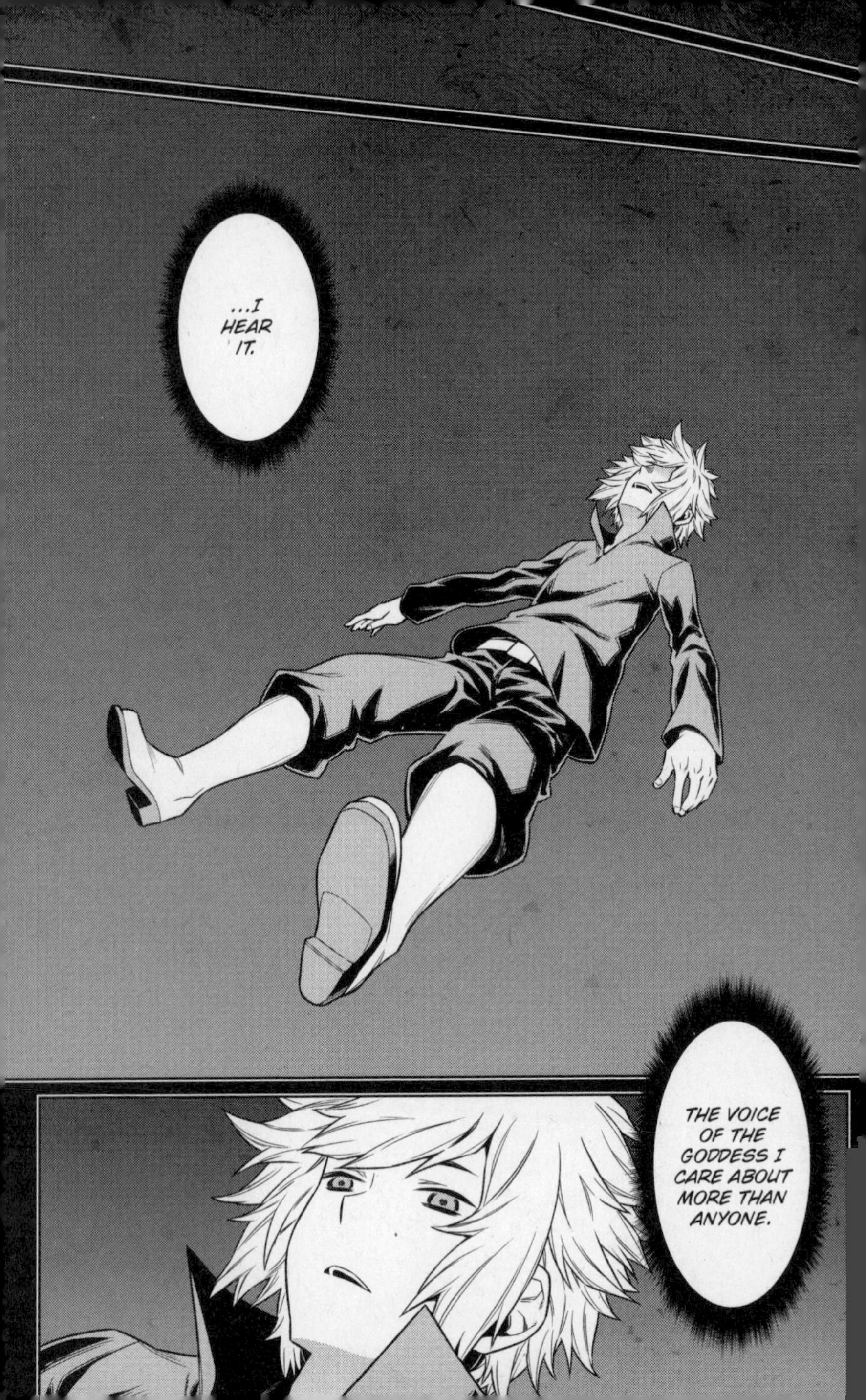
...I HEAR IT.
THE VOICE OF THE GODDESS I CARE ABOUT MORE THAN ANYONE.

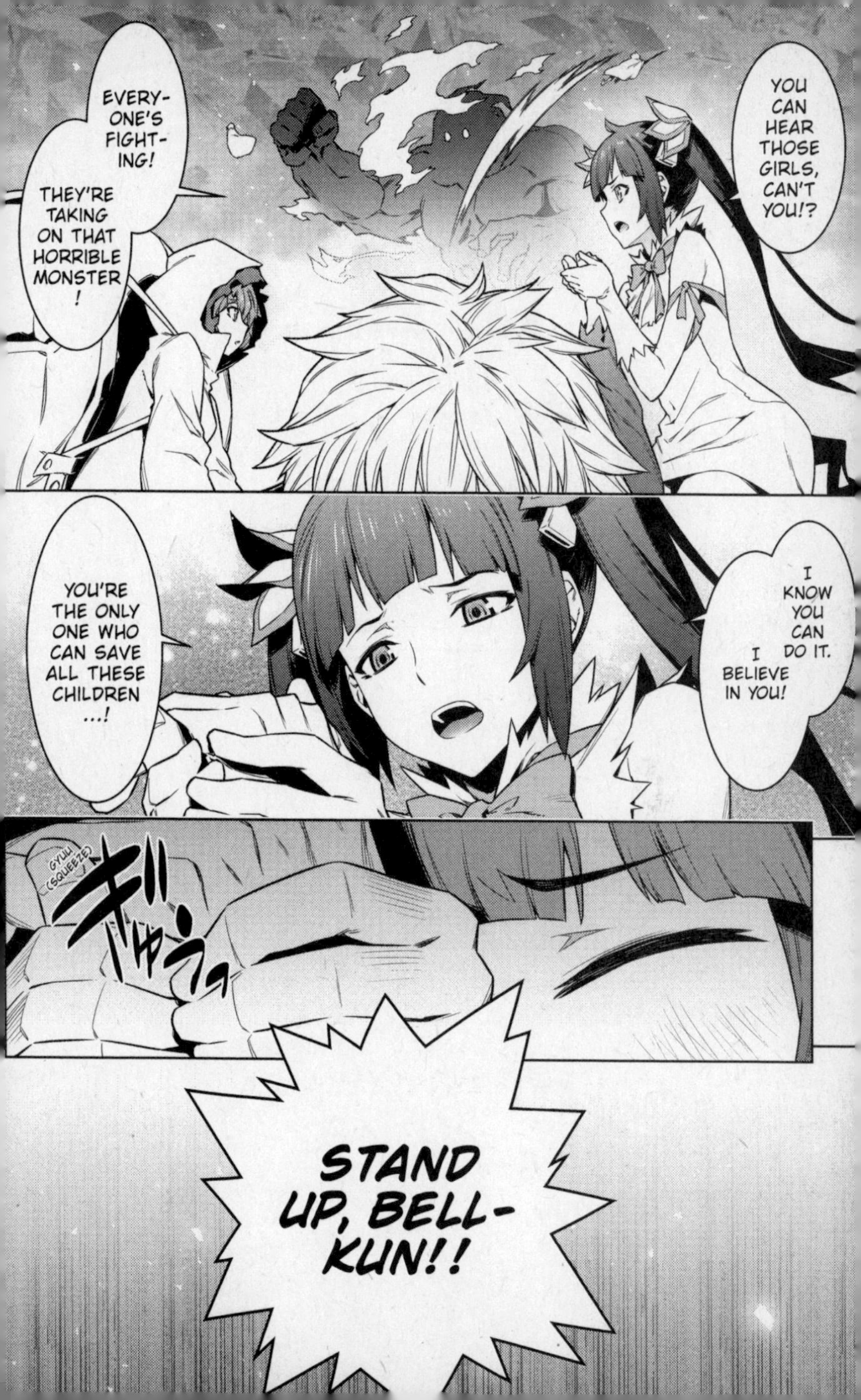
YOU CAN HEAR THOSE GIRLS, CAN'T YOU!?
EVERY-ONE'S FIGHT-ING!
THEY'RE TAKING ON THAT HORRIBLE MONSTER!
I KNOW YOU CAN DO IT. I BELIEVE IN YOU!
YOU'RE THE ONLY ONE WHO CAN SAVE ALL THESE CHILDREN...!
GYUU (SQUEEZE)
STAND UP, BELL-KUN!!

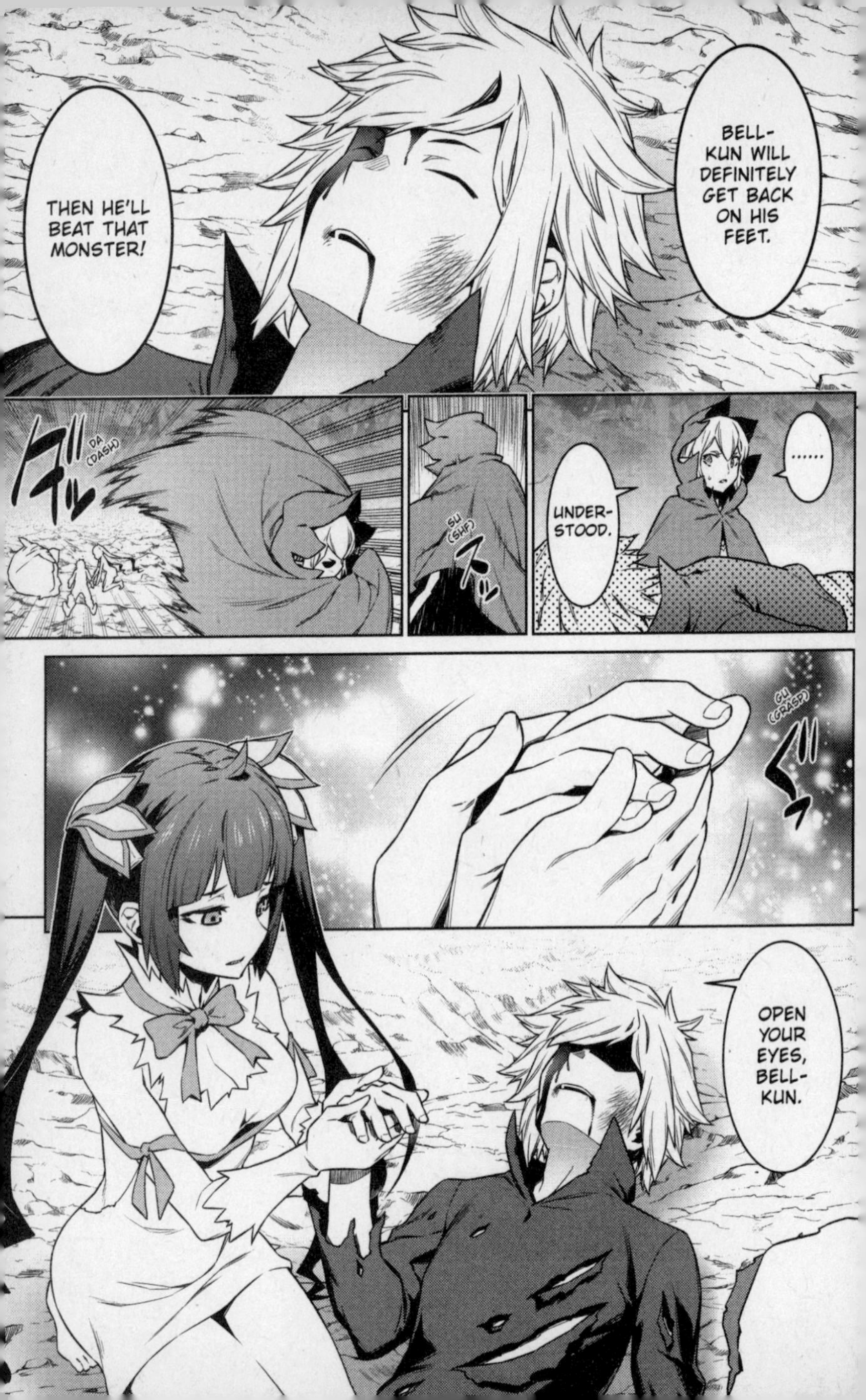
BELL-KUN WILL DEFINITELY GET BACK ON HIS FEET.
THEN HE'LL BEAT THAT MONSTER!
......
UNDERSTOOD.
SU (SHF)
DA (DASH)
GU (GRASP)
OPEN YOUR EYES, BELL-KUN.

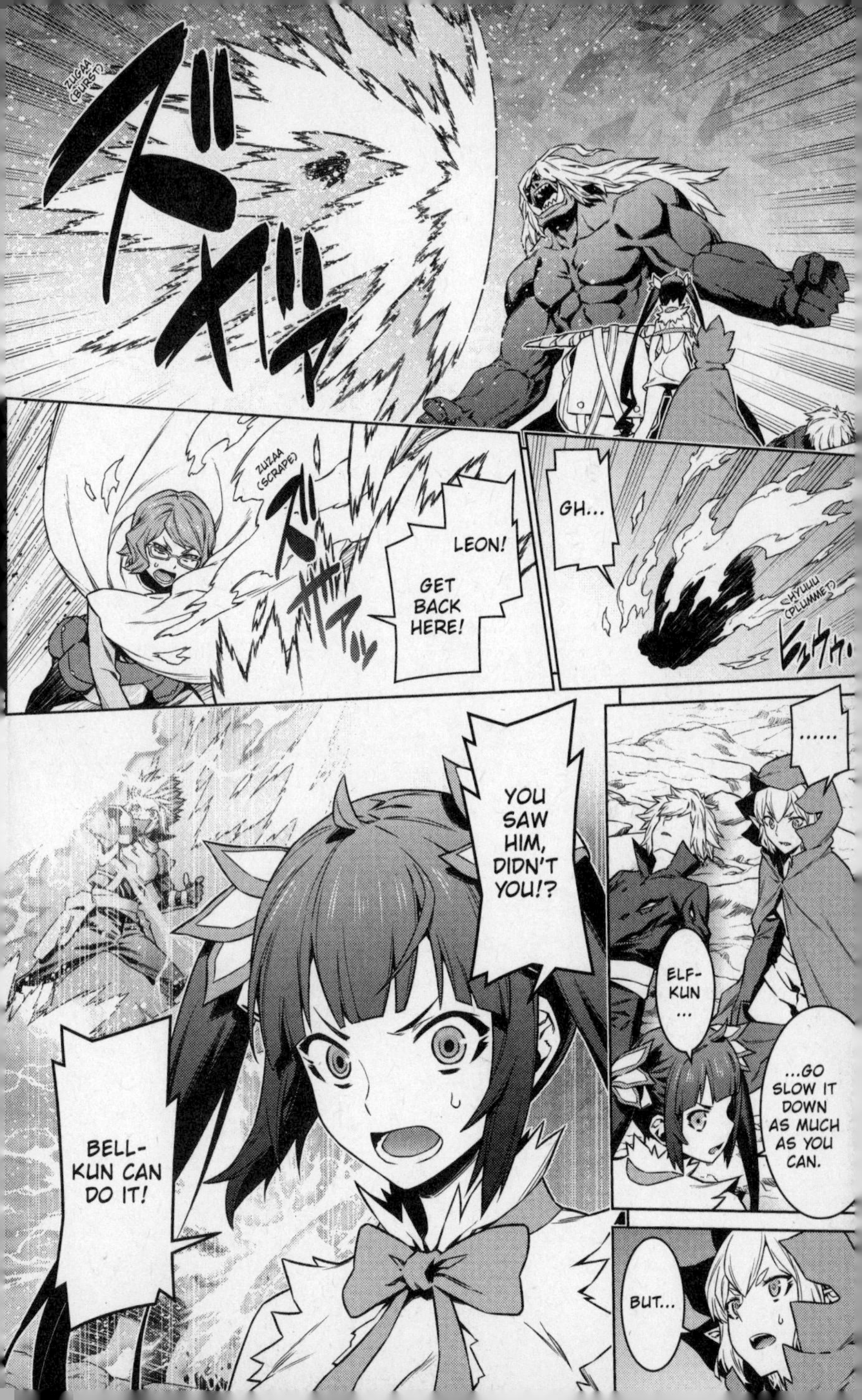
ZUGAA (BURST)
GH...
HYUUU (PLUMMET)
ZUZAA (SCRAPE)
LEON!
GET BACK HERE!
......
ELF-KUN...
...GO SLOW IT DOWN AS MUCH AS YOU CAN.
BUT...
YOU SAW HIM, DIDN'T YOU!?
BELL-KUN CAN DO IT!

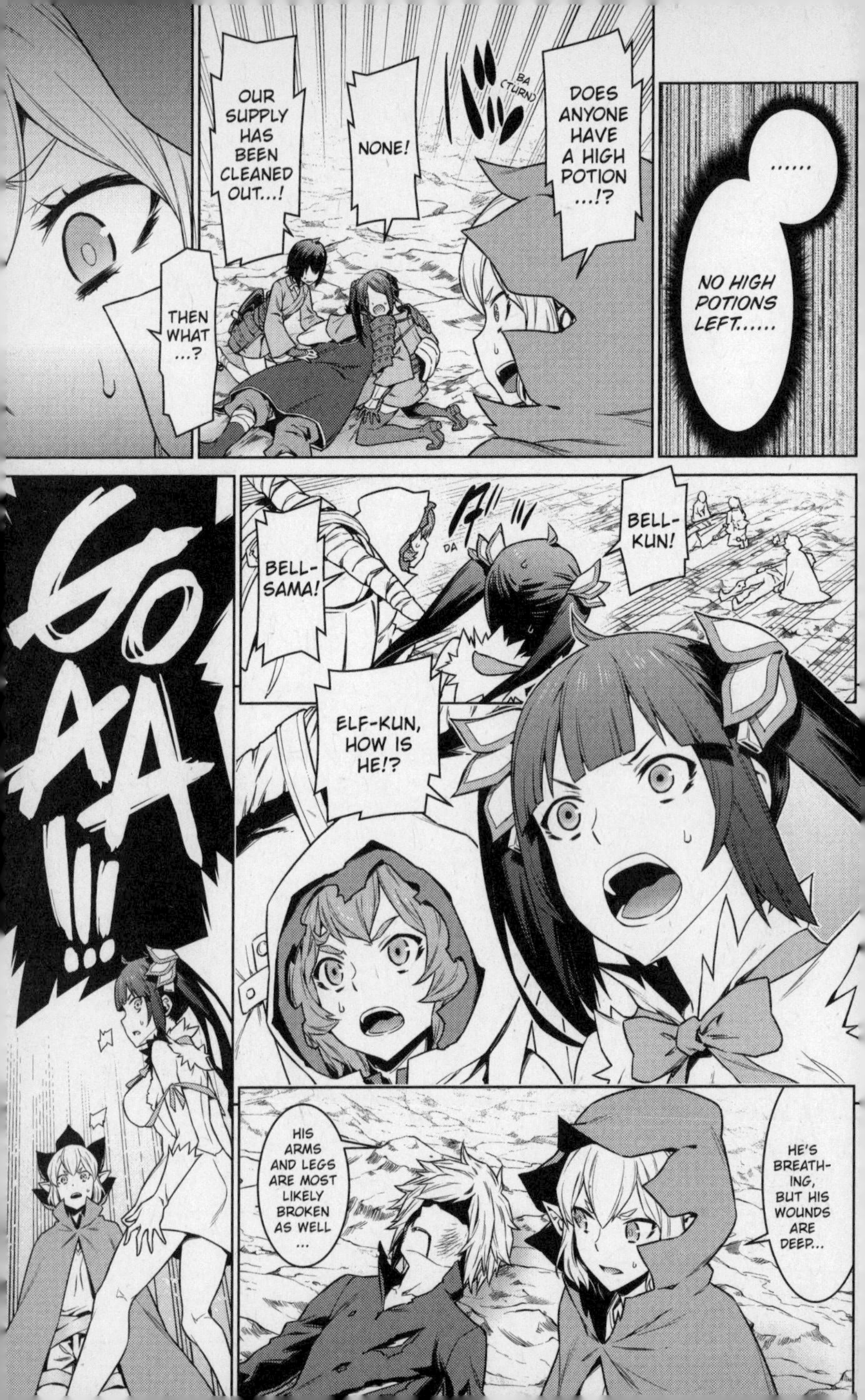
......
NO HIGH POTIONS LEFT......
DOES ANYONE HAVE A HIGH POTION ...!?
BA (TURN)
NONE!
OUR SUPPLY HAS BEEN CLEANED OUT...!
THEN WHAT ...?
BELL-KUN!
DA
BELL-SAMA!
ELF-KUN, HOW IS HE!?
HE'S BREATH-ING, BUT HIS WOUNDS ARE DEEP...
HIS ARMS AND LEGS ARE MOST LIKELY BROKEN AS WELL ...
GOAA!!!...

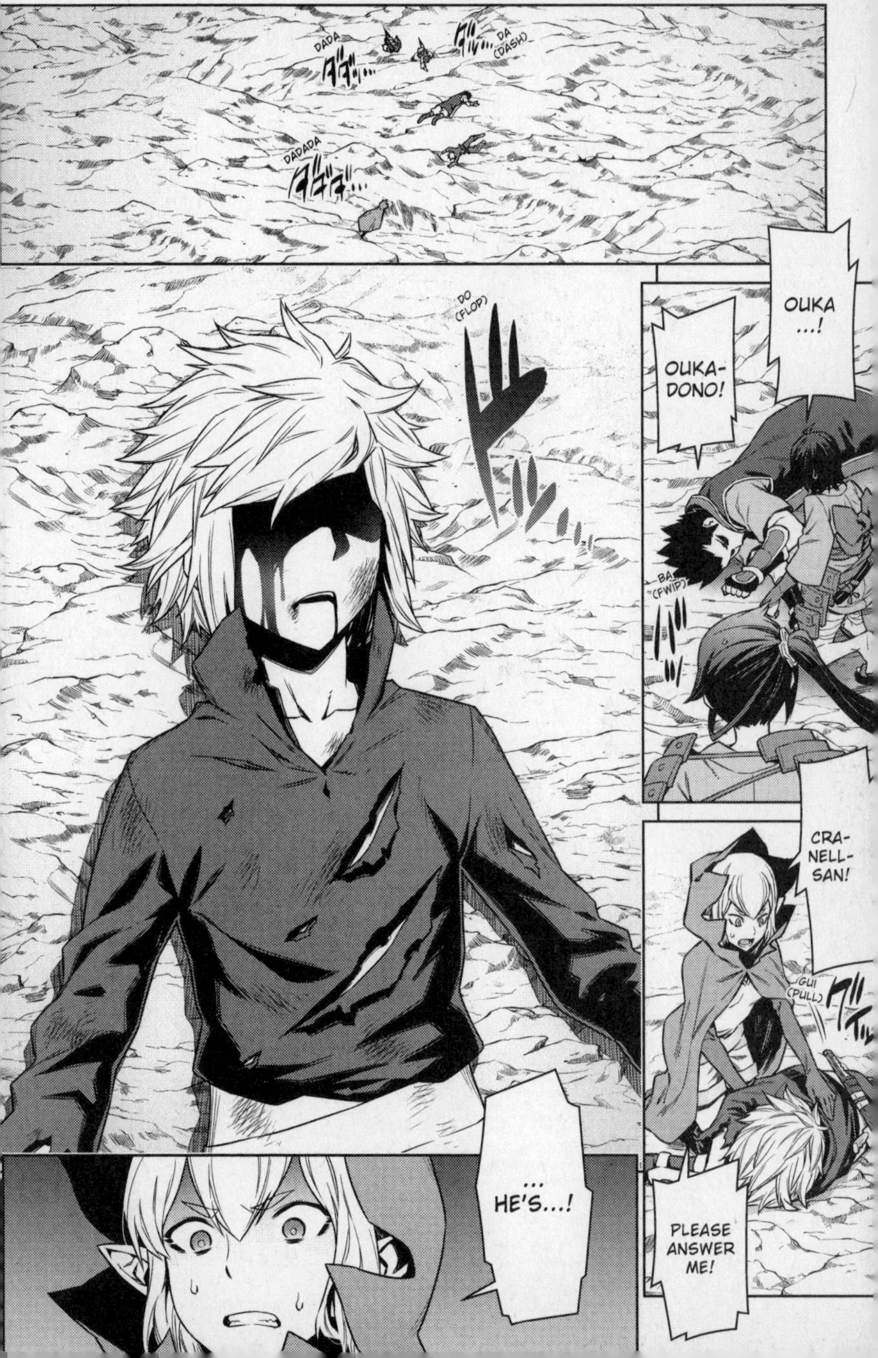
DA (DASH)
DADA
DADADA
OUKA...!
OUKA-DONO!
BA (FWIP)
CRA-NELL-SAN!
GUI (PULL)
PLEASE ANSWER ME!
DO (FLOP)
...HE'S...!

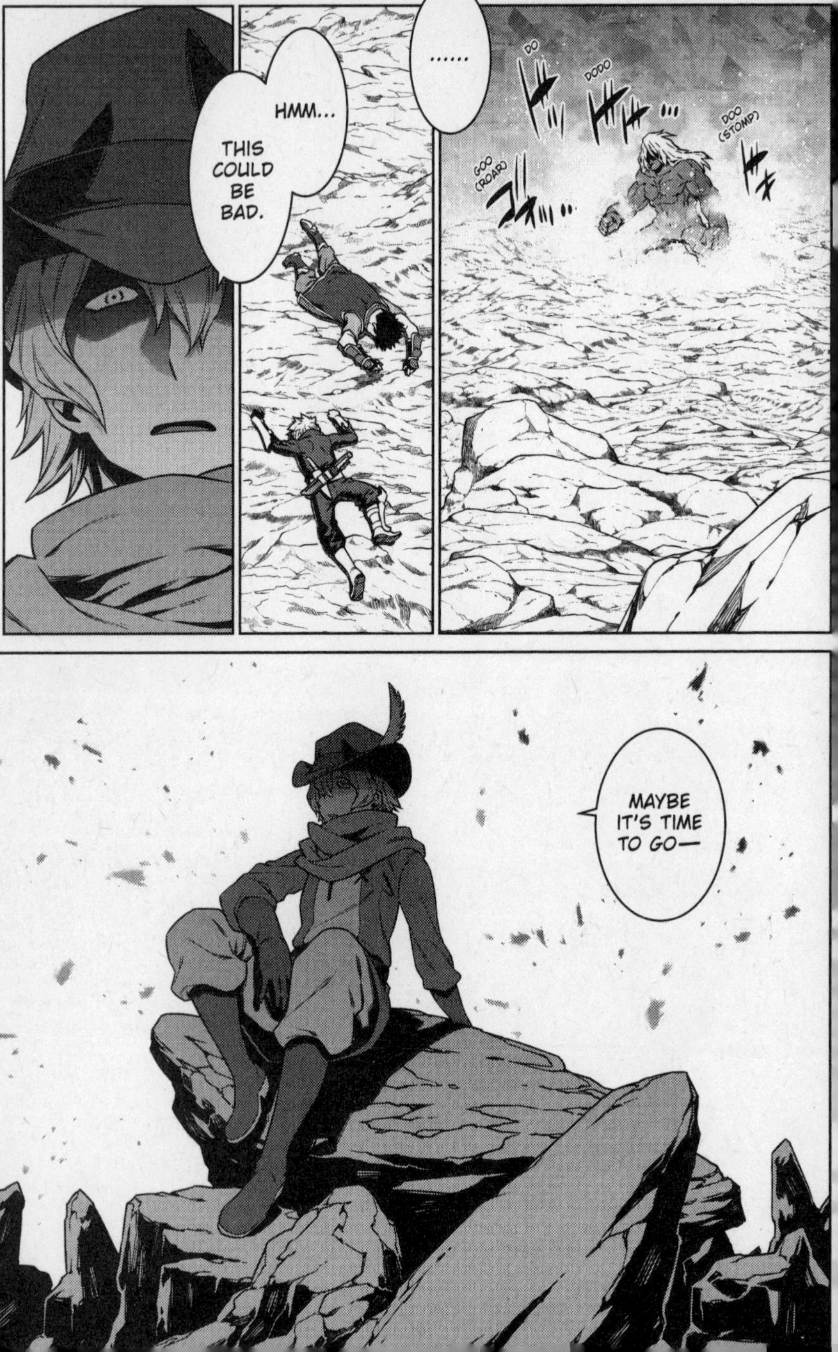
DOO (STOMP)
DODO
DO
GOO (ROAR)
......
HMM...
THIS COULD BE BAD.
MAYBE IT'S TIME TO GO—

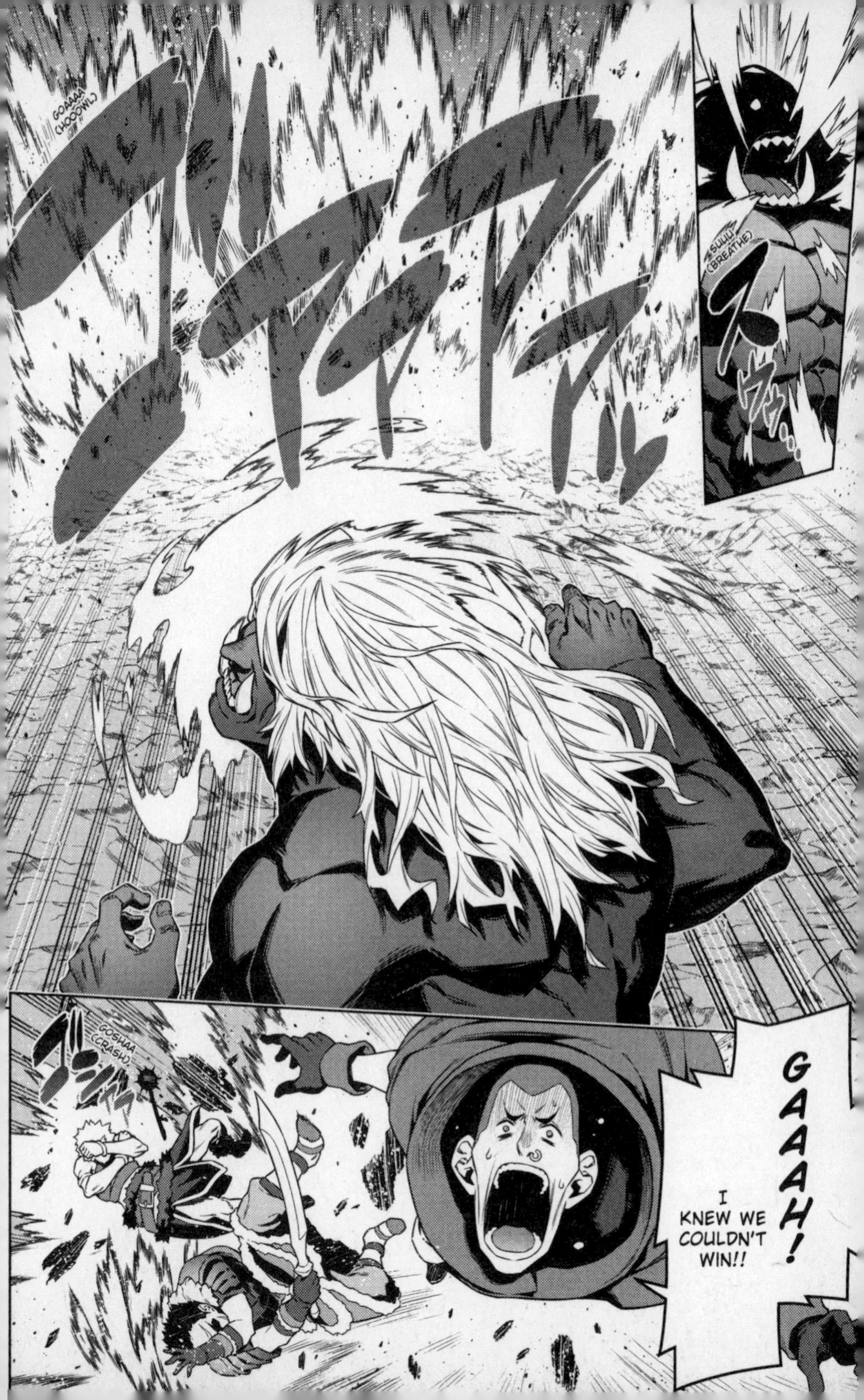
SUUU (BREATHE)
GOAAAA (HOOOWL)
GAAAAH!
I KNEW WE COULDN'T WIN!!
GOSHAA (CRASH)

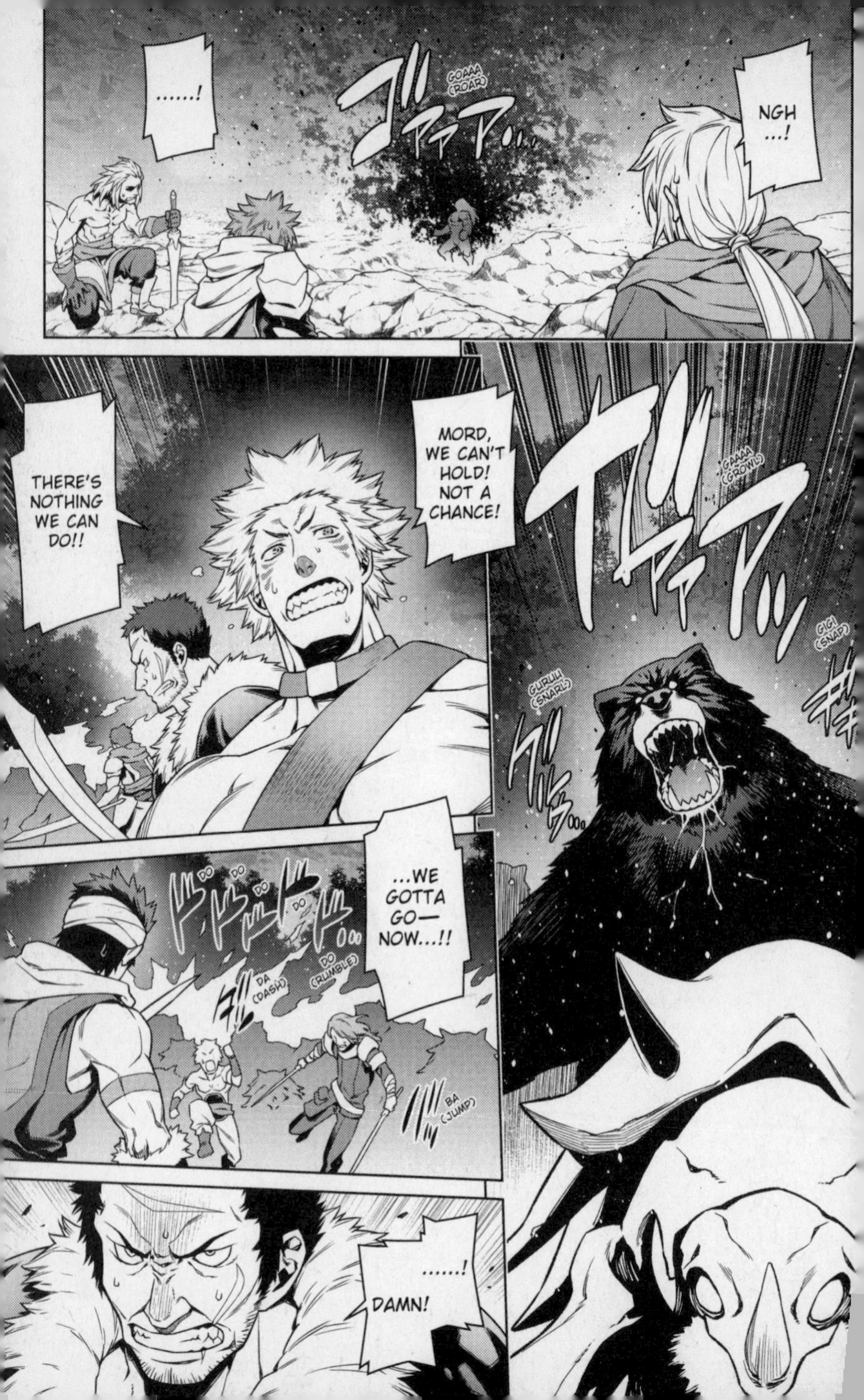
NGH ...!
GOAAA (ROAR)
......!
GAAAA (GROWL)
GIGI (SNAP)
GURUU (SNARL)
MORD, WE CAN'T HOLD! NOT A CHANCE!
THERE'S NOTHING WE CAN DO!!
...WE GOTTA GO— NOW...!!
DO DO DO DO
DO (RUMBLE)
DA (DASH)
BA (JUMP)
......!
DAMN!

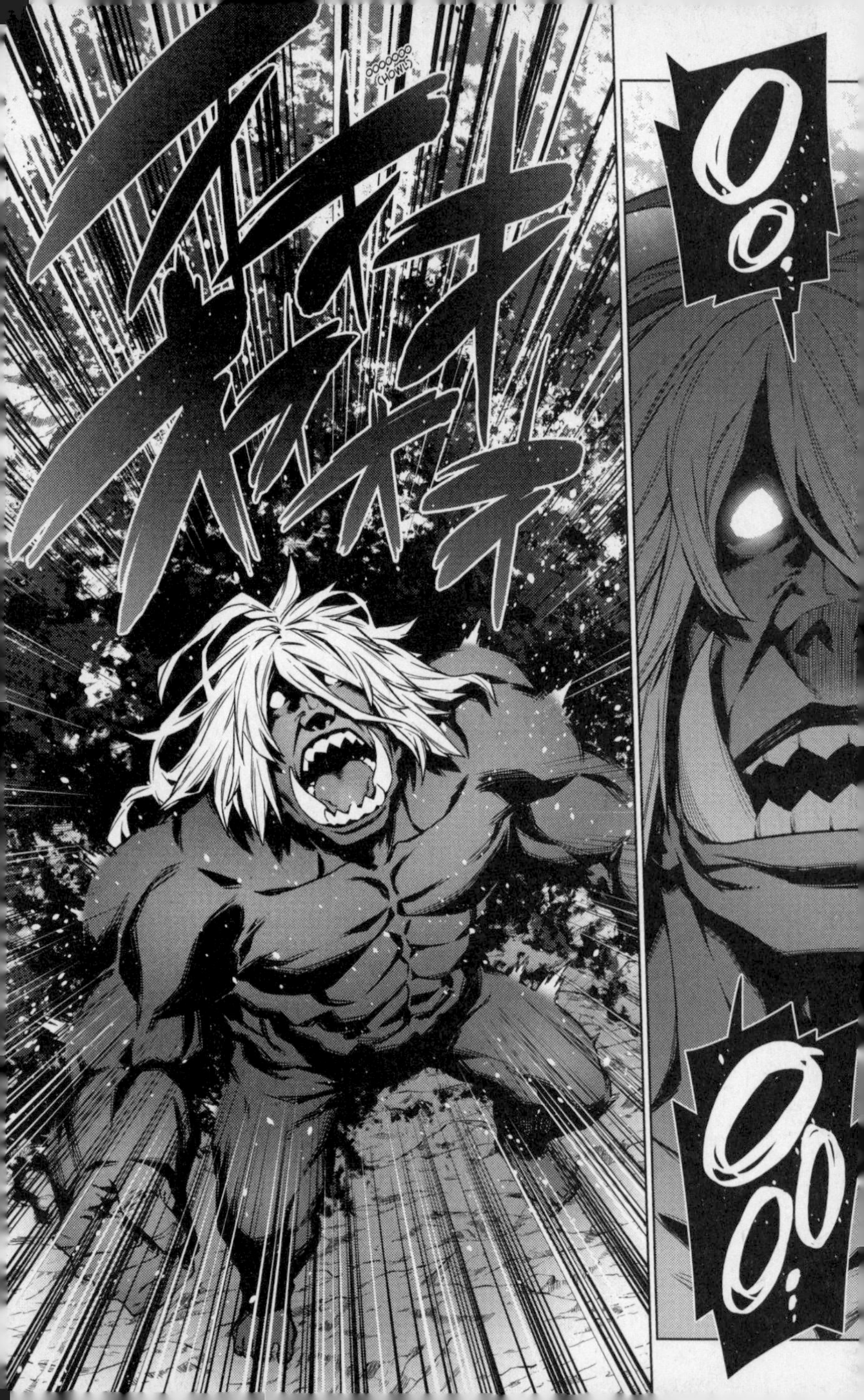
O...
OO...
(HOWL) OOOOOOO~

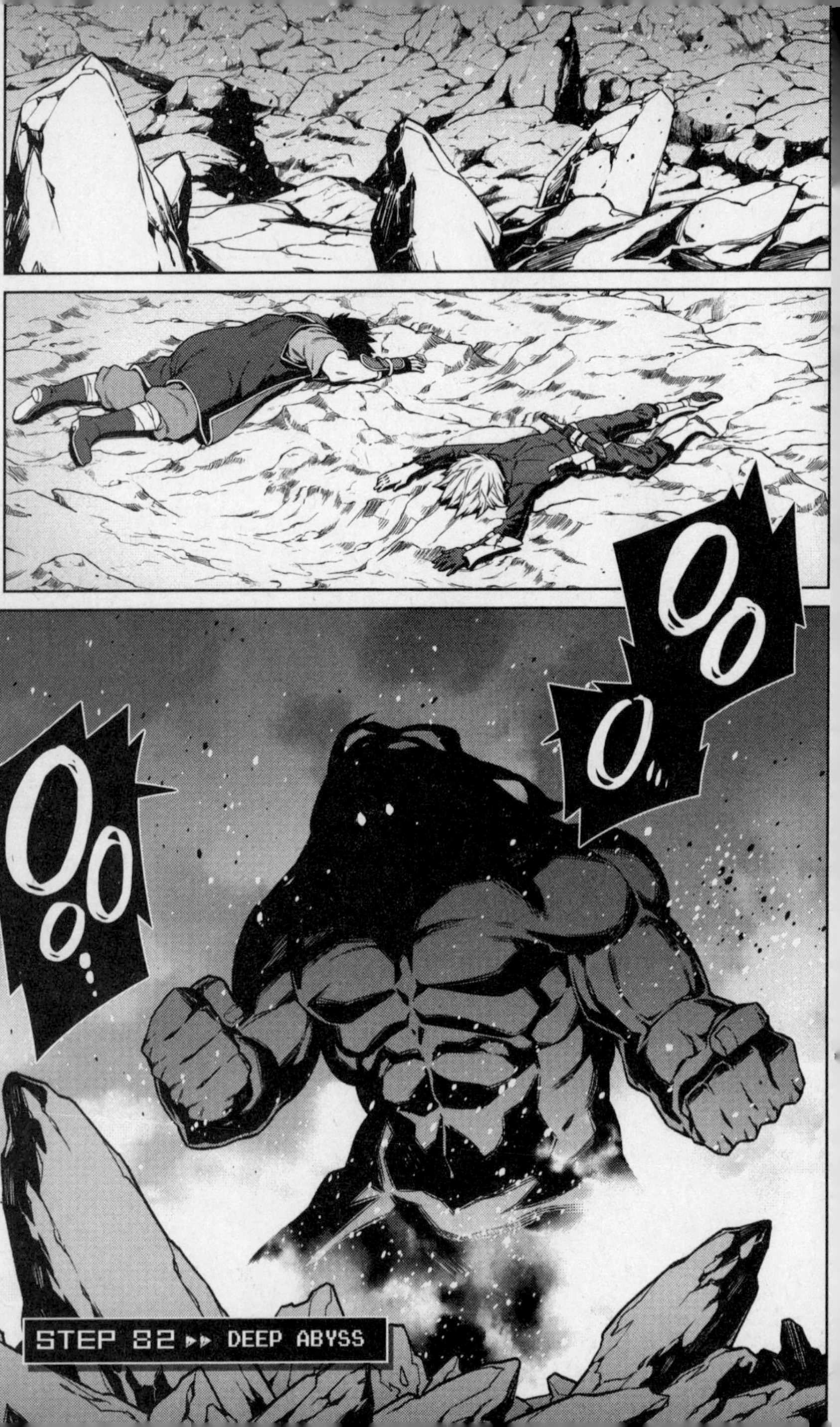
OOO...
OOO..
STEP 82 ▸▸ DEEP ABYSS

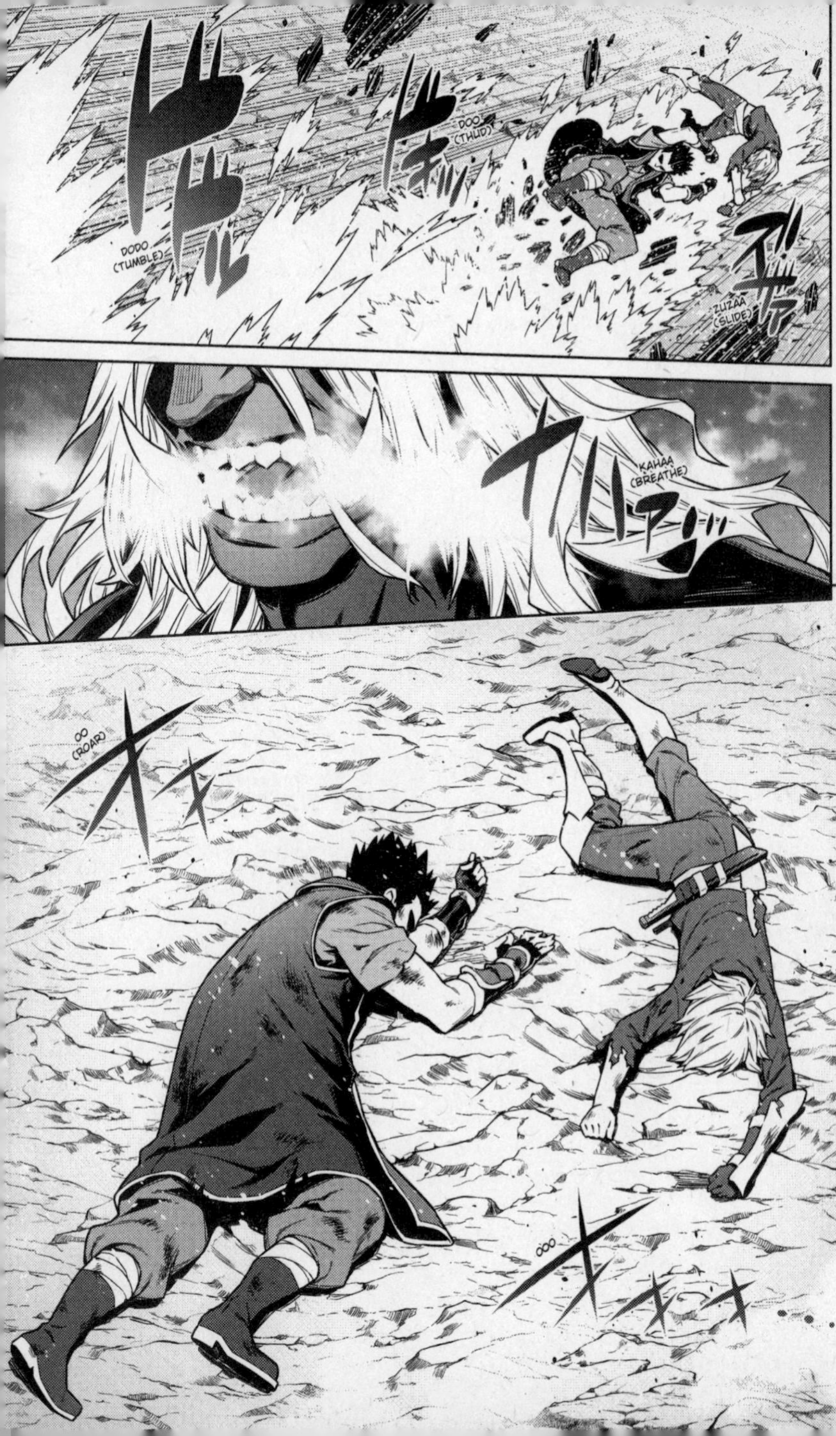
DOO (THUD)
DODO (TUMBLE)
ZUZAA (SLIDE)
KAHAA (BREATHE)
OO (ROAR)
OOO

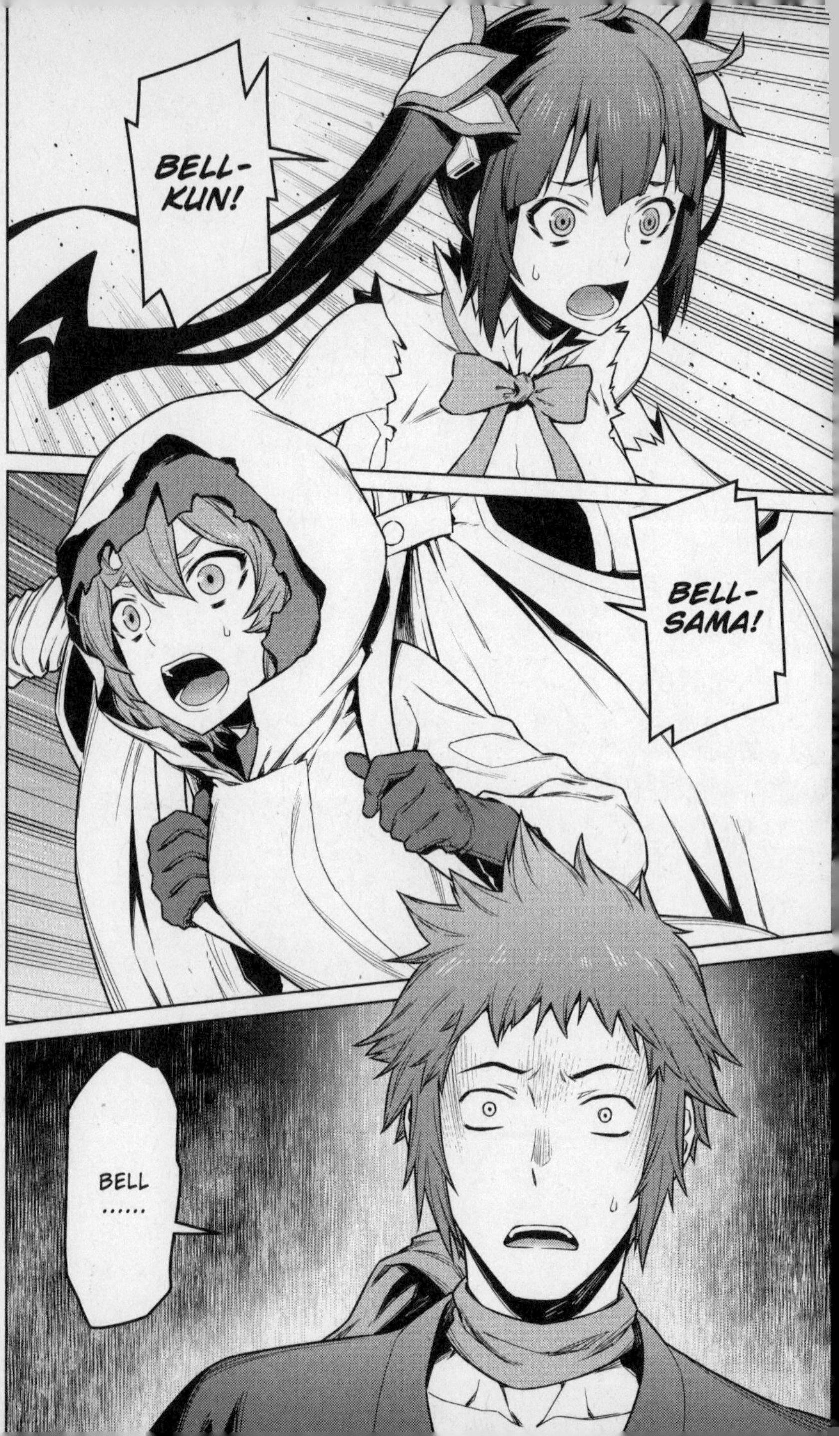
BELL-KUN!
BELL-SAMA!
BELL ......

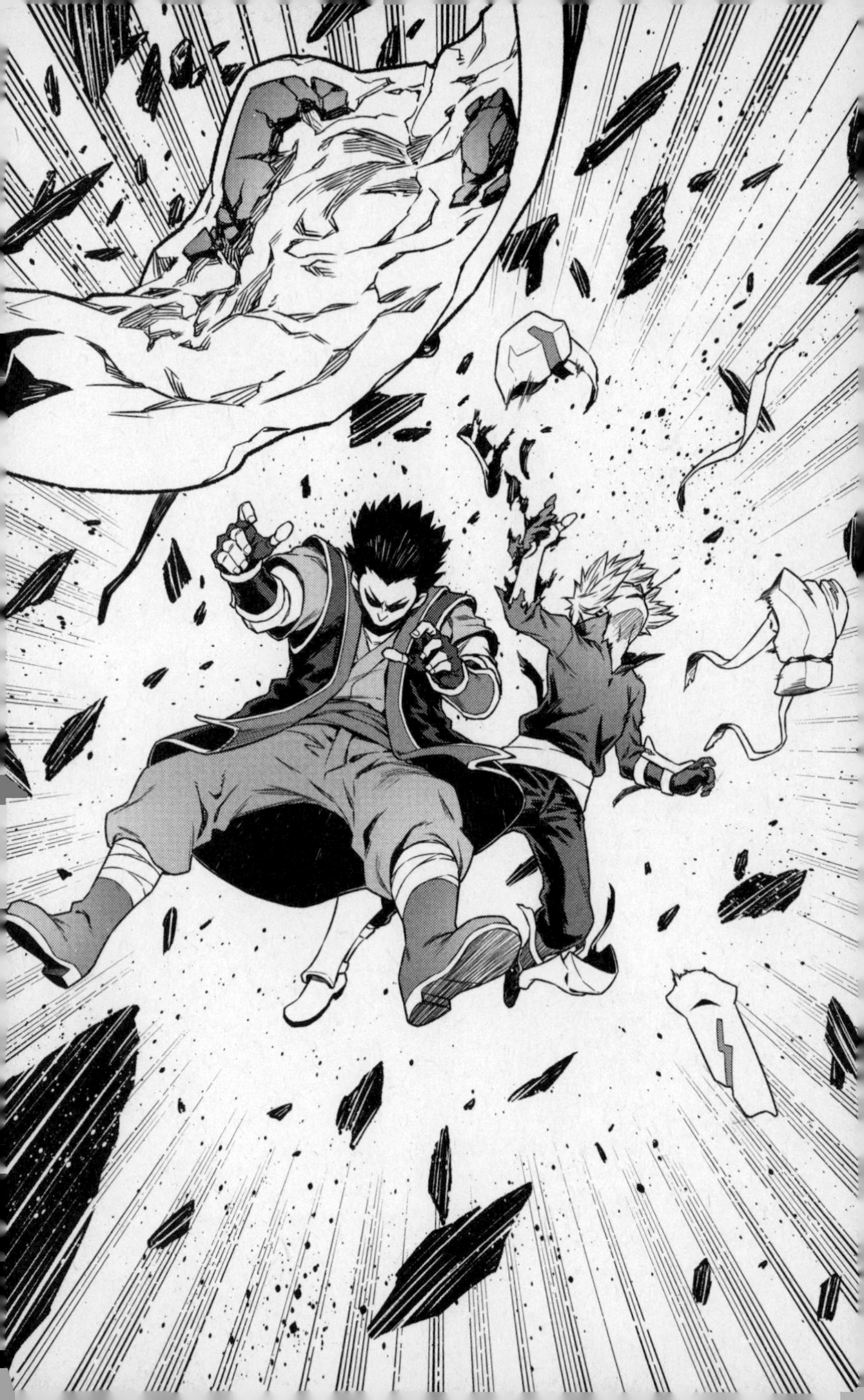

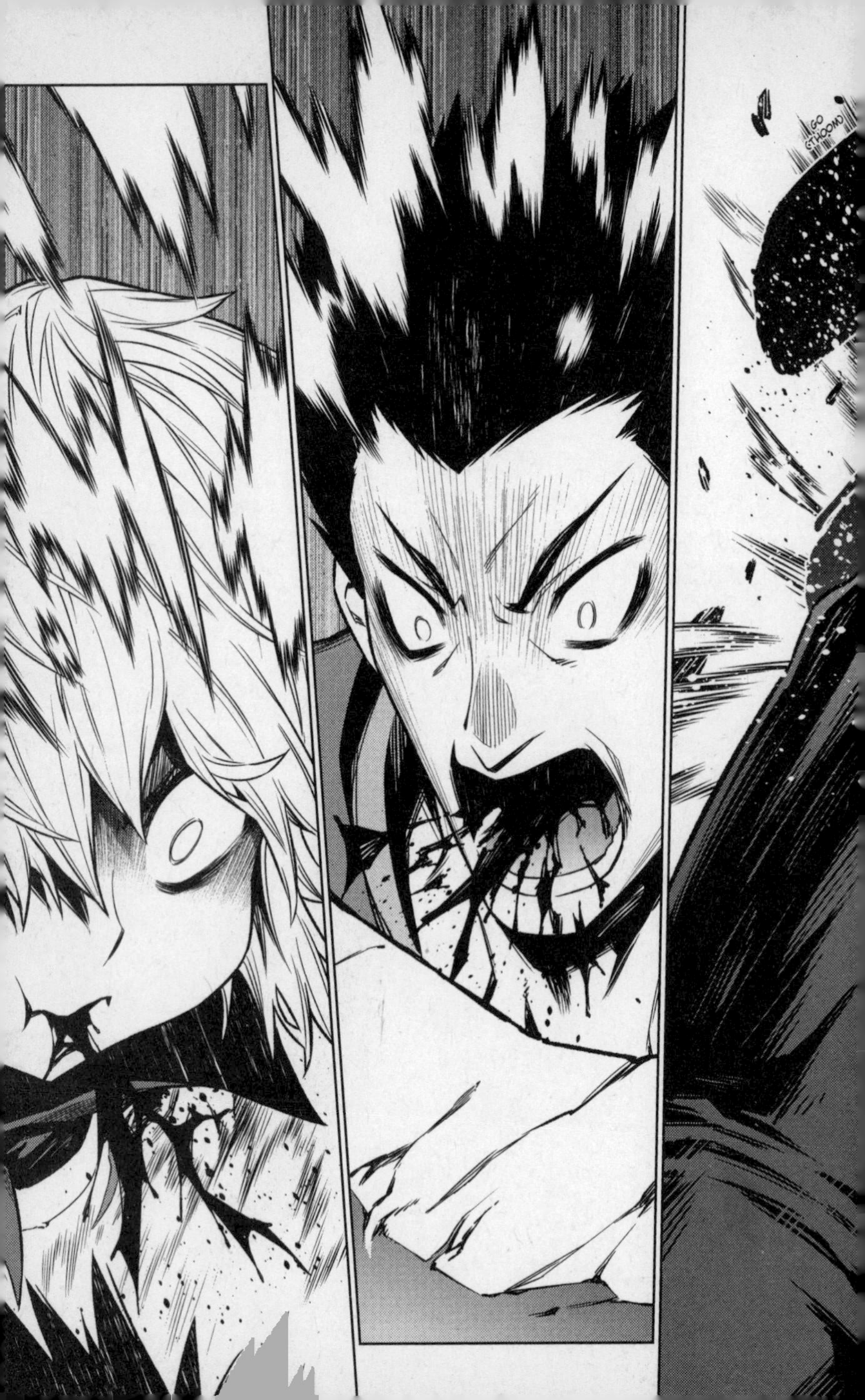
GO
GTHOOM

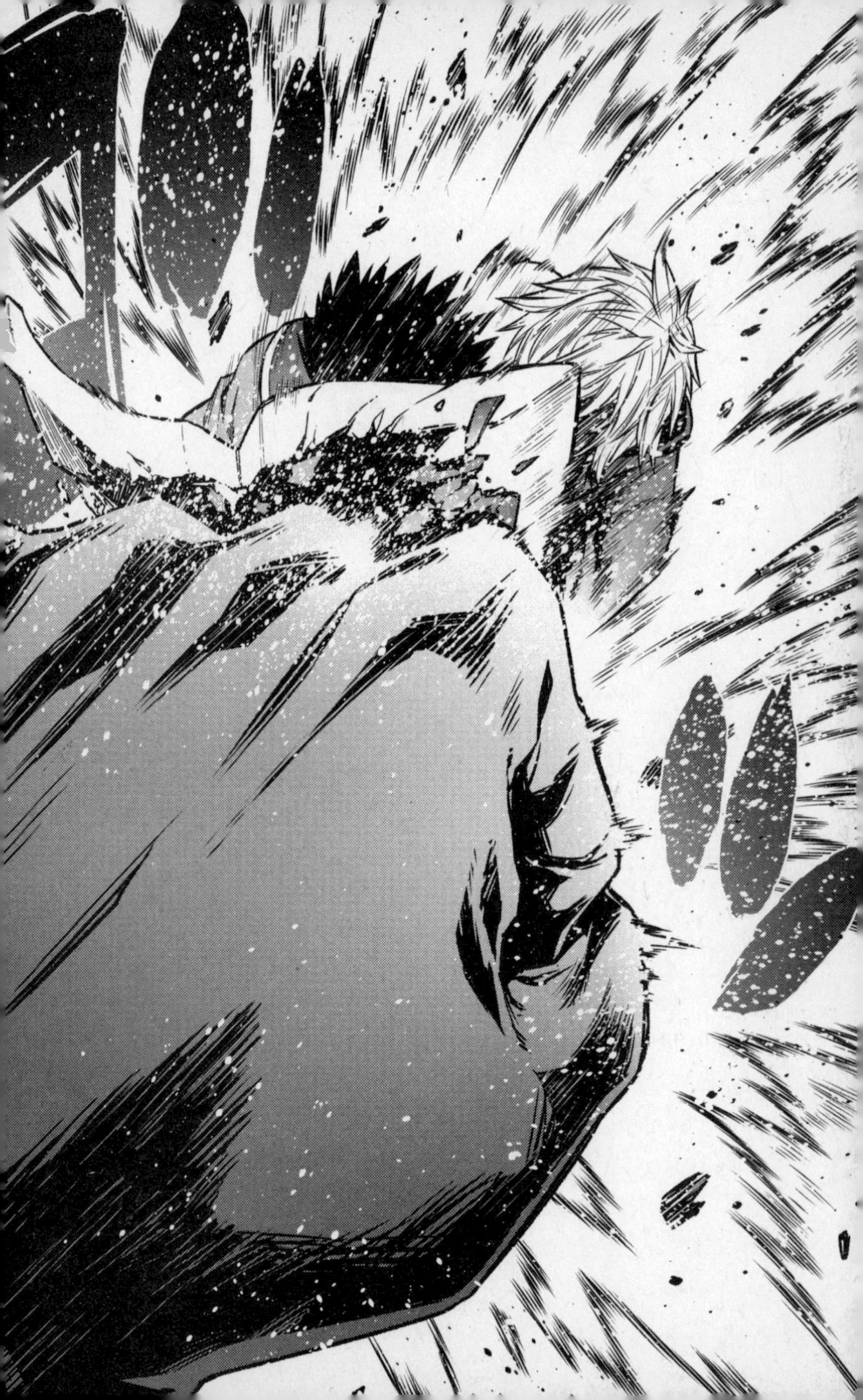

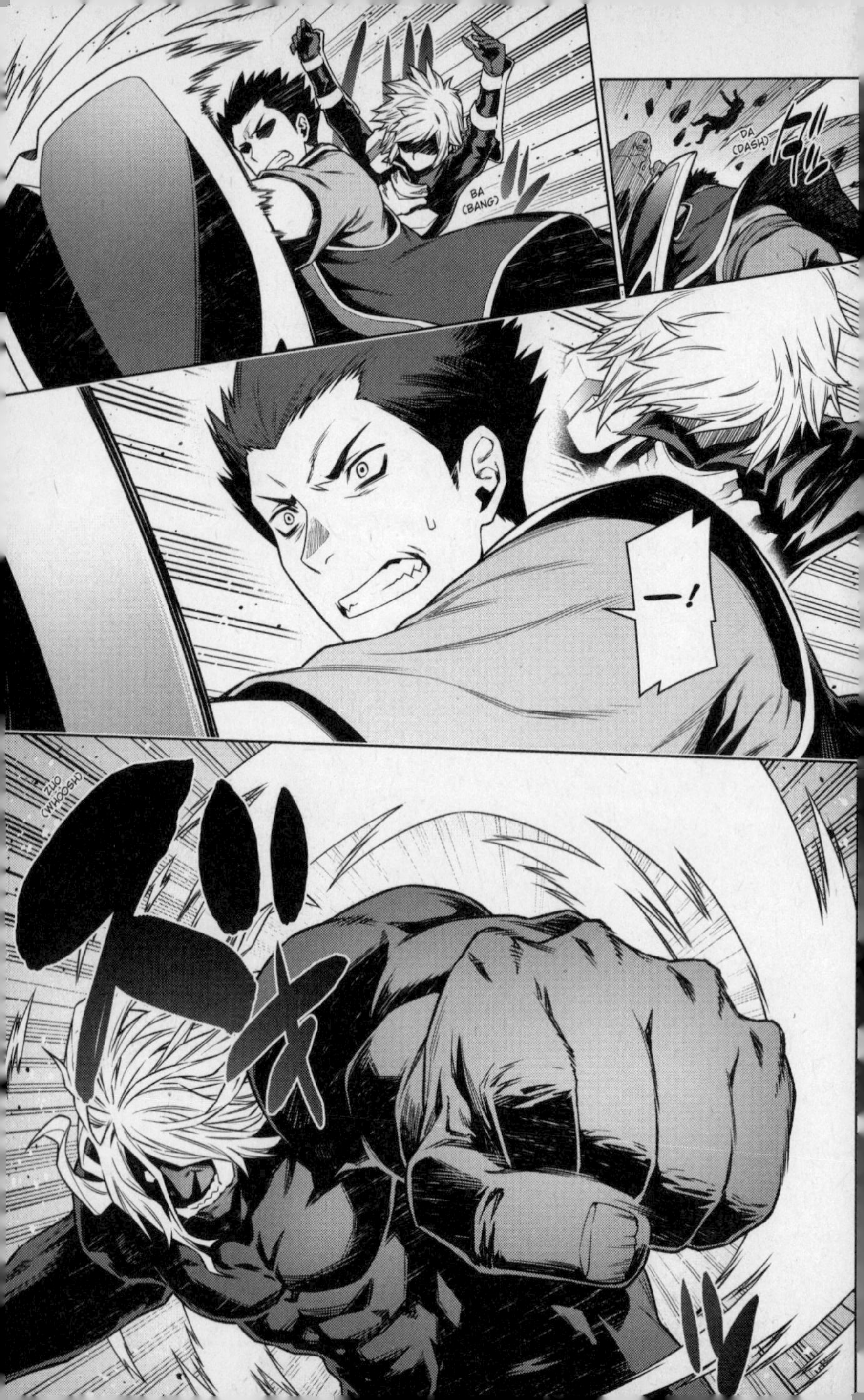
DA
(DASH)
BA
(BANG)
—!
ZUO
(WHOOSH)

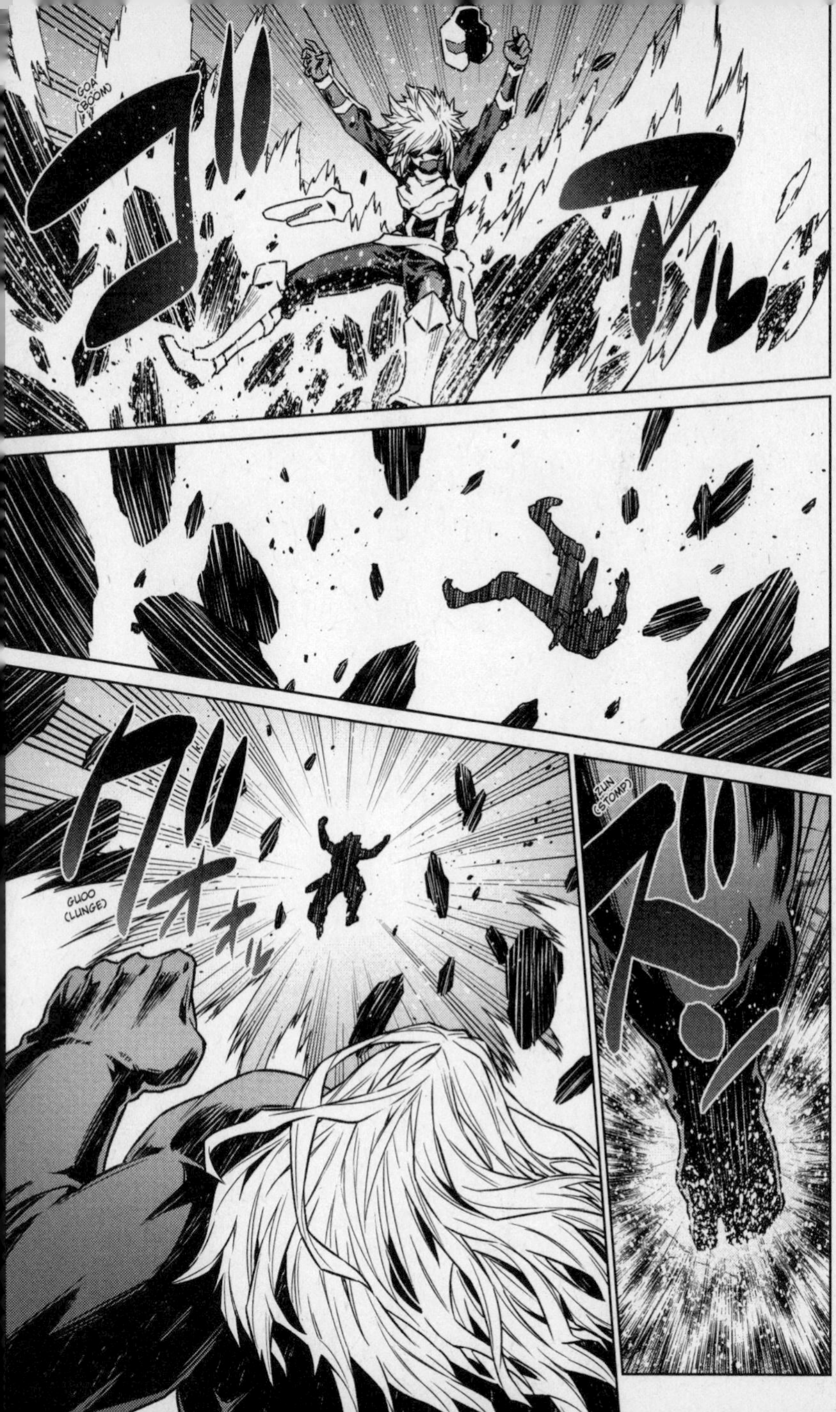
GOA (BOOM)
ZUN (STOMP)
GUOO (LUNGE)

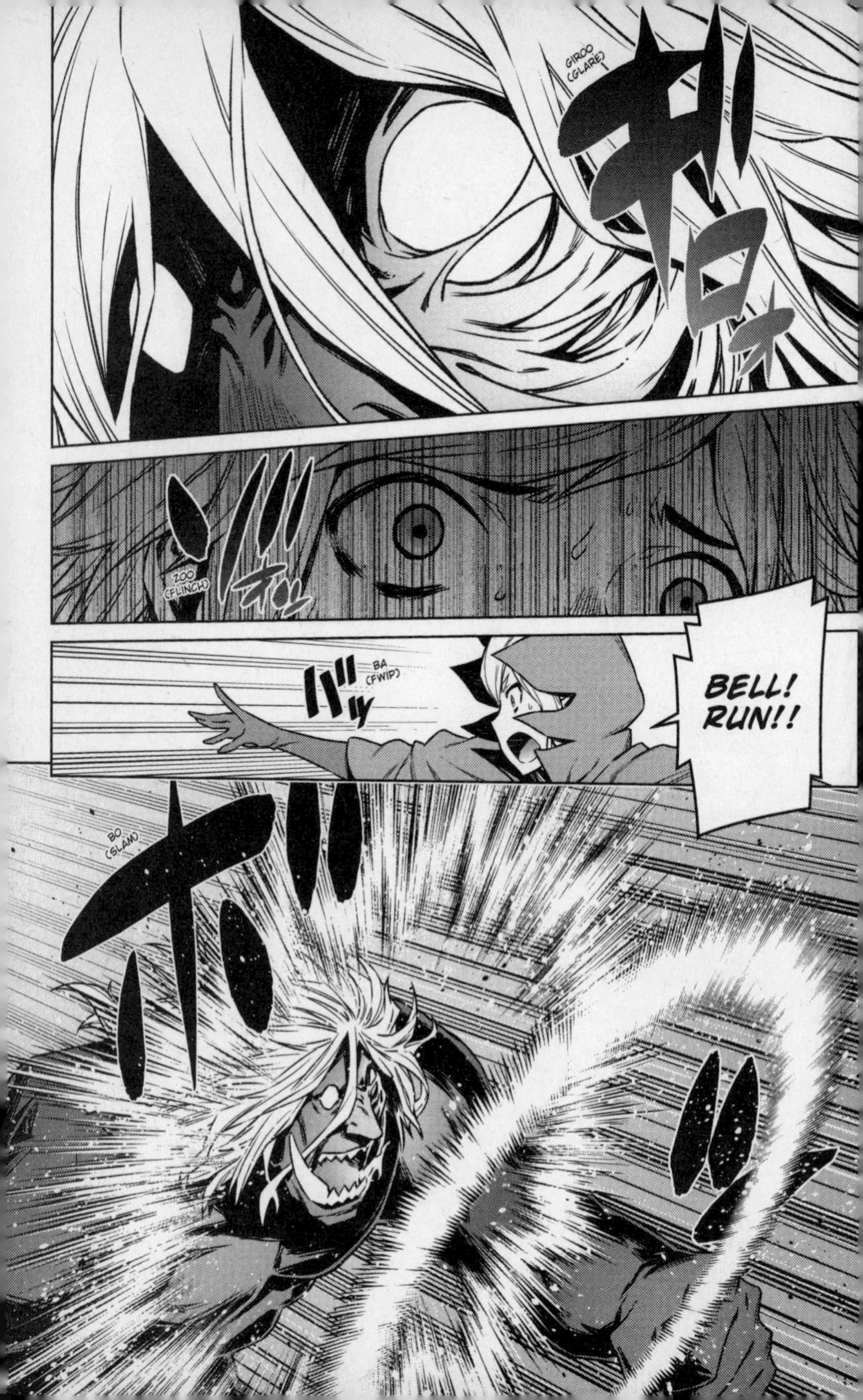
GIROO (GLARE)
ZOO (FLINCH)
BELL! RUN!!
BA (FWIP)
BO (SLAM)

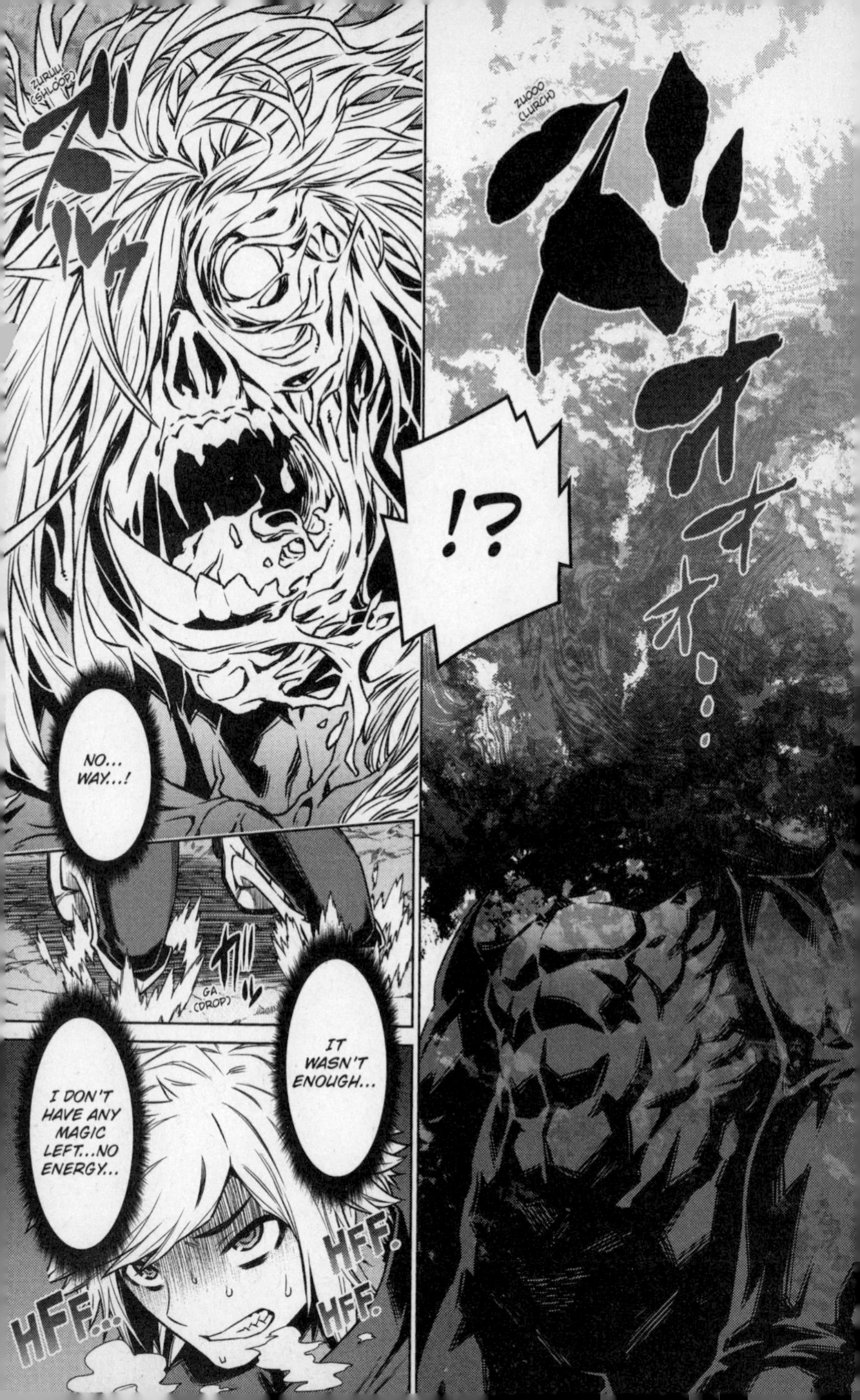
ZUOOO (LURCH)
!?
ZURUU (SHLOOP)
NO... WAY...!
GA (DROP)
IT WASN'T ENOUGH...
I DON'T HAVE ANY MAGIC LEFT...NO ENERGY...
HFF. HFF.
HFF...

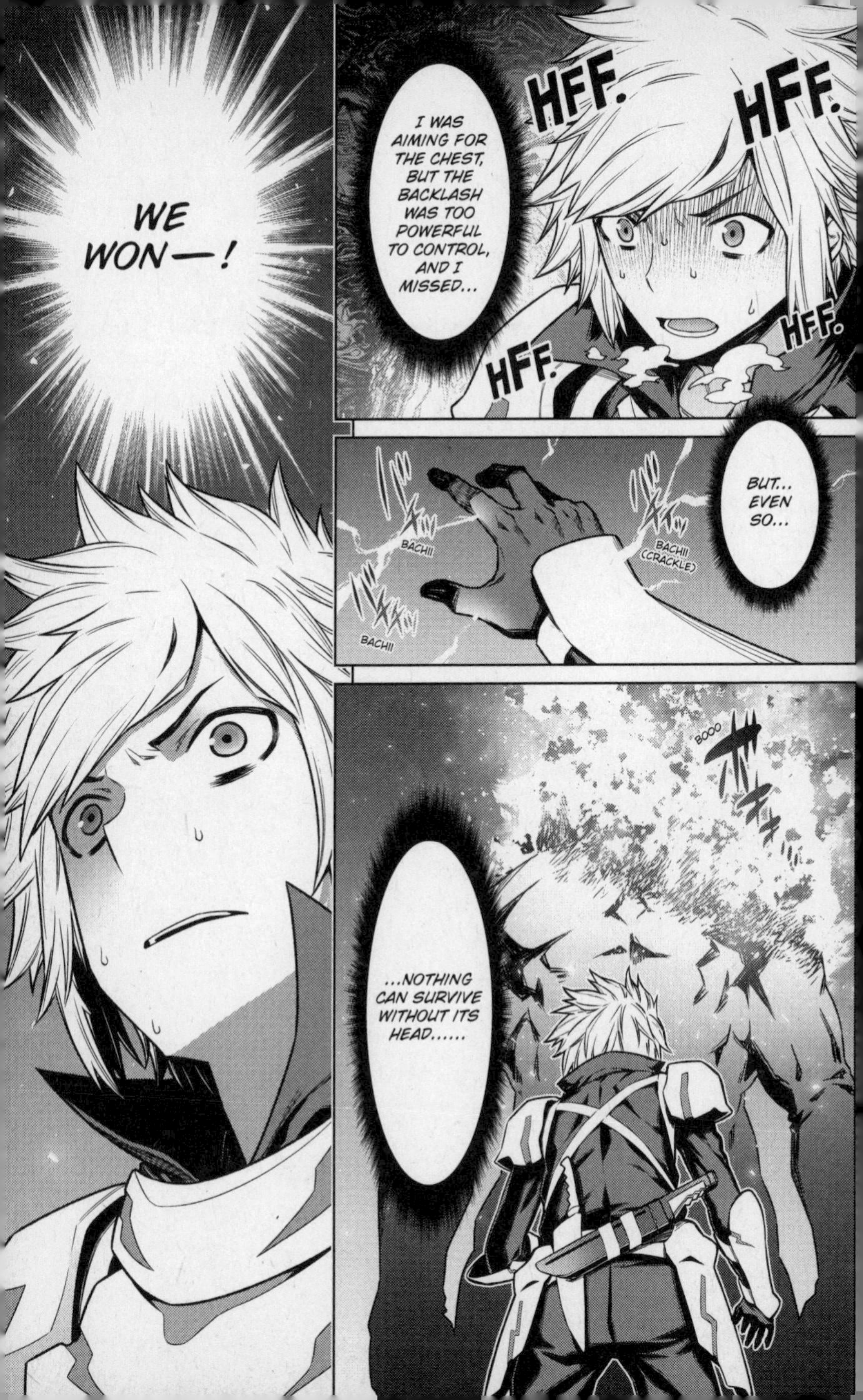
HFF.
HFF.
HFF.
HFF.
I WAS AIMING FOR THE CHEST, BUT THE BACKLASH WAS TOO POWERFUL TO CONTROL, AND I MISSED...
BUT... EVEN SO...
BACHII (CRACKLE)
BACHII
BACHII
BOOO
...NOTHING CAN SURVIVE WITHOUT ITS HEAD......
WE WON—!

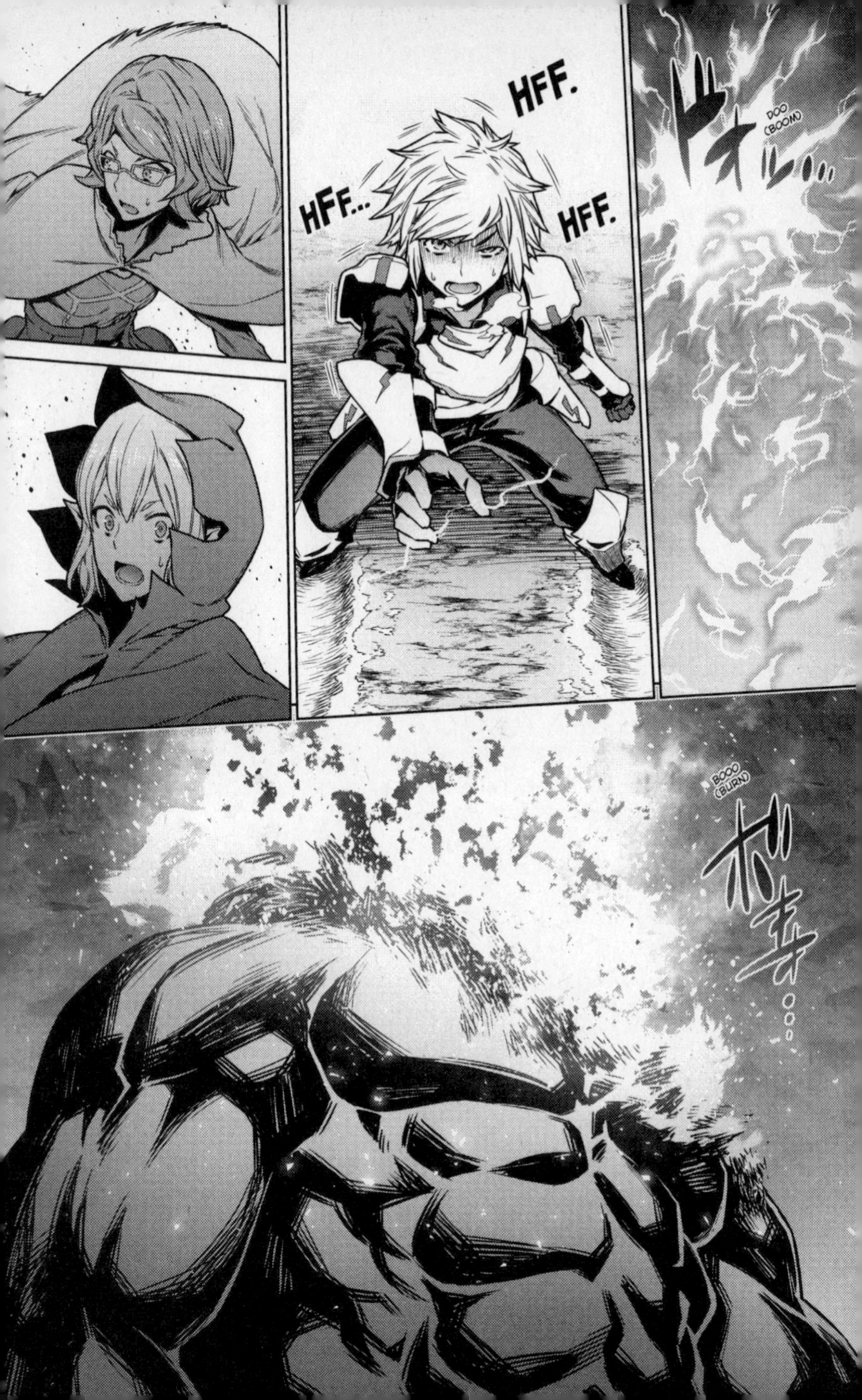
DOO (BOOM)
HFF.
HFF.
HFF...
BOOO (BURN)

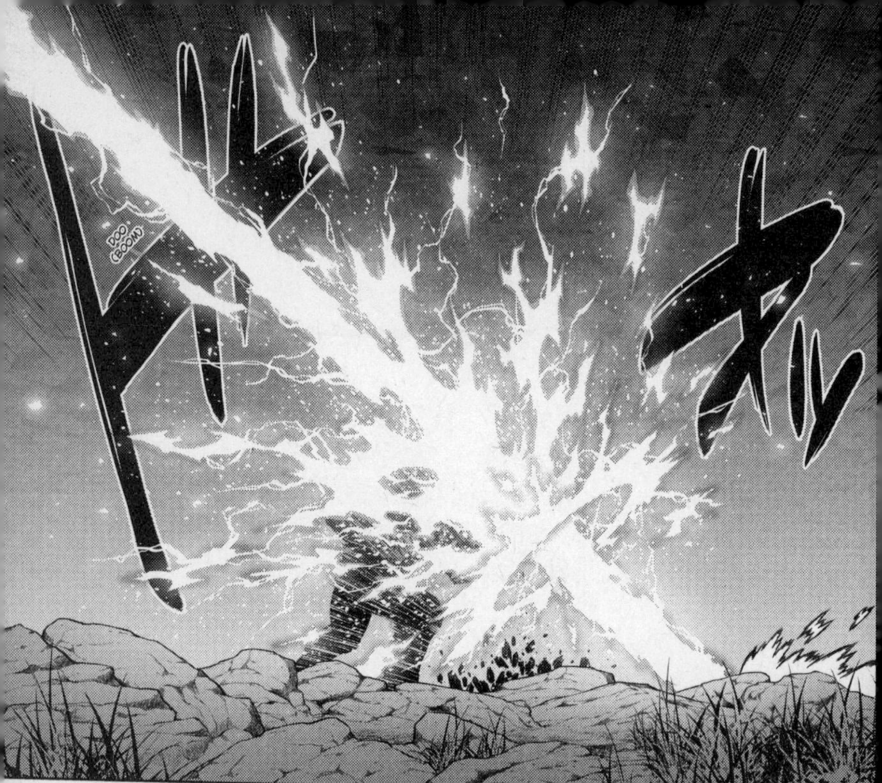
DOO (BOOM)
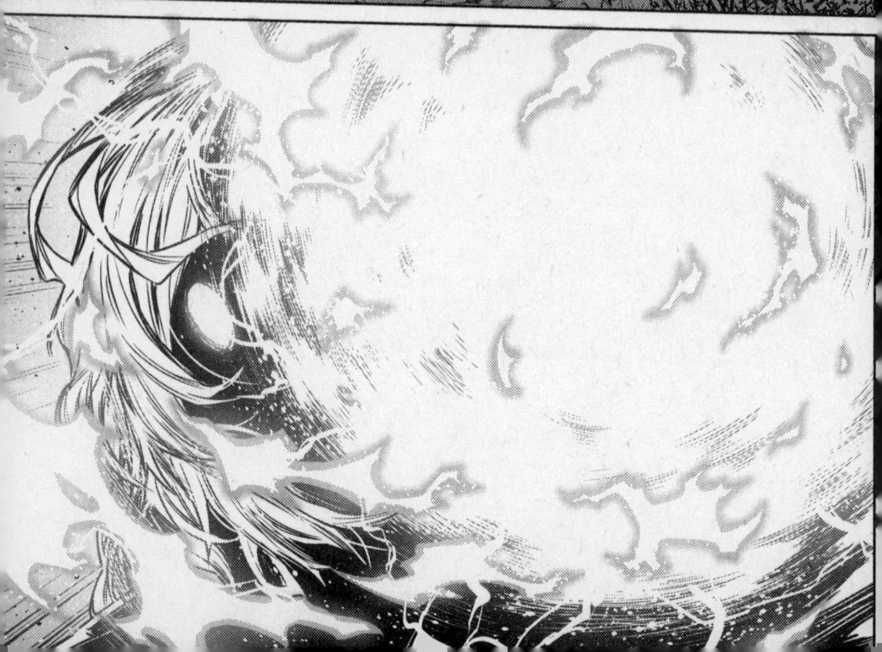

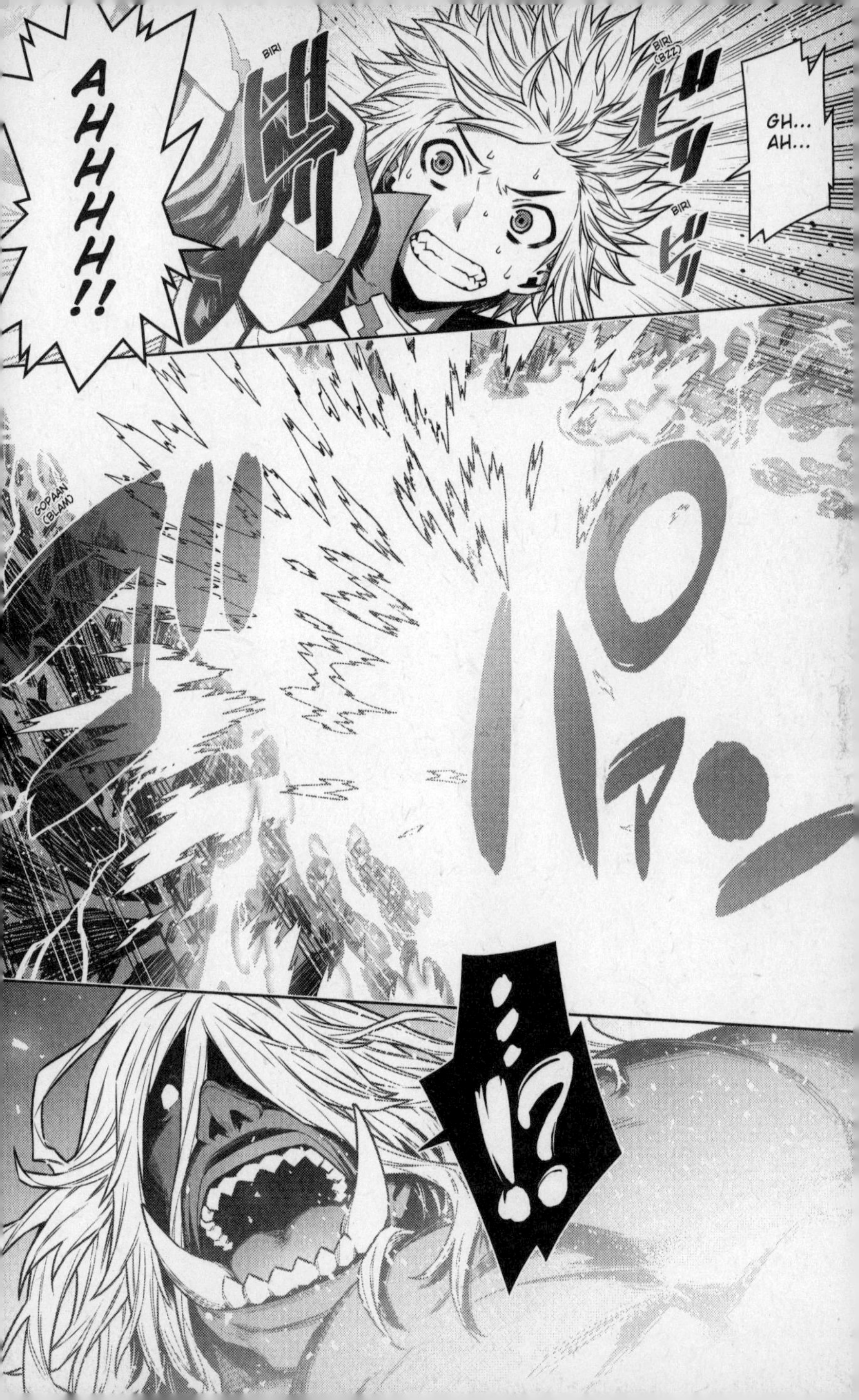
GH... AH...
BIRI (BZZ)
BIRI
BIRI
AHHHHH!!
GOPAAN (BLAM)
!?

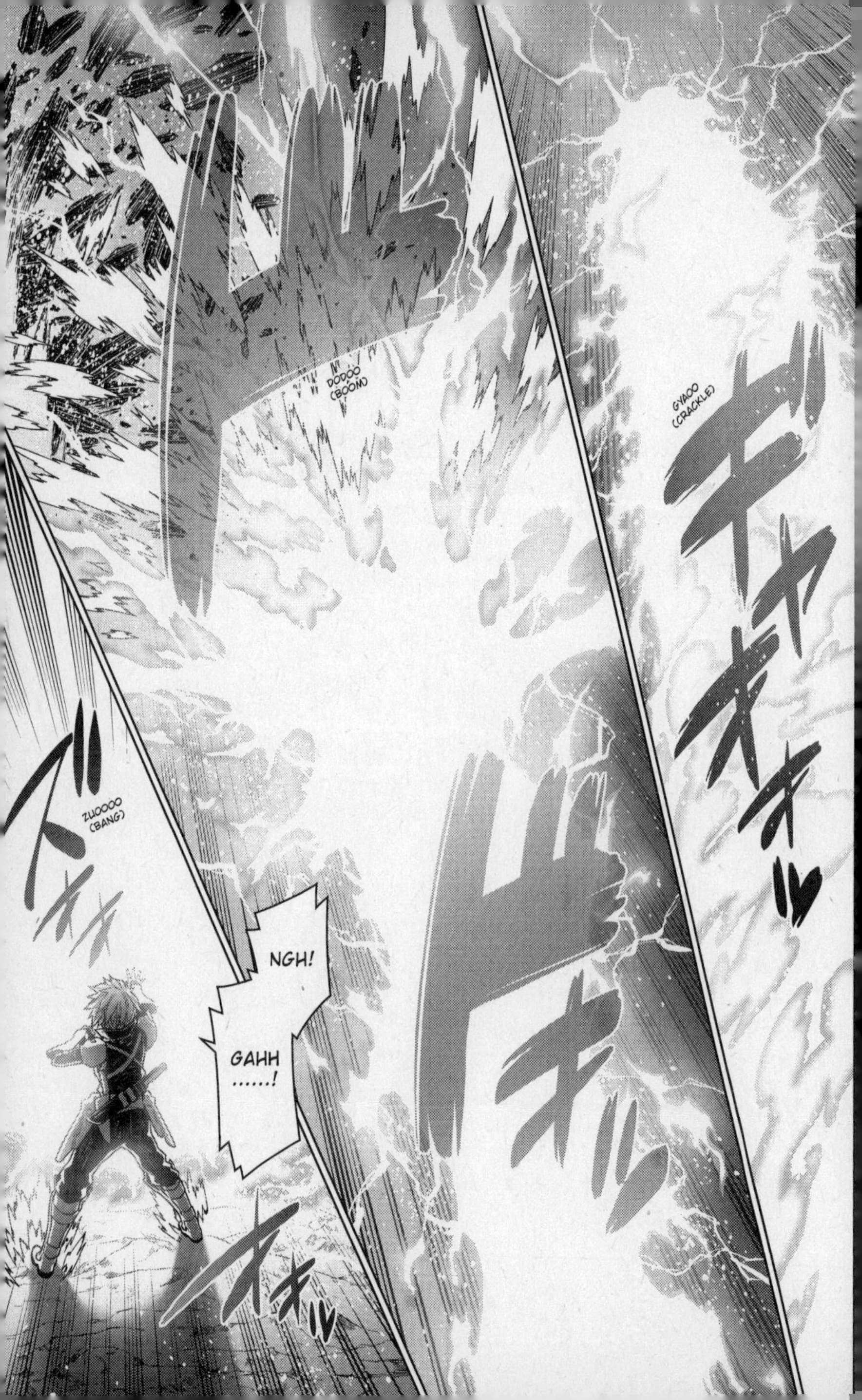
GYAOO (CRACKLE)
DODOO (BOOM)
ZUOOOO (BANG)
NGH!
GAHH ......!

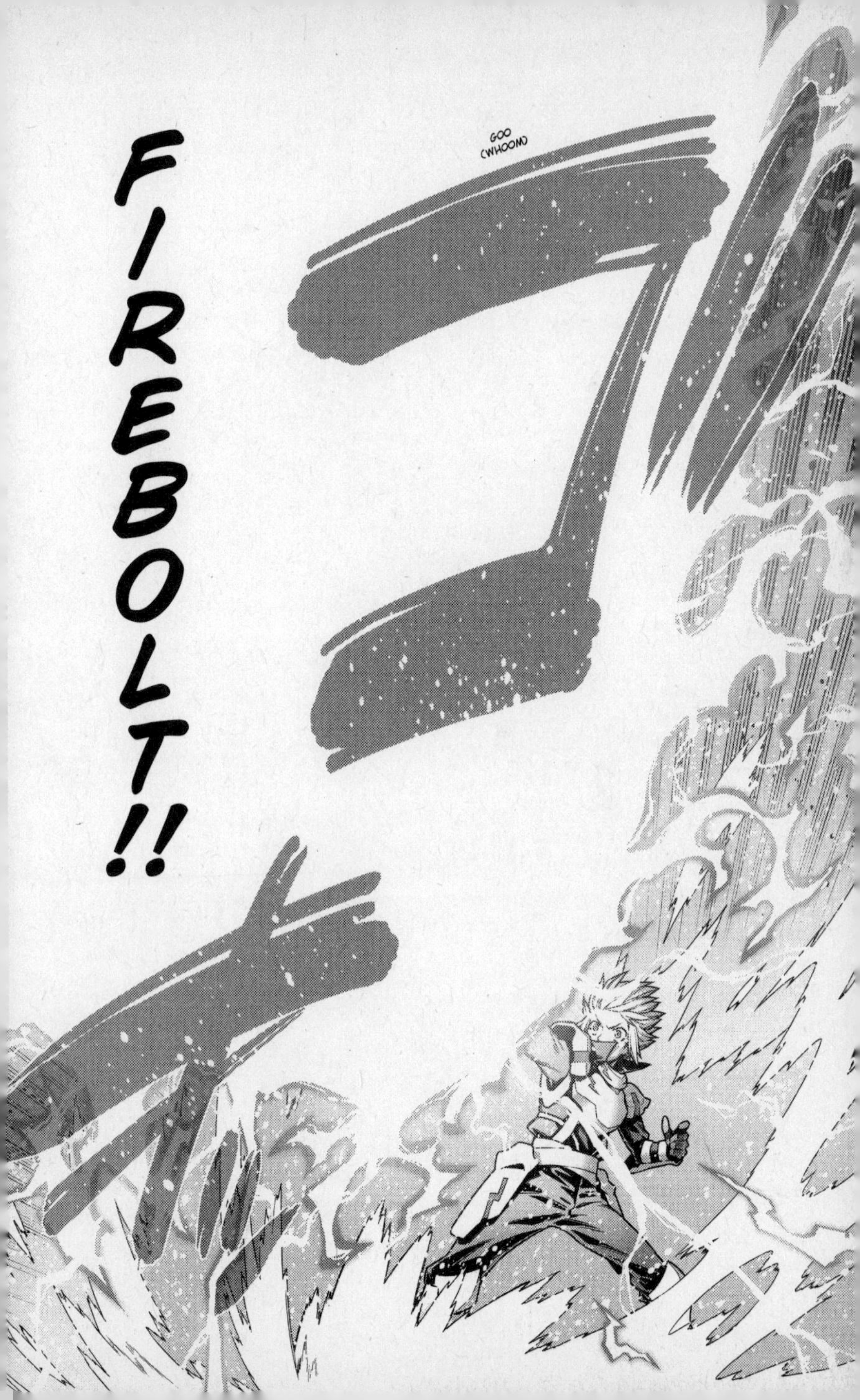
FIREBOLT!!
GOO
(WHOOM)

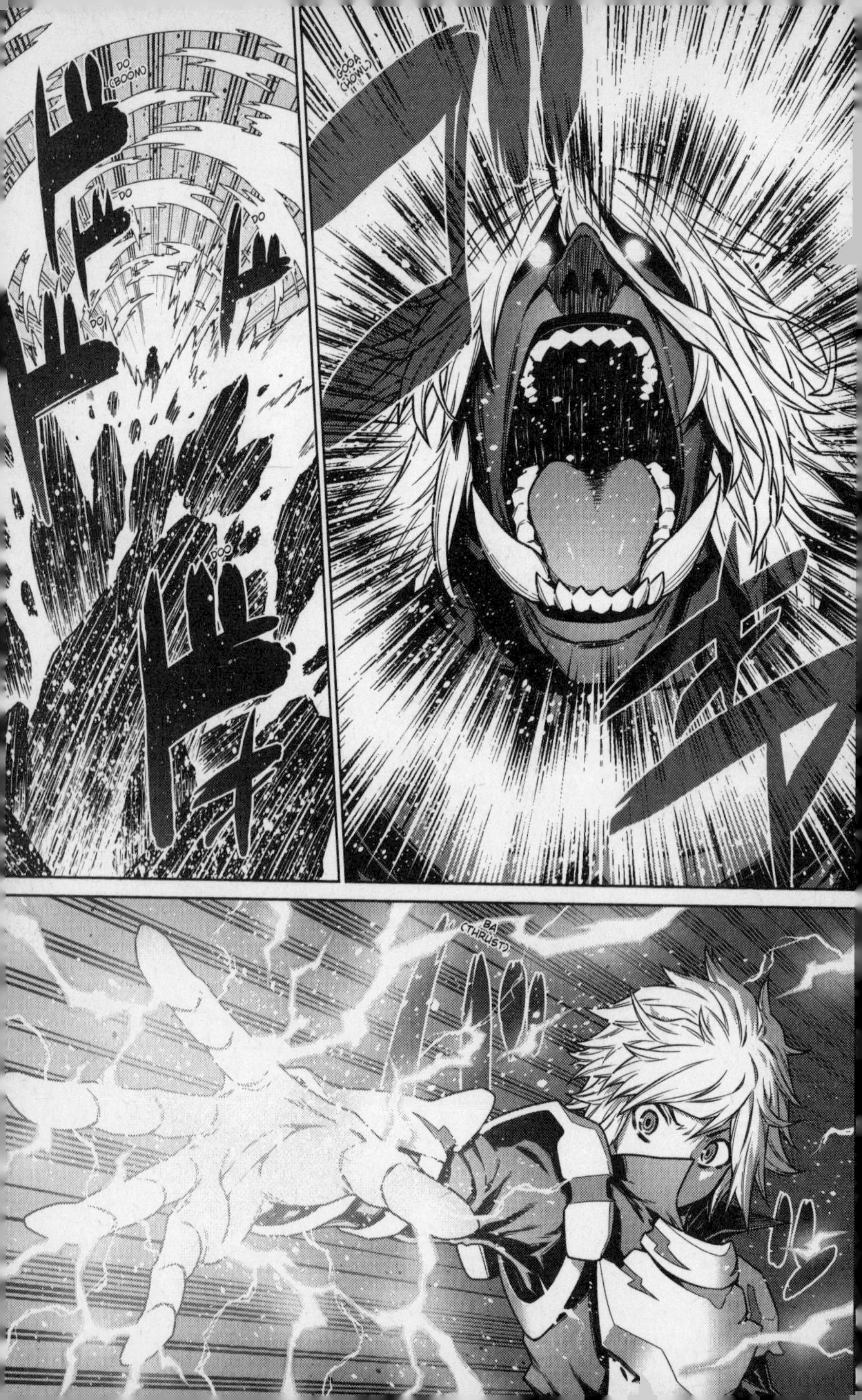
GOOA (HOWL)
DO (BOOM)
DO
DO
DO
DOO
BA (THRUST)

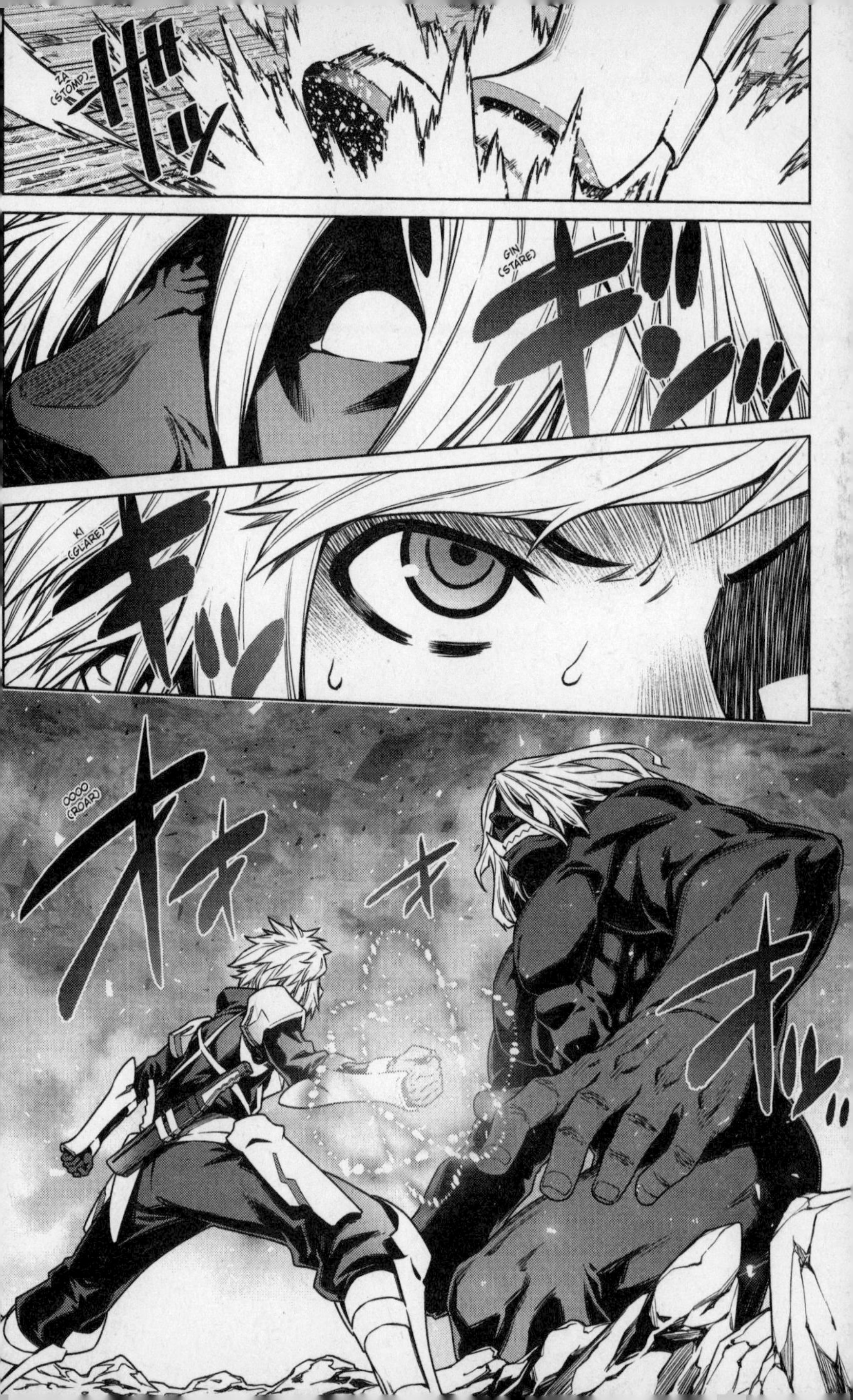
ZA (STOMP)
GIN (STARE)
KI (GLARE)
OOOO (ROAR)

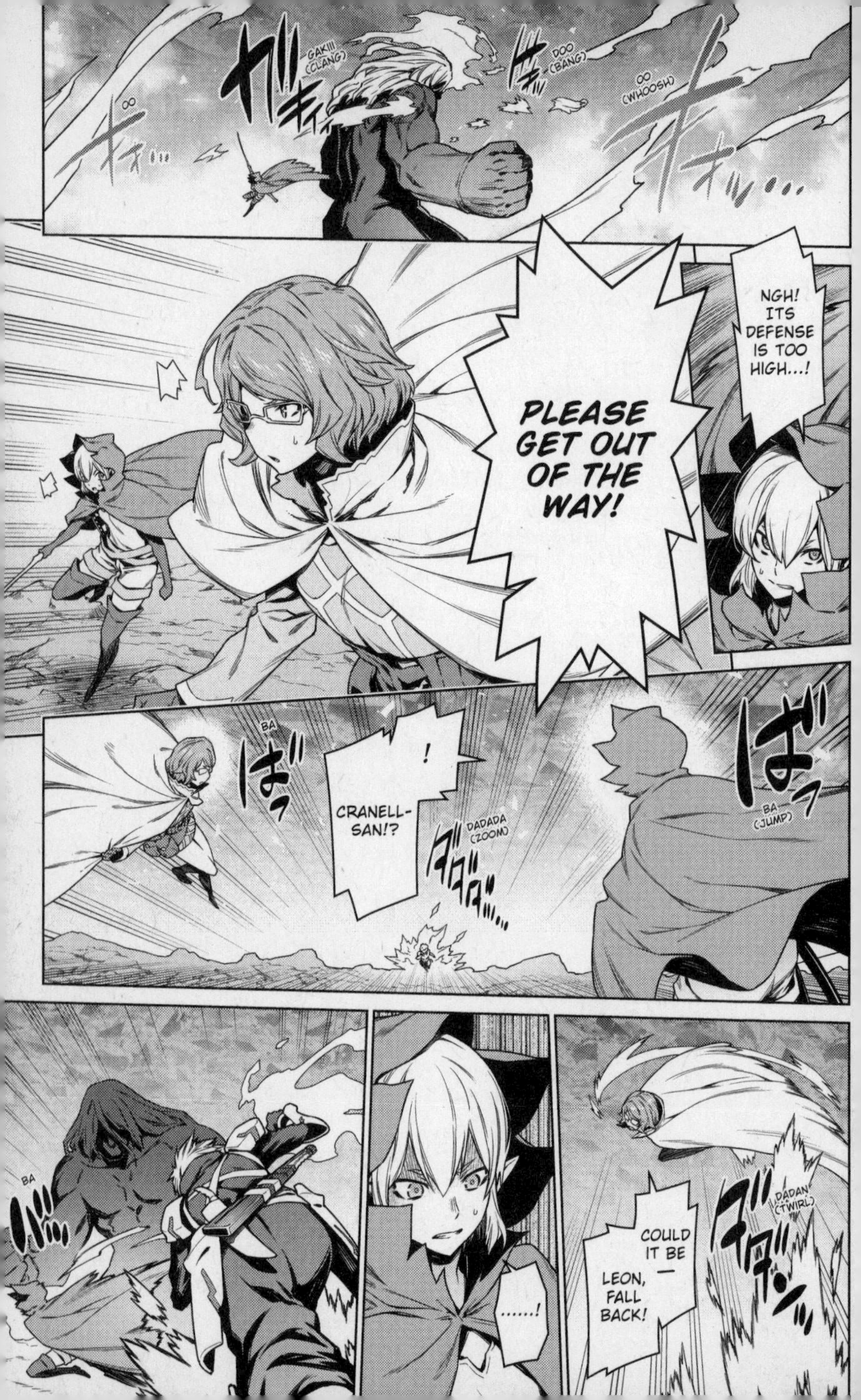
OO (WHOOSH)
DOO (BANG)
GAKIII (CLANG)
OO
NGH! ITS DEFENSE IS TOO HIGH...!
PLEASE GET OUT OF THE WAY!
BA (JUMP)
!
CRANELL-SAN!?
DADADA (ZOOM)
BA
DADAN (TWIRL)
COULD IT BE —
LEON, FALL BACK!
......!
BA

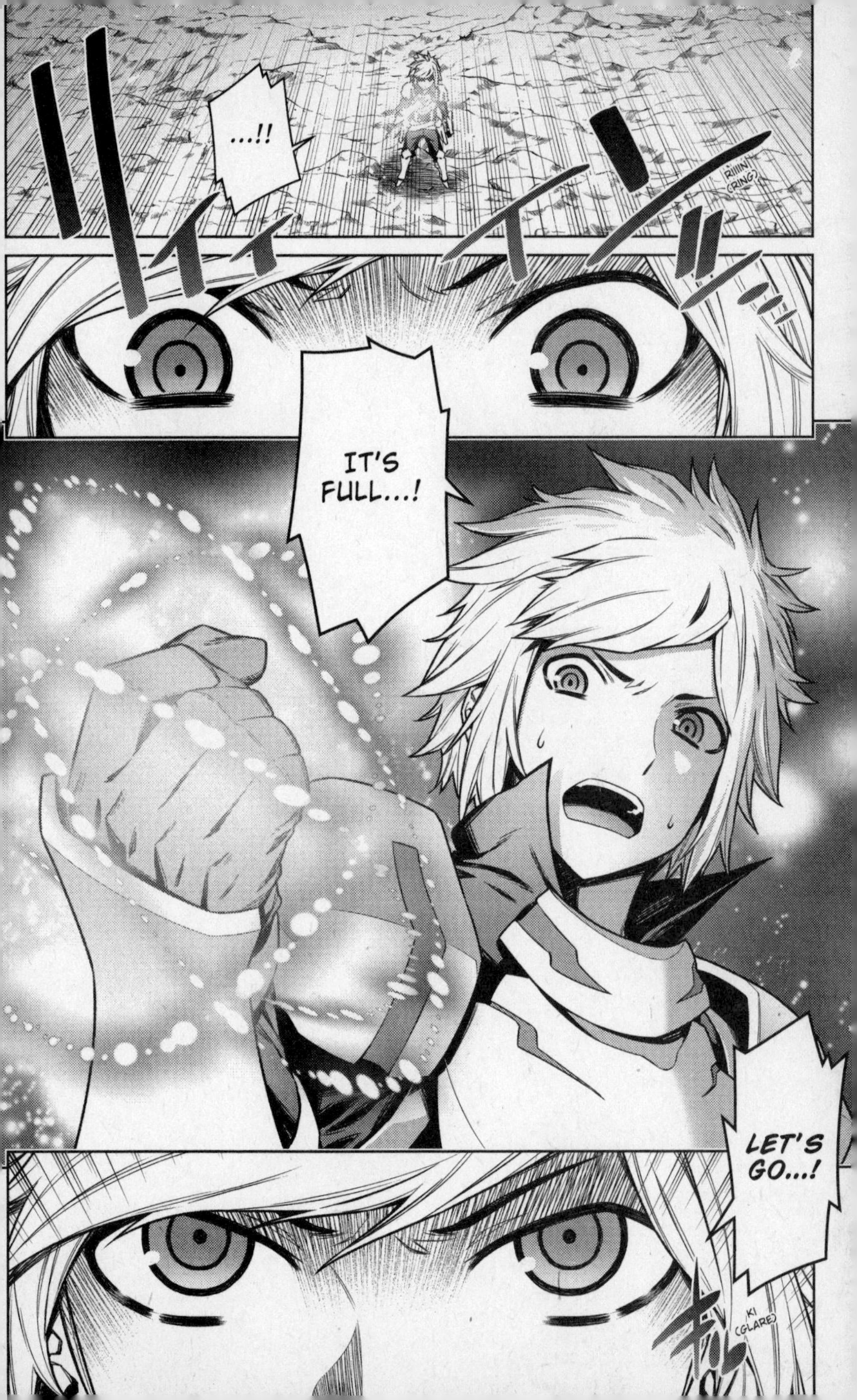
...!!
RIIIN! (RING)
IT'S FULL...!
LET'S GO...!
KI (GLARE)

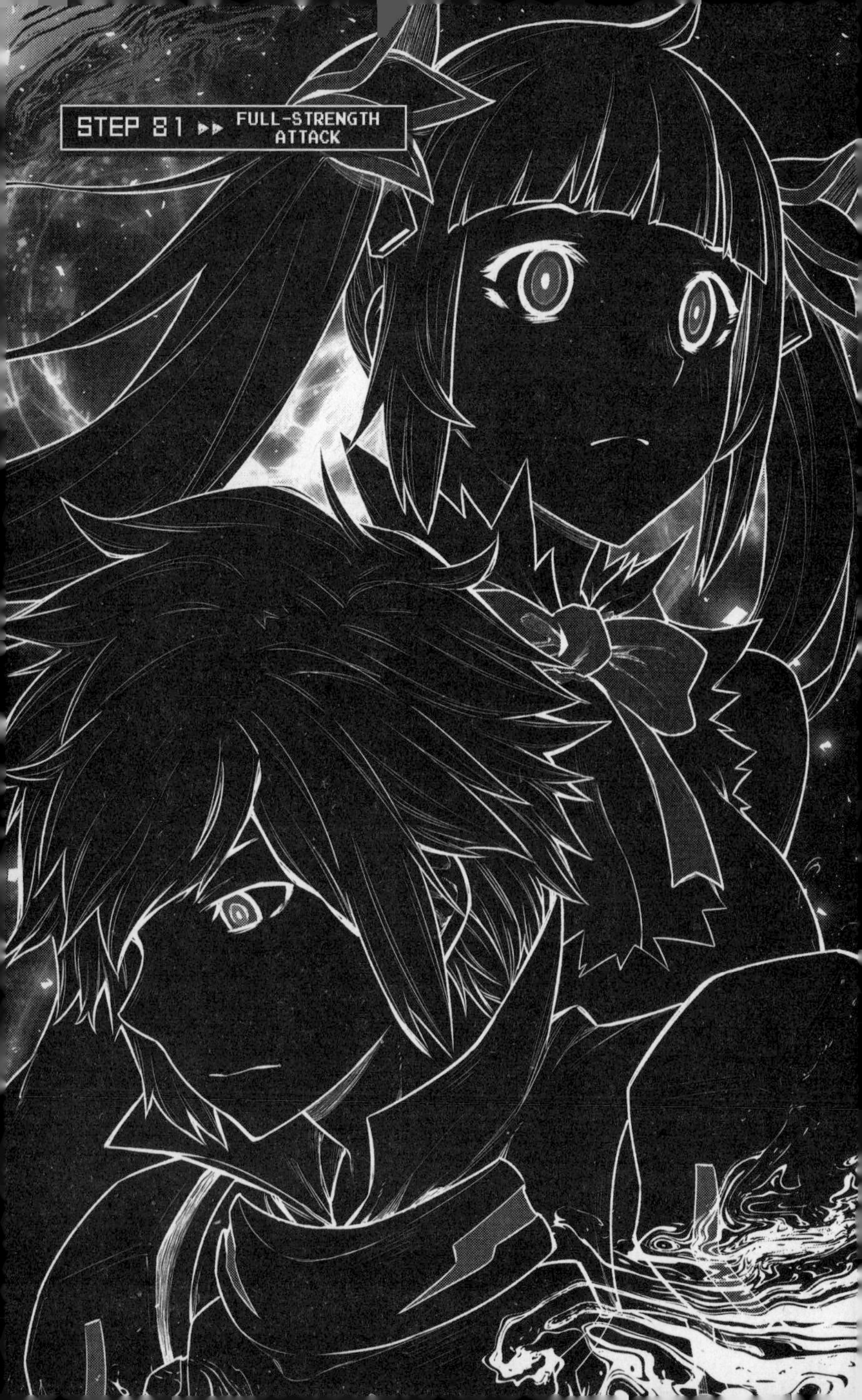
STEP 81 ▸▸ FULL-STRENGTH ATTACK

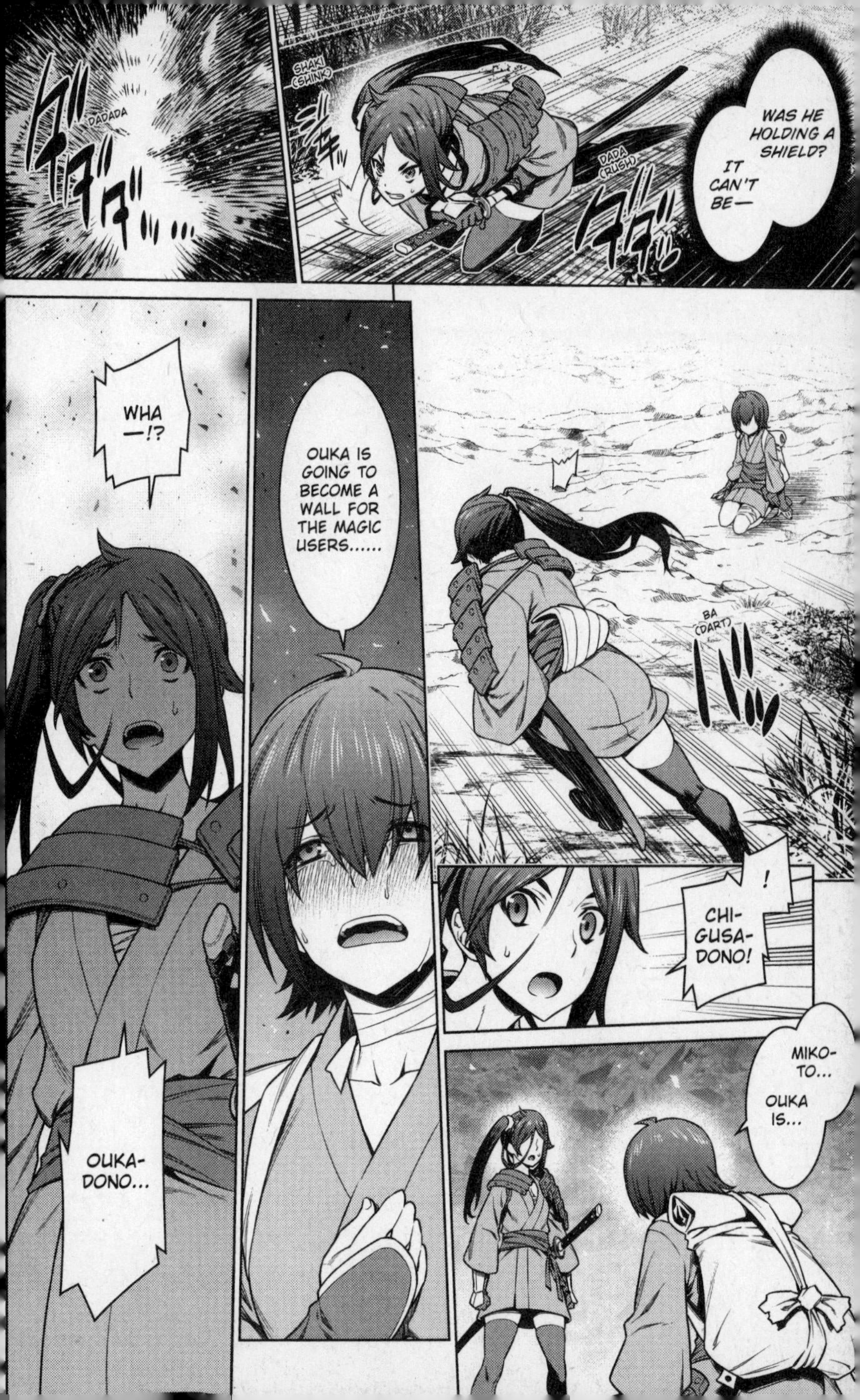
WAS HE HOLDING A SHIELD?
IT CAN'T BE—
DADA (RUSH)
SHAKI (SHINK)
DADADA
BA (DART)
!
CHI-GUSA-DONO!
MIKO-TO...
OUKA IS...
OUKA IS GOING TO BECOME A WALL FOR THE MAGIC USERS......
WHA—!?
OUKA-DONO...

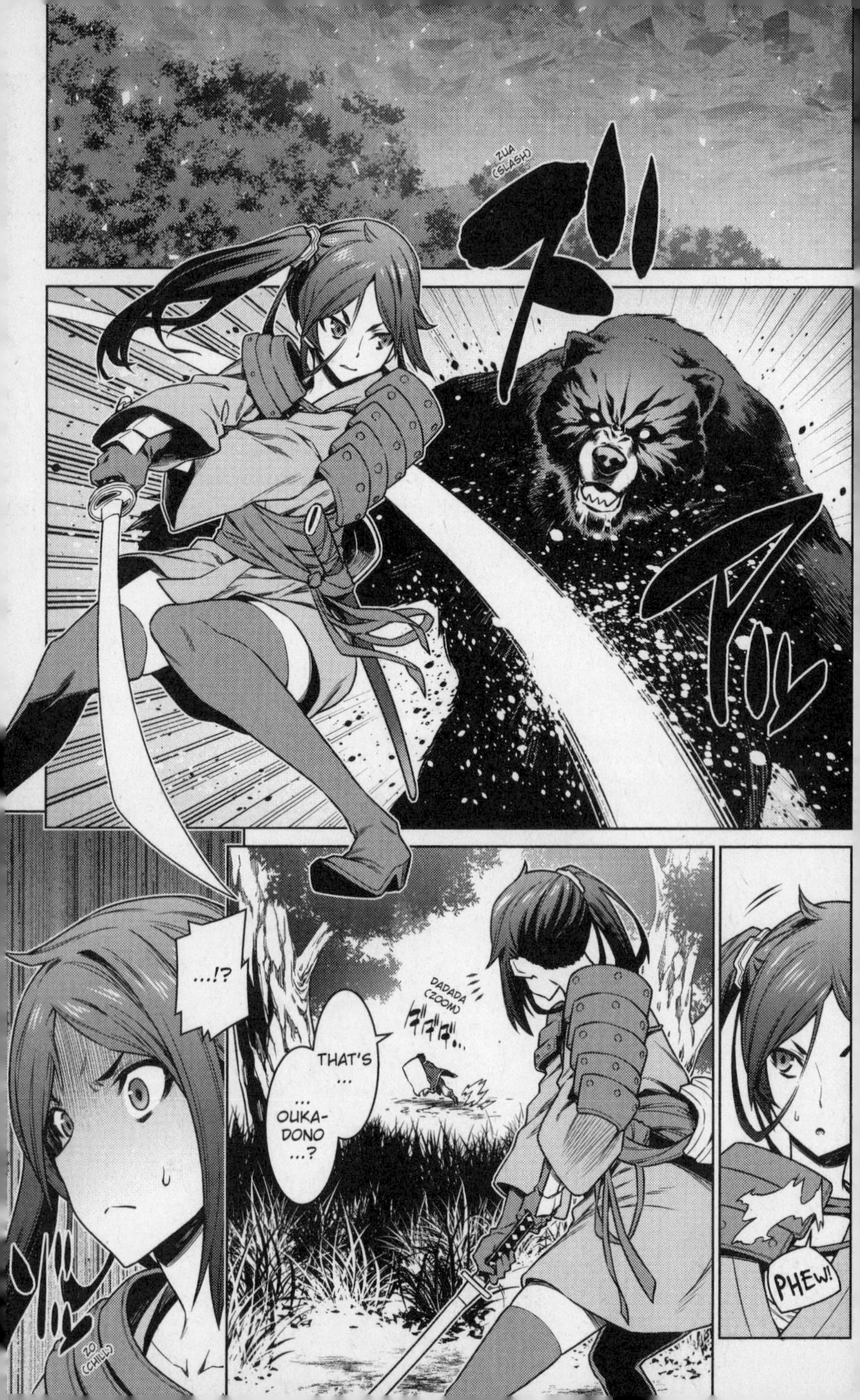
ZUA (SLASH)
PHEW!
DADADA (ZOOM)
THAT'S ... ... OUKA-DONO ...?
...!?
ZO (CHILL)

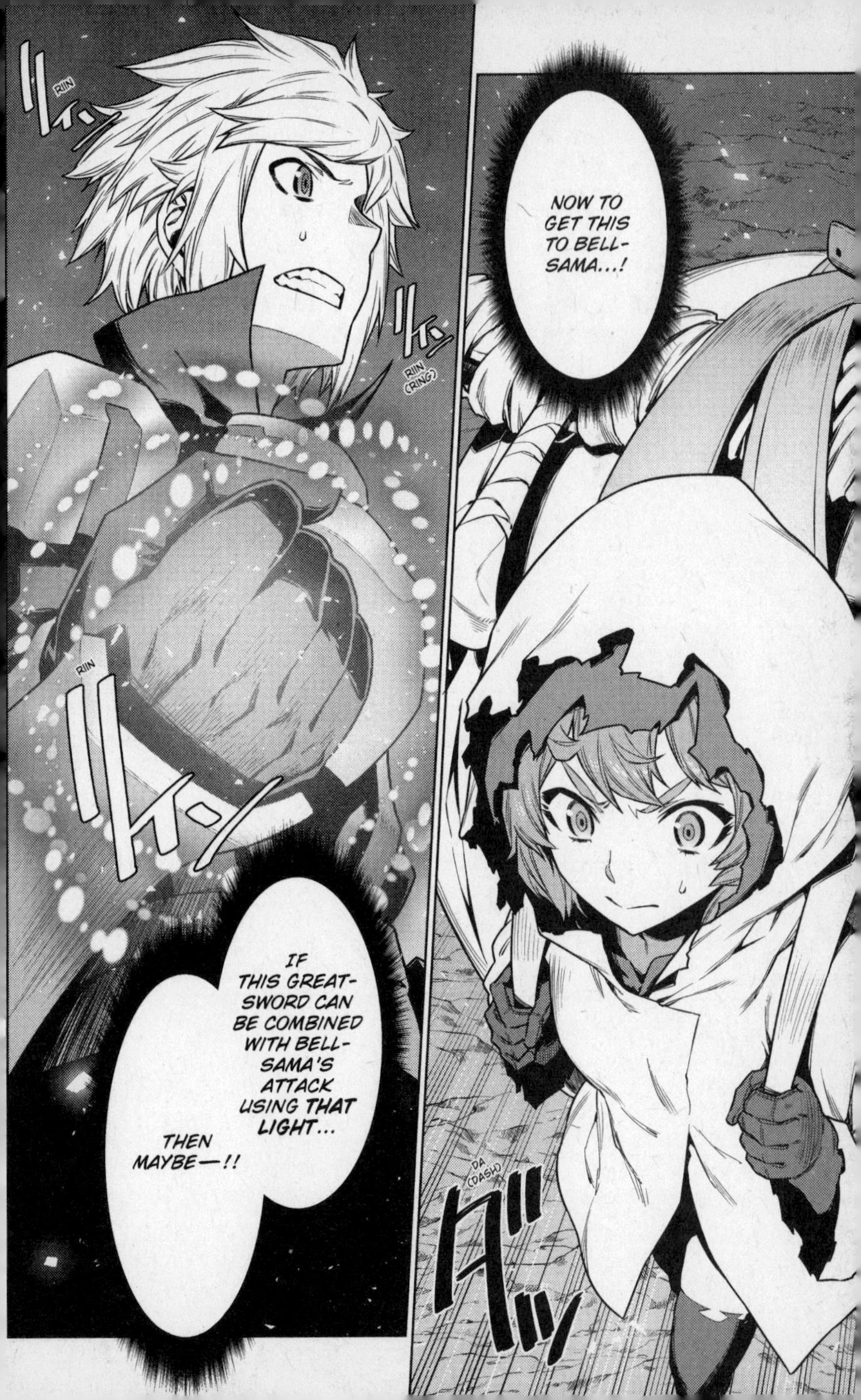
NOW TO GET THIS TO BELL-SAMA...!
DA (DASH)
RIIN
RIIN (RING)
RIIN
IF THIS GREAT-SWORD CAN BE COMBINED WITH BELL-SAMA'S ATTACK USING THAT LIGHT...
THEN MAYBE—!!

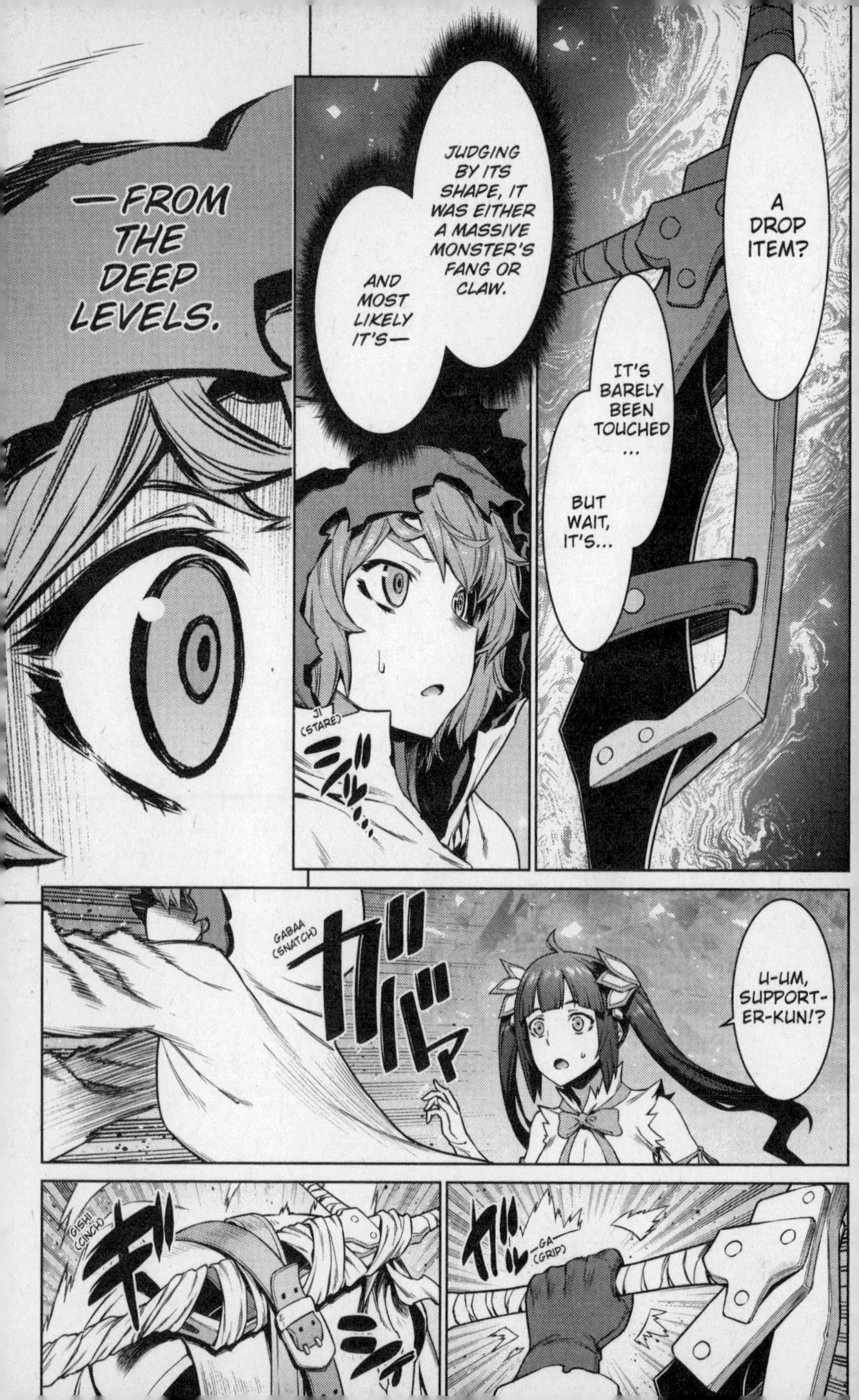
A DROP ITEM?
IT'S BARELY BEEN TOUCHED...
BUT WAIT, IT'S...
JUDGING BY ITS SHAPE, IT WAS EITHER A MASSIVE MONSTER'S FANG OR CLAW.
AND MOST LIKELY IT'S—
JI (STARE)
—FROM THE DEEP LEVELS.
U-UM, SUPPORTER-KUN!?
GABAA (SNATCH)
GA (GRIP)
GISHI (CINCH)

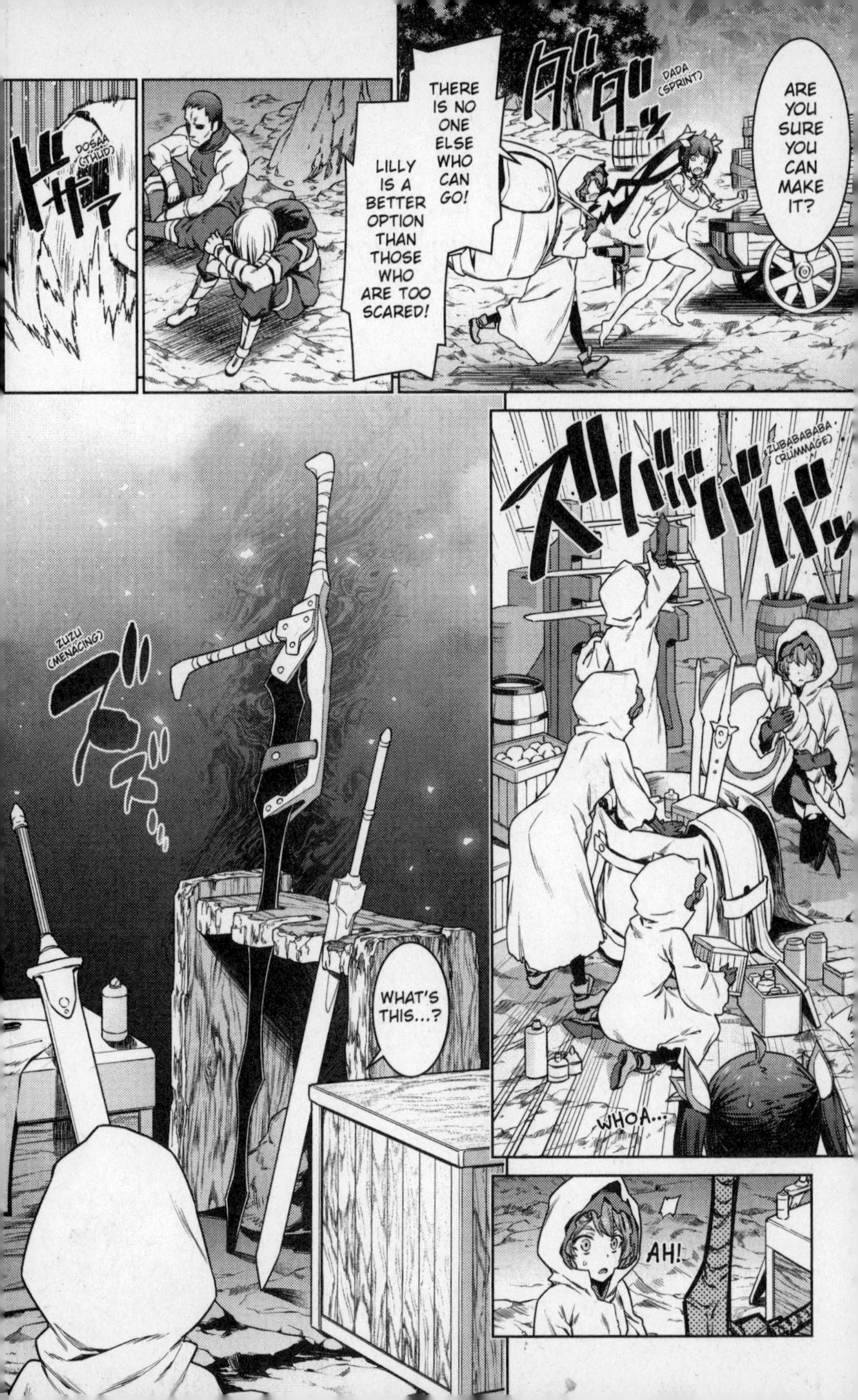
ARE YOU SURE YOU CAN MAKE IT?
DADA (SPRINT)
THERE IS NO ONE ELSE WHO CAN GO!
LILLY IS A BETTER OPTION THAN THOSE WHO ARE TOO SCARED!
DOSAA (THUD)
ZUBABABABA (RUMMAGE)
WHOA...
AH!
ZUZU (MENACING)
WHAT'S THIS...?

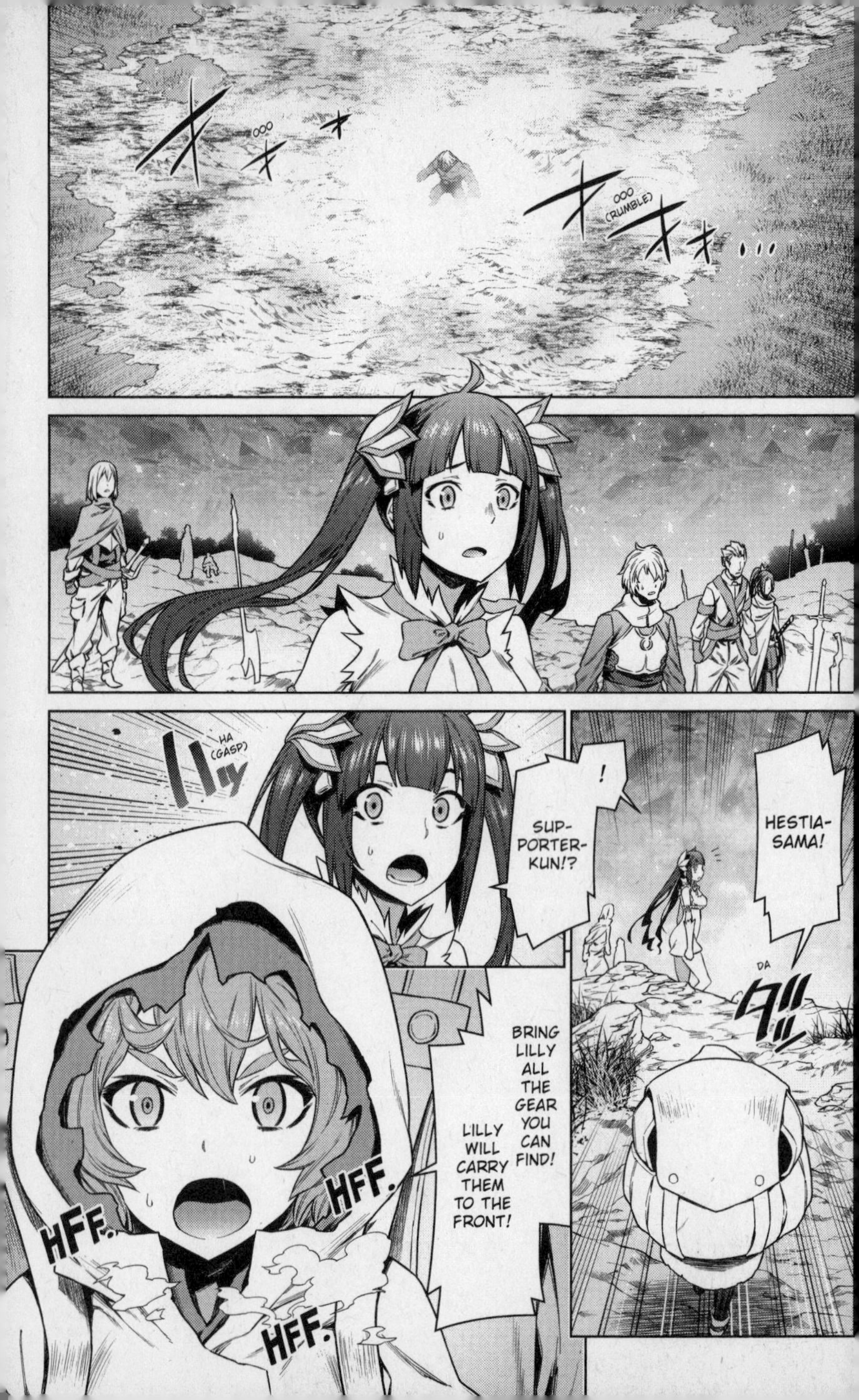
OOO
OOO (RUMBLE)
...
HA (GASP)
!
SUP-PORTER-KUN!?
HESTIA-SAMA!
DA
BRING LILLY ALL THE GEAR YOU CAN FIND!
LILLY WILL CARRY THEM TO THE FRONT!
HFF.
HFF..
HFF.

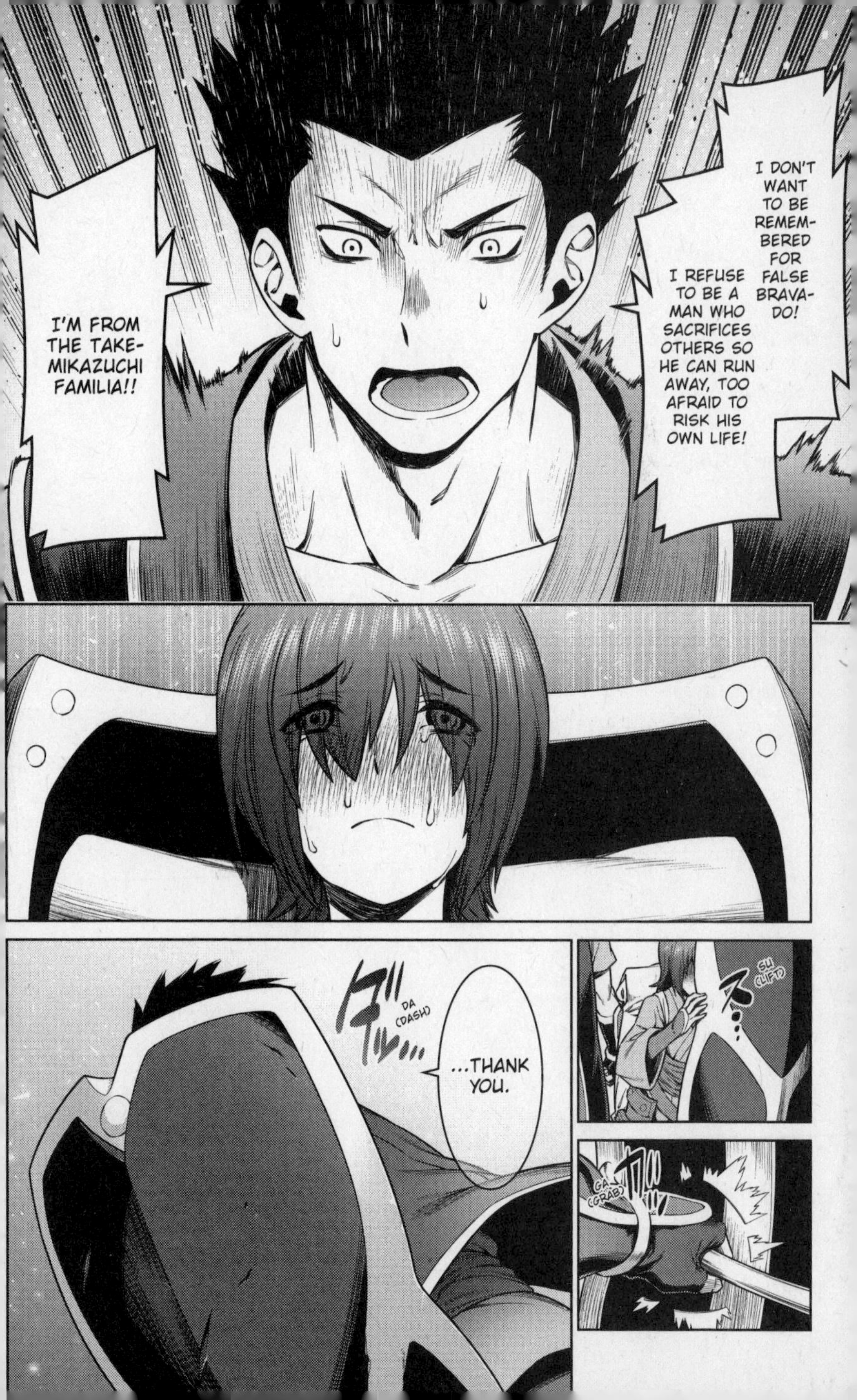
I DON'T WANT TO BE REMEMBERED FOR FALSE BRAVADO!
I REFUSE TO BE A MAN WHO SACRIFICES OTHERS SO HE CAN RUN AWAY, TOO AFRAID TO RISK HIS OWN LIFE!
I'M FROM THE TAKE-MIKAZUCHI FAMILIA!!
SU (LIFT)
GA (GRAB)
DA (DASH)
...THANK YOU.

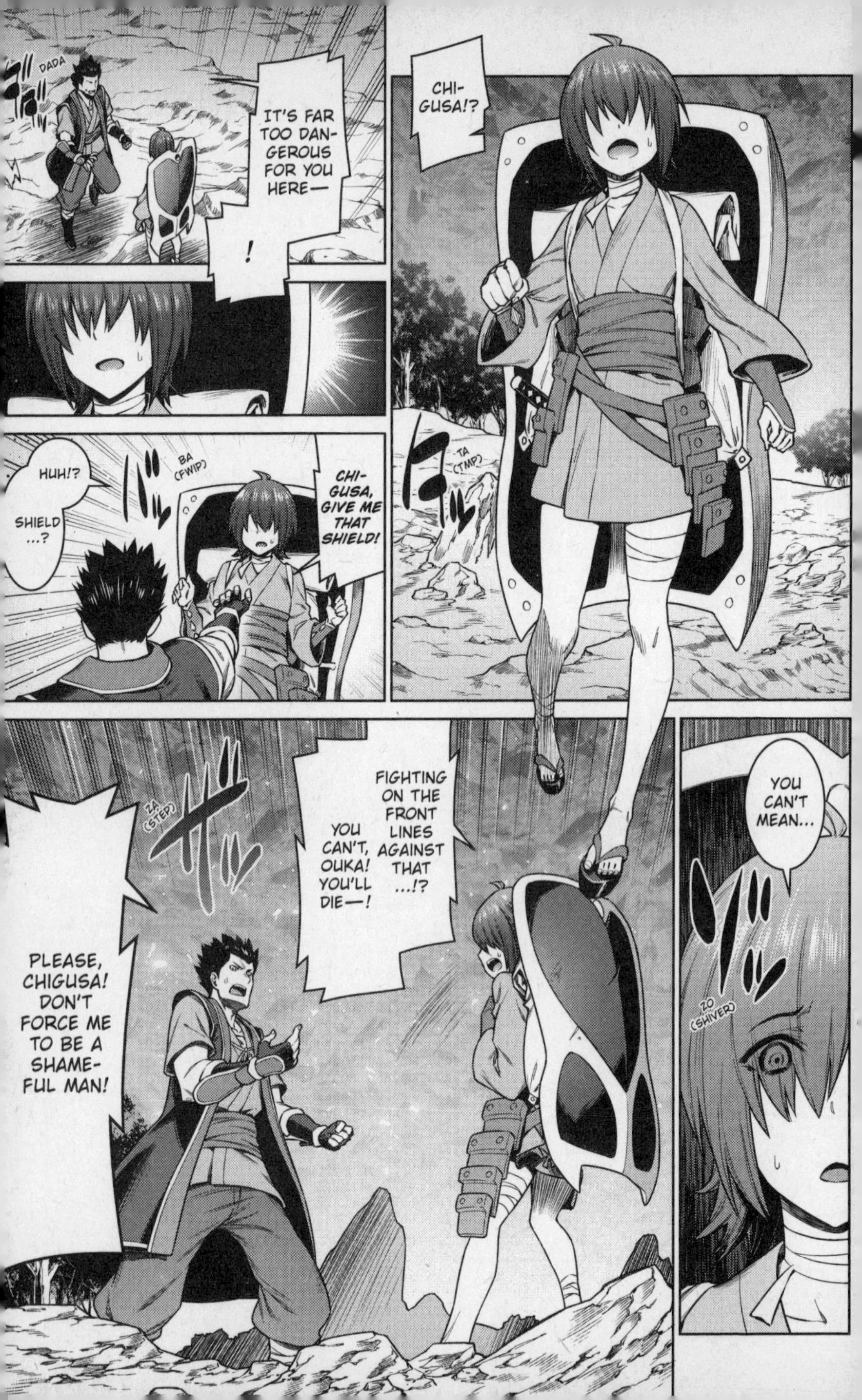
CHI-GUSA!?
TA (TMP)
DADA
IT'S FAR TOO DAN-GEROUS FOR YOU HERE—
!
CHI-GUSA, GIVE ME THAT SHIELD!
BA (FWIP)
HUH!?
SHIELD ...?
YOU CAN'T MEAN...
ZO (SHIVER)
FIGHTING ON THE FRONT LINES AGAINST THAT ...!?
YOU CAN'T, OUKA! YOU'LL DIE—!
ZA (STEP)
PLEASE, CHIGUSA! DON'T FORCE ME TO BE A SHAME-FUL MAN!

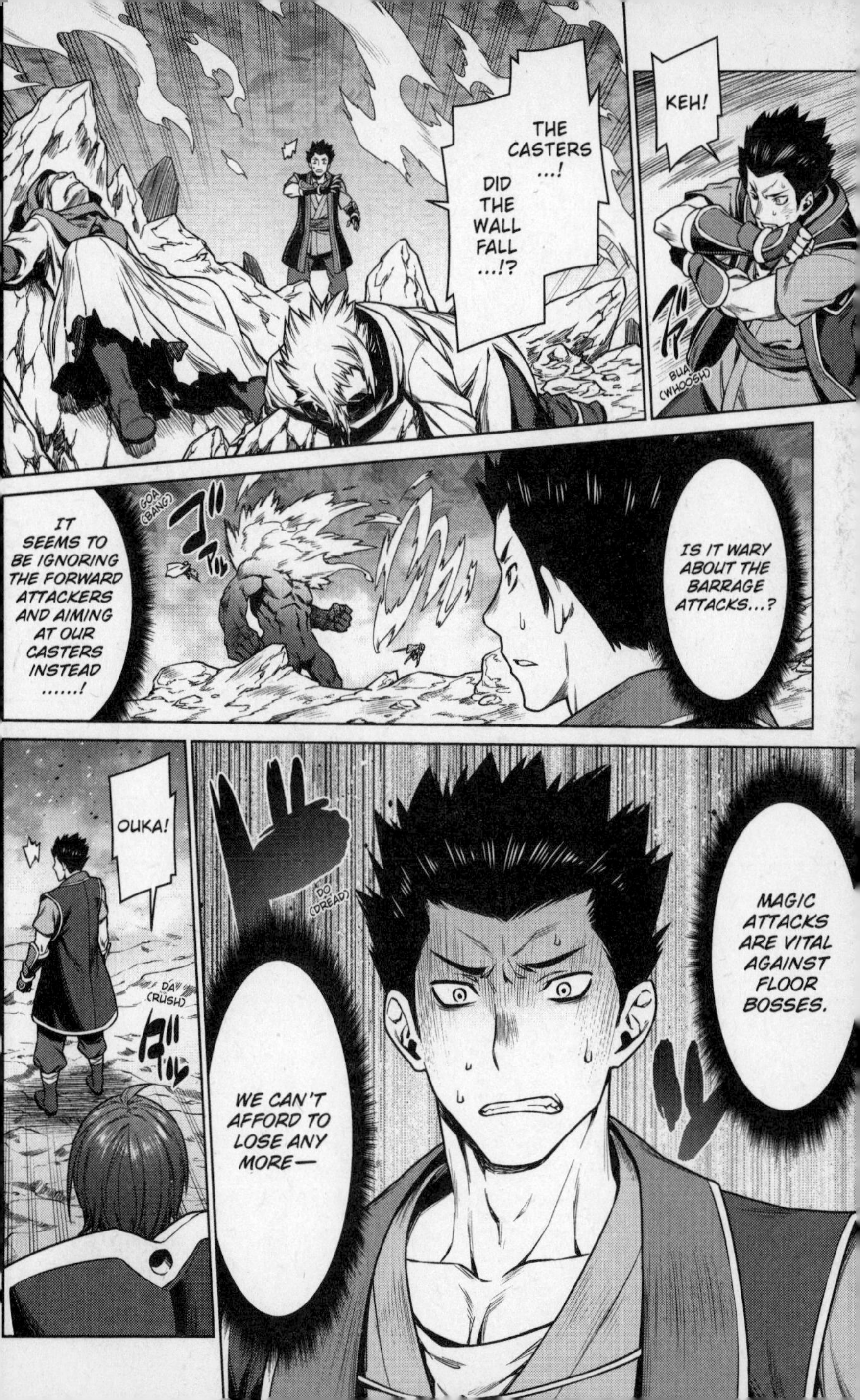
KEH!
BUA (WHOOSH)
THE CASTERS ...!
DID THE WALL FALL ...!?
IS IT WARY ABOUT THE BARRAGE ATTACKS...?
GOA (BANG)
IT SEEMS TO BE IGNORING THE FORWARD ATTACKERS AND AIMING AT OUR CASTERS INSTEAD ......!
MAGIC ATTACKS ARE VITAL AGAINST FLOOR BOSSES.
DO (DREAD)
WE CAN'T AFFORD TO LOSE ANY MORE—
OUKA!
DA (RUSH)

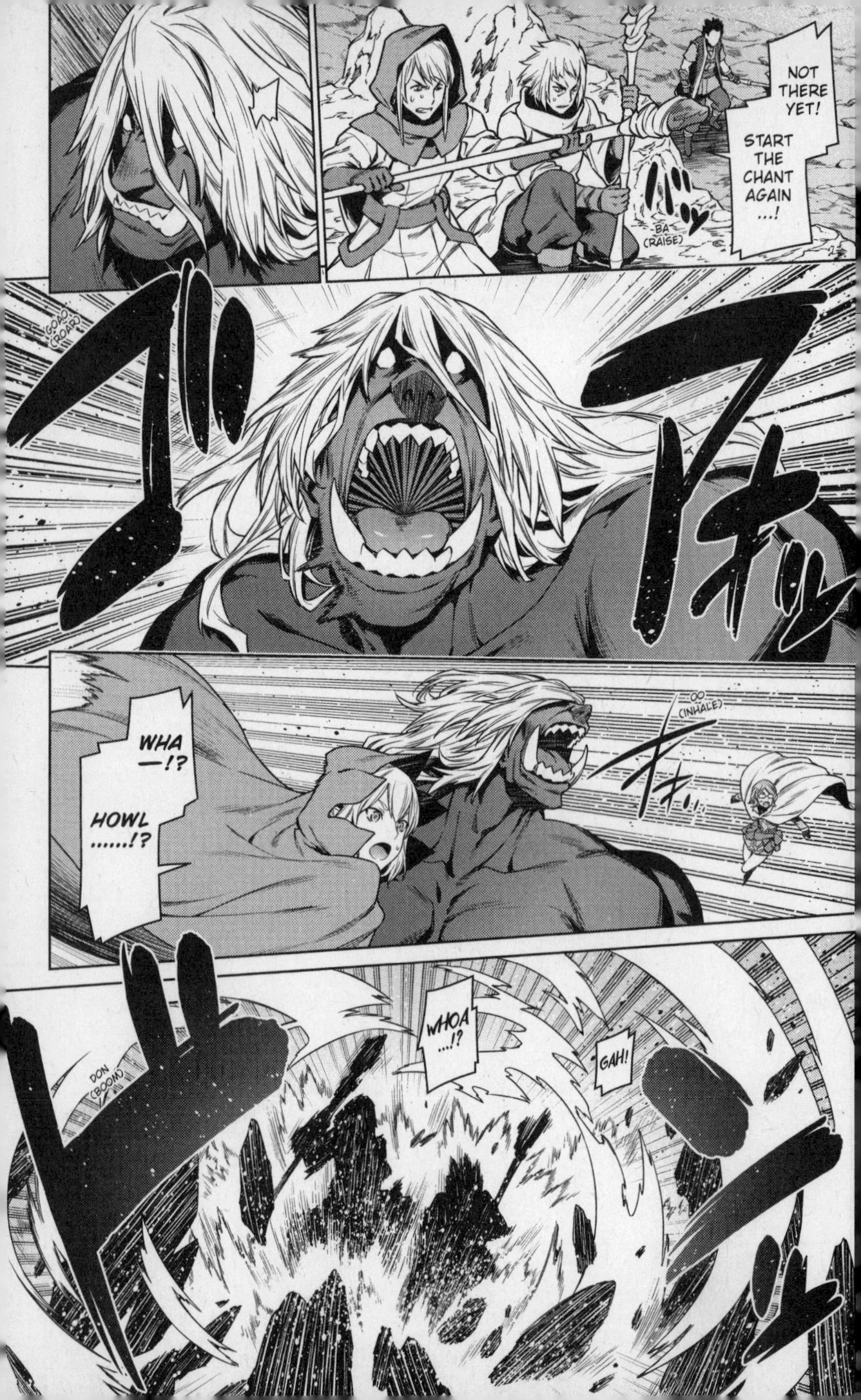
NOT THERE YET!
START THE CHANT AGAIN ...!
BA (RAISE)
GOAO (ROAR)
OO (INHALE)
WHA—!?
HOWL ......!?
GAH!
WHOA ...!?
DON (BOOM)

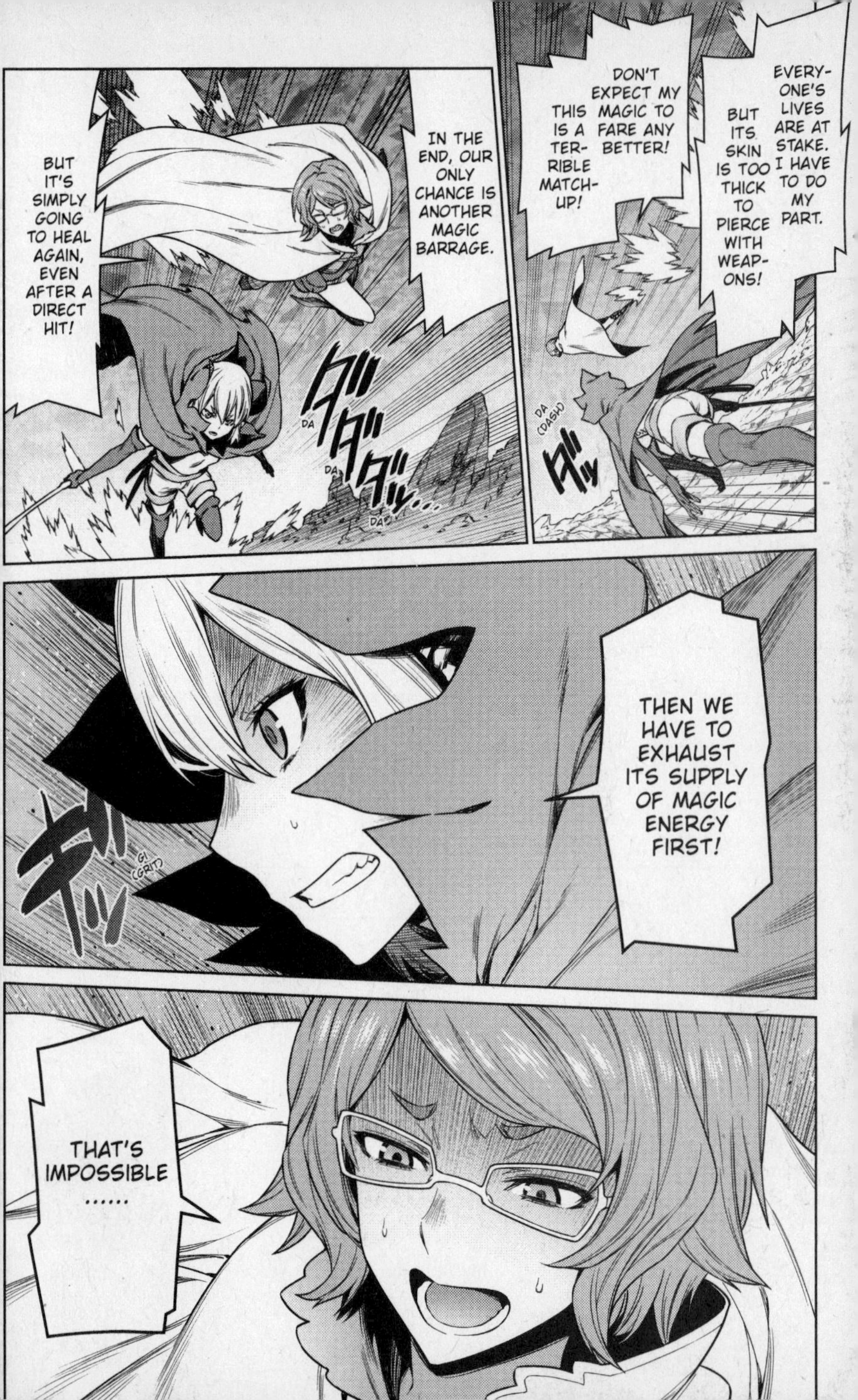
EVERYONE'S LIVES ARE AT STAKE. I HAVE TO DO MY PART.
BUT ITS SKIN IS TOO THICK TO PIERCE WITH WEAPONS!
DON'T EXPECT MY MAGIC TO FARE ANY BETTER!
THIS IS A TERRIBLE MATCH-UP!
DA (DASH)
IN THE END, OUR ONLY CHANCE IS ANOTHER MAGIC BARRAGE.
BUT IT'S SIMPLY GOING TO HEAL AGAIN, EVEN AFTER A DIRECT HIT!
DA DA DA
THEN WE HAVE TO EXHAUST ITS SUPPLY OF MAGIC ENERGY FIRST!
GI (GRIT)
THAT'S IMPOSSIBLE ......

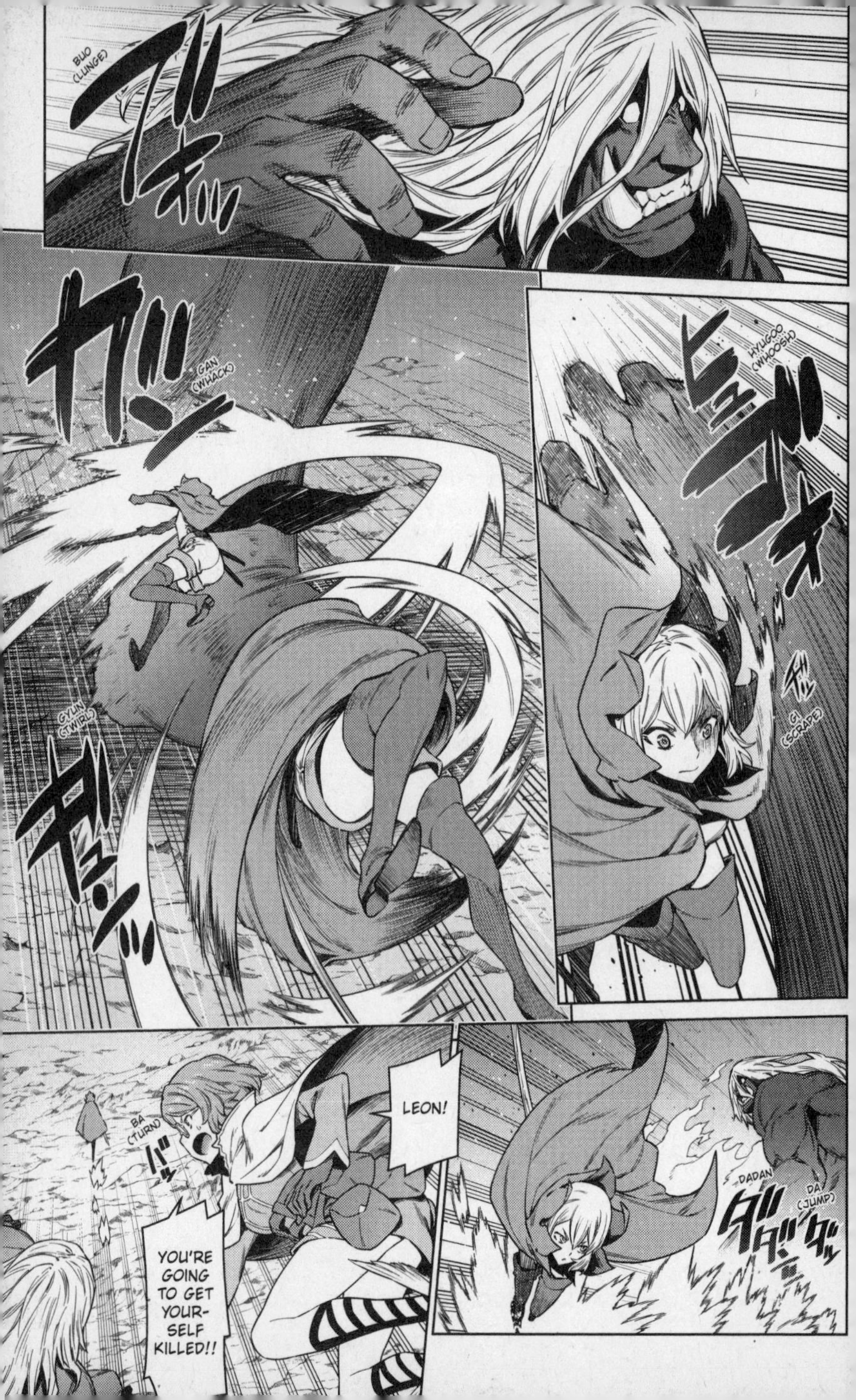
BUO (LUNGE)
HYUGOO (WHOOSH)
GI (SCRAPE)
GAN (WHACK)
GYUN (TWIRL)
DADAN
DA (JUMP)
LEON!
BA (TURN)
YOU'RE GOING TO GET YOURSELF KILLED!!

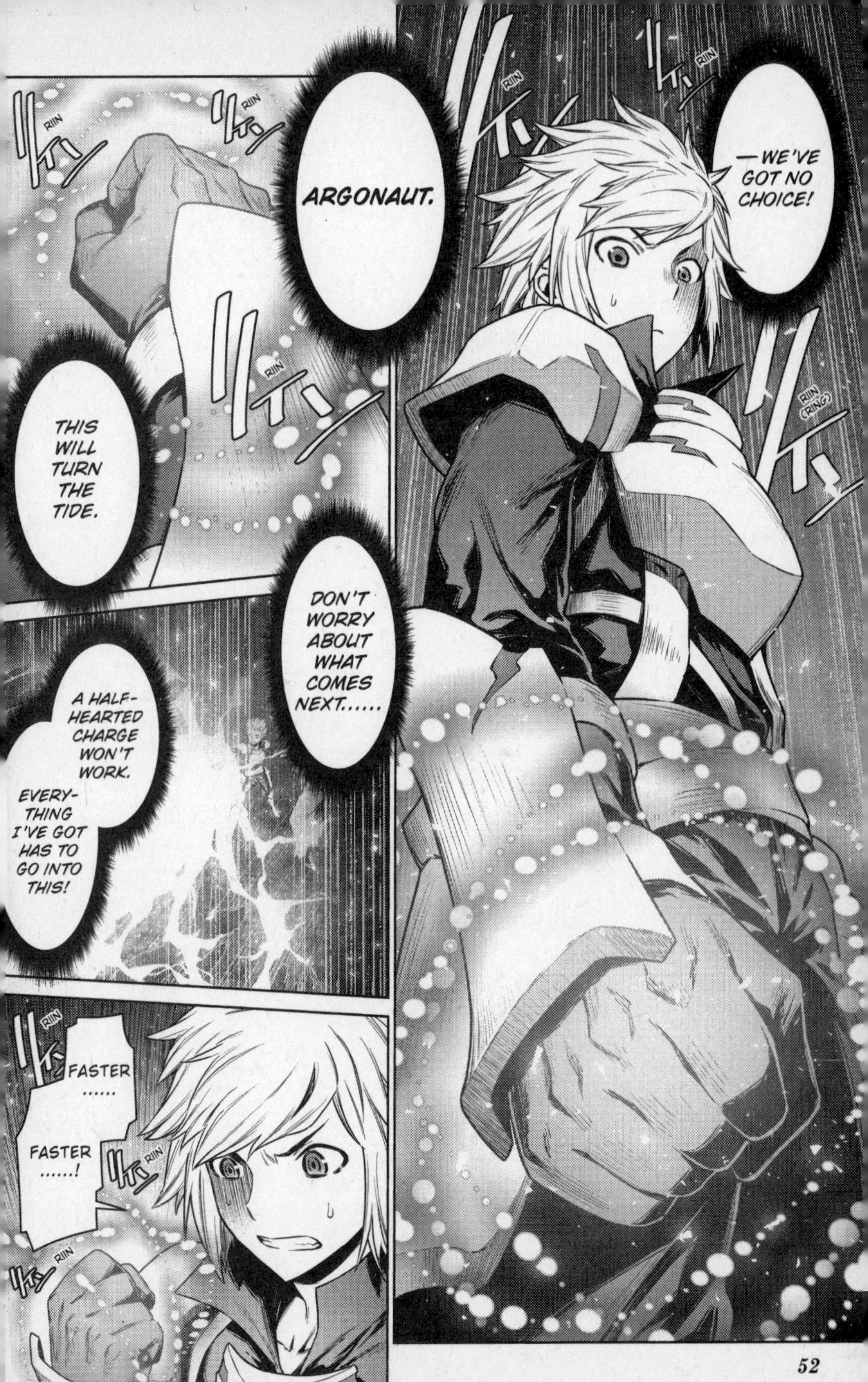
RIIN
RIIN
—WE'VE GOT NO CHOICE!
RIIN (RING)
DON'T WORRY ABOUT WHAT COMES NEXT......
ARGONAUT.
RIIN
RIIN
RIIN
THIS WILL TURN THE TIDE.
A HALF-HEARTED CHARGE WON'T WORK.
EVERY-THING I'VE GOT HAS TO GO INTO THIS!
RIIN
FASTER ......
FASTER ......!
RIIN
RIIN

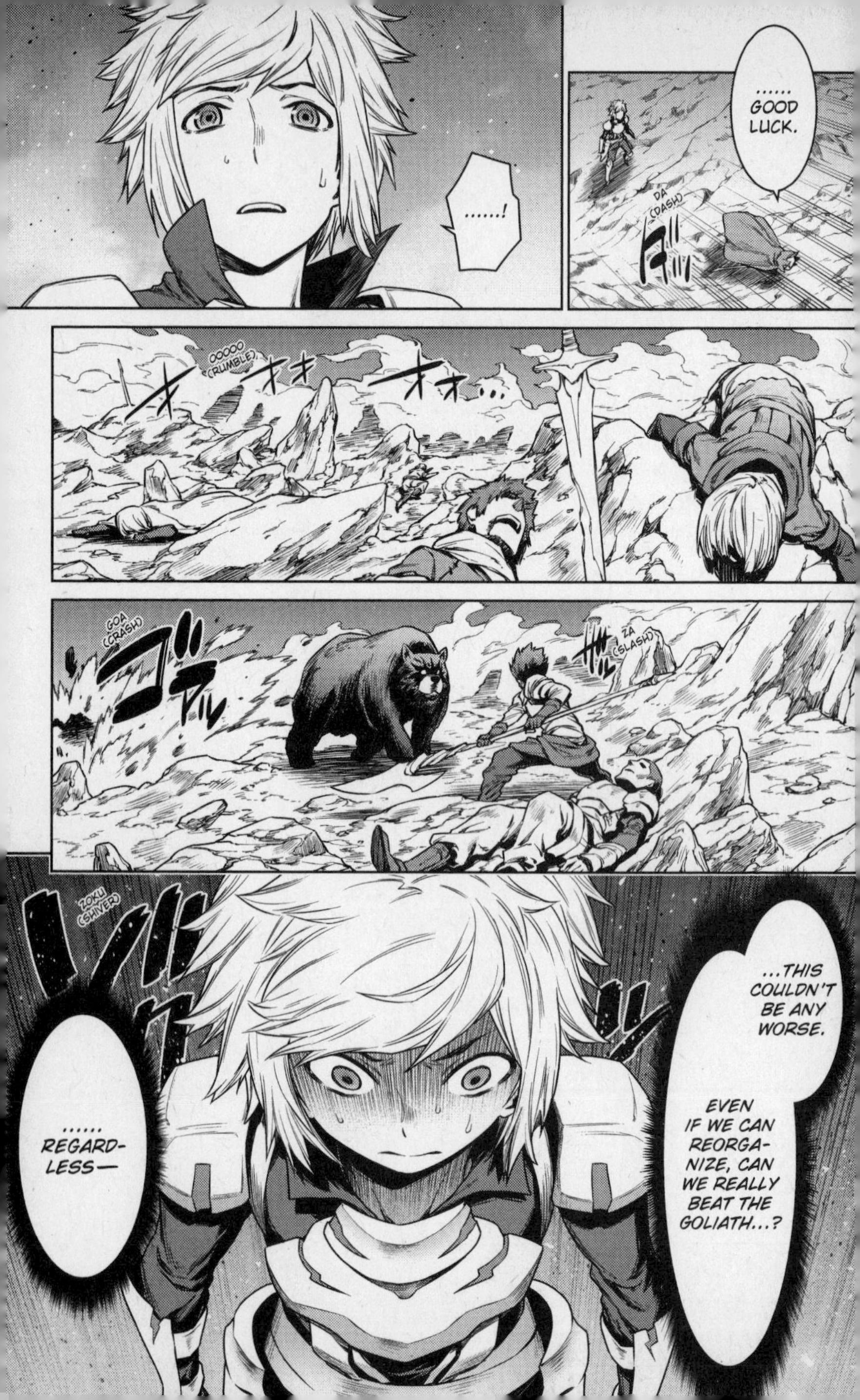
......GOOD LUCK.
DA (DASH)
......!
OOOOO (RUMBLE)
ZA (SLASH)
GOA (CRASH)
ZOKU (SHIVER)
...THIS COULDN'T BE ANY WORSE.
EVEN IF WE CAN REORGANIZE, CAN WE REALLY BEAT THE GOLIATH...?
......REGARDLESS—

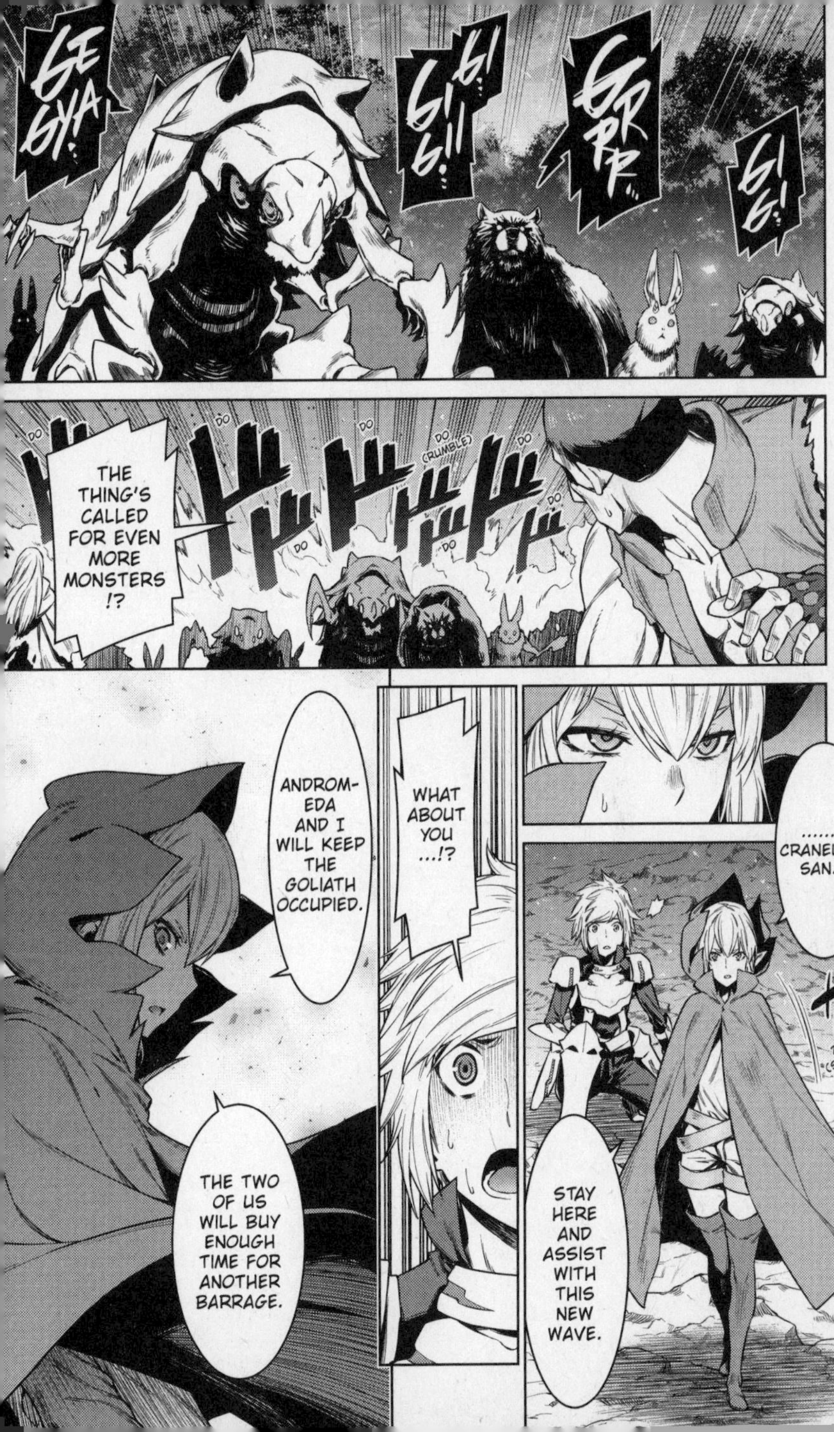
GIGI...
GRRR...
GIGI... GIGI...
GEGYA...
DO (RUMBLE)
THE THING'S CALLED FOR EVEN MORE MONSTERS !?
......CRANELL-SAN.
ZA (STEP)
STAY HERE AND ASSIST WITH THIS NEW WAVE.
WHAT ABOUT YOU ...!?
ANDROMEDA AND I WILL KEEP THE GOLIATH OCCUPIED.
THE TWO OF US WILL BUY ENOUGH TIME FOR ANOTHER BARRAGE.

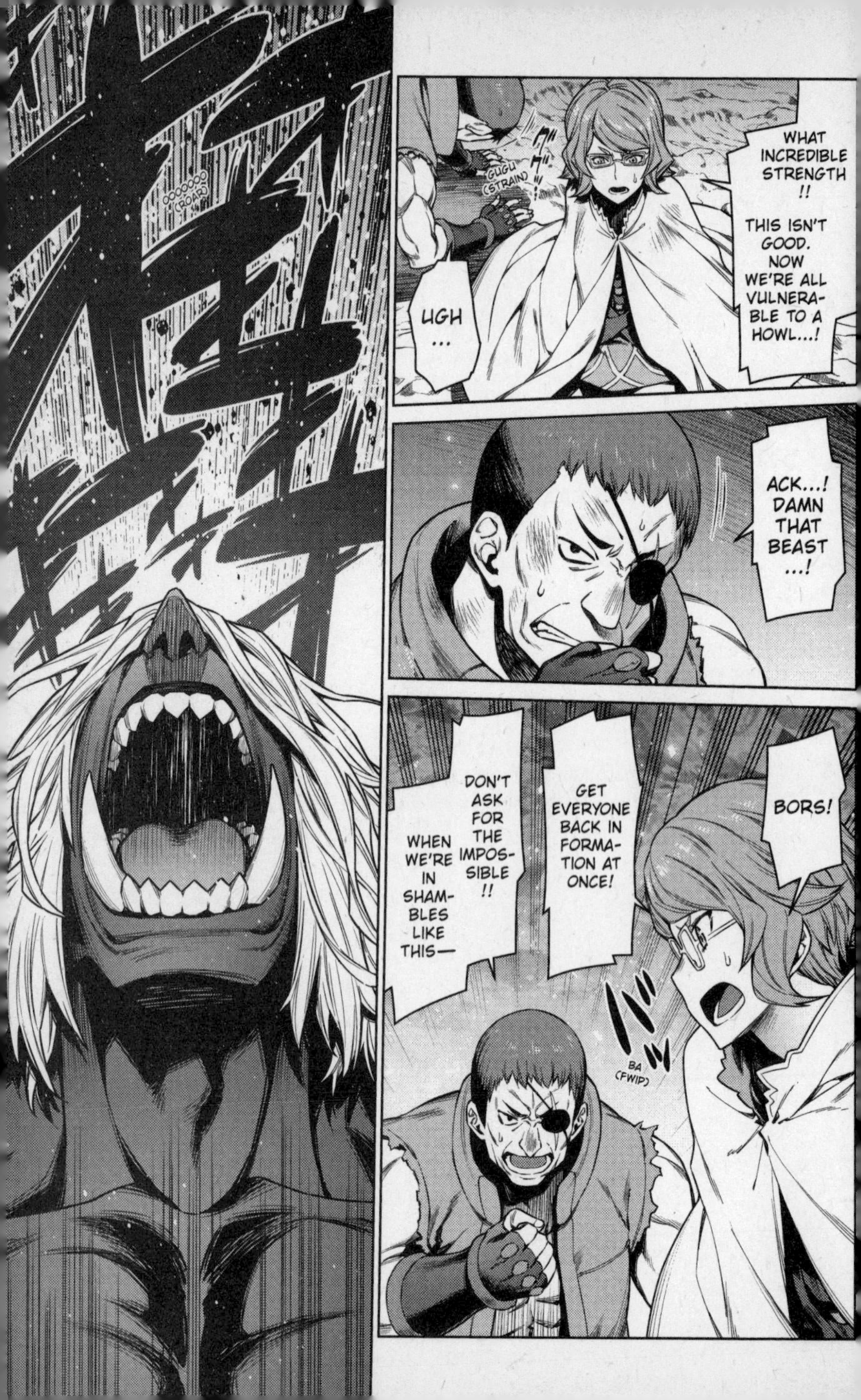
WHAT INCREDIBLE STRENGTH!!
THIS ISN'T GOOD. NOW WE'RE ALL VULNERA-BLE TO A HOWL...!
GUGU (STRAIN)
UGH...
ACK...! DAMN THAT BEAST...!
BORS!
GET EVERYONE BACK IN FORMA-TION AT ONCE!
DON'T ASK FOR THE IMPOS-SIBLE!!
WHEN WE'RE IN SHAM-BLES LIKE THIS—
BA (FWIP)
OOOOOOO (ROAR)

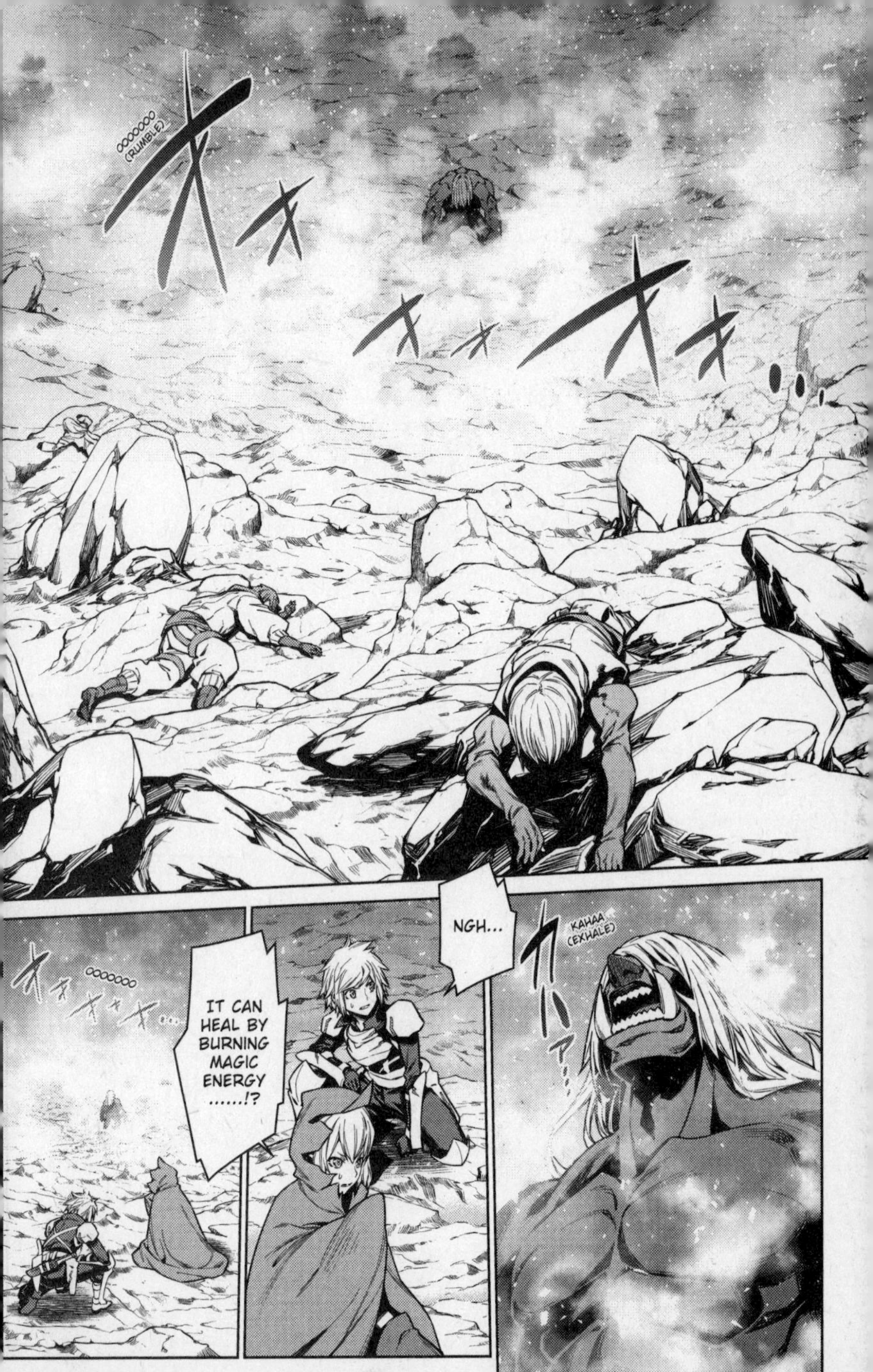
OOOOOOO (RUMBLE)
KAHAA (EXHALE)
NGH...
IT CAN HEAL BY BURNING MAGIC ENERGY ......!?
OOOOOOO

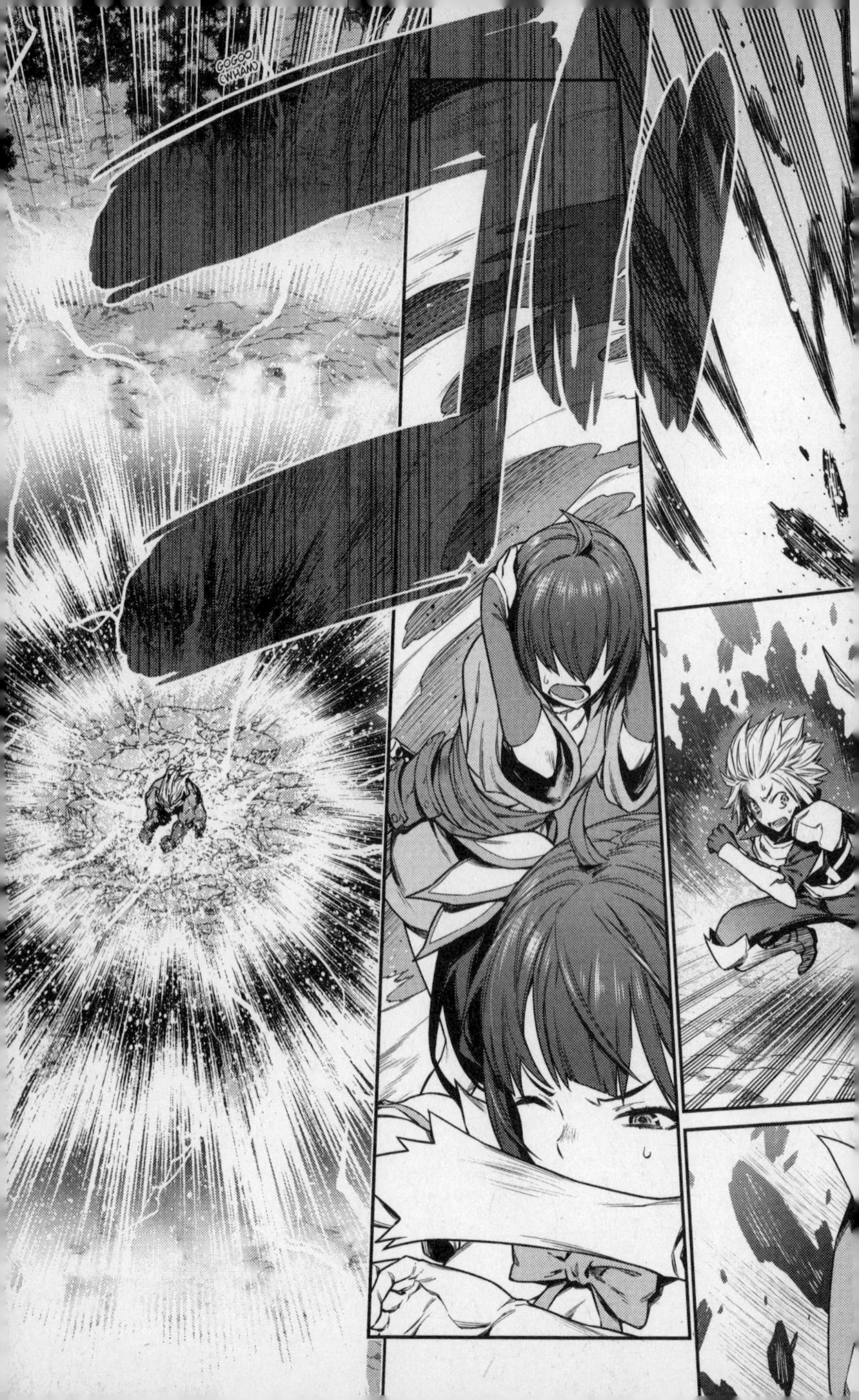
GOGOO!
(WHAM)

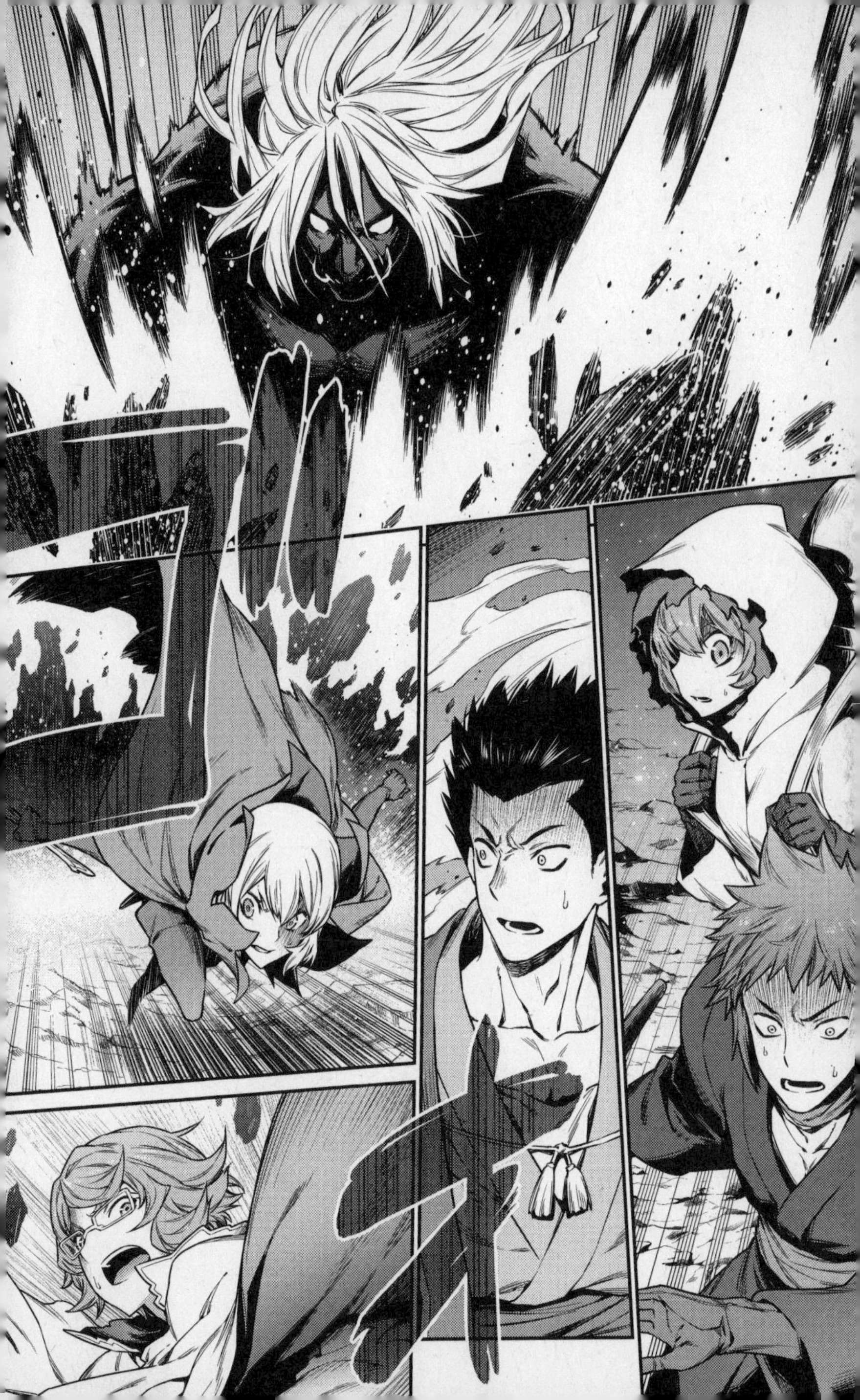

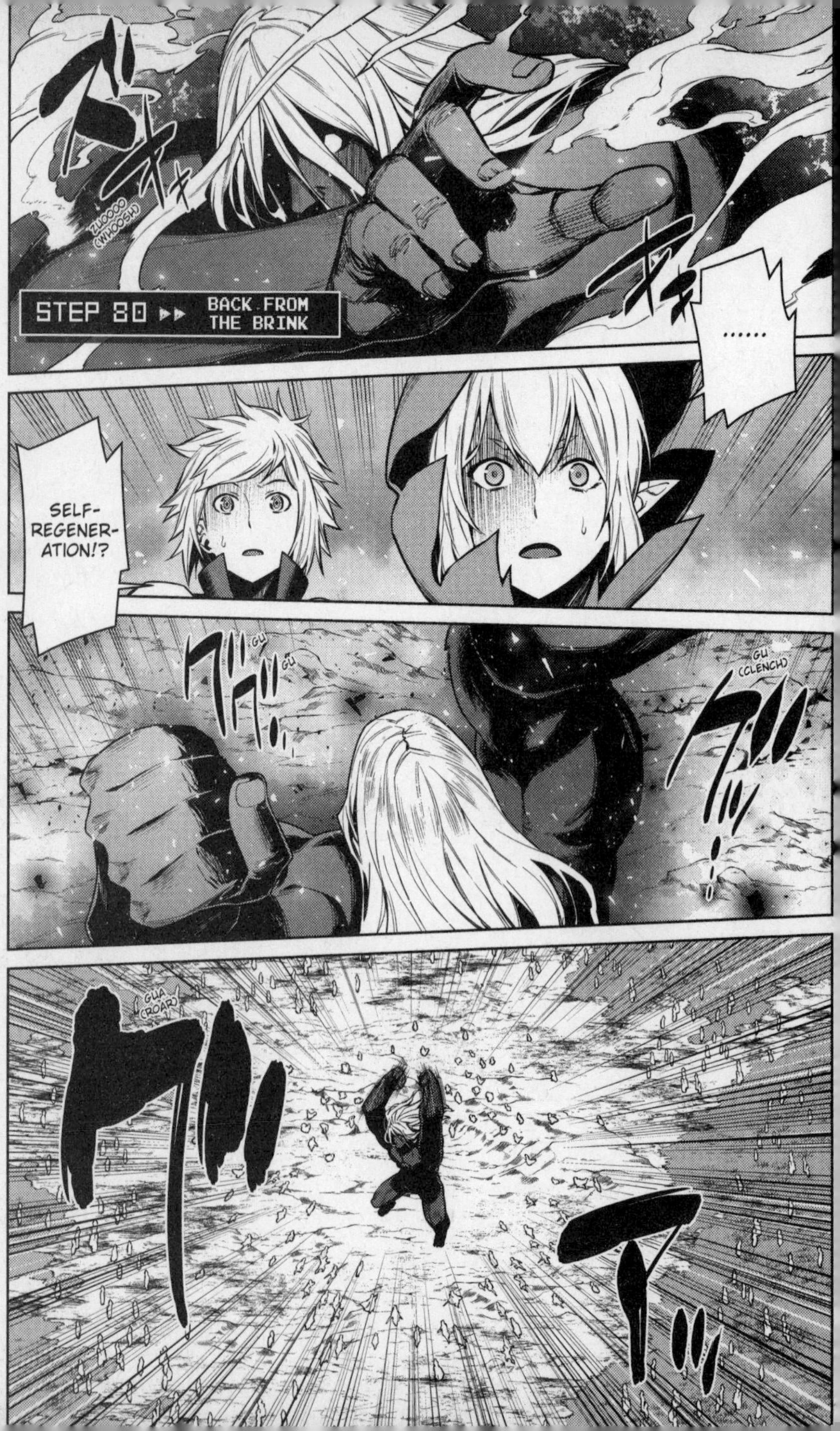
......
ZUOOOO (WHOOSH)
STEP 80 ▸▸ BACK FROM THE BRINK
SELF-REGENERATION!?
GU (CLENCH)
GU GU
GUA (ROAR)

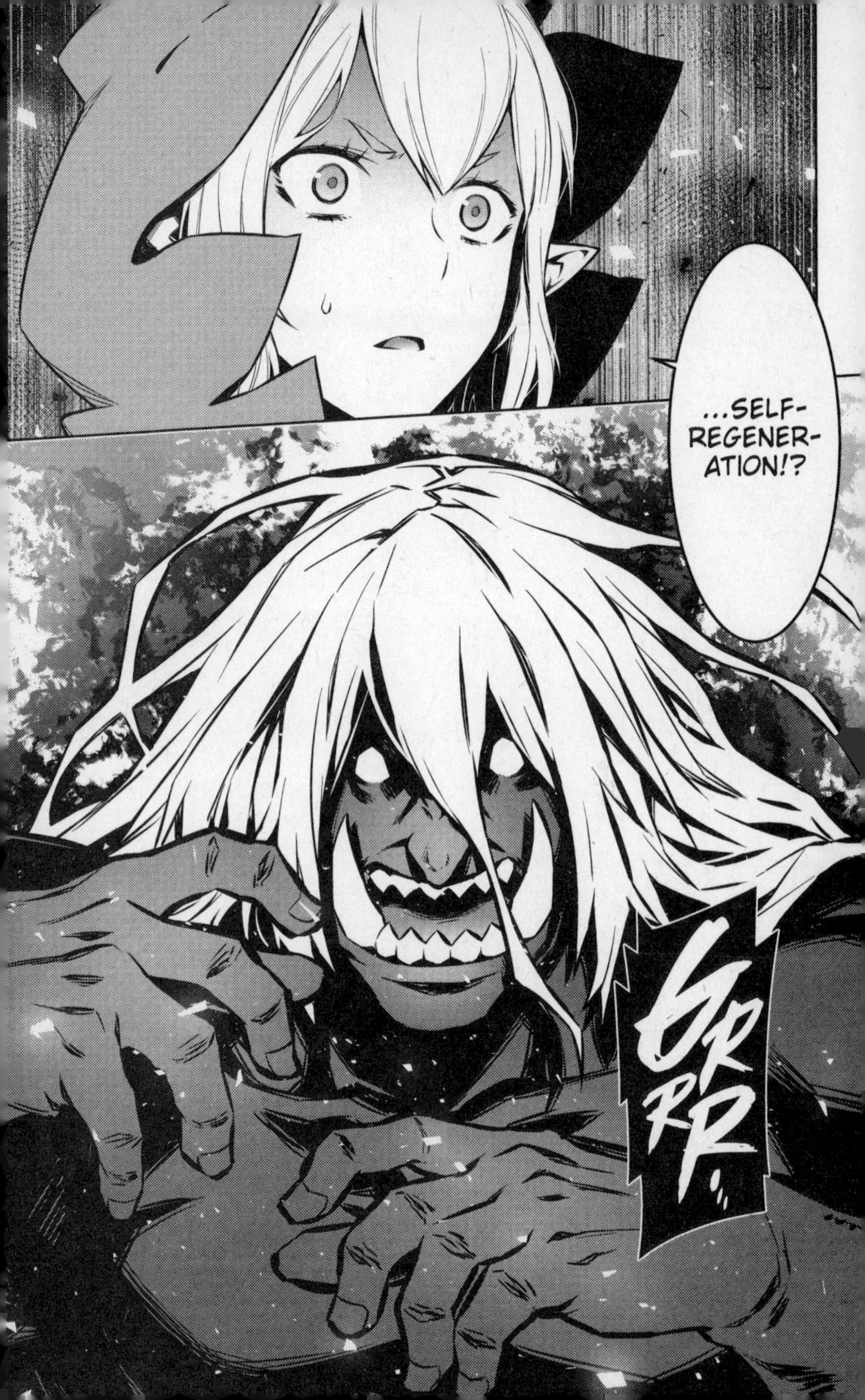
...SELF-REGENERATION!?
GRRR...

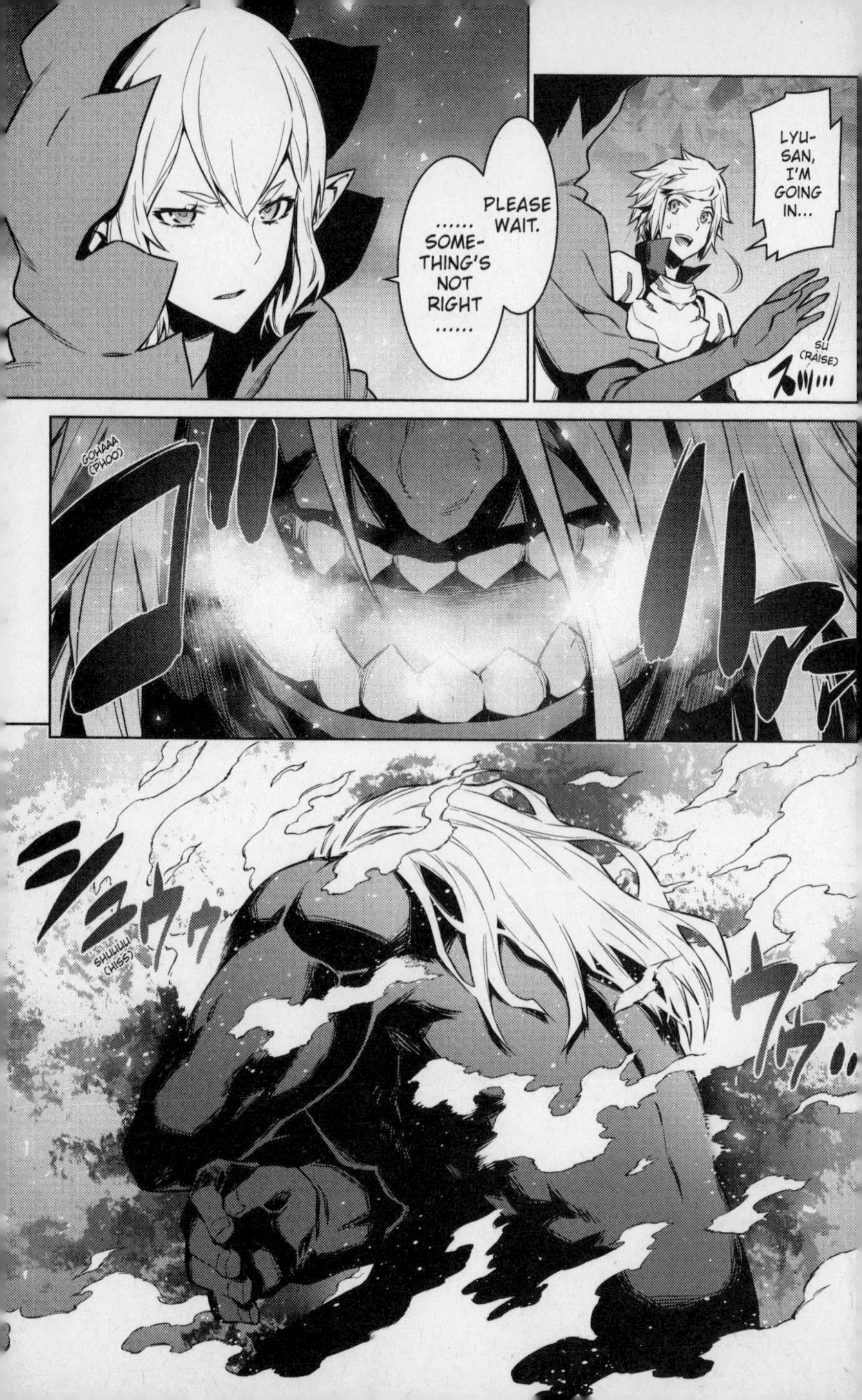
LYU-SAN, I'M GOING IN...
SU (RAISE)
PLEASE WAIT.
...... SOMETHING'S NOT RIGHT ......
GOHAAA (PHOO)
SHUUUU (HISS)

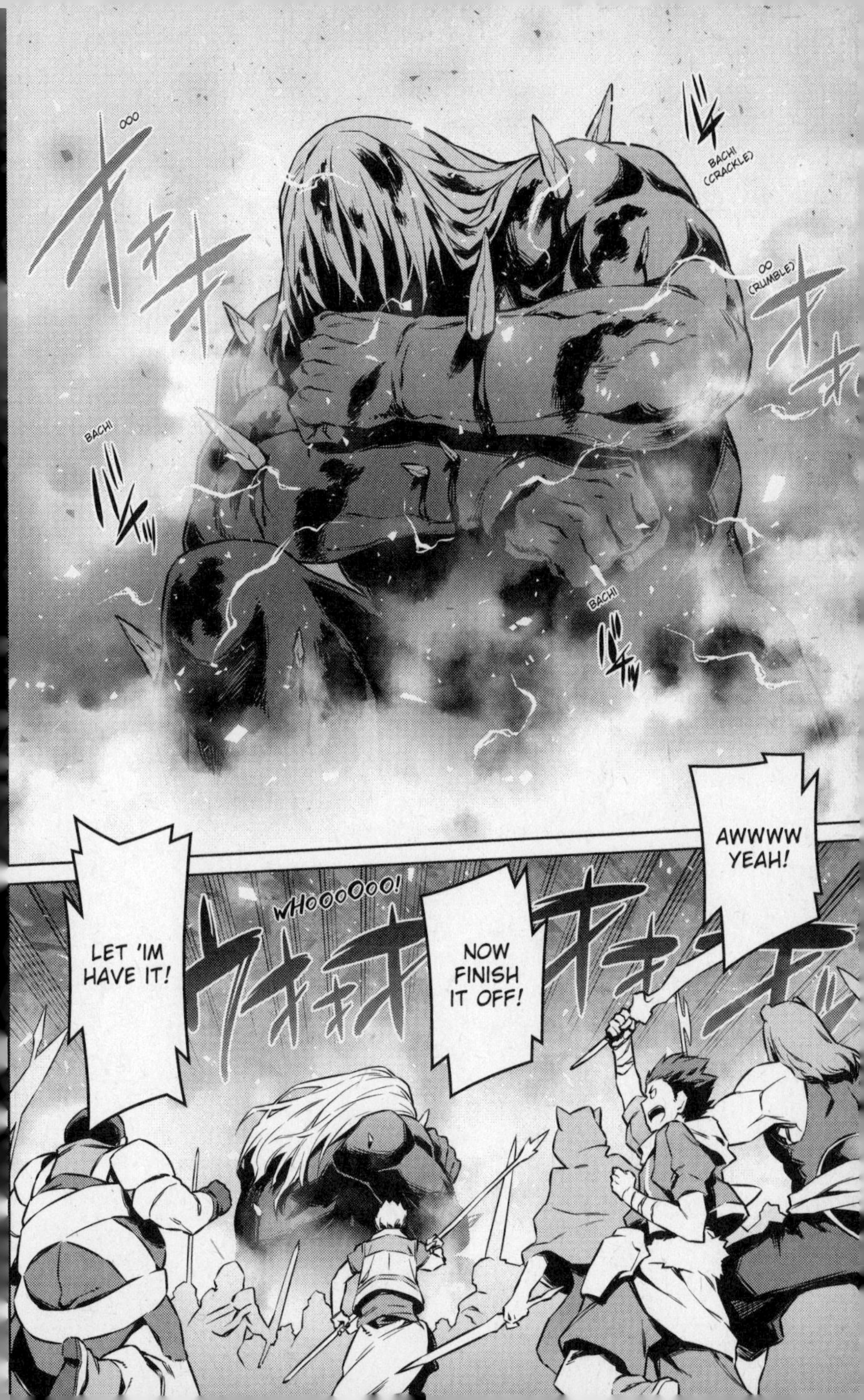
BACHI (CRACKLE)
OOO
OO (RUMBLE)
BACHI
BACHI
AWWWW YEAH!
NOW FINISH IT OFF!
WHOOOOOO!
LET 'IM HAVE IT!

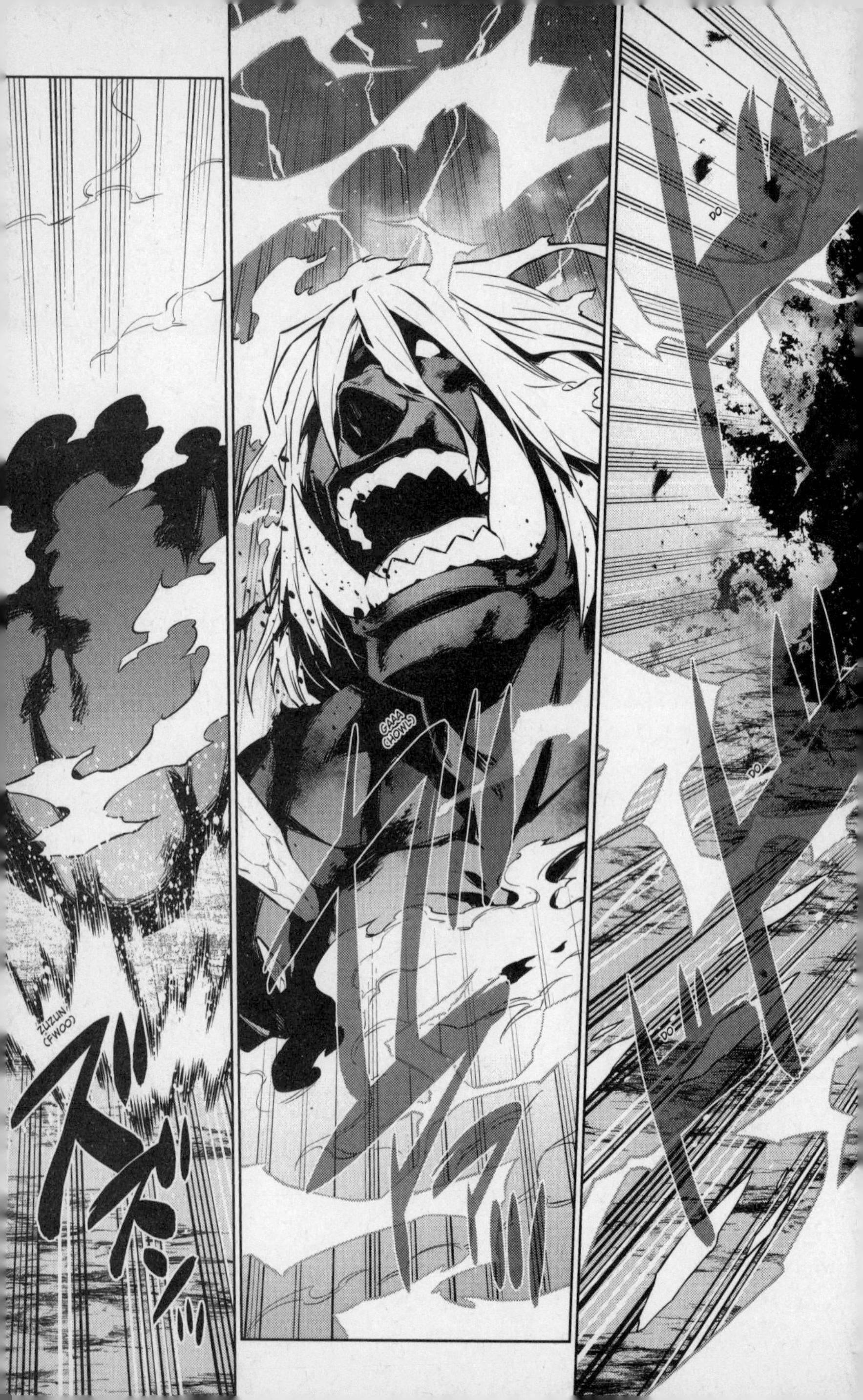
DO
DO
DO
GAAA (HOWL)
ZUZUN (FWOO)

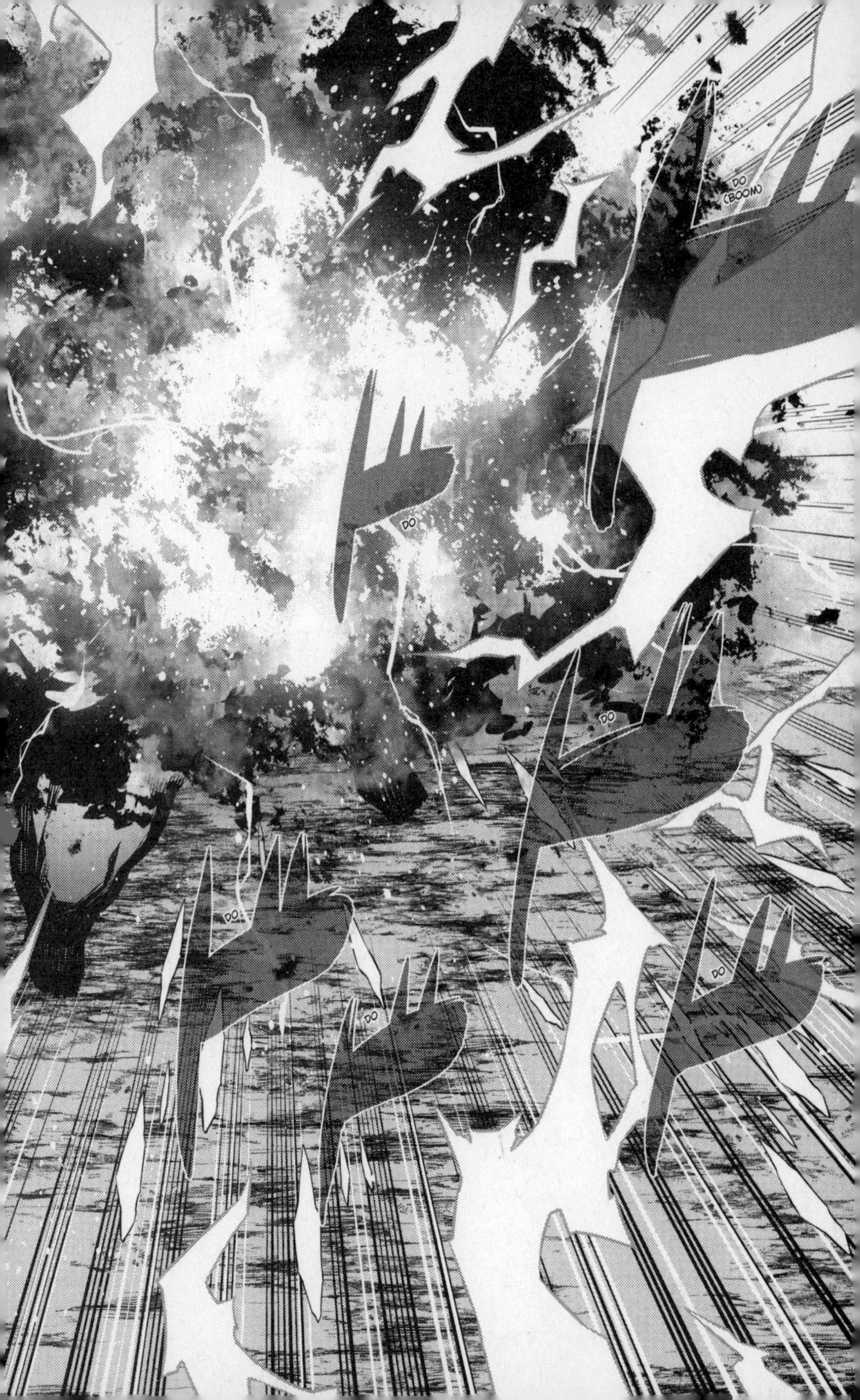
DO (BOOM)
DO
DO
DO
DO
DO

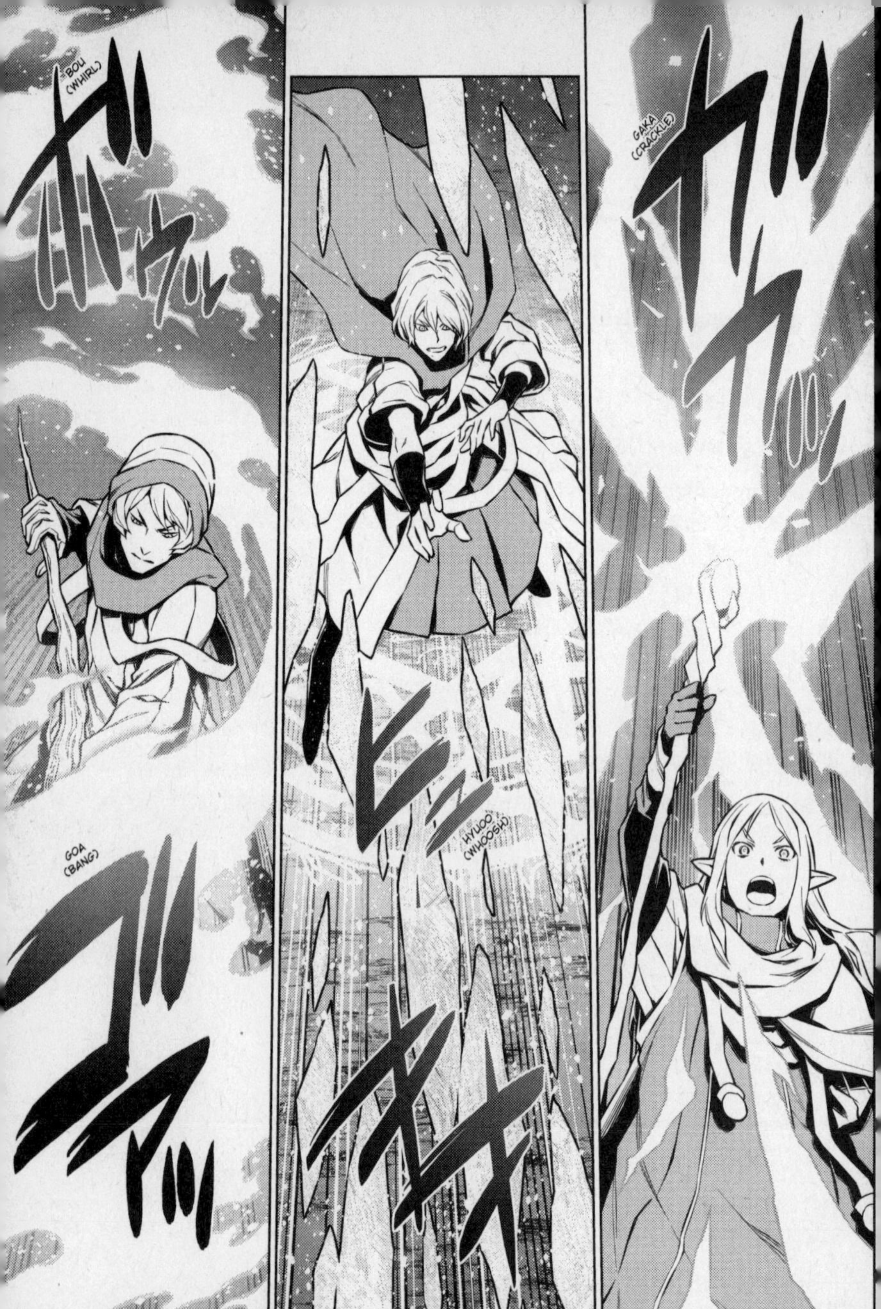
GAKA (CRACKLE)
HYUOO (WHOOSH)
BOU (WHIRL)
GOA (BANG)

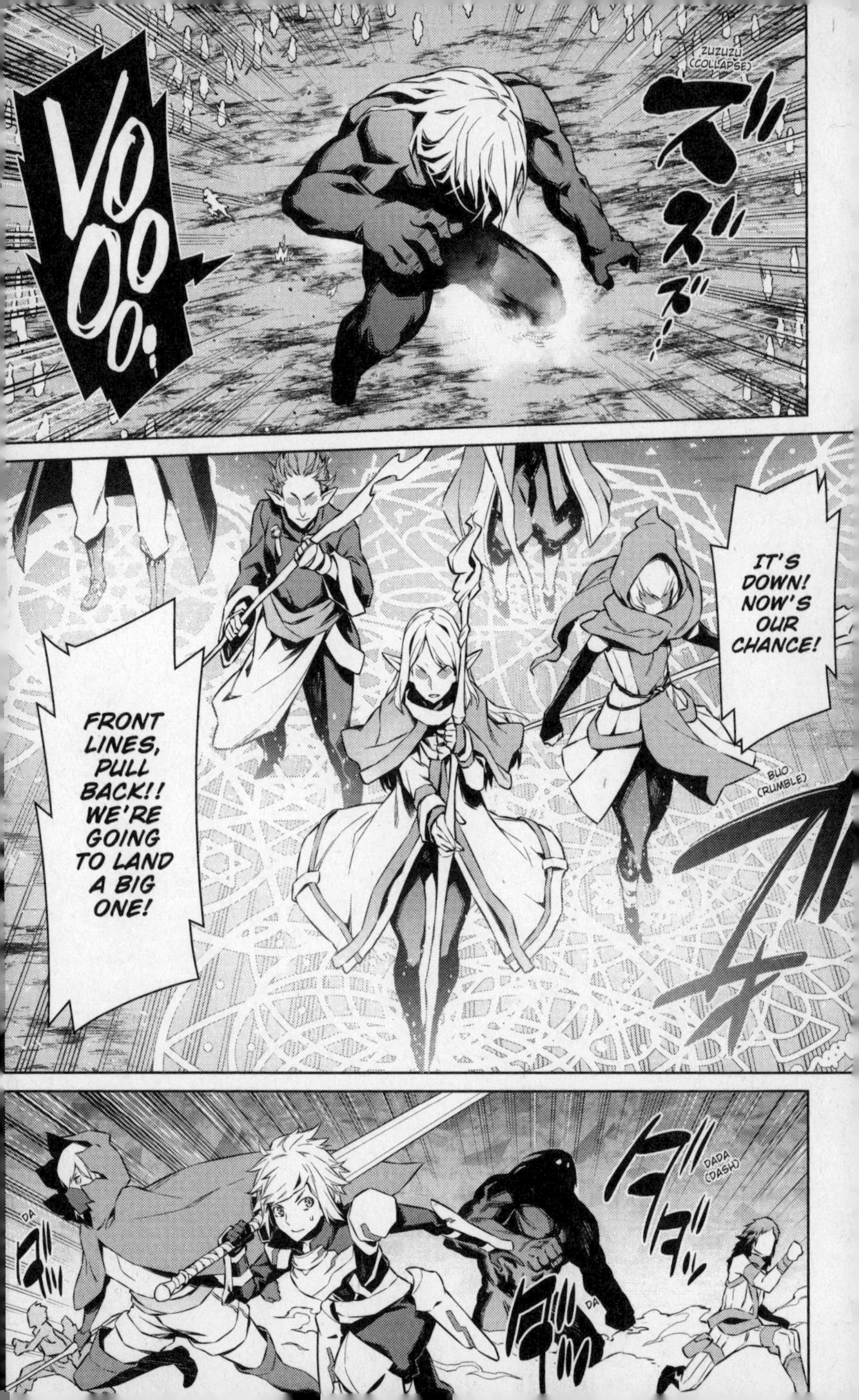

ZUZUZU (COLLAPSE)
VOOOO!!
IT'S DOWN! NOW'S OUR CHANCE!
BUO (RUMBLE)
FRONT LINES, PULL BACK!! WE'RE GOING TO LAND A BIG ONE!
DADA (DASH)
DA
DA

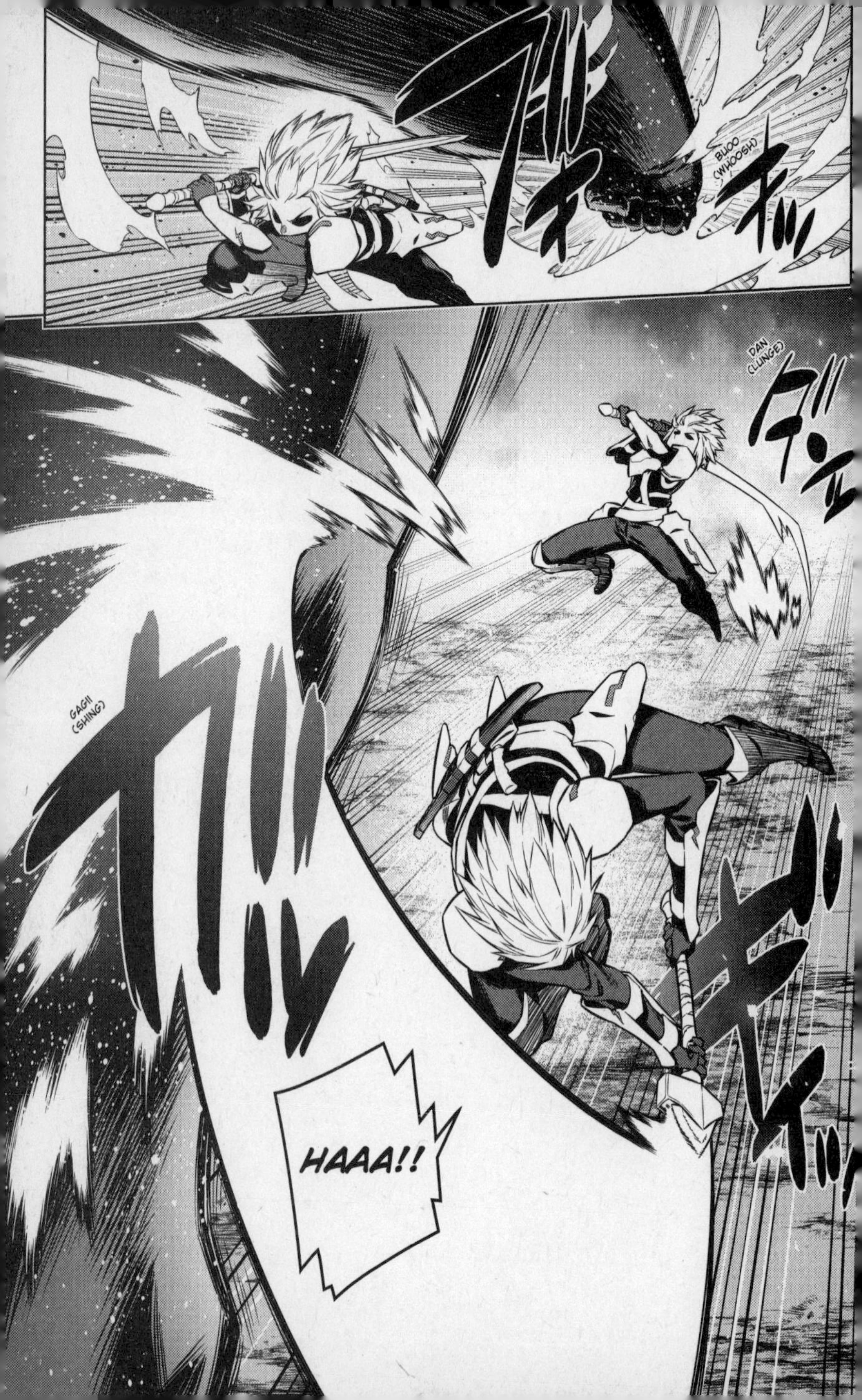
BUOO (WHOOSH)
DAN (LUNGE)
HAAA!!
GAGII (SHING)

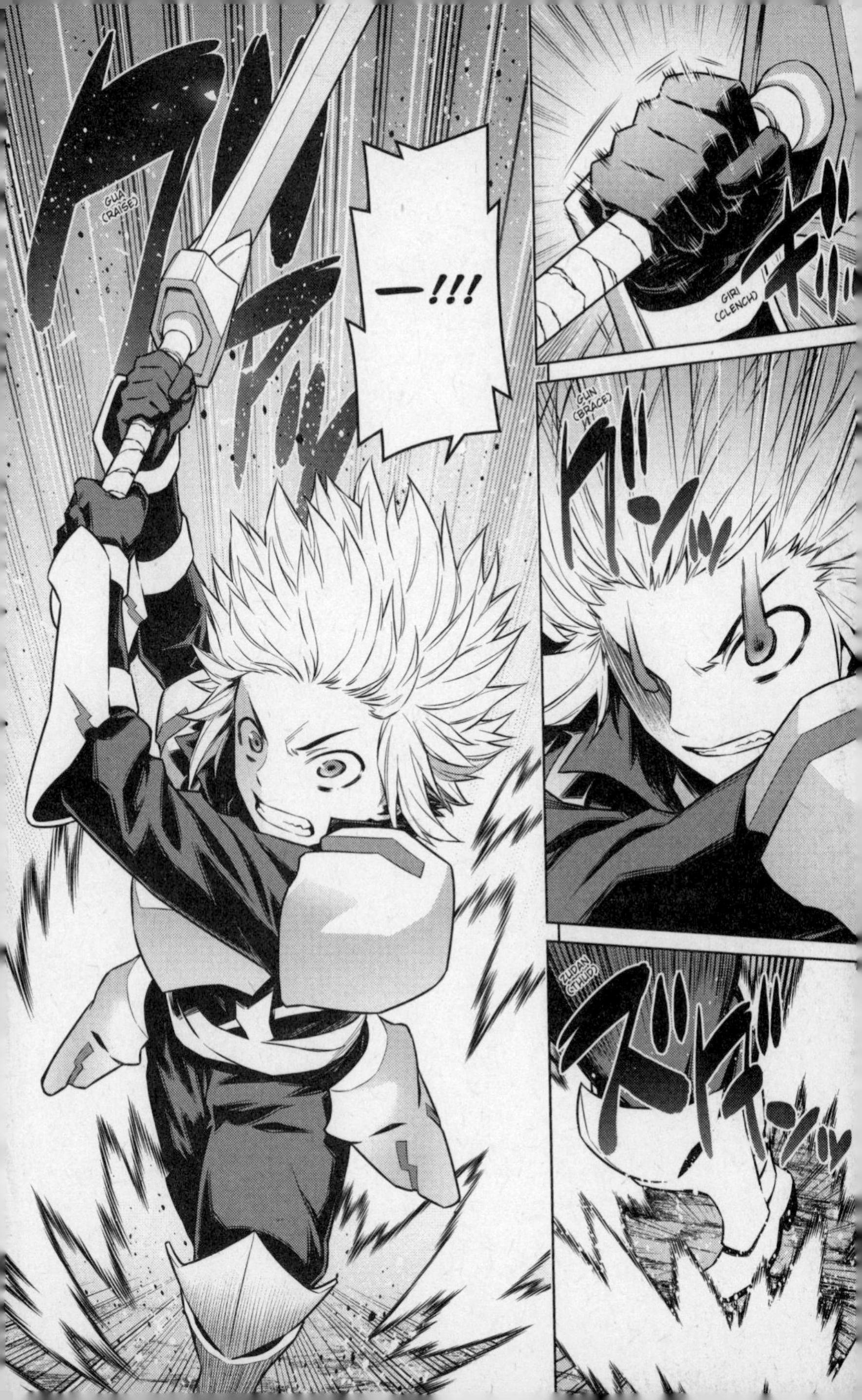
GIRI (CLENCH)
GUN (BRACE)
ZUDAN (THUD)
—!!!
GUA (RAISE)

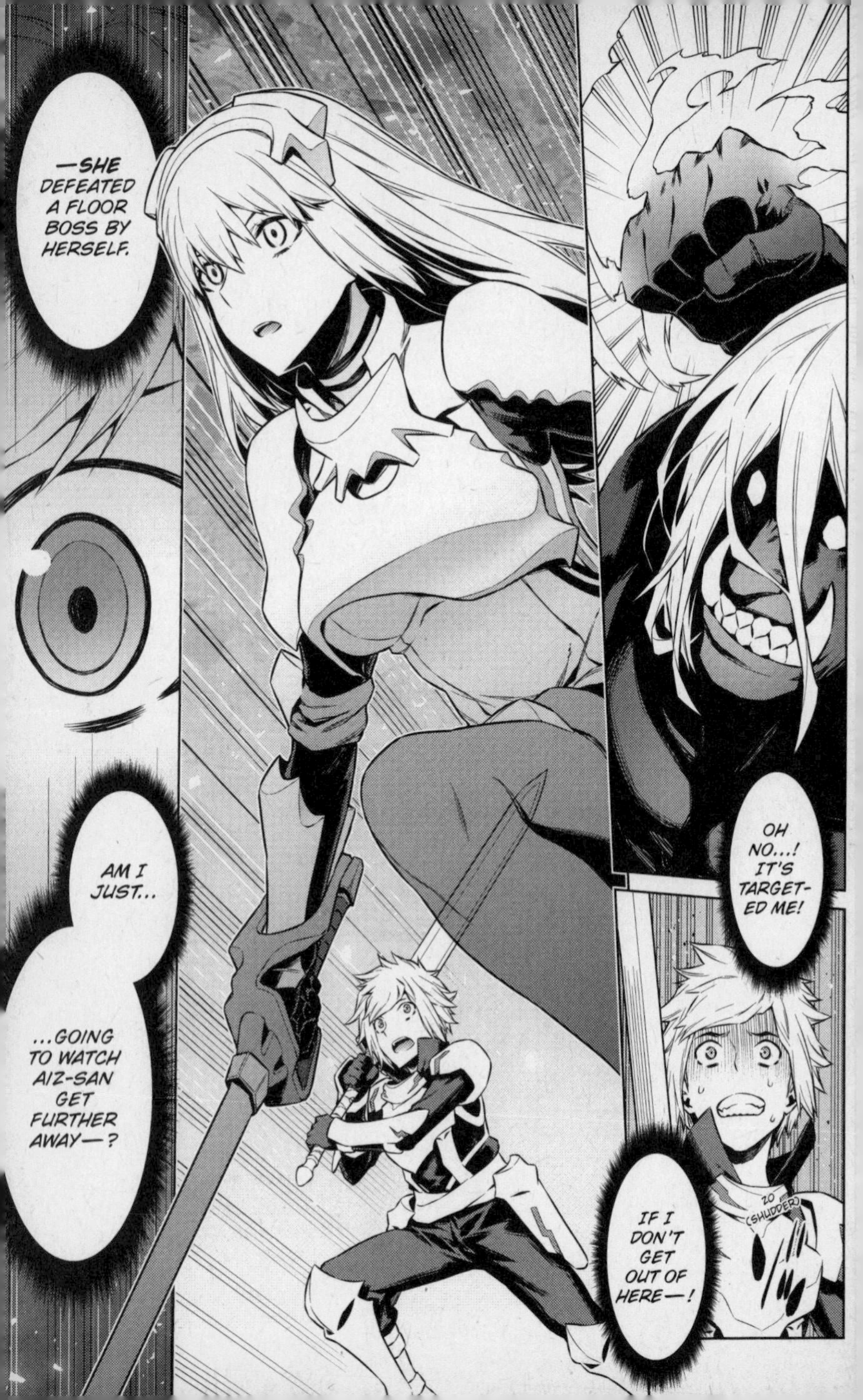
OH NO...! IT'S TARGET-ED ME!
ZO (SHUDDER)
IF I DON'T GET OUT OF HERE—!
—SHE DEFEATED A FLOOR BOSS BY HERSELF.
AM I JUST...
...GOING TO WATCH AIZ-SAN GET FURTHER AWAY—?

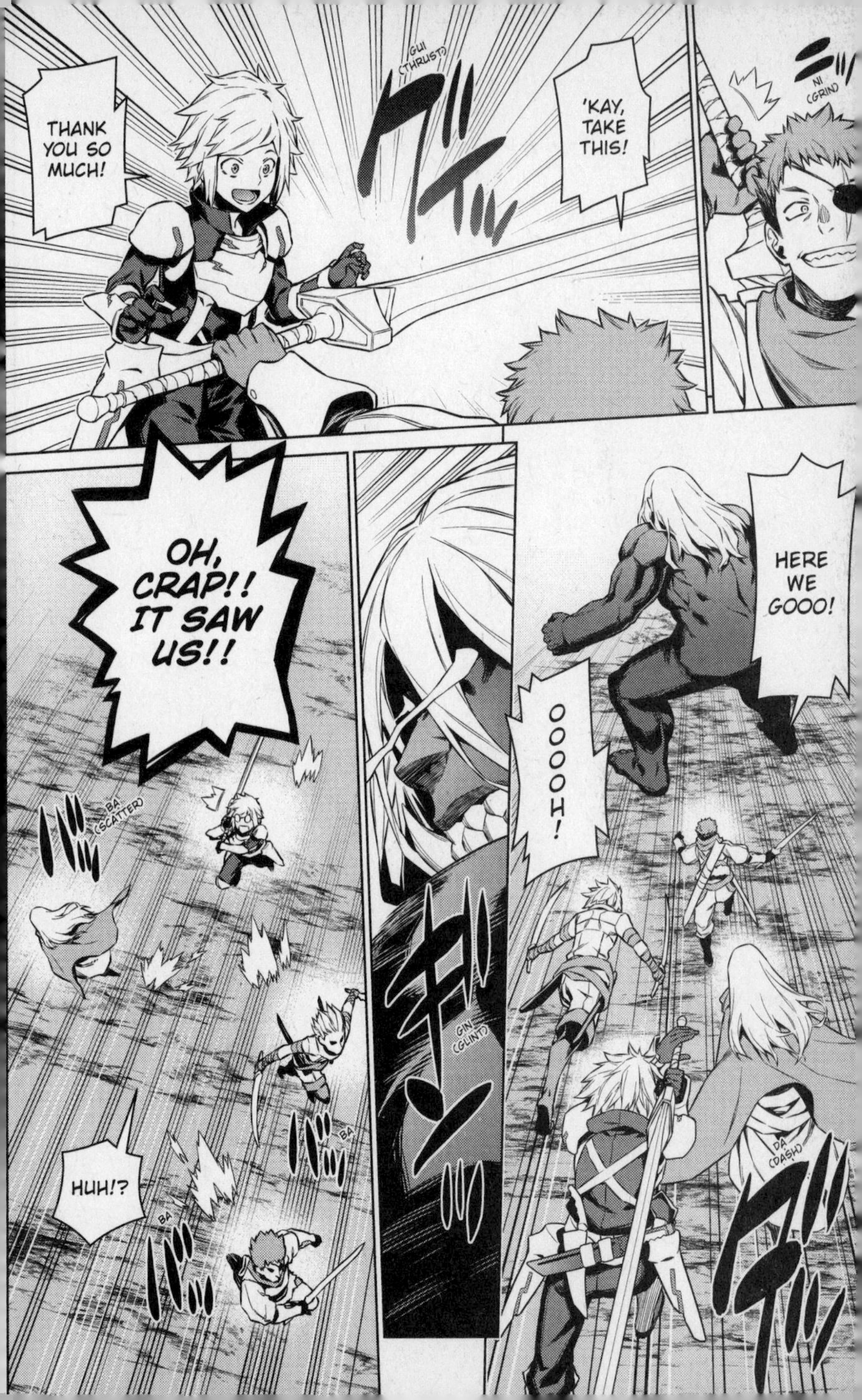
NI (GRIN)
'KAY, TAKE THIS!
GUI (THRUST)
THANK YOU SO MUCH!
HERE WE GOOO!
OOOOOH!
DA (DASH)
GIN (GLINT)
OH, CRAP!! IT SAW US!!
BA (SCATTER)
BA
HUH!?
BA

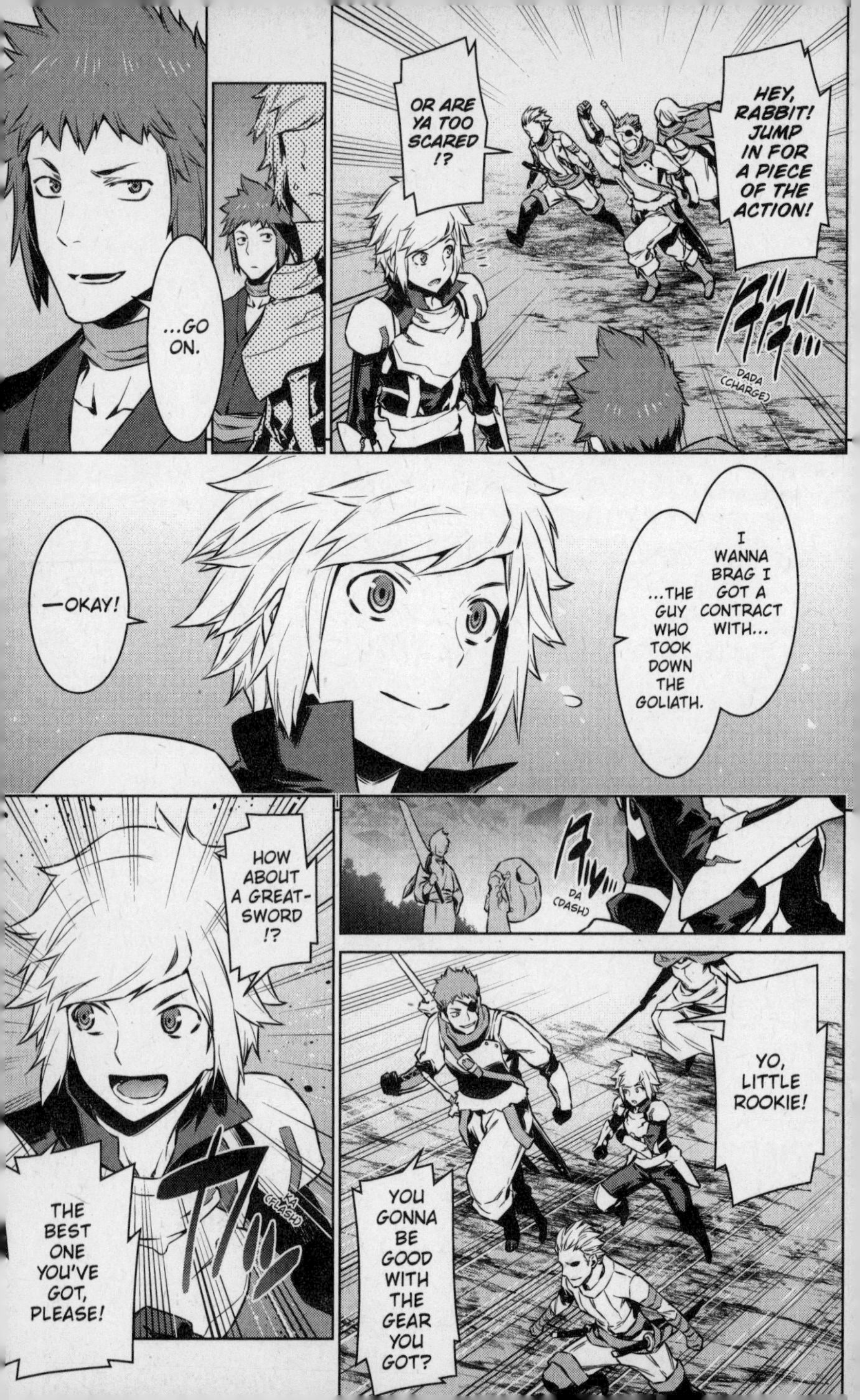
HEY, RABBIT! JUMP IN FOR A PIECE OF THE ACTION!
OR ARE YA TOO SCARED !?
DADA (CHARGE)
...GO ON.
I WANNA BRAG I GOT A CONTRACT WITH...
...THE GUY WHO TOOK DOWN THE GOLIATH.
—OKAY!
DA (DASH)
YO, LITTLE ROOKIE!
YOU GONNA BE GOOD WITH THE GEAR YOU GOT?
HOW ABOUT A GREAT-SWORD !?
KA (FLASH)
THE BEST ONE YOU'VE GOT, PLEASE!

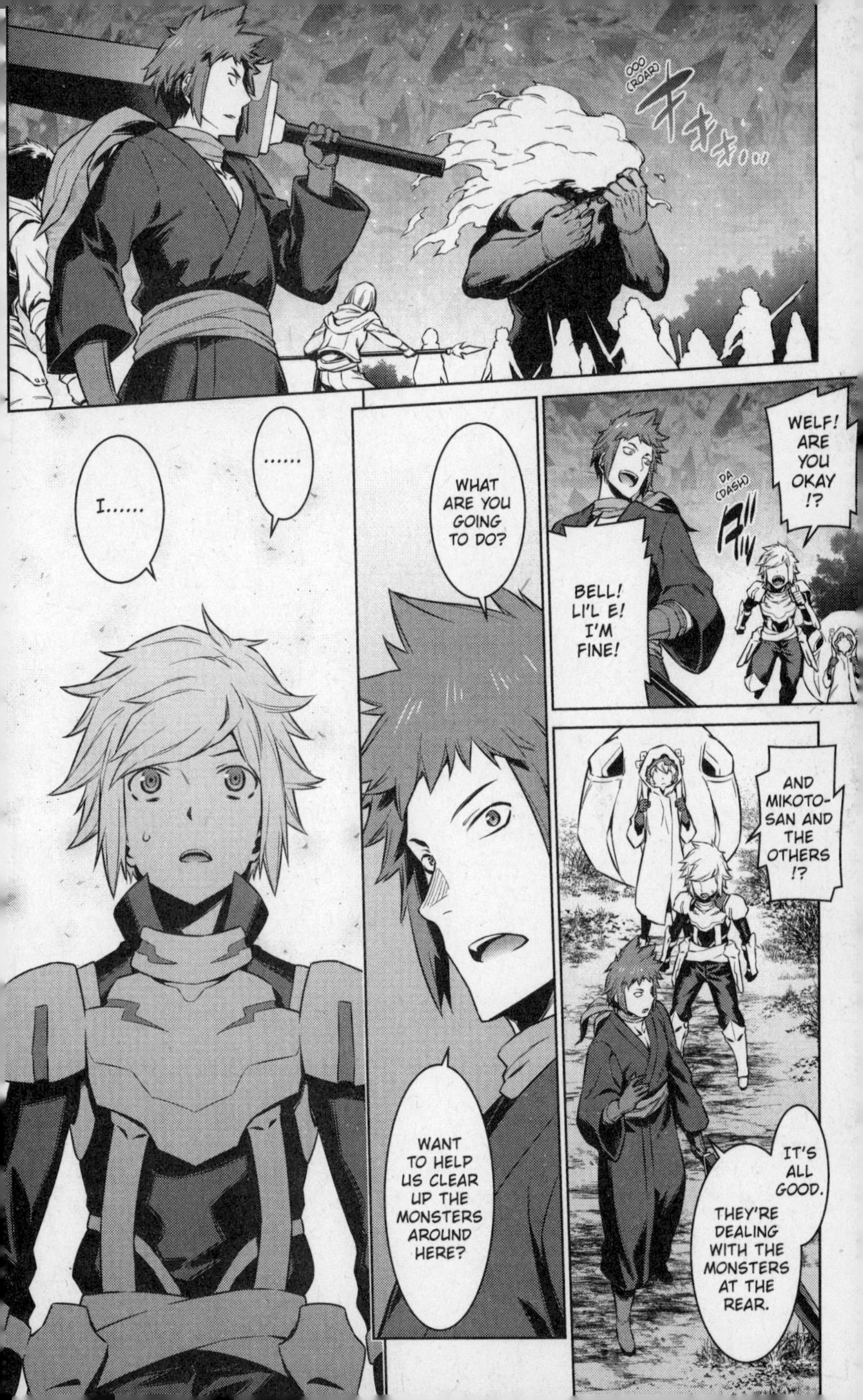
OOO (ROAR)
WELF! ARE YOU OKAY!?
DA (DASH)
BELL! LI'L E! I'M FINE!
AND MIKOTO-SAN AND THE OTHERS!?
IT'S ALL GOOD.
THEY'RE DEALING WITH THE MONSTERS AT THE REAR.
WHAT ARE YOU GOING TO DO?
WANT TO HELP US CLEAR UP THE MONSTERS AROUND HERE?
......
I......

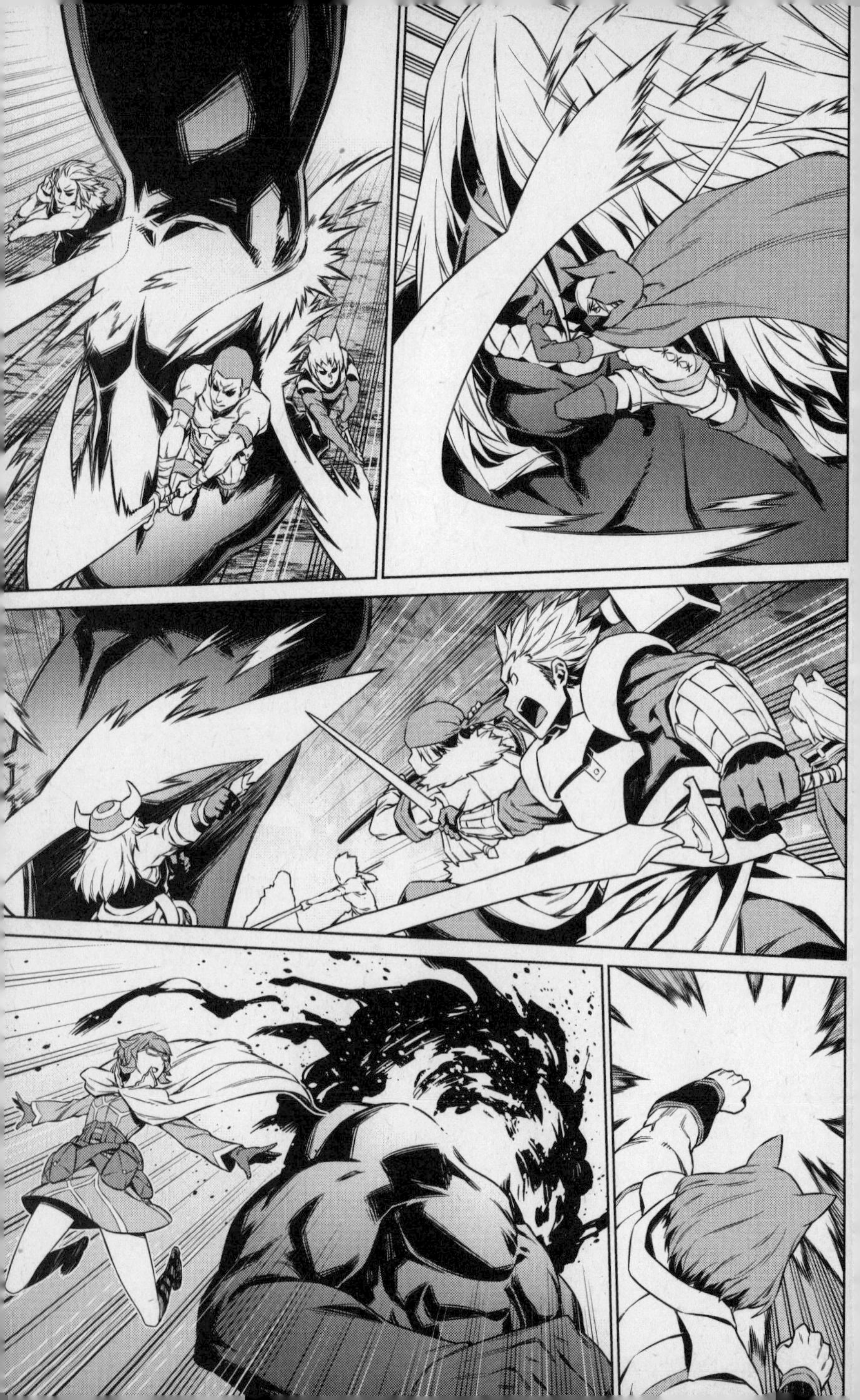

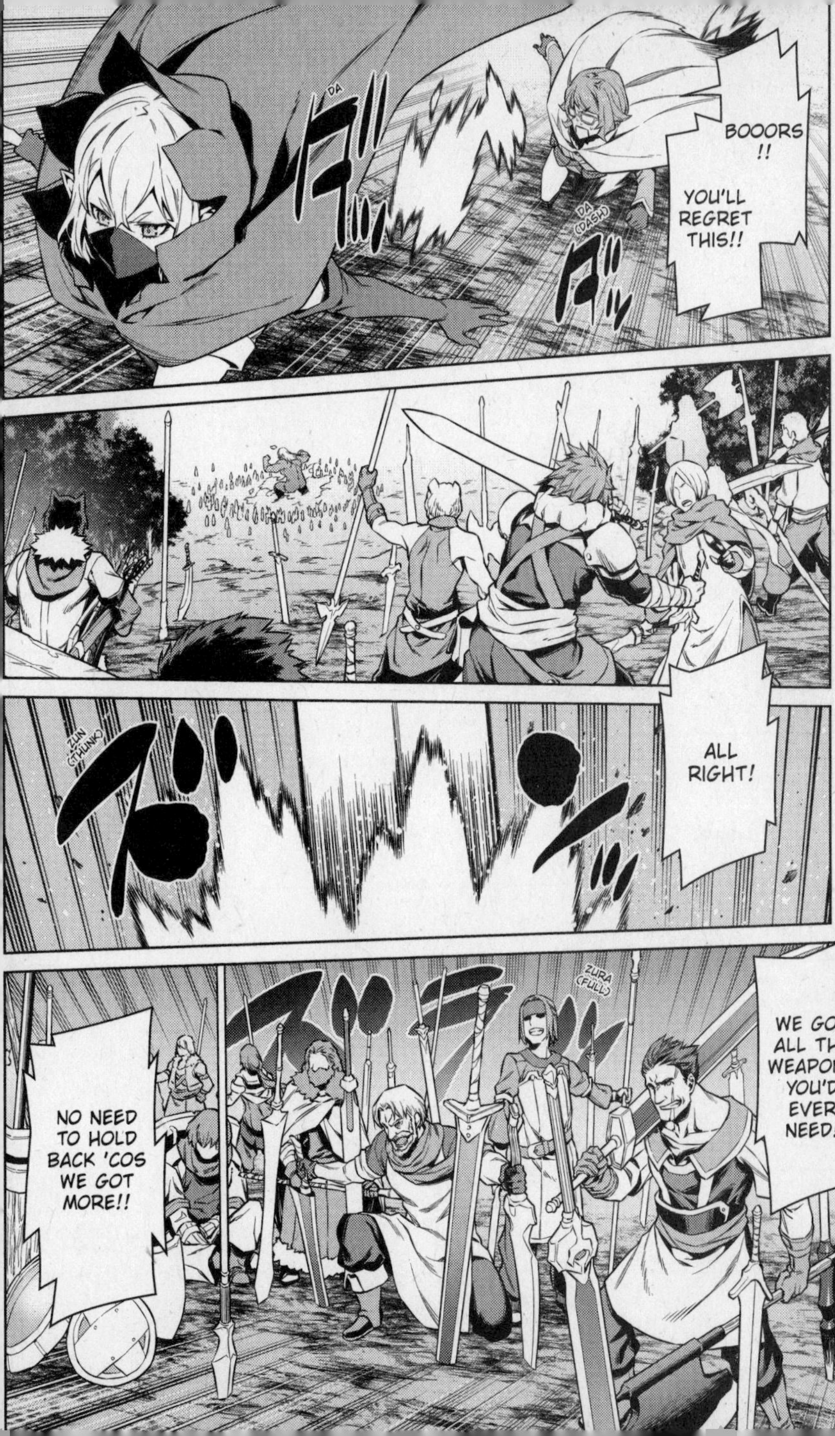
BOOORS !!
YOU'LL REGRET THIS!!
DA (DASH)
DA
ALL RIGHT!
ZUN (THUNK)
WE GOT ALL THE WEAPONS YOU'D EVER NEED!
ZURA (FULL)
NO NEED TO HOLD BACK 'COS WE GOT MORE!!

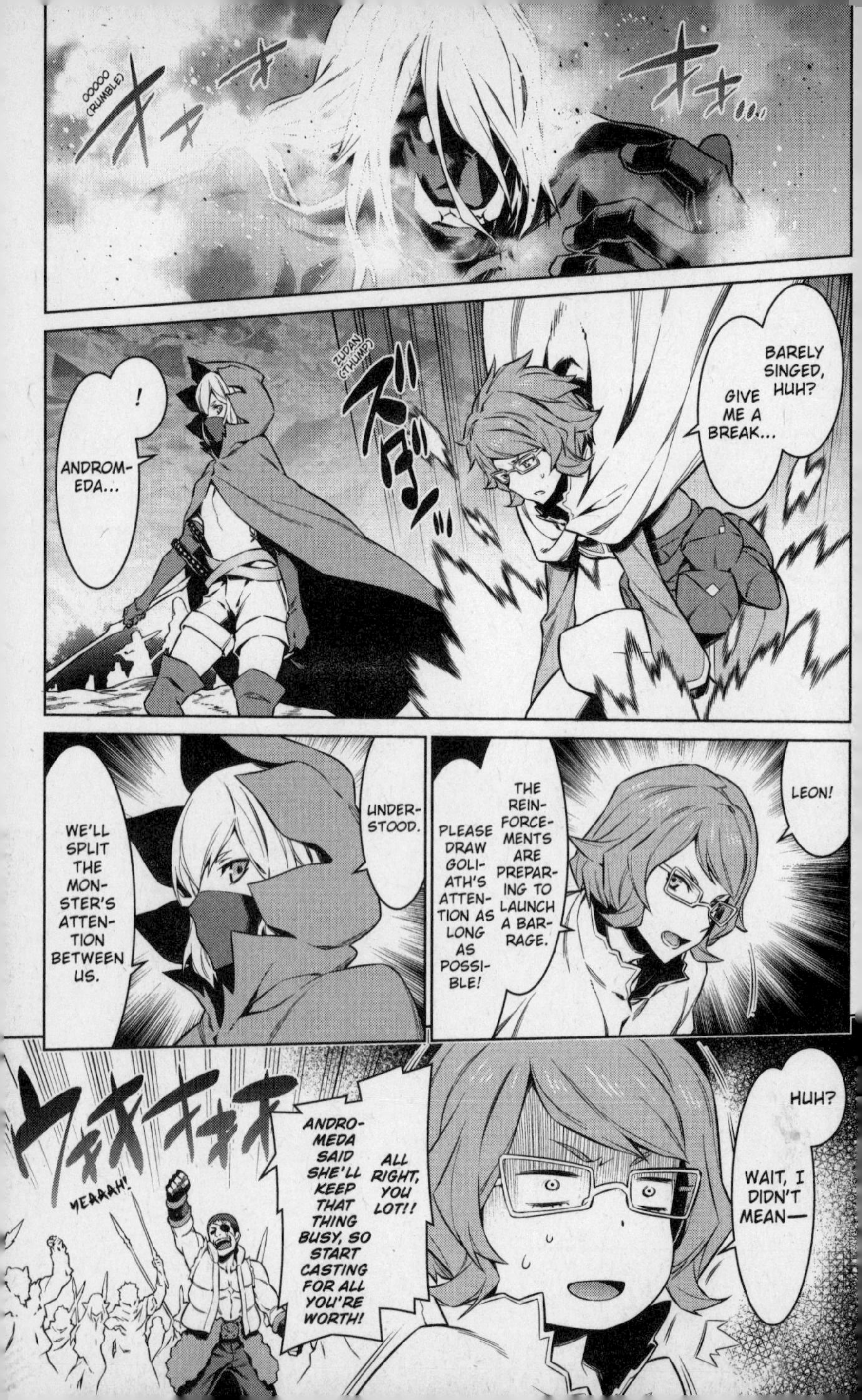

OOOOO (RUMBLE)
BARELY SINGED, HUH?
GIVE ME A BREAK...
ZUDAN (THUMP)
!
ANDROMEDA...
LEON!
THE REINFORCEMENTS ARE PREPARING TO LAUNCH A BARRAGE.
PLEASE DRAW GOLIATH'S ATTENTION AS LONG AS POSSIBLE!
UNDERSTOOD.
WE'LL SPLIT THE MONSTER'S ATTENTION BETWEEN US.
HUH?
WAIT, I DIDN'T MEAN—
ALL RIGHT, YOU LOT!!
ANDROMEDA SAID SHE'LL KEEP THAT THING BUSY, SO START CASTING FOR ALL YOU'RE WORTH!
YEAAAH!

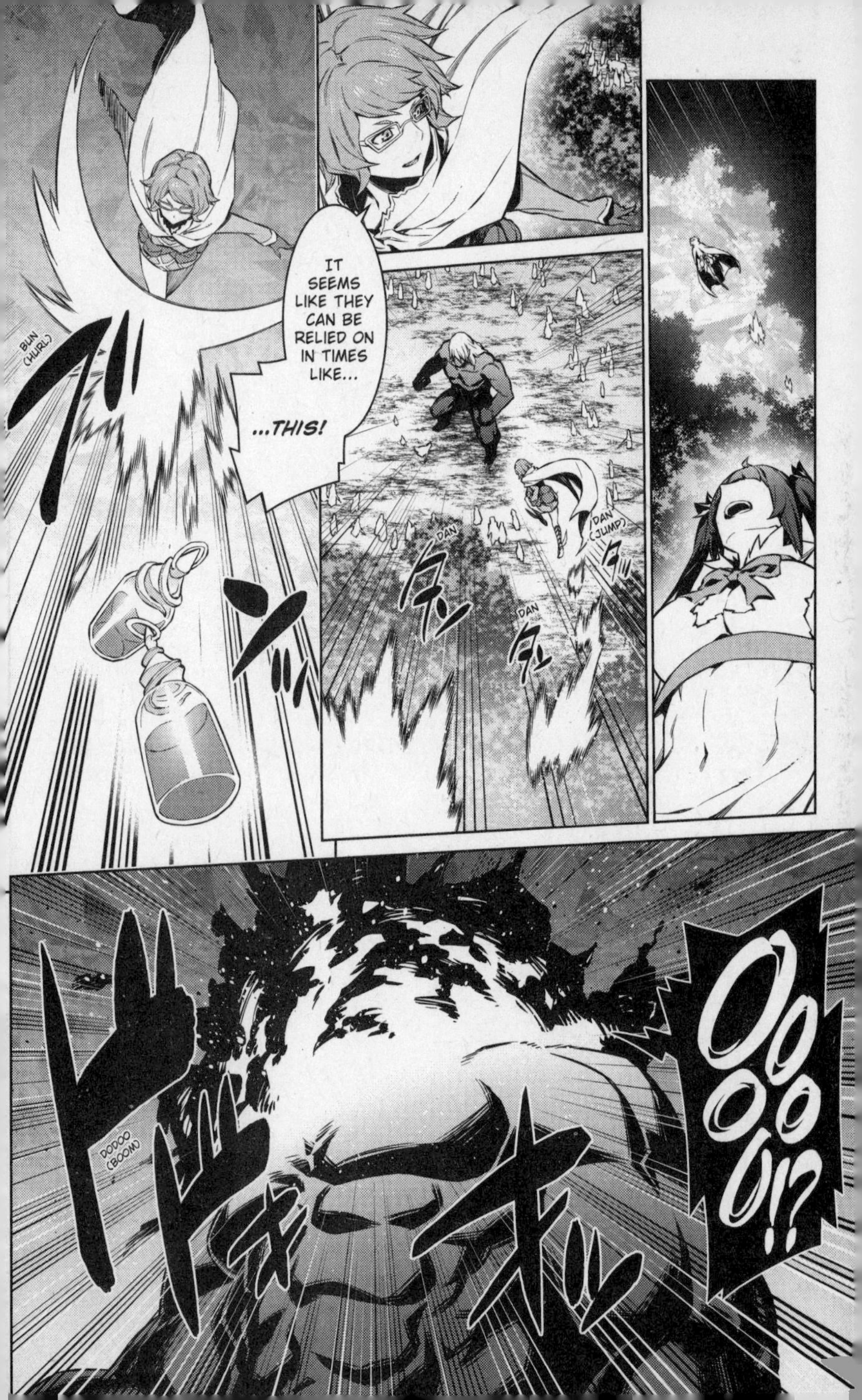
IT SEEMS LIKE THEY CAN BE RELIED ON IN TIMES LIKE...
...THIS!
DAN (JUMP)
DAN
DAN
BUN (HURL)
OOOOO!?
DODOO (BOOM)

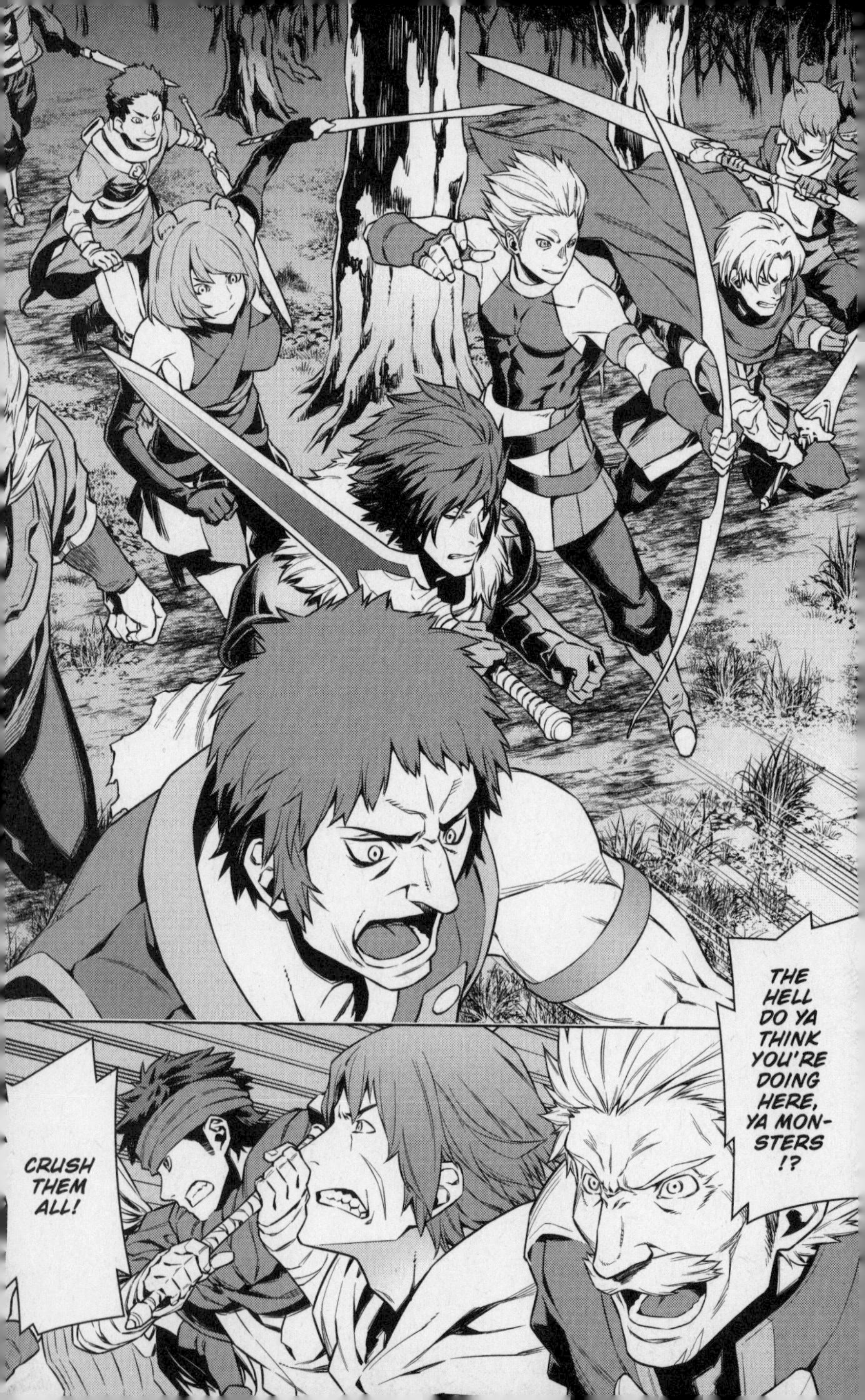
THE HELL DO YA THINK YOU'RE DOING HERE, YA MONSTERS!?
CRUSH THEM ALL!

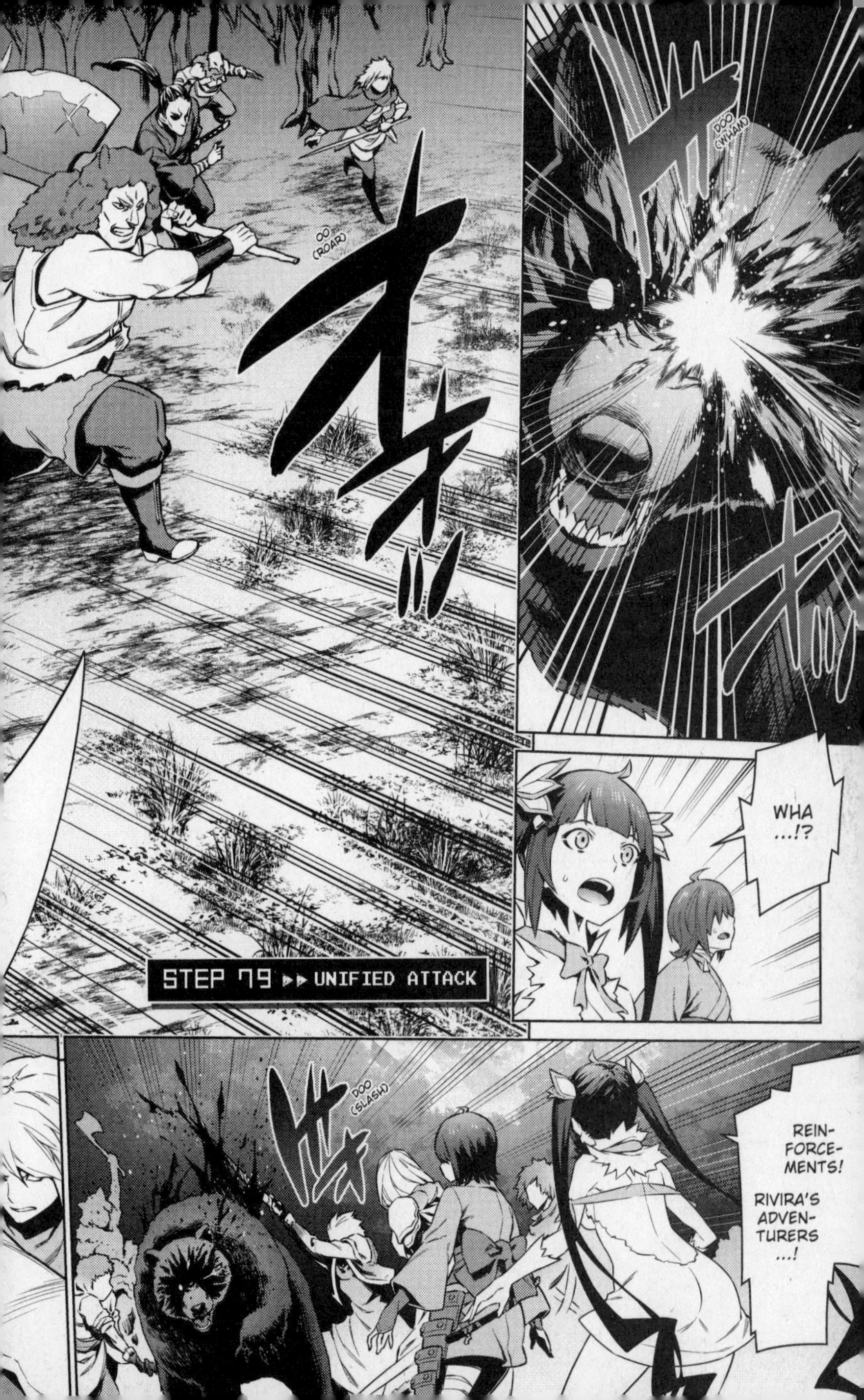
DOO (WHAM)
WHA ...!?
OO (ROAR)
STEP 79 ▸▸ UNIFIED ATTACK
REIN-FORCE-MENTS!
RIVIRA'S ADVEN-TURERS ...!
DOO (SLASH)

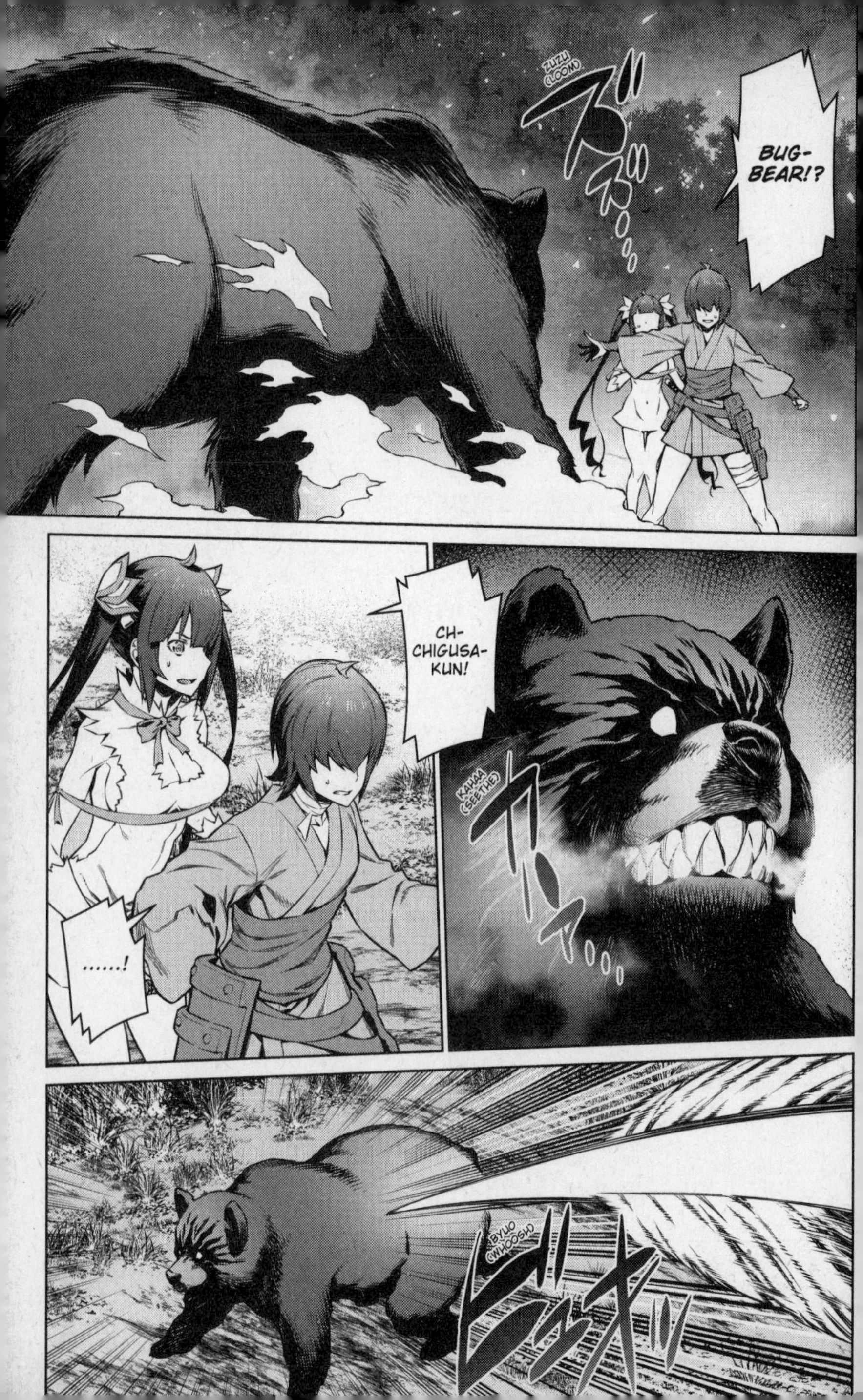
ZUZU (LOOM)
BUG-BEAR!?
CH-CHIGUSA-KUN!
KAHAA (SEETHE)
......!
BYUO (WHOOSH)

Is it WRONG to TRY to PICK UP GIRLS IN A DUNGEON?

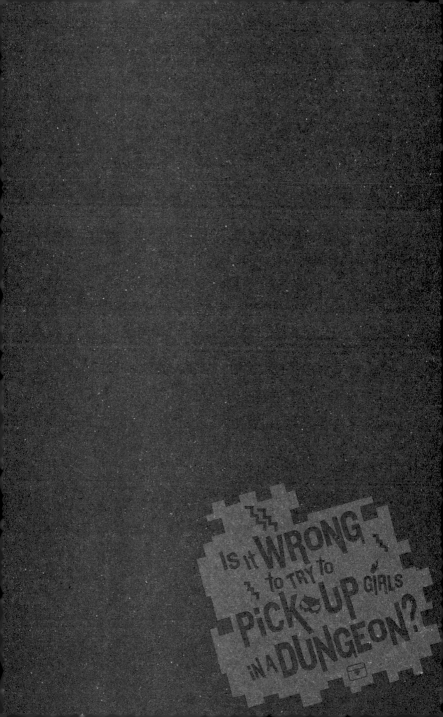

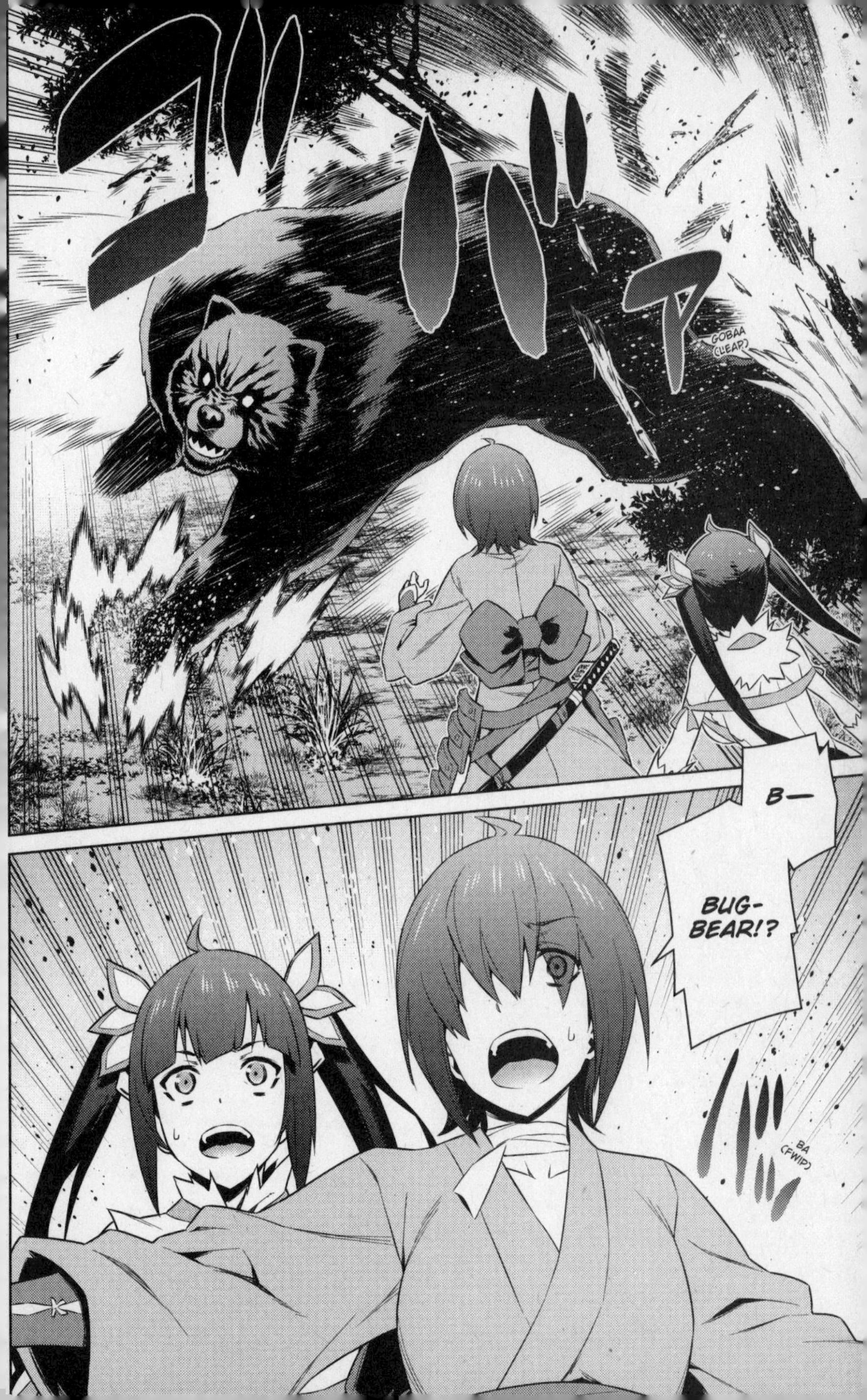
GOBAA (LEAP)
B—
BUG-BEAR!?
BA (FWIP)

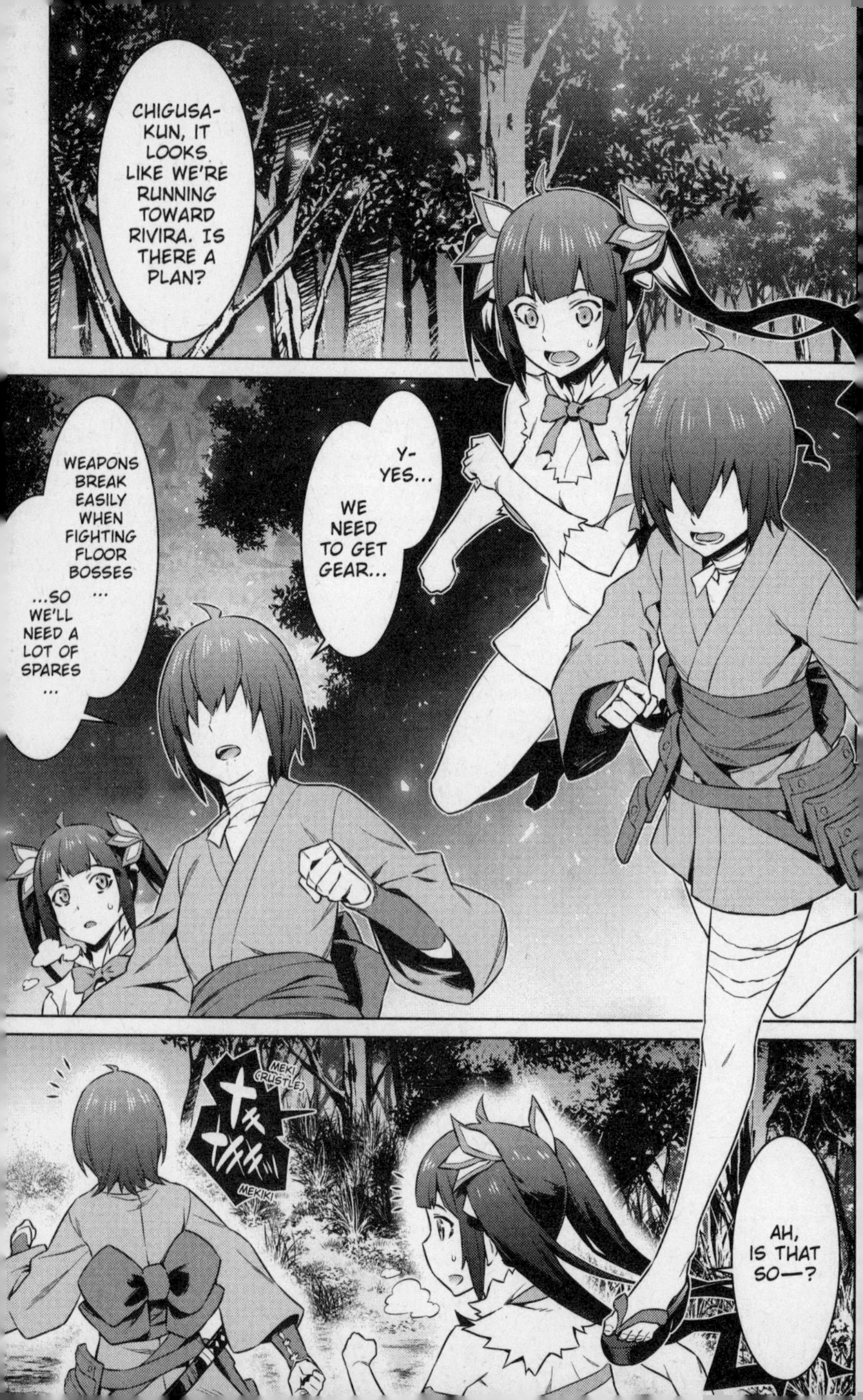
CHIGUSA-KUN, IT LOOKS LIKE WE'RE RUNNING TOWARD RIVIRA. IS THERE A PLAN?
Y-YES...
WE NEED TO GET GEAR...
WEAPONS BREAK EASILY WHEN FIGHTING FLOOR BOSSES ...
...SO WE'LL NEED A LOT OF SPARES ...
AH, IS THAT SO—?
MEKI (RUSTLE)
MEKIKI

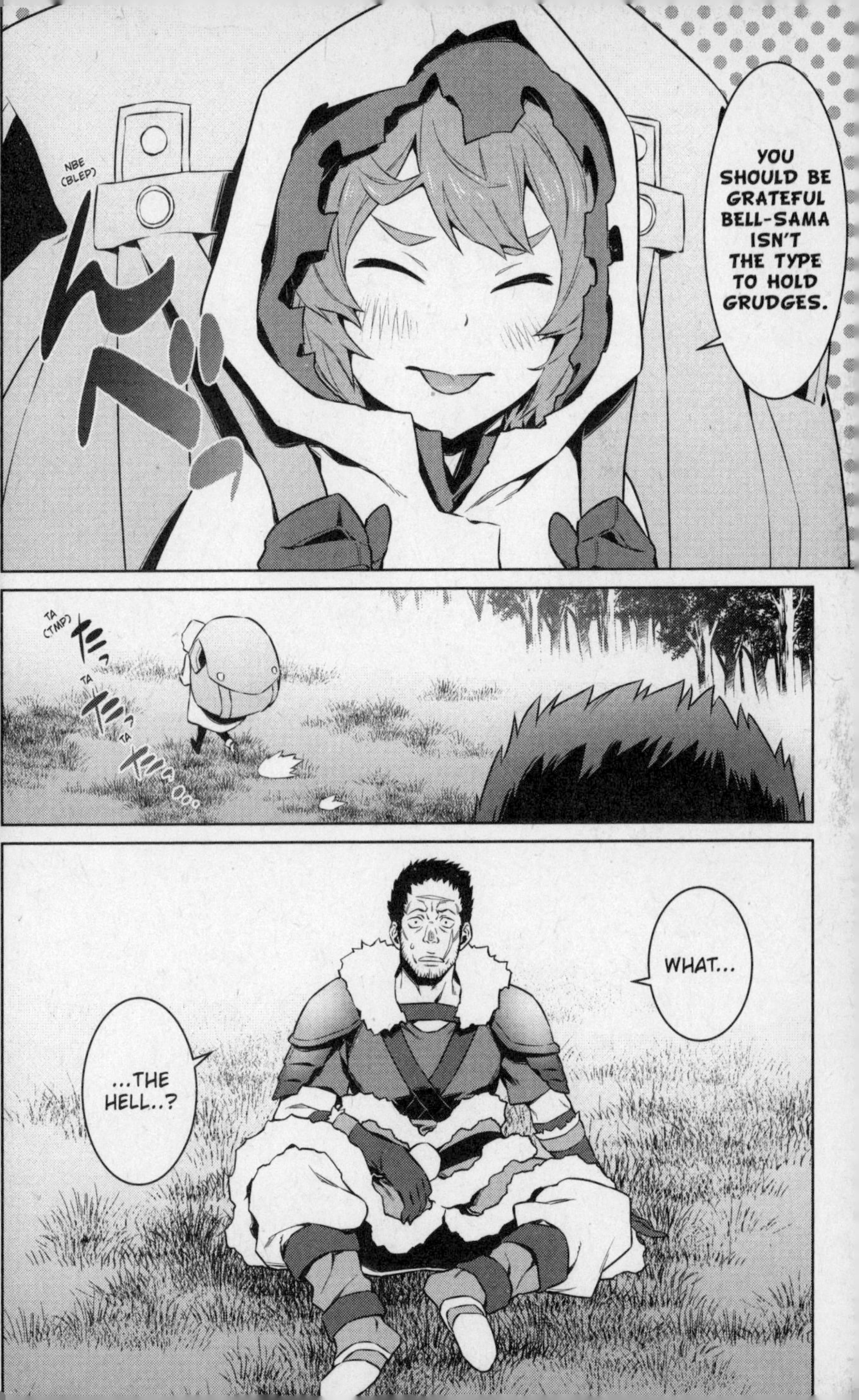
YOU SHOULD BE GRATEFUL BELL-SAMA ISN'T THE TYPE TO HOLD GRUDGES.
NBE (BLEP)
TA (TMP)
TA
TA
WHAT...
...THE HELL..?

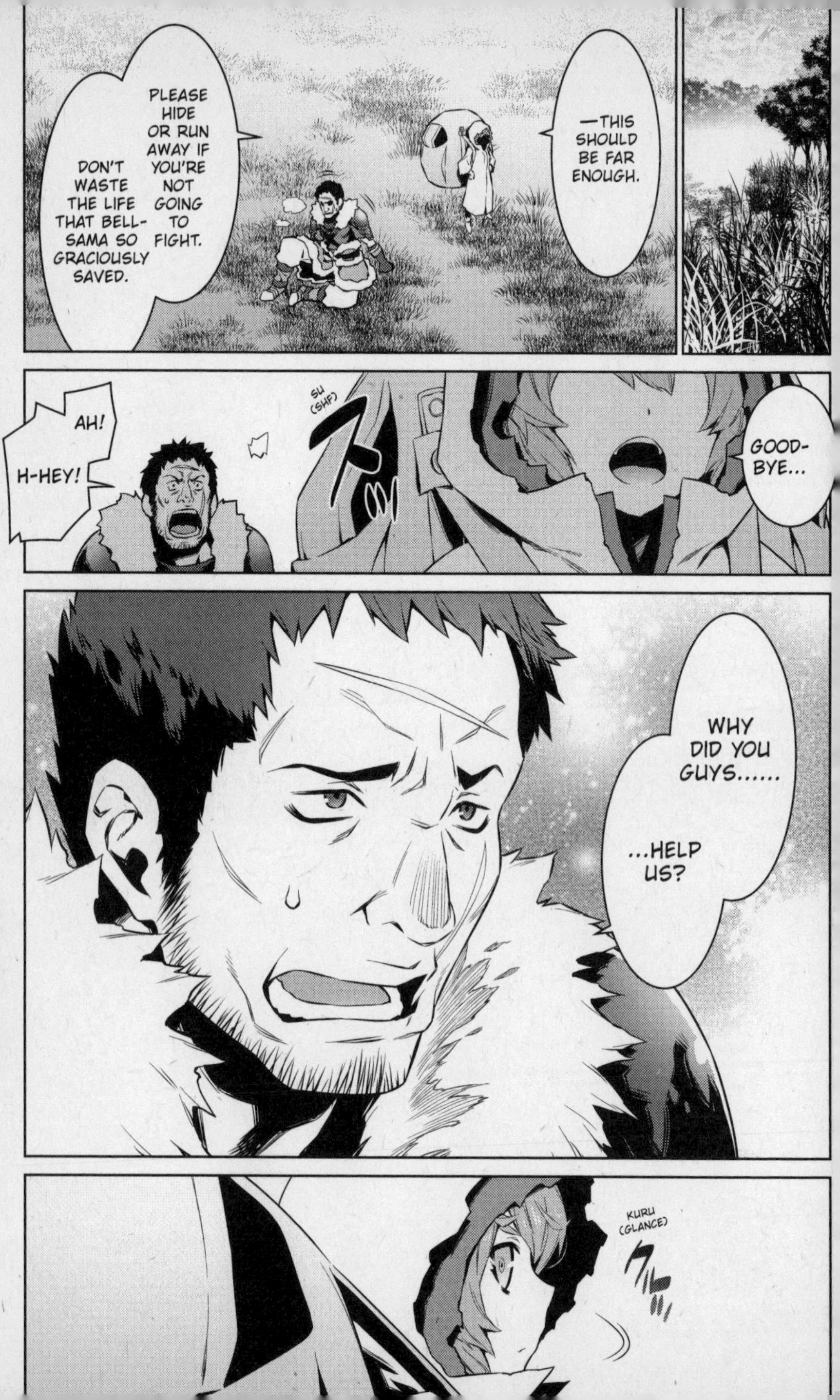
—THIS SHOULD BE FAR ENOUGH.
PLEASE HIDE OR RUN AWAY IF YOU'RE NOT GOING TO FIGHT.
DON'T WASTE THE LIFE THAT BELL-SAMA SO GRACIOUSLY SAVED.
GOOD-BYE...
SU (SHF)
AH!
H-HEY!
WHY DID YOU GUYS......
...HELP US?
KURU (GLANCE)

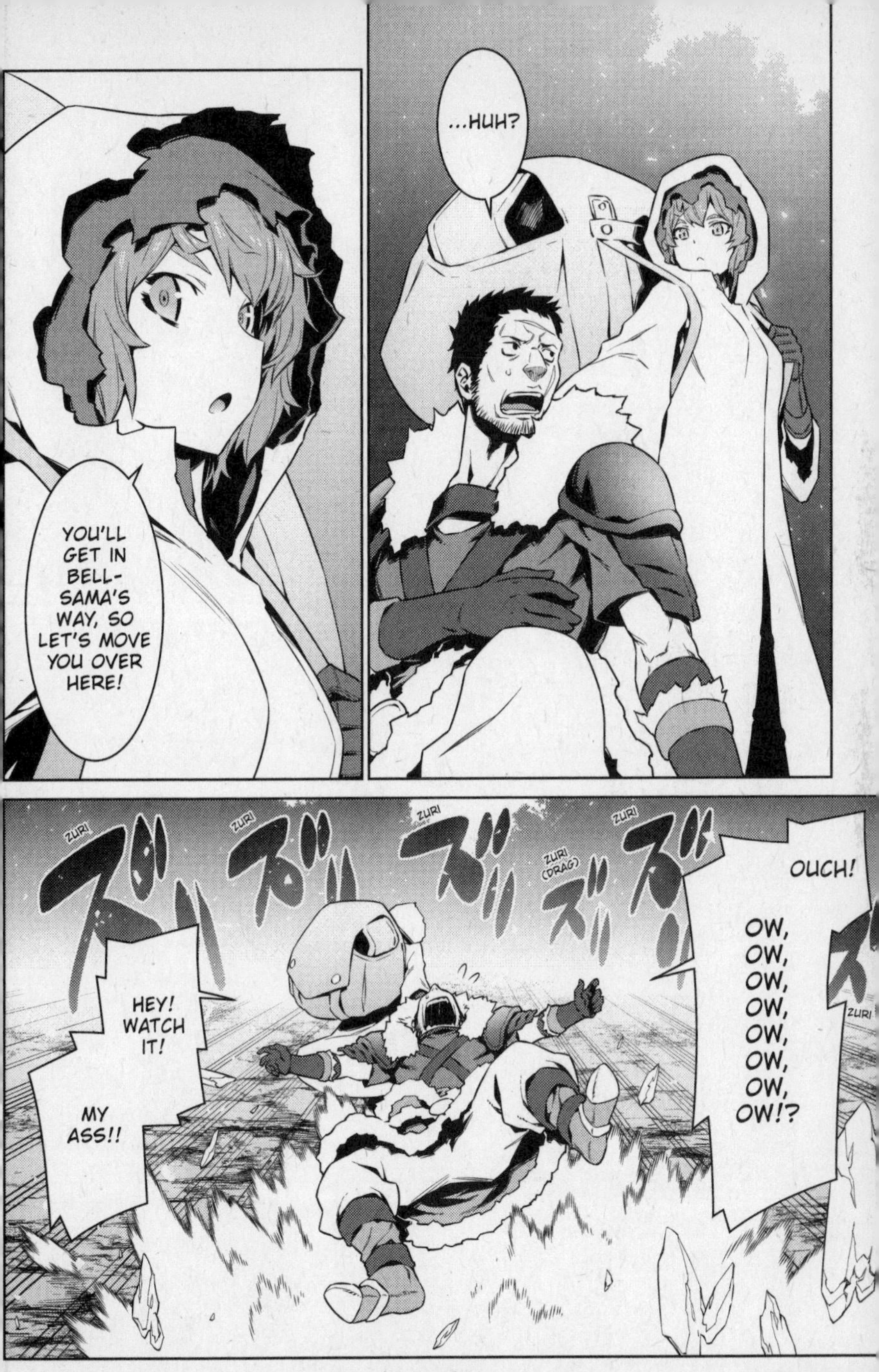
...HUH?
YOU'LL GET IN BELL-SAMA'S WAY, SO LET'S MOVE YOU OVER HERE!
ZURI
OUCH!
OW, OW, OW, OW, OW, OW, OW, OW!?
ZURI
ZURI (DRAG)
ZURI
ZURI
ZURI
HEY! WATCH IT!
MY ASS!!

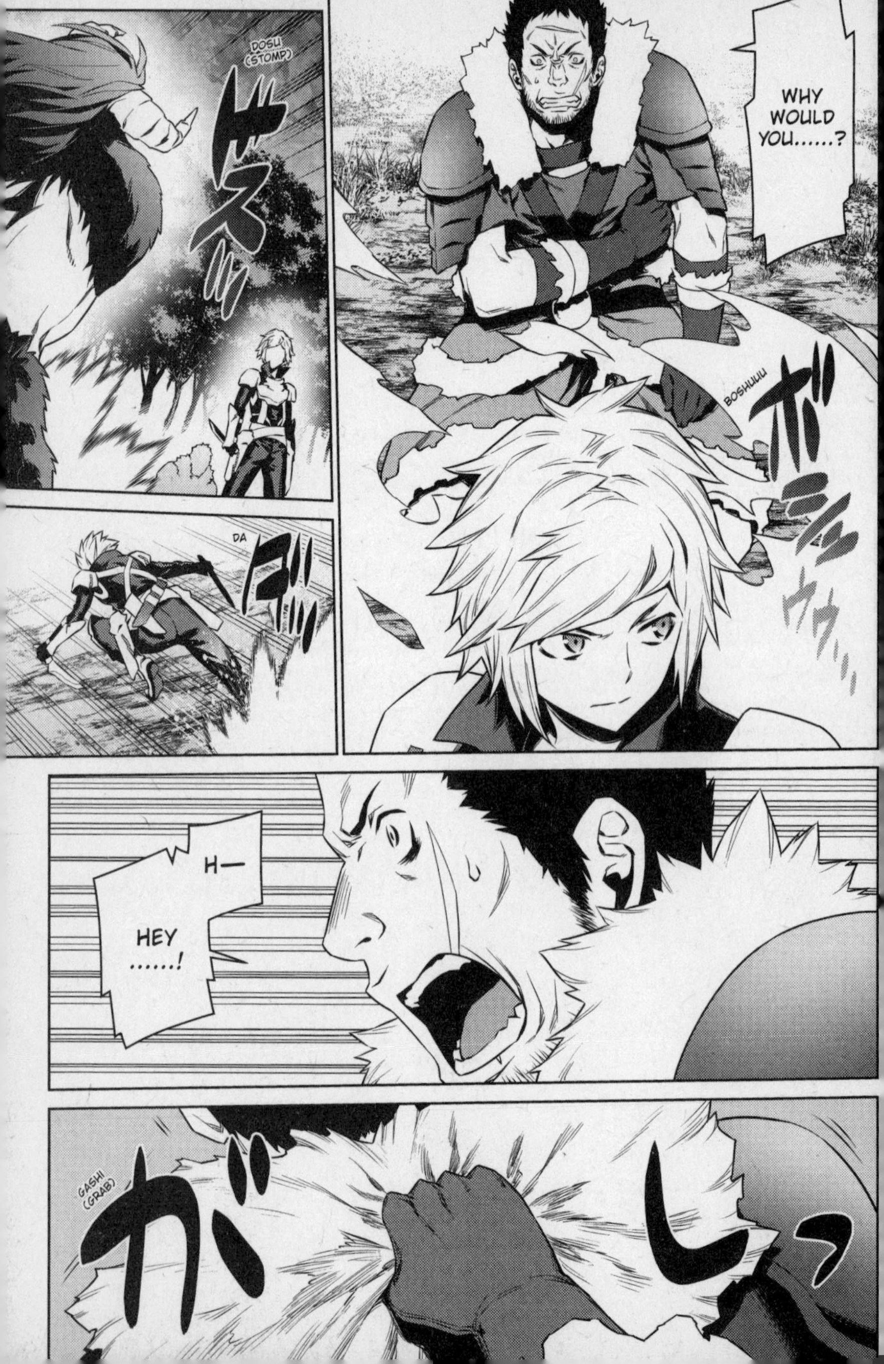
WHY WOULD YOU......?
BOSHUUU
DOSU (STOMP)
DA
H—
HEY ......!
GASHI (GRAB)

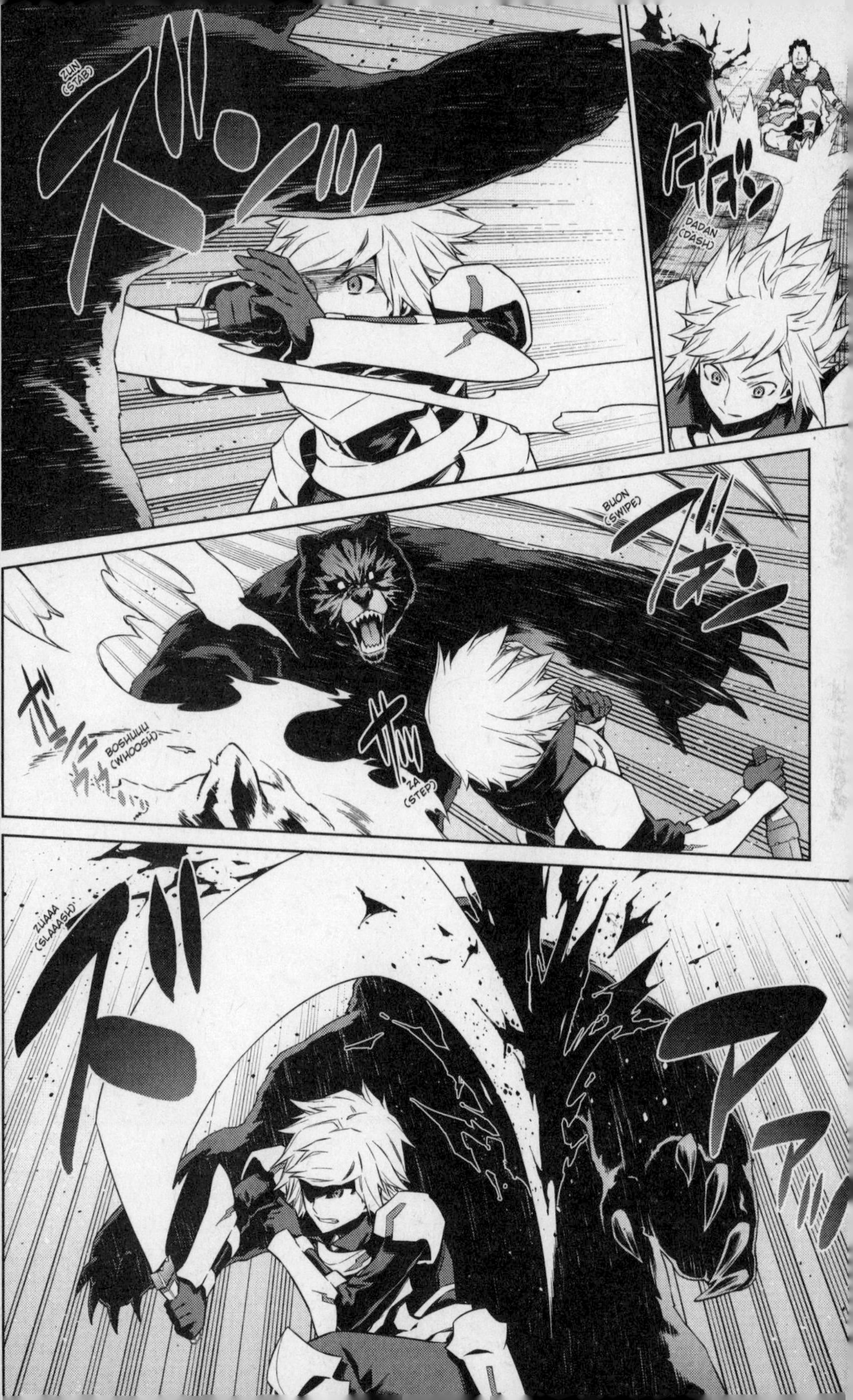
DADAN (DASH)
ZUN (STAB)
BUON (SWIPE)
ZA (STEP)
BOSHUUU (WHOOSH)
ZUAAA (SLAAASH)

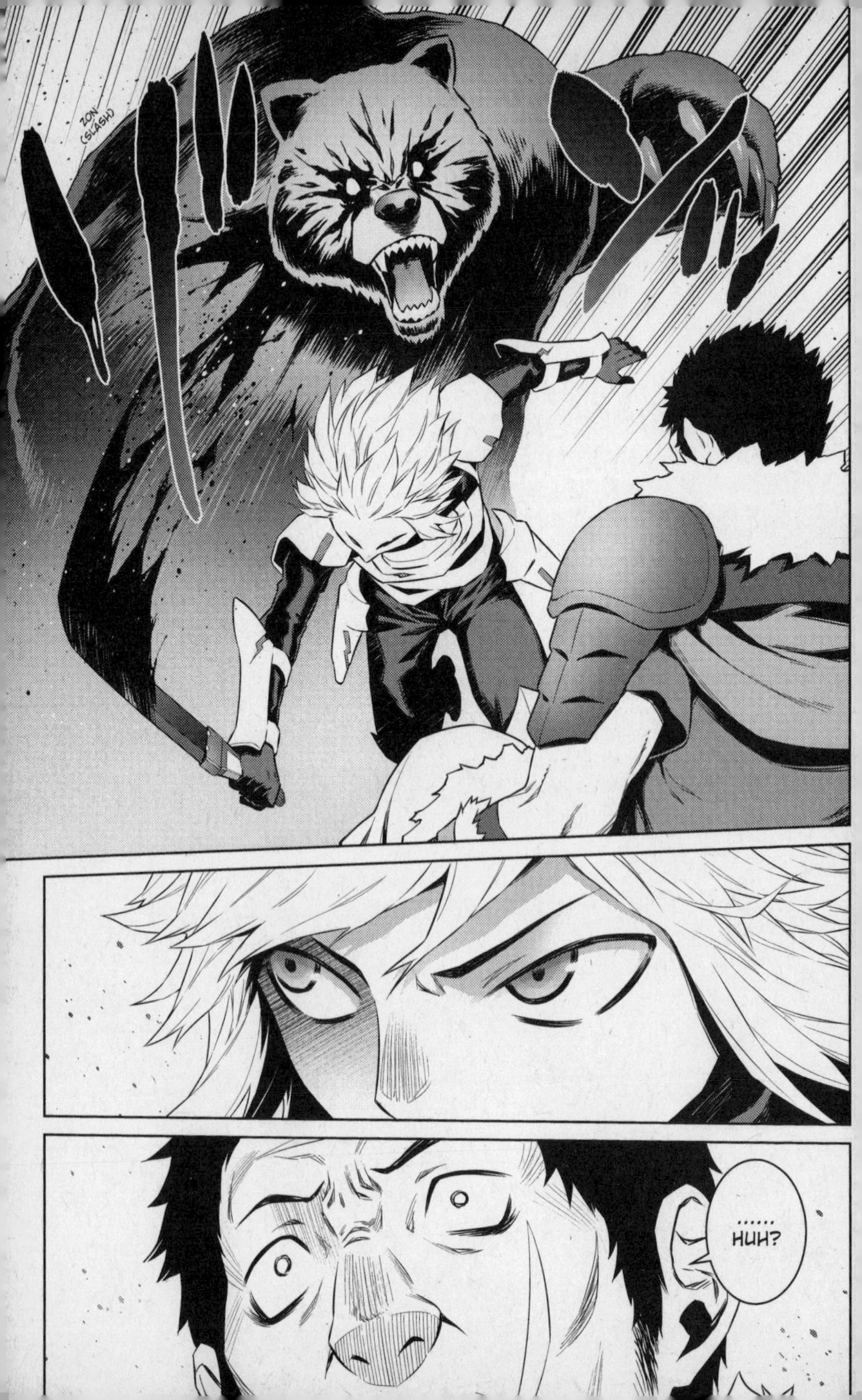
ZON (SLASH)
...... HUH?

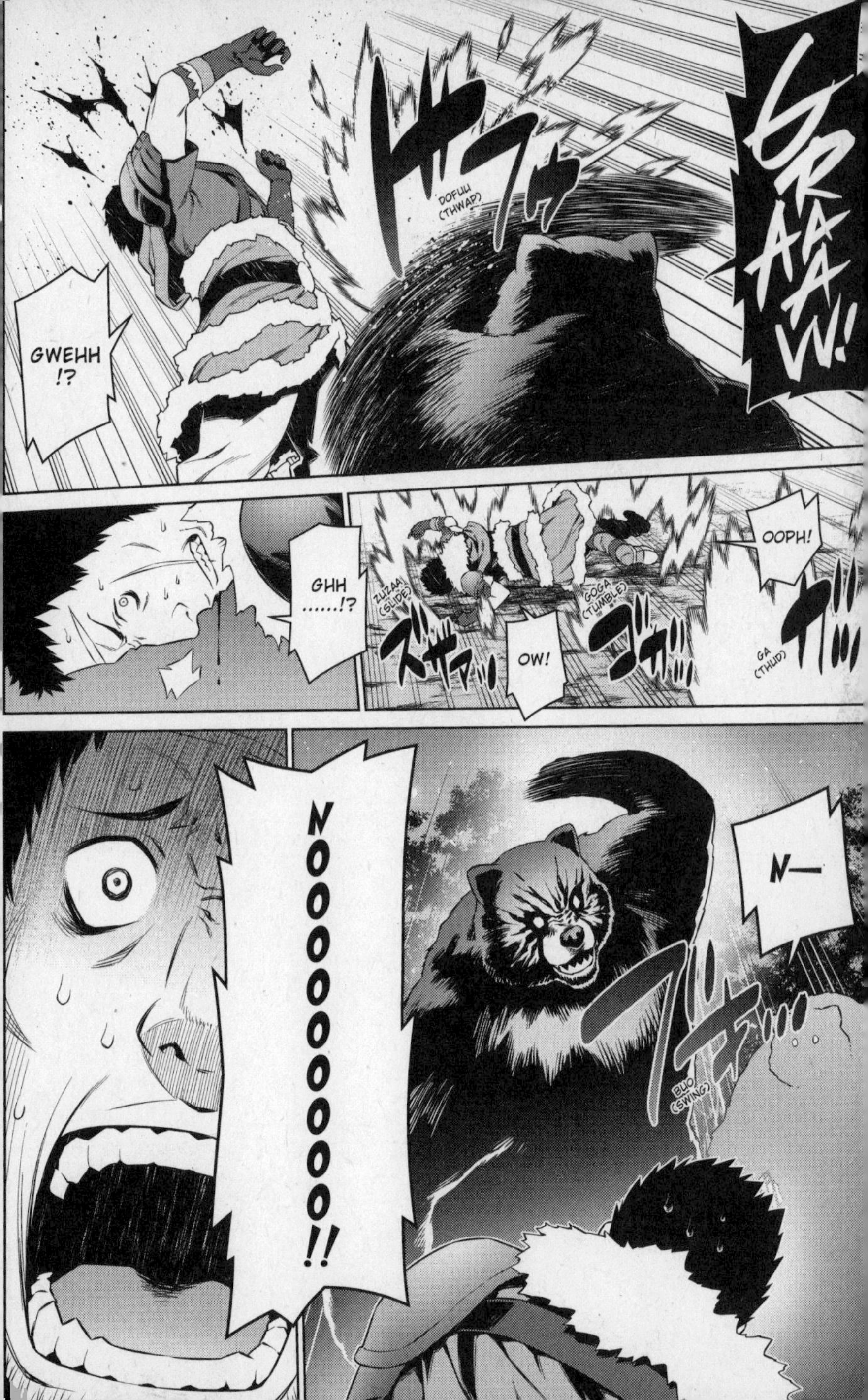
GRAAAAW!
DOFUU (THWAP)
GWEHH !?
OOPH!
GA (THUD)
GOGA (TUMBLE)
OW!
ZUZAA (SLIDE)
GHH ......!?
N—
BUO (SWING)
NOOOOOOOOOOOO!!

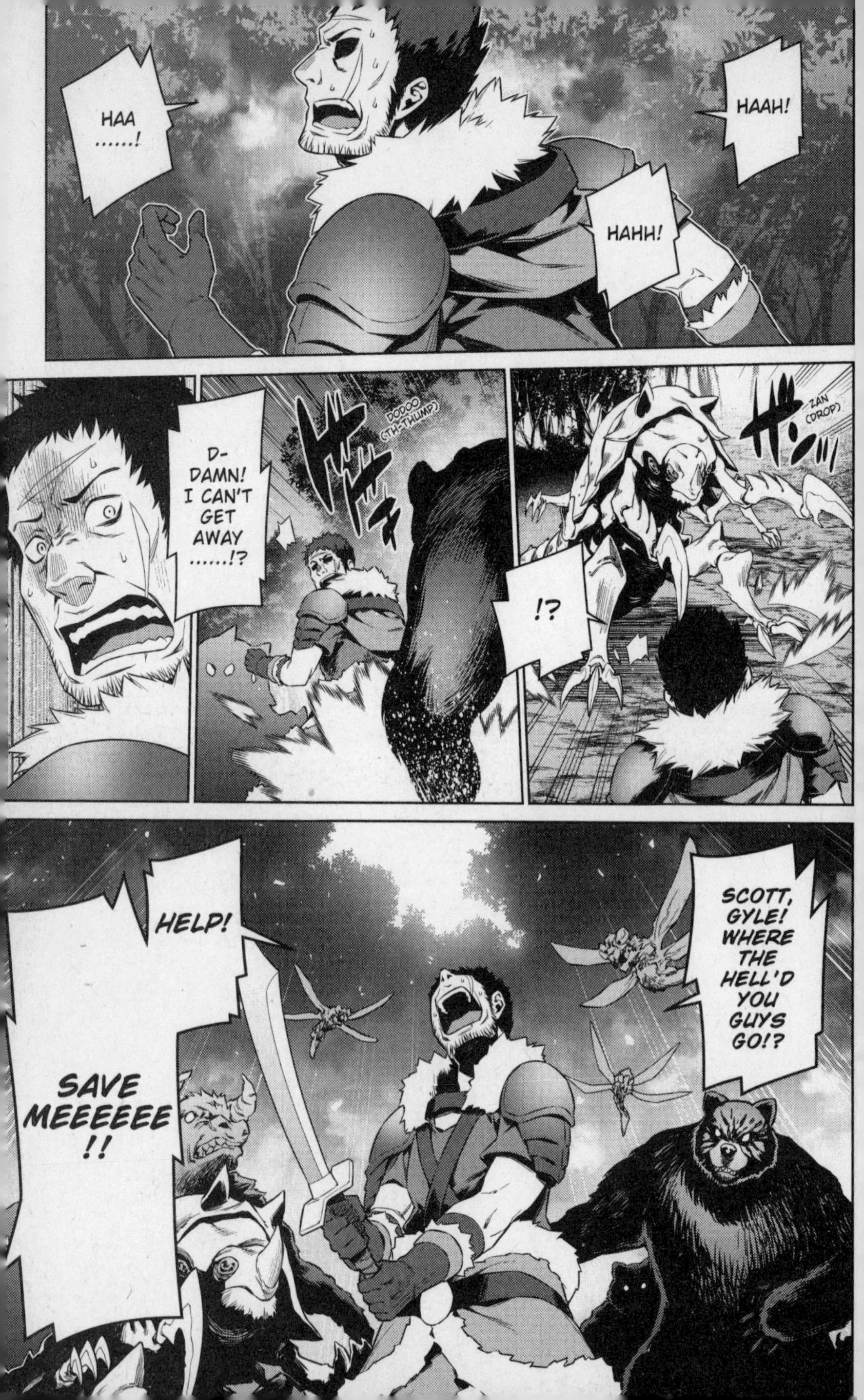
HAAH!
HAHH!
HAA......!
ZAN (DROP)
!?
DODOO (TH-THUMP)
D-DAMN! I CAN'T GET AWAY......!?
SCOTT, GYLE! WHERE THE HELL'D YOU GUYS GO!?
HELP!
SAVE MEEEEEE!!

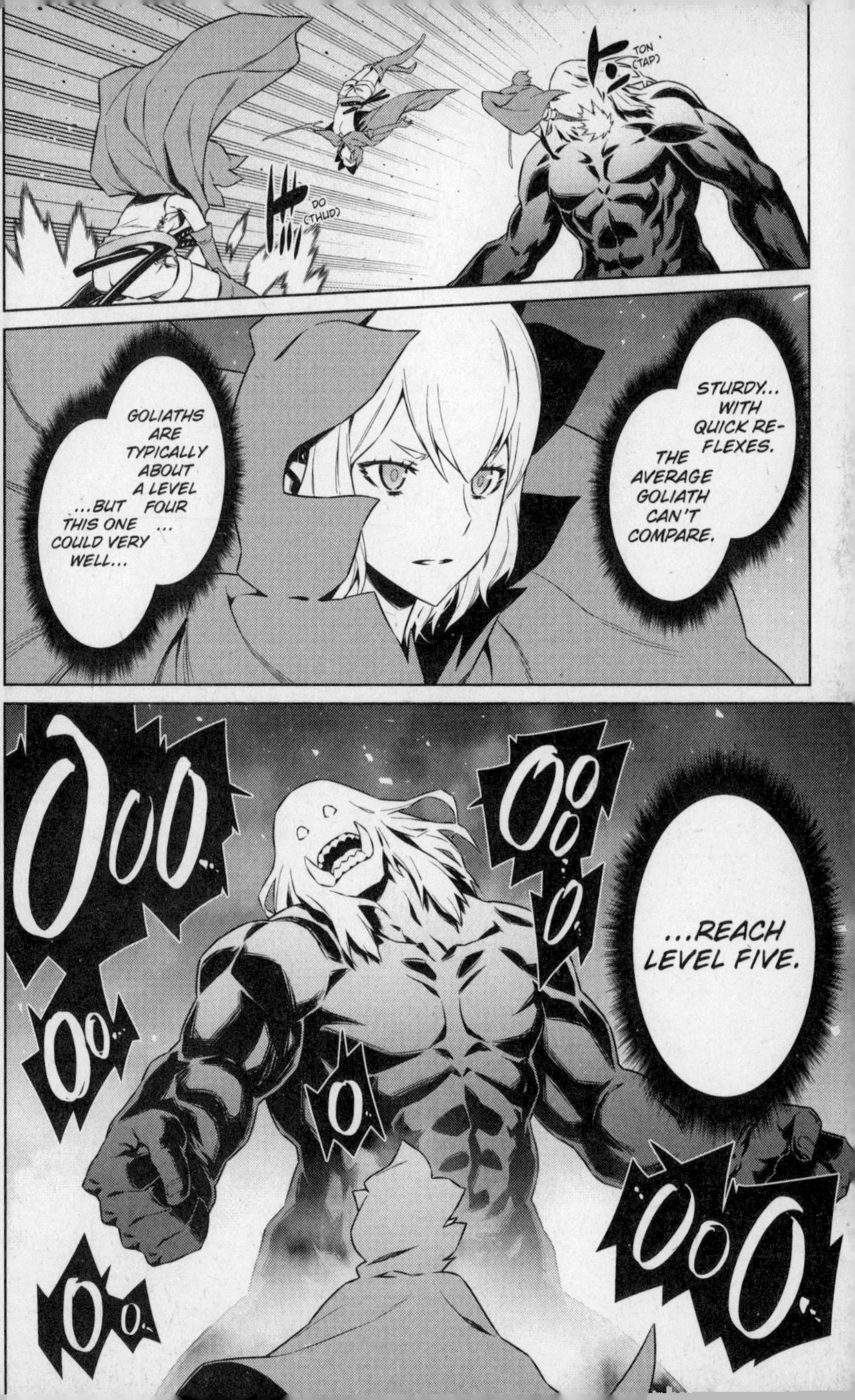

TON (TAP)
DO (THUD)
STURDY... WITH QUICK REFLEXES. THE AVERAGE GOLIATH CAN'T COMPARE.
GOLIATHS ARE TYPICALLY ABOUT A LEVEL FOUR...
...BUT THIS ONE COULD VERY WELL...
...REACH LEVEL FIVE.
OOOOO...
OOO.
OO..
O..
OOO.
OO..

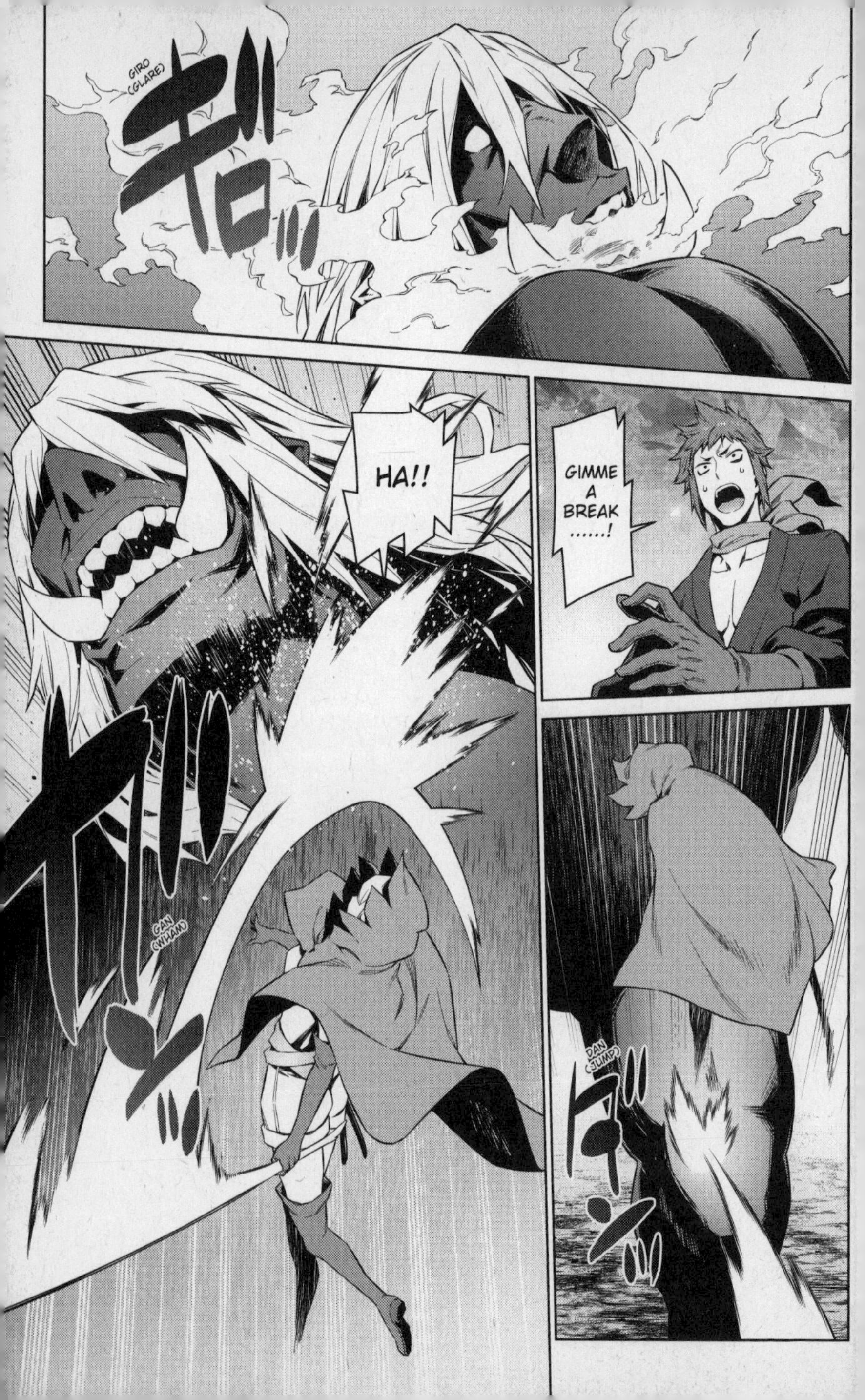
GIRO (GLARE)
GIMME A BREAK ......!
DAN (JUMP)
HA!!
GAN (WHAM)

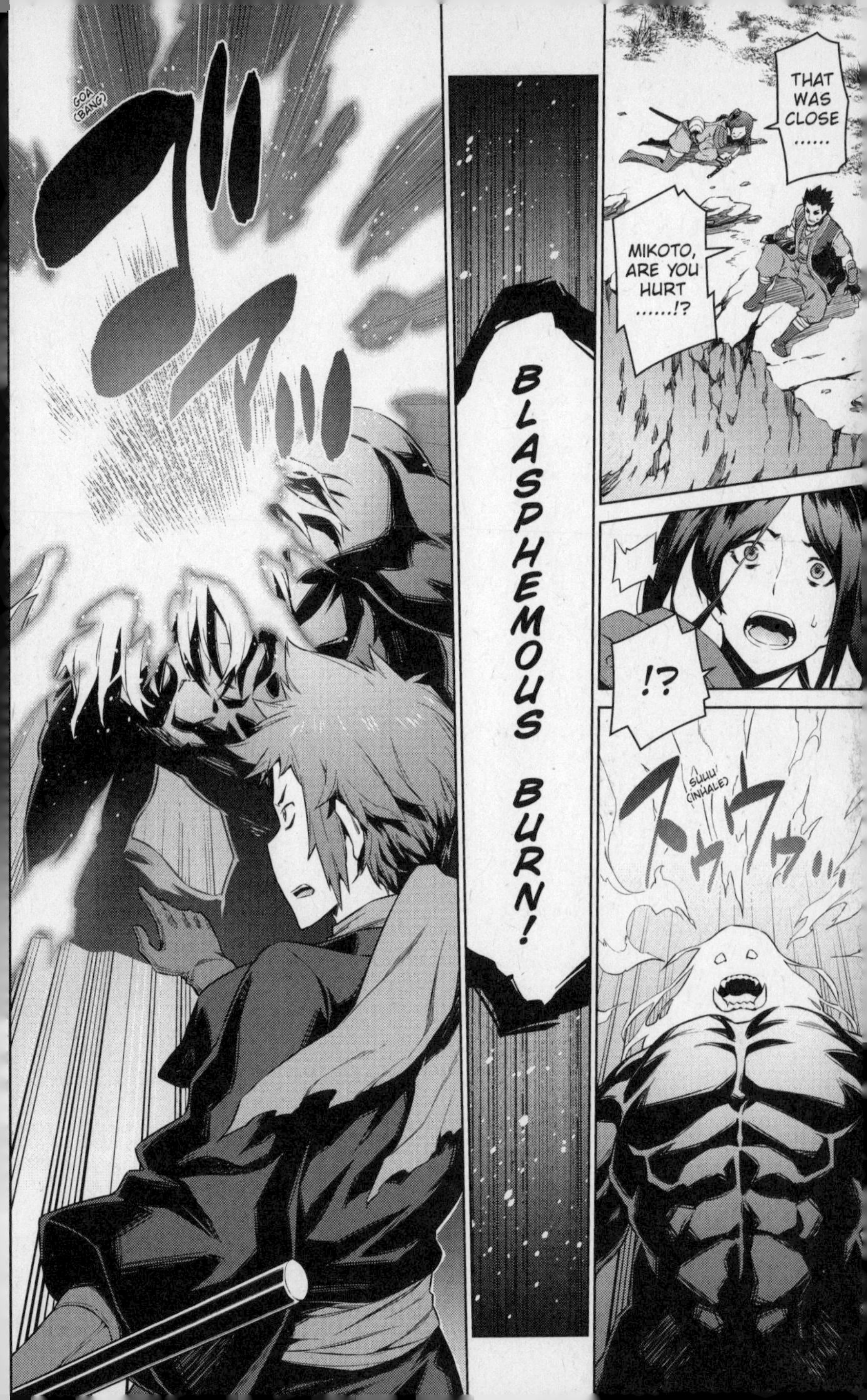
THAT WAS CLOSE ......
MIKOTO, ARE YOU HURT ......!?
!?
SUUU (INHALE)
BLASPHEMOUS BURN!
GOA (BANG)

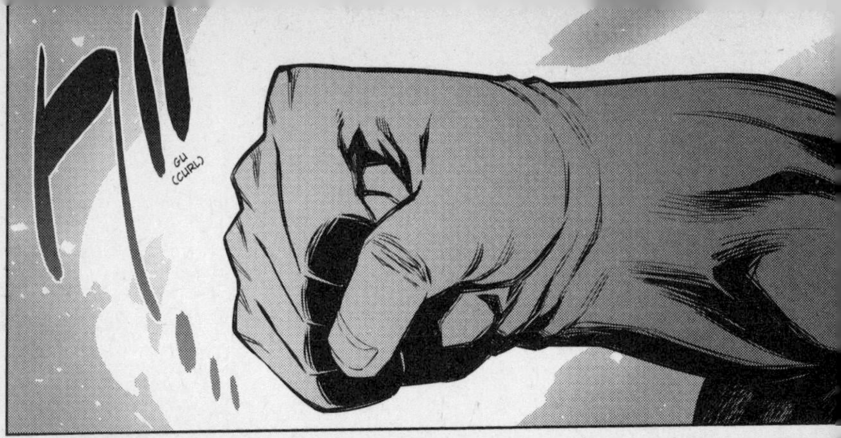
GU (CURL)
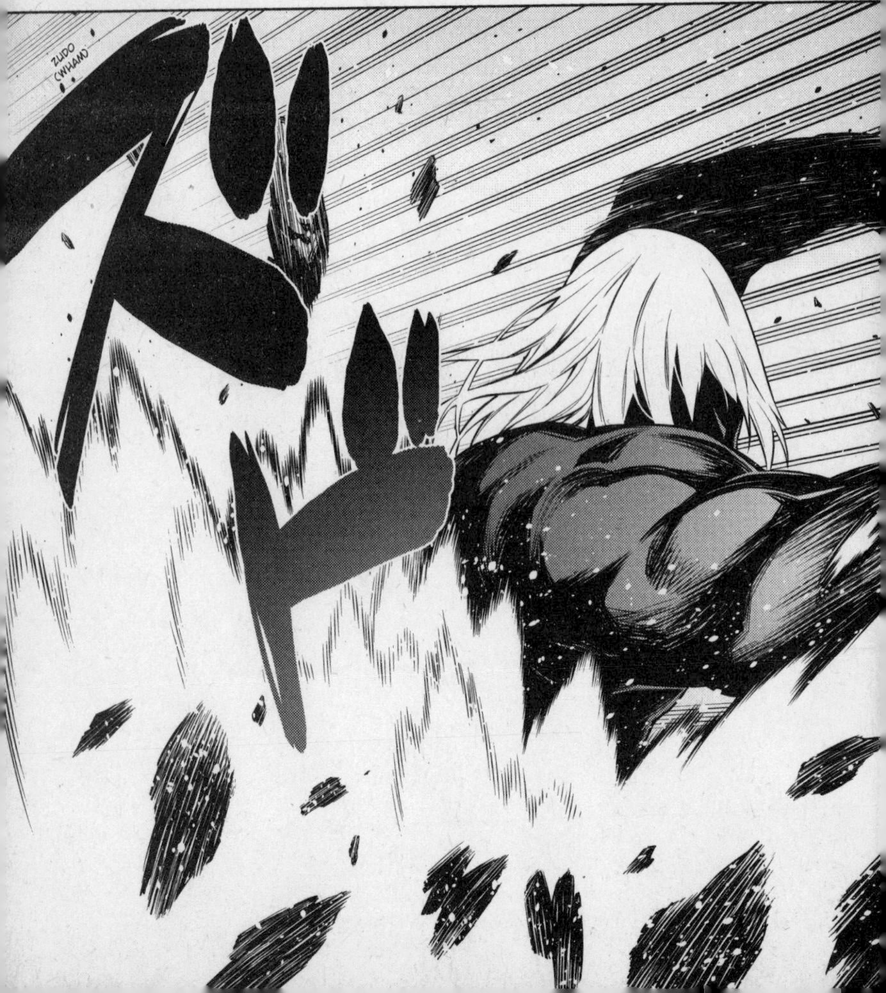
ZUDO (WHAM)

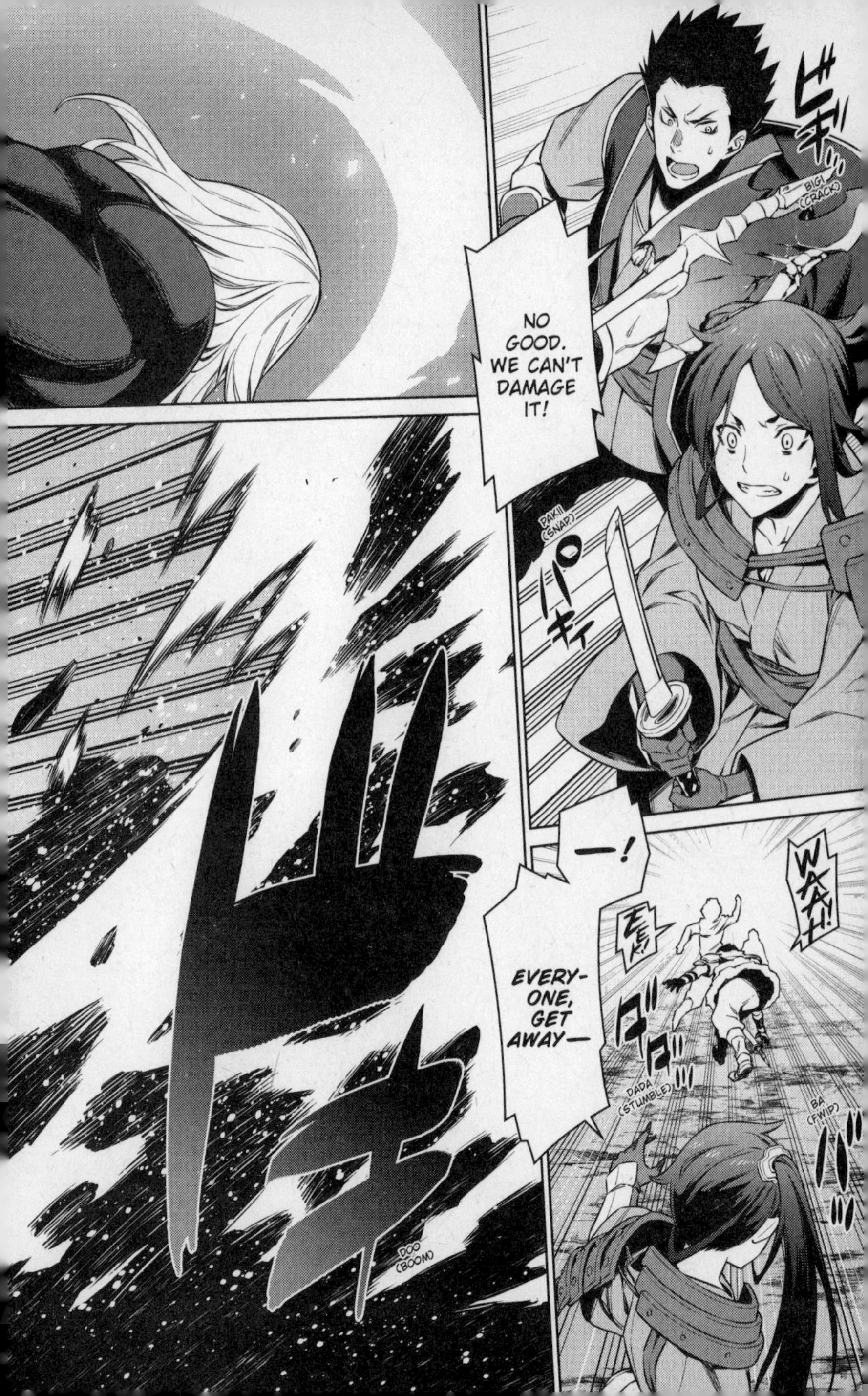
BIGI (CRACK)
NO GOOD. WE CAN'T DAMAGE IT!
PAKII (SNAP)
—!
EVERY-ONE, GET AWAY—
WAAAH!
EEK!
DADA (STUMBLE)
BA (FWIP)
DOO (BOOM)

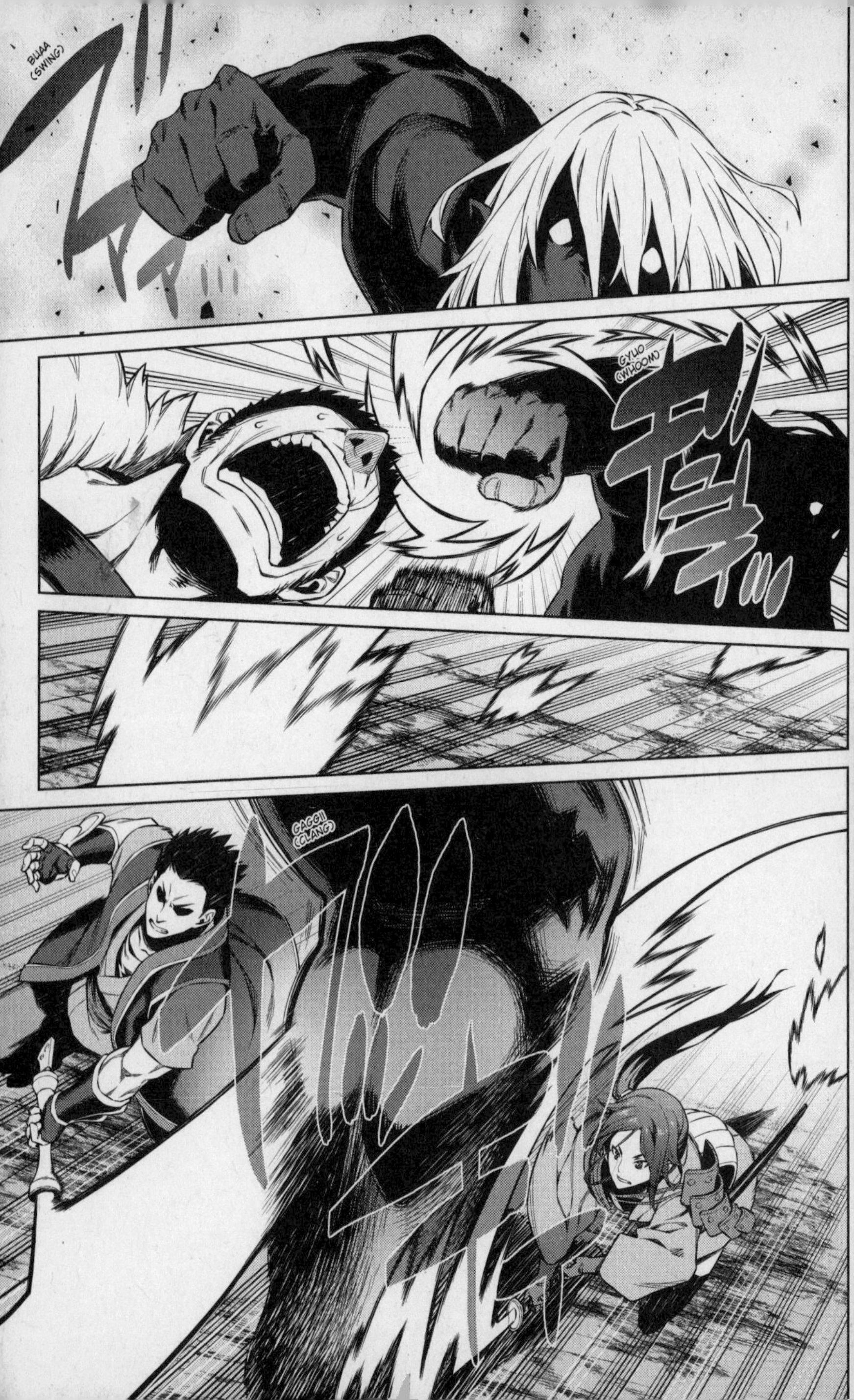
BUAA (SWING)
GYUO (WHOOM)
GAGGII (CLANG)

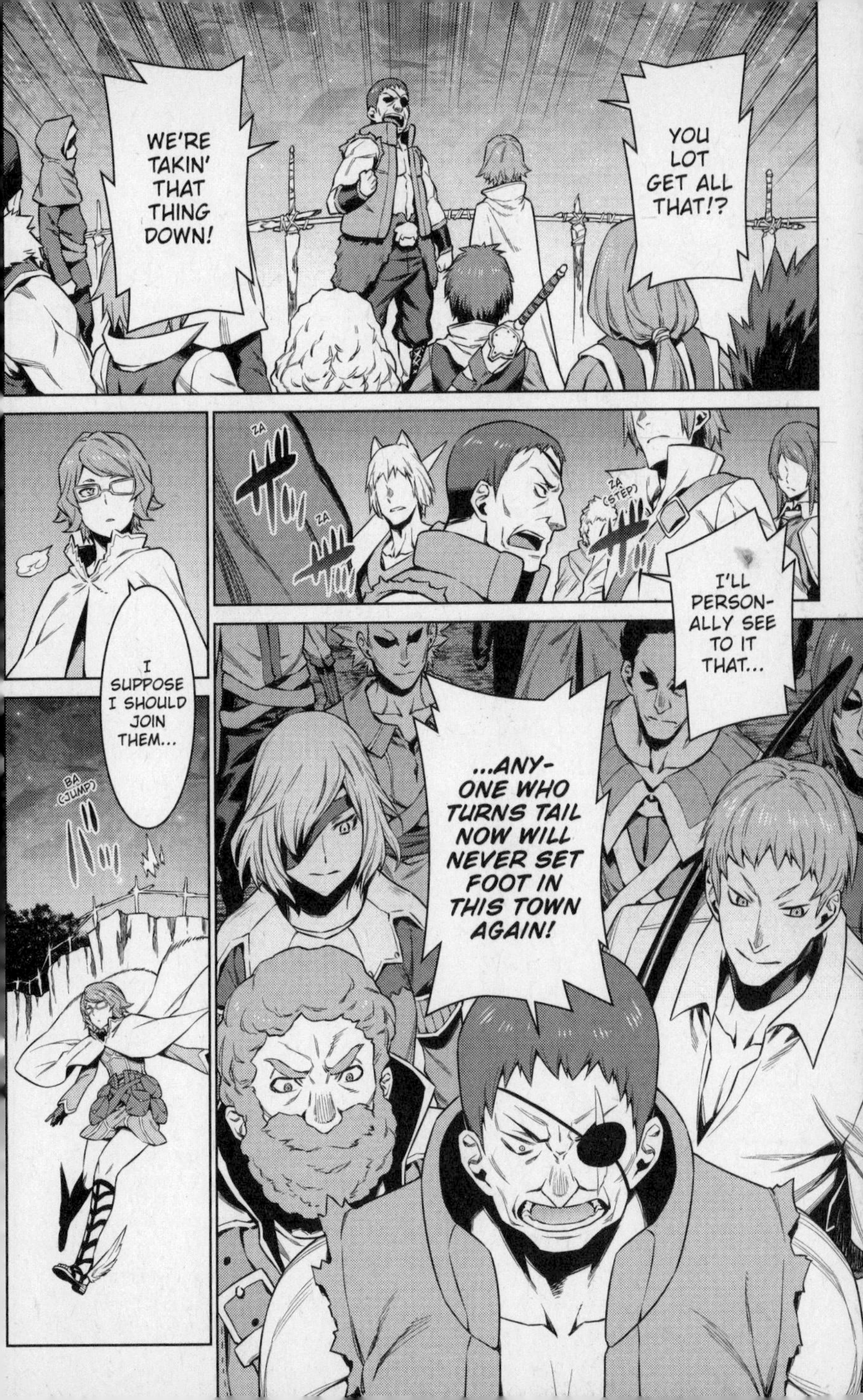
YOU LOT GET ALL THAT!?
WE'RE TAKIN' THAT THING DOWN!
ZA
ZA
ZA (STEP)
I'LL PERSONALLY SEE TO IT THAT...
...ANYONE WHO TURNS TAIL NOW WILL NEVER SET FOOT IN THIS TOWN AGAIN!
I SUPPOSE I SHOULD JOIN THEM...
BA (JUMP)

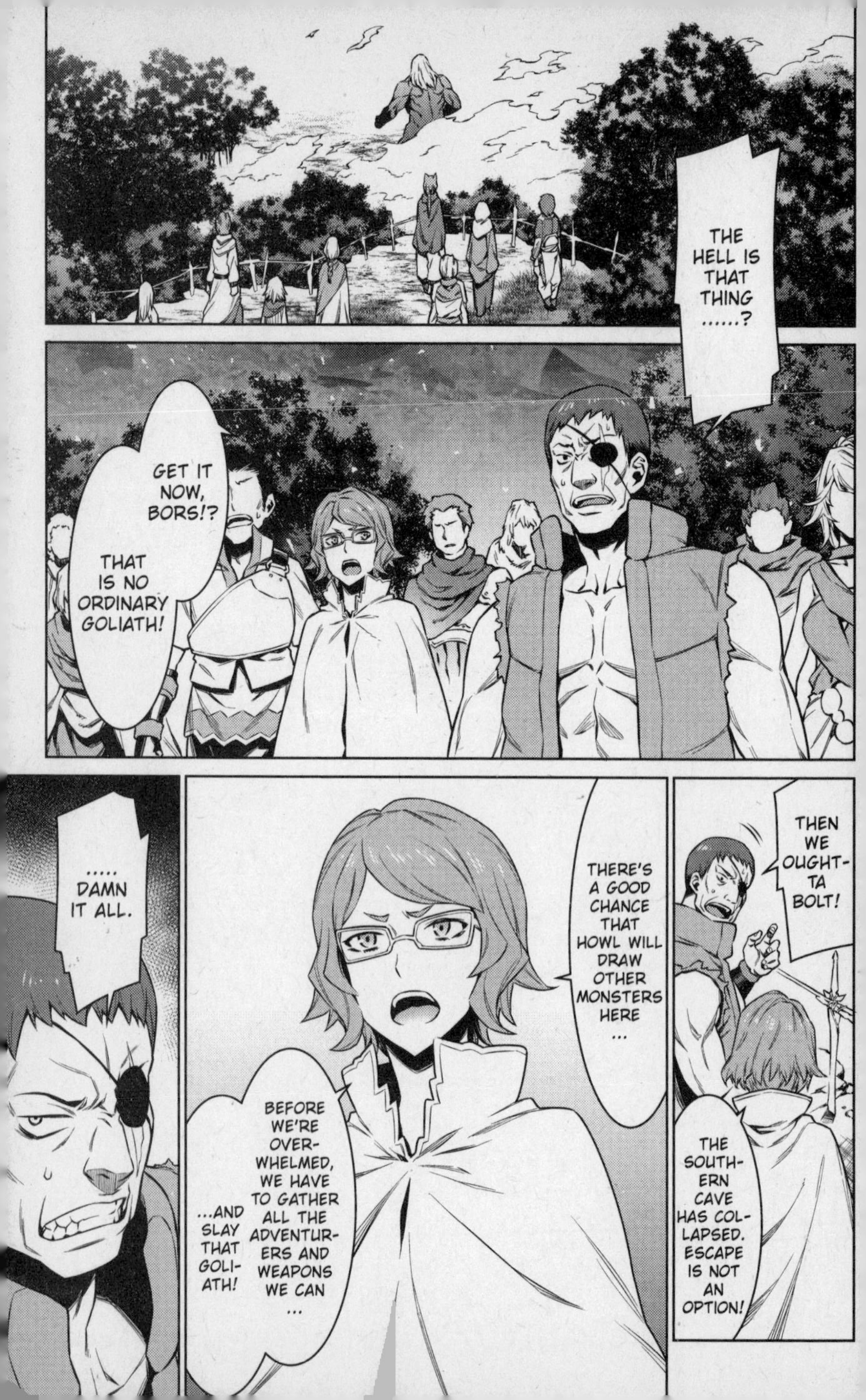

THE HELL IS THAT THING ......?
GET IT NOW, BORS!?
THAT IS NO ORDINARY GOLIATH!
THEN WE OUGHT-TA BOLT!
THE SOUTHERN CAVE HAS COLLAPSED. ESCAPE IS NOT AN OPTION!
THERE'S A GOOD CHANCE THAT HOWL WILL DRAW OTHER MONSTERS HERE ...
BEFORE WE'RE OVERWHELMED, WE HAVE TO GATHER ALL THE ADVENTURERS AND WEAPONS WE CAN ...
...AND SLAY THAT GOLIATH!
..... DAMN IT ALL.

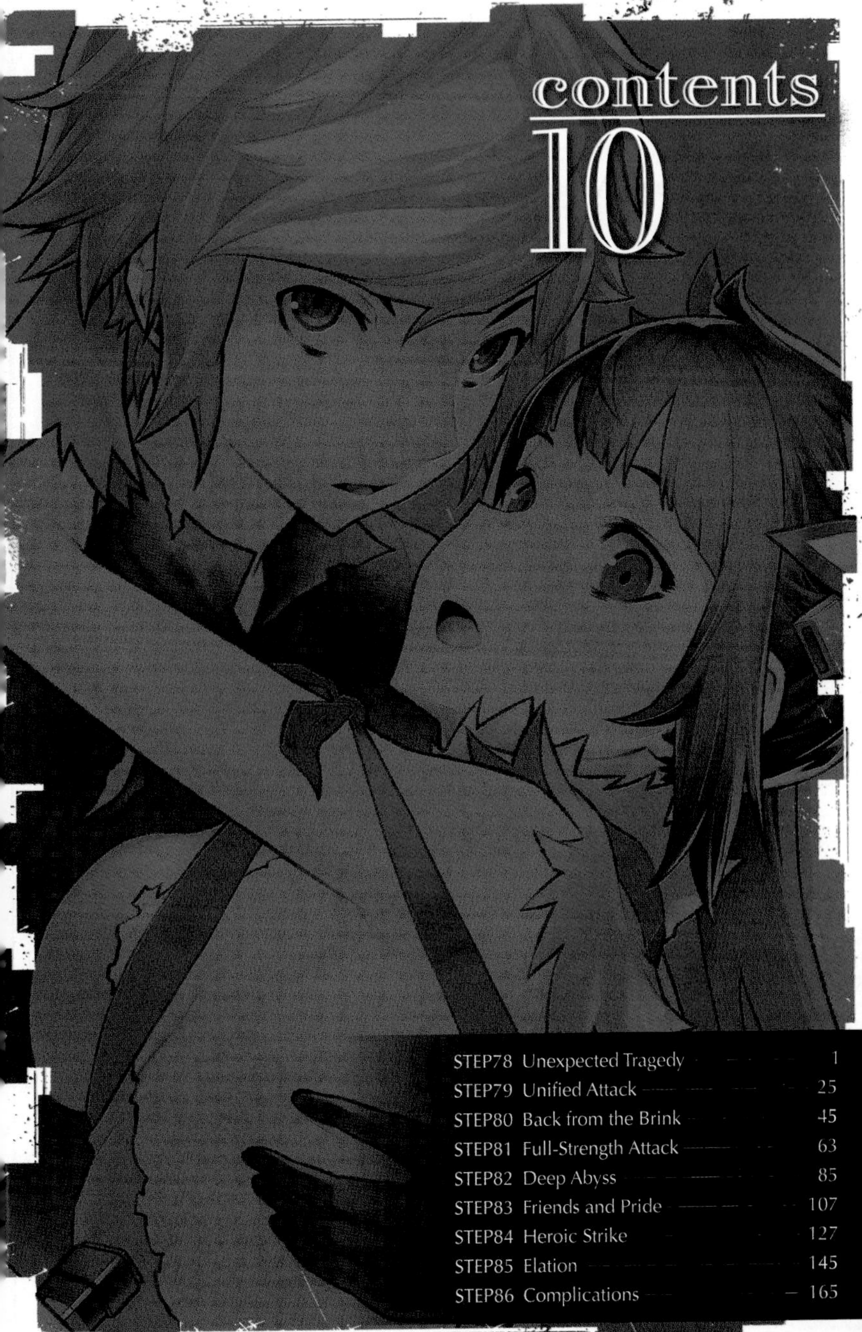

contents 10

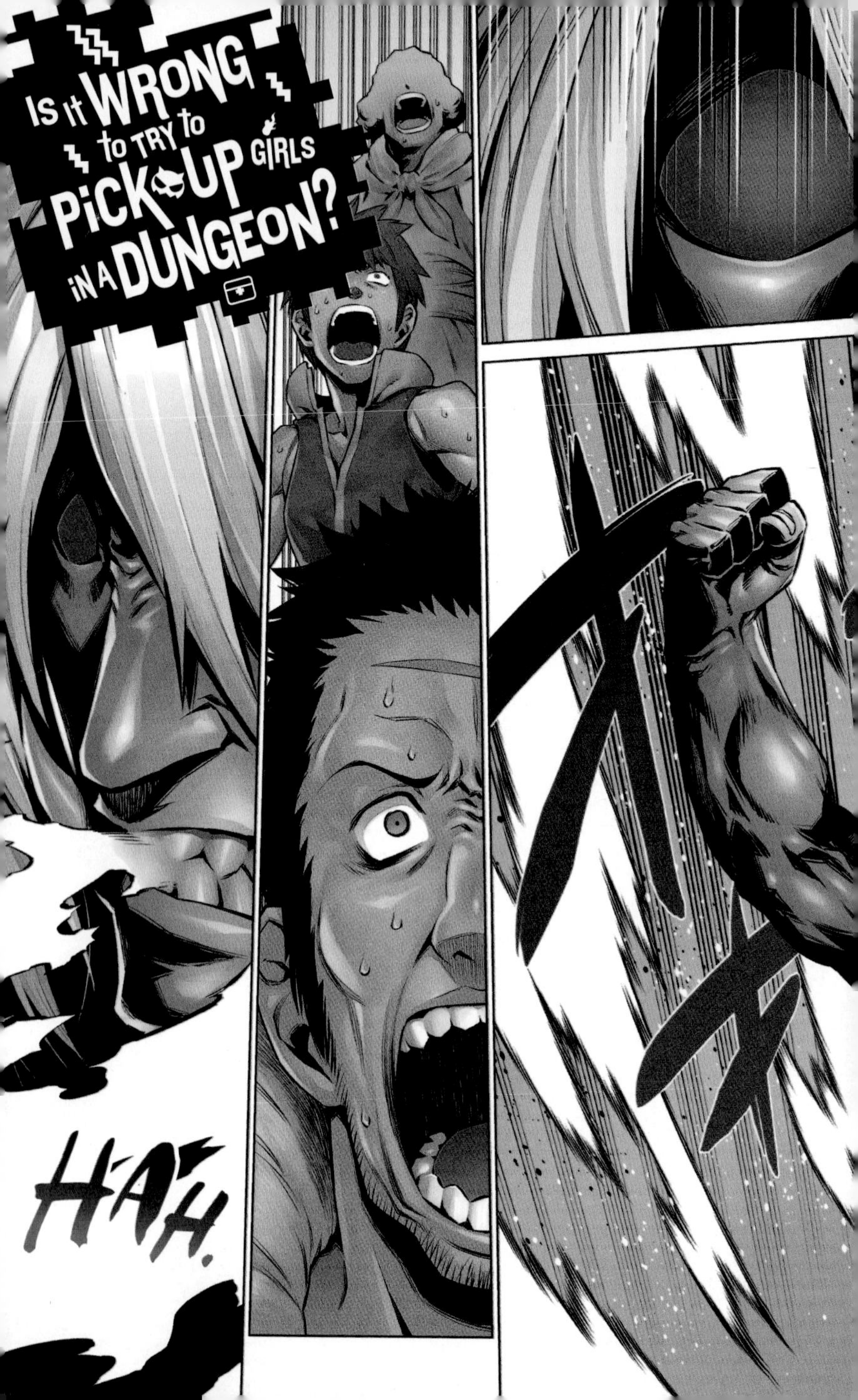
Is it WRONG to try to PICK UP GIRLS in a DUNGEON?
HAH.

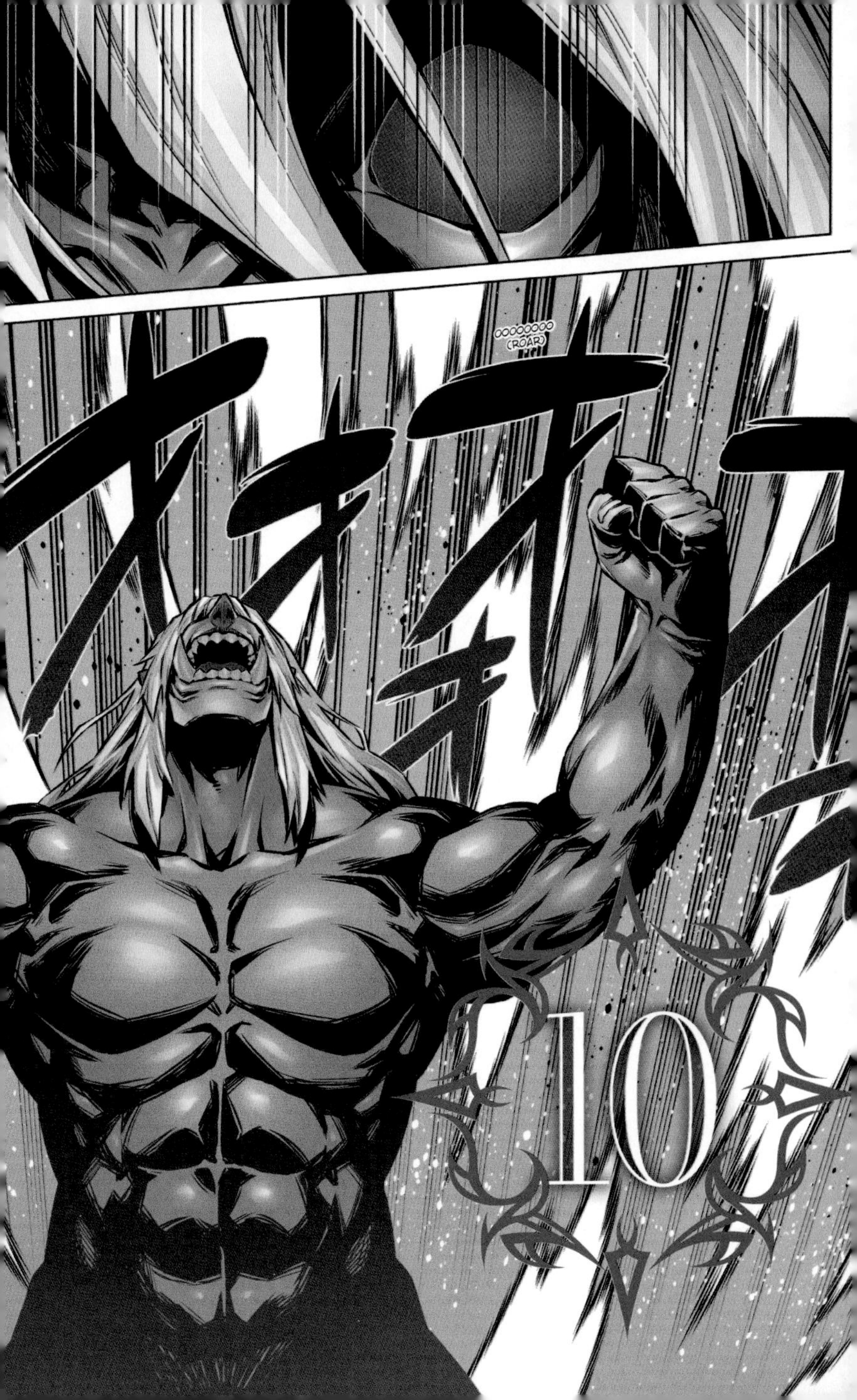
OOOOOOOO
(ROAR)
10

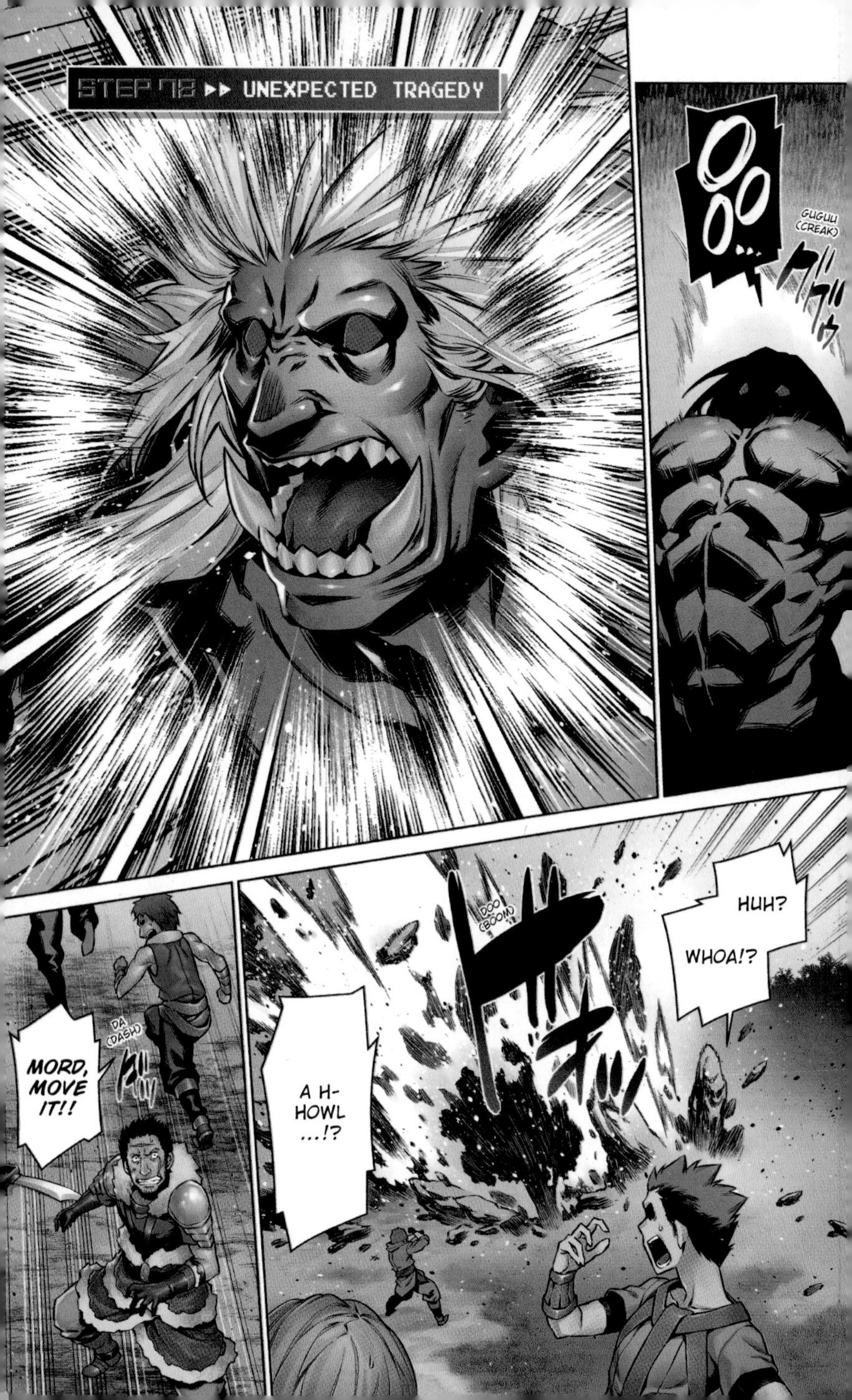
GUGUU (CREAK)
STEP 78 ▸▸ UNEXPECTED TRAGEDY
HUH?
WHOA!?
DOO (BOOM)
A H-HOWL ...!?
DA (DASH)
MORD, MOVE IT!!